IN THE SHADOW OF THE MILL

This book traces the socio-spatial transformation of workers' neighbourhoods in Ahmedabad over the course of the twentieth and early-twenty-first centuries—during which the city witnessed dramatic and disturbing transformations. It follows the multiple histories of Ahmedabad's labour landscapes from when the city acquired prominence as an important site of Gandhian political activity and as a key centre of the textile industry, through the decades of industrial collapse and periods of sectarian violence in recent years. Taking the working-class neighbourhood as a scale of social practice, the question of urban change is examined along two axes of investigation: the transformation of local political configurations and forms of political mediation, and the shifts in the social geography of the neighbourhood as reflected in the changing regimes of property.

In the Shadow of the Mill combines both archival and ethnographic methods to write a historical ethnography of two workers' neighbourhoods. Many of Ahmedabad's economic, social and political transformations—the decline of large-scale manufacturing, intensification of urban planning, rapid rise of politicised religion and spatial segregation—have mirrored national and global shifts and a study of the city's history presents a way of approaching broader historical processes while engaging with specifically local questions.

Rukmini Barua is a researcher at the Centre for the History of Emotions, Max Planck Institute of Development, Berlin. Prior to this she held fellowships at re:work, International Research Center, 'Work and Human Lifecycle in Global History', Humboldt University, and the M.S. Merian-R. Tagore International Center for Advanced Studies, New Delhi. Her research interests coalesce around questions of labour, urbanism, politics and emotions in modern and contemporary India.

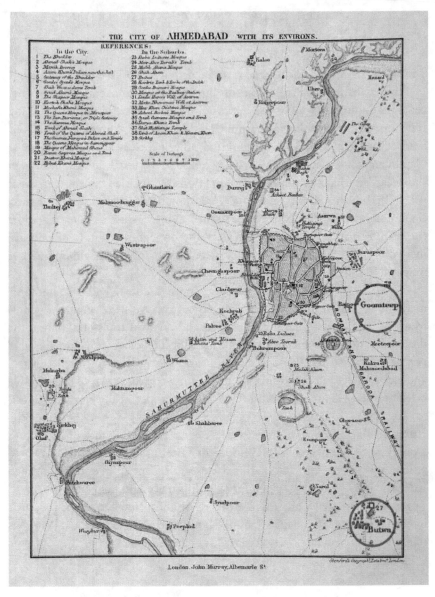

Map of Ahmedabad (1866) showing the location of Gomtipur and Vatva

Source: British Library commons.

IN THE SHADOW
OF THE MILL

Workers' Neighbourhoods in Ahmedabad,
1920s to 2000s

RUKMINI BARUA

CAMBRIDGE
UNIVERSITY PRESS

CAMBRIDGE
UNIVERSITY PRESS

University Printing House, Cambridge CB2 8BS, United Kingdom

One Liberty Plaza, 20th Floor, New York, NY 10006, USA

477 Williamstown Road, Port Melbourne, vic 3207, Australia

314 to 321, 3rd Floor, Plot No.3, Splendor Forum, Jasola District Centre, New Delhi 110025, India

103 Penang Road, #05–06/07, Visioncrest Commercial, Singapore 238467

Cambridge University Press is part of the University of Cambridge.

It furthers the University's mission by disseminating knowledge in the pursuit of education, learning and research at the highest international levels of excellence.

www.cambridge.org
Information on this title: www.cambridge.org/9781108838115

First published 2022

Printed in India by Thomson Press India Ltd.

A catalogue record for this publication is available from the British Library

ISBN 978-1-108-83811-5 Hardback

CONTENTS

List of Figures vii
List of Tables ix
Acknowledgements xi

INTRODUCTION
1

1. SETTING THE STAGE
A Brief Political History of Ahmedabad, 1920s to 2000s
31

PART I. INCARNATIONS OF THE
POLITICAL INTERMEDIARY
63

2. THE TLA AND *DADAGIRI*
Mediation in the Mill Neighbourhoods
70

3. THE UNDERGROUND ECONOMY, THE STATE AND
THE POLITICAL INTERMEDIARY
96

4. CIVIL SOCIETY, 'SOCIAL WORK' AND
POLITICAL MEDIATION
134

PART II. PROPERTY AND PRECARITY
173

5. *CHAWLS* WITHOUT CHIMNEYS
178

6. VIOLENCE, LAW AND 'GHETTOISATION'
213

7. SECURITY AND TENANCY AT THE MARGINS OF THE CITY
238

CONCLUSION
266

Appendix 273
Glossary 275
Bibliography 277
Index 297

FIGURES

Map of Ahmedabad (1866) showing the location of
Gomtipur and Vatva   frontispiece

1.1   Map highlighting the growth of the municipal limits
and indicating the location of the two neighbourhoods
under study   7

5.1   Map of Rajpur–Gomtipur   189

7.1   Map showing the major landmarks and architectural
forms of the south-western parts of Vatva   244

7.2   Town Planning Scheme No. 86, showing the areas of
Jain Ashram, Darbar Nagar, Navapura and
Jafar Row House   252

7.3   Promotional brochure of Navjivan Apartments   258

TABLES

1.1   Population of Ahmedabad   3

1.2   Growth of municipal limits   8

1.3   Population growth in the wards of Vatva, Gomtipur and Rajpur   8

A.1   Sample of property tax information for Darbar Nagar   273

A.2   Sample of property tax information for Jafar Row House   274

ACKNOWLEDGEMENTS

This book has been many years in the making and sustained by so many along the way. It began as my doctoral research at the Centre for Modern Indian Studies, Goettingen. My PhD supervisor, Ravi Ahuja, whose patience and attention to my work throughout the undeniably onerous task of supervision has been truly generous. He read through countless drafts and helped bring coherence to my arguments. His incisive comments stayed with me, as I revised the dissertation into the monograph. I am fortunate to have a teacher like him. Research for this book was supported by the Erasmus Mundus PhD scholarship and the German Historical Institute, London. I am grateful to Cambridge University Press for permission to use for this book 'The Textile Labour Association and Dadagiri: Power and Politics in the Working-class Neighbourhoods of Ahmedabad', *International Labour and Working-Class History* 87 (2015): 63–91. Chapter 5 draws on material previously published as 'Legacies of Housing in Ahmedabad's Industrial East: The *Chawl* and the Slum' in Felicitas Hentschke and James Williams (eds.), *To Be at Home: House, Work, and Self in the Modern World* (De Gruyter Oldenbourg, 2018). I thank the editors for their comments and the publisher, De Gruyter Oldenbourg, for permission to use this piece.

The History Research Group at CeMIS was where this work first took shape, and I am very grateful for all the engagement and critique. Some of its early members not only offered sustenance and succour through the weary process of submission, revision and publication but also continued to perform the absolutely essential task of asking when the book was coming out. But for this, I may have never summoned the perseverance that was so necessary to complete the manuscript. Aditya Sarkar, Anna Sailer, Stefan Tetzlaff, Sumeet Mhaskar and Neena Mahadev, who made my life in Goettingen and beyond so much richer and more fun. Especially, Ahmad Azhar, thank you being part of a decade long conversation with me and for all these years of friendship and companionship.

Chitra Joshi, Prabhu Mohapatra and Rana Behal, who have been so inspiring as scholars and whose warmth and encouragement I am so thankful for. Dilip Simeon and Jamal Kidwai, who sparked my early interest in the questions that form the core of this book, have remained not only involved in my work but also incredibly generous with their help and support with my fieldwork in Ahmedabad.

I am truly grateful to Fehmida Malik, who helped me make sense of much of what I saw and felt in Ahmedabad and continued to weigh in on my questions for years after. Thanks to Achyut Yagnik, Ashok Shrimali and Kiran Nanavati, for sharing their formidable knowledge of the city with me and for so patiently engaging with all my questions. Jan Breman, whose work has been a compass for this project, offered practical and theoretical insights, which helped me navigate Ahmedabad and its history. My friends and interlocutors in Ahmedabad, many of whom you will meet in the book, allowed me into their lives and so generously shared their time, stories and experiences. I would also like to thank the various institutions— particularly, the Textile Labour Association, the Ahmedabad Municipal Corporation, the British Library, the Centre for Environment Planning and Technology, the Ahmedabad Millowners Association, the Nehru Memorial Museum and Library—that have been so helpful with their time and resources. Especially, thanks to Siddhi Shah for tracking down sources and for all your help with translations.

I am grateful for the support of the Max Planck Institute for Human Development, where I am now based. Ute Frevert, Margrit Pernau, and my colleagues and friends Yaara Benger Alaluf, Steffi Lämmert, Alex Oberländer, Julia Wambach, Esra Sariouglu and all the participants of the South Asia and Beyond colloquium, thank you for inspiring new directions in my work and for your engagement and encouragement.

Qudsiya Ahmed, Sohini Ghosh, Anwesha Rana and Aniruddha De— so patient with the delays, and so considerate of the trials of the last few years—thank you for seeing the potential in this book and whipping it into shape. The anonymous reviewers provided the meaningful critique that was so necessary for revising the manuscript and the encouragement that was so crucial for seeing the book through.

Aheli Chowdhury, Suvritta Khatri, Riddhi Bhandari, Sarath Jakka, Monisha Behal, my cousins, Nandita and Nayantara, thank you for being a steadfast source of support. Nayara, especially, who has lifted my spirits in more ways than she knows. My greatest intellectual debt is perhaps to my father, whose curiosity about the world and the rigour with which he explores this, continues to amaze me. My mother's unwavering love has seen me through the good times and the bad. I am so grateful to my mother-in-law for her support and encouragement. In the years that I was working on this book, many people that I care for left this world too soon and too suddenly. My father-in-law, my grandparents, my uncle and Piku, I miss you and I know how happy you would have been to see this book completed. My biggest thanks are for Ron, for sharing every bit of the happiness, the miseries and the messiness that life offers. He has borne too many of my bad moods and dour days, and must be as relieved and as pleased as I am that this book is out in the world.

INTRODUCTION

A fable about the founding of Ahmedabad reflects the recurring pattern of change in the city. When in the early fifteenth century, Sultan Ahmad Shah began building the city walls, the day's construction would be mysteriously destroyed every night and the next morning, work would have to begin anew. Legend had it that a local saint, Manek Nath, unhappy with these developments, had cast a spell. As the walls were being built during the day, Manek Nath would weave a magical blanket. Every night, he would then unravel the blanket, this magical gesture bringing down the city walls. There are different versions of the resolution of this conflict. In one, Manek Nath relented because Ahmad Shah agreed to name a part of the city after him. In another, the saint was tricked into trapping himself in a bottle. The constant dynamic of weaving and unweaving recurs through the city's history.[1] It is visible in the partial disintegration of the handloom industry and the growth of the textile mills from the mid-nineteenth century onwards. The motif reappears when the textile industry collapsed in the mid-1980s and industrial restructuring enabled the expansion of power-looms and other industries. It is visible again in the settling and unsettling of city spaces, in the knitting and unspooling of social relations. As Ahmedabad's neighbourhoods grew, its socio-spatial relations transformed. Older spatial and social forms and practices were not simply supplanted by newer ones. Instead, as this research demonstrates, they were overlaid and, in turn, were often enmeshed with the newer forms and practices. While the analogy of weaving and unravelling offers us a productive lens through which to view the city's history, it was not an unambiguous, unidirectional process. It is this tension—of the often simultaneous and interlinked processes of building and dismantling—that this book is set against.

Two broad historical processes—industrial transformation and communalisation—frame the questions that I seek to address. The expansion and decline of the textile industry, the acceleration of informalised work regimes and an extensive ethno-religious mobilisation that appeared as a particularly violent form of Hindutva shape the contours of this book. The key theme that this book grapples with revolves around how the urban working classes attempted to make a life in the city through the course of the twentieth and the early years of the twenty-first century: how is a foothold established upon the city; what claims were asserted and how; what actors emerge as mediators in this process; what forms of material and political avenues appear through which to stake a claim on urban resources and state processes.

I follow this question from the 1920s to the 2000s with a focus on two interrelated themes of inquiry, which correspond to the two parts of the book. First, I examine the forms and practices of local politics, tracing the dynamics of political mediation and the constitution of social power and authority, as it is made and remade in a countervailing field of forces. This examination of how local constellations of power fluctuate offers some clues about the ways in which the urban working classes accessed and negotiated with state processes. It presents a view into the workings of political mediation, the nitty-gritties of local political involvement, as they straddle the realm of formal and informal politics. Second, I focus on the social geography of workers' housing as a way of understanding how material claims on space are effected. A closer look at the dynamics of changing property regimes allows, on the one hand, to reconstruct and empirically illustrate how working-class housing was produced, the conflicts and tensions it generated and, on the other hand, to analyse the politics of spatial marginalisation and differential access to the city. This research contends that the interconnections between the histories of industrial transformations and the histories of communal pogroms can be only grasped against the background of evolving, contingent and, to some extent, continuous structures of political mediation and property relations.

Certain qualifications should be laid out at the outset. While this book is about the city's industrial areas, it does not take as its object of study the textile mills or the industrial estates themselves, the work sites around it or their labour processes. While communalism and religious violence are crucial to the structure and organisation of this study, I do not focus at length on the actual unfolding of violence. Rather, it is a study of the ambiguous relationships of power and conflict that undergird the making and remaking of Ahmedabad's worker districts, offering a view into the geographies of urban change, social segregation and the links between the realms of formal (state-born) and informal (often extra-legal) regulation.

THE CITY, ITS INDUSTRIES AND ITS NEIGHBOURHOODS

Ahmedabad was founded in 1411 by Sultan Ahmad Shah. The citadel of Bhadra on the eastern bank of the Sabarmati River formed the original nucleus, with *pol*s growing around it. The pols were clusters of houses, intersected with narrow winding streets and open spaces. Often gated and usually organised around caste, religion or occupation, pols took the form of a spatially contained 'residential street', governed by a *pol panch*, or council.[2] Transactions of pol property were collectively regulated and sociality in these spaces, as other observers have remarked, was stamped with a 'warm or oppressive coziness'.[3] At the edges of the walled city centre grew a number of suburbs or *pura*s. In 1572, Ahmedabad came under the Mughals. By the early 1700s, Maratha rule was established over the city, and by the early nineteenth century the city came under British colonial control. Ahmedabad's morphology, which had been influenced by both Muslim and Hindu conceptions of space, changed considerably by the late nineteenth century.[4] This was due to several reasons: the volume of trade to and from the city intensified; the growth of railways recalibrated Ahmedabad's position in relation to other commercial centres; certain sectors of the urban economy expanded, accompanied by an increase in population (Table I.1).[5] However, the most significant change in Ahmedabad during this period was the growth of the textile mill industry, which was central in reshaping the city's spatial and social organisation.

Table I.1 Population of Ahmedabad

Year	Population
1881	127,621
1891	148,412
1901	185,889
1911	216,777
1921	274,007
1951	837,163
1971	1,585,544
1981	2,059,725
1991	2,876,710
2001	3,520,085
2011	5,577,904

Source: AMC Statistical Outline 2003–04;
Census of India (Ahmedabad city), 2011.

We begin our story about five decades after the establishment of the first textile mill in 1861. In this time, Ahmedabad had gained prominence as the 'Manchester of the East'—an industrial centre that could compete with Bombay (present-day Mumbai). Through the late nineteenth and early twentieth centuries, textile mills were established in a semicircle around the walled city and beyond. The nascent textile industry met with little opposition from the city's economic elite and was backed by prominent financiers as well as by the merchants' guilds, the *mahajan*s. The mill owners, as Gillion writes, 'cooperated rather than competed', many of them sharing caste, kinship and marriage ties.[6] By 1921, there were fifty-three textile mills in the city, employing on an average nearly 49,000 workers daily.[7] Ahmedabad's textile workers at this point accounted for almost 18 per cent of the total population and, according to colonial sources, formed a remarkably urban workforce.[8] Compared to other industrial centres, such as Bombay or Kanpur, a large proportion of textile workers in Ahmedabad were drawn from the city and Ahmedabad district.[9] While those workers who came from the city were said to have 'no contact with the villages at all', others, especially those from the Deccan and Konkan regions, were recorded as 'permanently settled' in Ahmedabad.[10]

Following strikes against wage cuts in 1917–18, the Textile Labour Association (henceforth the TLA) was established in 1920. Instrumental in its formation were Mahatma Gandhi, Anasuyaben Sarabhai[11] and Shankarlal Banker.[12] The Gujarati name for the union—Majoor Mahajan Sangh—retained a link with the caste-based merchants' guilds (the mahajans) of pre-industrial Ahmedabad. Through this name, in a sense, the same status and dignity were symbolically assigned to the worker and the merchant alike and a partnership envisaged between the employer and employee.[13] Prodigiously powerful in the first half of the twentieth century, the union remained committed to a Gandhian ideology of labour relations. At the heart of Gandhian philosophy lay the notions of dignity and justice, which shaped his conceptualisations of labour relations. Thus, the interdependence of labour and capital was based on a set of mutual rights and obligations. The rights of workers, such as a basic standard of living for the satisfaction of their economic, social and cultural needs, were seen as obligations of the employers; while conversely, the obligations of the workers towards the employers were seen in terms of a moderation of their demands in relation to the health of the industry.[14]

In the initial years of the textile industry, caste and community distinctions permeated onto the workfloor, with various departments drawing labour from particular groups.[15] In historical sources and other academic writings, we can trace the concentration of certain communities in specific occupations within the textile mills. Of these, Dheds and Vankars (Dalit sub-castes) were employed primarily in the spinning departments, Vaghris in the frame departments, and upper castes such as Brahmins and Banias in bundling and reeling.[16] The weaving sheds were staffed mainly by Muslim workers, with a gradual increase in the middle-caste Patel and Patidar component, as well as by workers from the United Provinces and Padmashalis from Andhra.[17] Among others, Bavchas, Marathas and Kolis (a numerically dominant but lower-caste group) also formed a fair proportion of the workforce.[18] While there were changes in the caste-based occupational groupings in the textile mills, much of the earlier segmentation remained and was, in fact, even strengthened by the TLA's structure as a federation of various departmental unions and by its mode of organising.[19] From contemporary newspaper sources, we can surmise that the union's support base, especially in the early years, was segmented likewise—nearly 65 per cent of spinners aligned with the TLA, while only 25 per cent of the weavers were union members.[20]

The mill owners came from the city's social and mercantile elite and banded together to form the Ahmedabad Millowners Association (AMA), which went on to play an influential role in city politics in the first half of the twentieth century.[21] As the textile mills flourished, workers settled around the mills, partly accommodated by the mill owners and partly by private landlords. New property arrangements emerged in the pols, with increasing numbers of renters, modifications in customary regulations and changes in their caste compositions.[22] Tenements and the new architectural form of the *chawl*—one- or two-room dwellings, with shared facilities—sprouted across the landscape of eastern Ahmedabad. The mill neighbourhoods acquired a distinct spatial form over the years and amassed considerable political clout, to a large extent propelled by the TLA.

In 1960, a new state of Gujarat was carved out of the Bombay Presidency;[23] until the new capital was established in Gandhinagar, Ahmedabad remained the administrative centre of the state. From the late 1960s onwards, investments were directed towards small-scale, power-loom and chemical industries—processes which were concentrated in the industrial estates established in the eastern peripheries of the city: Naroda, Odhav and Vatva. When the mill industry entered a crisis in the late 1970s and eventually collapsed by the mid-1980s, over 100,000 workers lost their jobs.[24] Women's participation in the textile industry had already been whittled down by the time the mills finally closed—accounting for less than 2 per cent of the total workforce, with a coeval increase in informal sector work participation.[25] This loss of what a former mill worker called 'gentleman *naukriyan*'[26] entailed a dramatic transformation of the social, spatial and economic fabric of the industrial east. The strong urban base of the city's workers was highlighted again, as retrenched millworkers remained in Ahmedabad even in the face of grave socio-economic dispossession.[27]

The liberalisation policies of 1991 opened up the country's economy more directly to forces of global capital.[28] The decline of the textile industry was not indicative of an overall slump in Gujarat's economy. Instead, the 1990s witnessed a growth in investments, but not in employment.[29] The chemical industry, in particular, was the site of the most impressive growth—the number of registered units increased from 10,919 in 1980 to 29,661 in 1991, and then made a phenomenal jump to 58,332 in 2000.[30] Furthermore, large parts of former textile mill areas such as Bapunagar and Amraiwadi grew as important sites of the diamond polishing industry, as small workshops were established by Patidar entrepreneurs from Saurashtra. The intensity of investments in the industrial estates, and the willingness of the government to ignore non-compliance with legal regulations, allowed these spaces to grow unregulated.[31] Retrenched mill workers thus found poorly paid jobs in such precarious and scantily regulated work environments, entering employment relationships that were considerably more insecure.[32] The mill closures and the repeated episodes of communal violence (most significantly, in 1941, 1946, 1969, 1981, 1985–86, 1991–92, 2002), accompanied by changes in political ideology and forms of political practice, contributed to a substantial remaking of Ahmedabad's labour spaces.

It is in these neighbourhoods of the city's industrial east that I locate my explorations (Figure I.1 and Table I.2). While the archival material used relate to Ahmedabad's worker neighbourhoods in general, the ethnographic evidence has been collected from two such localities—Gomtipur and Vatva. Both of these grew around sites of production. In the case of Gomtipur, the neighbourhood grew with the establishment of the textile mills in the early twentieth century and the neighbourhood of Vatva grew around the industrial estate established in the late 1960s (Table I.3). Gomtipur, located in the heart of the mill districts,[33] continues to have a mixed population, mainly of lower-caste Hindus and Muslims. The neighbourhood of Vatva is situated in the south-eastern periphery of the city and lies adjacent to a Gujarat Industrial Development Corporation (GIDC) estate that specialises in chemicals. An important Sufi shrine—the fifteenth-century mausoleum of Qutub-e-Alam— imbues the area with some cultural significance. Incorporated into

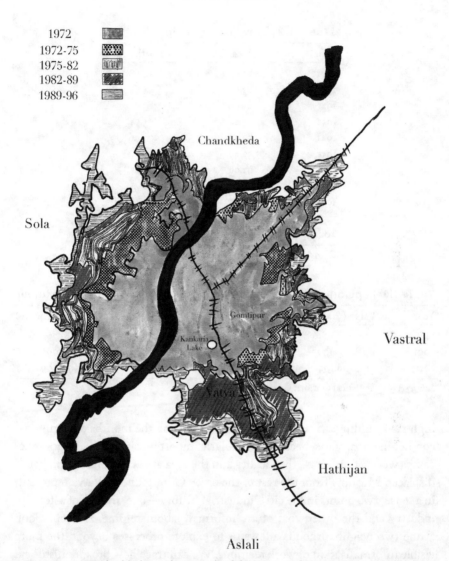

Figure I.1 Map highlighting the growth of the municipal limits and indicating the location of the two neighbourhoods under study

Source: Prepared from Ahmedabad City Development Plan, 2006–12.

the municipal limits only in the late 1980s, Vatva has grown as a residential area with every successive episode of communal violence, especially since the early 1990s. The locality at present includes the vast industrial estate, scattered workshops and factories, shanties and worker settlements, and a few

Table 1.2 Growth of municipal limits

Year	Area	Growth rate
1901	14.93	30.68
1911	23.08	54.59
1921	23.96	3.82
1932	25.29	5.54
1941	52.47	102.46
1951	52.47	–
1961	92.98	77.22
1971	92.98	–
1981	98.15	5.56
1991	190.84	94.44
2001	190.84	–

Source: AMC Statistical Outline 2006–07.

Table 1.3 Population growth in the wards of Vatva, Gomtipur and Rajpur

Year	Vatva (32.82 sq. km)	Gomtipur (1.88 sq. km)	Rajpur (3 sq. km)
1991	52,816	41,090	85,706
2001	121,725	68,476	73,096
2011	164,730	70,015	79,409

Source: AMC Statistical Outline; Census 2011.

high-rise buildings. Systematically targeted during the months of communal conflict in 2002, Vatva became particularly important since three major relief camps were set up across the locality and the area attracted a large number of displaced Muslims from the rest of the city.[34] Gomtipur and Vatva represent, in a sense, two points in the city's industrial history—one, the site of a 'formal' industry and the other, that of an 'informal' labour regime. A deeper look at the two neighbourhoods allows us to explore processes beyond the more visible informalisation of work relations. We can trace how broader historical tendencies of electoral arithmetic, communalisation and religious violence, and more localised and specific implementation of urban policies and legal measures have contributed to the production of the city's labour spaces.

WHY THE NEIGHBOURHOOD?

What does it mean when we talk of the neighbourhood? Simply taken as a territorial unit, it serves a limited purpose for analysis. The neighbourhood appears in many forms—as an administrative category, as a unit of urban planning, as a delineated element in urban cartographies, and as a web of social relations. These various maps of the neighbourhood do not always neatly correspond; indeed, they may coincide at various points, while conflict at others.

In recent scholarship, the working-class neighbourhood in India has been viewed as a site where subsistence strategies of the worker's household are forged, as a site of social reproduction and as the locus of political action and popular movements.[35] A dominant view has tended to hold these neighbourhoods as spaces where rural ties and primordial connections are easily reproduced in an urban context—in a sense, 'villages transplanted to the city'.[36] Implicit in this conceptualisation is an idea of a seamless continuity with the rural—a sense that social relations in the urban working-class spaces were constituted by inherited village ties. A 'shared urban experience', as Chandavarkar points out, was assumed to foster a moral consensus and social harmony within the neighbourhood. Instead, he argues for an understanding of the social relations of the neighbourhood as constituted by conflict and competition, rather than by an inherent social harmony brought on by proximity.[37]

The working-class neighbourhood, in this book, appears as a 'scale' of social practice that is constituted and transformed by sociopolitical dynamics. I use scale not merely to delineate the geographical and empirical level of investigations, but more as an operational one, which refers to the levels at which social processes and practices work.[38] Crucial in this regard is the attention devoted to forms of state practices, the shifting trajectories of urban governance and the range of political actors. In locating the interactions and the intersections between these various dimensions, we see the neighbourhood as an ever-forming, ever-dynamic category embedded within wider hierarchies and relations. Brenner identifies two significant ways in which the notion of scale has been employed in recent literature. The first uses it in the sense of a 'boundary', differentiating the object in question from other geographical units. The second deploys it more in reference to processes by which different spatial units are hierarchised and recalibrated. In this research, the scale of the neighbourhood is not seen as a nested spatial container within ever-widening geographical units (such as the regional, national or global), but is constituted equally by shifting vertical hierarchies and horizontally dispersed relations and processes and is itself a product of multi-scalar networks.[39] The two lines of inquiry that this book follows—the transformation of urban political practice and the shifts in property regimes—aims to demonstrate how socio-spatial relations within the neighbourhood are enmeshed in broader spaces and processes. Implicit in structures and processes of political mediation are questions of connections, of networks and circuits that linked the workers' neighbourhoods to various nodes in the wider city. At one level, this speaks to how the state manages and regulates urban resources and what forms of socio-spatial distinctions arise in the process. At another, it relates to the struggles and engagements 'from below' with state processes.

Spatial qualifiers with regard to politics appear throughout this book—in terms of the 'local', the 'turf', the 'neighbourhood', the 'municipal', and so on. Cox's distinction between spaces of dependence and spaces of engagement is useful in laying out in more precise terms the spatiality of politics. Spaces of dependence, as he conceptualises it, refers to 'those more or less localized social relationships upon which we depend for the realization of essential interests and for which there are no substitutes elsewhere; they define place specific conditions for our material well-being and our sense of significance'.[40] In order to secure a space of dependence, engagement with other centres of social power is necessary and through this is constructed what he calls spaces of engagement. This formulation, in a sense, captures the embeddedness of local political practice within different sites and processes, pointing towards the ways in which social power and authority circulate through and are altered at various linked levels. Scale, in this conceptualisation, is not seen as an exclusively areal or territorial unit but rather in terms of networks.[41] This reading of scale runs implicitly through this book in its focus on the enmeshed and interconnected registers of socio-spatial practice.

The mechanisms of urban planning work at a fundamental level with categories of scale, as heterogeneous spatial arrangements are refracted through cartographic isolation and abstraction, land zoning, and so on. These mapping practices in Ahmedabad were deeply tied to administrative policies of urban governance and the legal regimes of the land and property market. The cartographies of planning, the allocation of urban resources via the intended patterns of land use is one way in which the state produces the scale of local urban development. Sectarian violence produced other connected scales of urban settlements and networks of mobility. The structures of property in the city, the regulation of social space and the enforcement or circumvention of planning policies reveal the interlinkages between formal and informal registers of social control. Thus, a historically contingent and fluid hierarchical order of socio-spatial processes emerges. These scaled processes or the production of the scale itself cannot be divorced from the production of space.[42] As a produced 'social metric' that differentiates spaces, scale is not space per se. Marston and Smith argue that 'the production of scale is integral to the production of space, all the way down. Scaled social processes pupate specific productions of space while the production of space generates distinct structures of geographical scale'.[43]

The neighbourhood in this book is therefore important as a lens into the multi-layered and polyrhythmic nature of social realities. On the one hand, we see how the transformation of political practice and the structures of political mediation relate to changing spatial hierarchies. On the other, we tease out the ways in which the social space of the neighbourhood is simultaneously a product and (re)producer of social practice. As Ahuja argues, this dynamic relationship is necessarily underpinned by conflict as different social groups influence, in contradictory ways (as per their social resources and interests), the production of social space. Inherent in this process of production is a reworking rather than a supplanting of earlier social spaces. Social space is not, to use Lefebvre's formulation, 'innocent'.[44] It is fundamentally political and ideological. Space as a 'political instrument of primary importance' for the state is a mode of social control and regulation and is, in effect, hierarchised.[45]

Thus, the space of the neighbourhood in this reading emerges not just as a site, but also as a dimension and a scale of social practice.[46] In other words, it allows us to explore the neighbourhood not just as a discrete bit of land, but also as a part of a fine filigree of social and spatial relations. It allows us to read the tensions over planning and mapping of these areas; it provides a lens with which to address the transforming social relations of property and the precarity of urban life and presents insights into the overlapping and conflicting rhythms of social life in these localities. The neighbourhood, in this view, emerges not so much as a microcosm of urban life, but as an inherently unstable socio-spatial formation. With this focus, we can explore the interplay of micro-politics (in terms of concrete conflicts over urban resources, networks of power and patronage, and social experiences) with broader social and economic shifts.

A short digression here to discuss the usage of the term 'working-class' neighbourhood—the term in this book is used largely as a descriptive one. As such, the phrase 'working class' is often substituted by the term 'worker' or 'labouring poor', which are more open-ended and flexible. Alternatively, I have also used the terms 'mill neighbourhoods' and 'industrial neighbourhoods' for the same localities. In employing these categories, one must also take into account the self-identification of its residents. For instance, inhabitants of Gomtipur would consistently refer to the neighbourhood as a 'mazdoor area', literally translated, a 'labour area'. Discussions in Vatva bring up other categories with which to describe their living spaces—slum, *basti* or Muslim basti being some of the most common. The shift in terminology already hints at the changing perception and experience of urban living, which will be explored in greater detail in the monograph.

AHMEDABAD AND ITS HISTORIOGRAPHY

Academic interest on Ahmedabad has been fairly recent, though sustained.[47] Broadly, we can identify two historiographic tendencies. One deals with the city's industrial history. In this, the focus has been largely on the rise of the textile industry and its subsequent collapse, with some attention devoted to exploring questions of informalisation. The second focuses on the city's 'violent' history—that is, it follows the regular and increasingly organised episodes of communal rioting. This is a fairly new body of work that has engendered productive conversations about the questions of communalism both in terms of ideology as well as in practice.

Partly, some of this scholarly interest was generated due to the city's seeming uniqueness. This has been reflected in the existing literature on the city in various ways—in the emphasis on a remarkably urbanised workforce and the growth of 'indigenous' capital; in the focus on the Gandhian project of trade unionism and the amicable relationship between labour and capital; and more recently, in the dramatic shift from a peaceful urban ethos to one marked by violence. In his history of the city, Gillion writes, 'To those who believe Western influence and example was decisive in Indian industrialisation, Ahmedabad must seem like a strange case.[48] To be sure, the Bombay textile industry was equally shaped by Indian capital.[49] However, as some scholars have pointed out, unlike many other industrial cities, Ahmedabad's industrial and social elite had an antagonistic relationship with the colonial authorities.[50] The 'strange case' of Ahmedabad, for instance, appears in Salim Lakha's work as an emphasis on the striking contrast that the city posed to many other colonial industrial centres. Not only was the textile industry shaped by Indian industrial capital, but it also boasted an urbanised and proletarianised workforce.[51]

In Spodek's treatment of the city's history, the stress on Ahmedabad's uniqueness is reflected in his argument that it is India's 'shock city'. By this, he suggests that Ahmedabad has been at the frontlines of many of the country's social, economic and political transformations of the twentieth century.[52] In Gandhi's residence in the city from 1915 to 1930, his involvement in labour issues, the formation of a strong and autonomous civic body and in a trade union that formed a model for national-level labour regulations, Spodek identifies the making of a 'shock city'. Equally important in his conceptualisation of the 'shock city' are the dramatic and often disturbing shifts in the urban social fabric—for instance, the political agitations against corruption in 1970s, the ascent of Hindutva politics, industrial restructuring and the rise of communal conflict.[53]

While Spodek's masterly survey charts the city's history at several levels— most notably, through an exploration of institutions and influential figures— it wavers in its attention to the more plebeian social groups. His examination of the textile industry, similarly, focuses on the AMA and the elite leadership of the TLA, often obscuring the micro-level tensions, negotiations and struggles that governed the lives of those who laboured in the mills. Thus, in Spodek and other scholars, we are often presented with a nuanced though somewhat laudatory picture of Ahmedabad until the late 1960s—as a vibrant site of Gandhian politics with an enterprising local elite, a peaceful trade union and a large but pliant workforce.[54]

Sujata Patel unveils the tensions underlying the formalisation of the arbitration machinery, which has partly contributed to the image of Ahmedabad's working classes as peaceful or even 'passive'.[55] In the institutionalisation of the model of negotiation and arbitration, Patel identifies a process of hegemonic domination, which, in turn, was only made possible because of the worker militancy of the early years.[56] Central to the project of hegemonic domination was the role of Gandhian ideology. Tracing an inherent inconsistency in Gandhian ideology of labour, she suggests that, on the one hand, it called for a relationship of co-operation and mutual interdependence; on the other, it advocated a struggle for the basic rights of workers. This, Patel argues, allowed for a dual movement—one, which was based on conflict with capital, and the other, premised on an 'understanding' between labour and capital. According to Patel, these two movements occurred in sequence, with the former unfolding between 1920 and 1923 and the later, in the period following.[57] Operating within the specific colonial context, this was able to simultaneously deflect class conflict into a struggle against imperialism, as well as formalise a relationship between labour and capital and 'make it part of the ideological precepts emanating from the national movement'.[58] This entailed a transformation of the structures and processes of mediation that retained continuities rather than pose a rupture with the older traditions of the mahajans.

The TLA, whose origins can be traced to Gandhi's first political fast in 1918, established itself by the early 1920s at the forefront of the labour struggle, a move that Breman points out was actively encouraged by the industrialists.[59] The union, in turn, cast the mill workers as the *parivar*—as part of the large family of the owners and managers and workers—and sought to instil obedience and docility by emphasising the duty of workers towards their employers and a reciprocal responsibility of the management towards the workers. The language of kinship thus worked to imbricate the control of workers' lives and spaces with a sort of filial duty. The labour–capital relations in Ahmedabad were not necessarily predicated on an 'equality of interests' and therefore somehow 'special', as conventionally thought.[60] As part of its 'righteous struggle', much of the union's efforts were directed towards the moral and social upliftment of textile workers. The very concept of trusteeship or, for that matter, the civilising mission of the union was underwritten with and tended to reinforce social hierarchies. It is important to keep in mind that textile mill workers did not present a unified body, but rather were striated with fissures and conflicting political positions.

The militancy that engendered the formation of the TLA was gradually replaced by an unwavering commitment to arbitration that did not sway even during the crisis of the textile industry. Patel suggests that the corporatist framework of industrial relations that the union followed thwarted the growth of class-based alliances. Thus, when the TLA adopted a conciliatory stand in the face of the mill closures of the mid-1980s, workers, by and large, were not drawn to other unions who advocated more militant struggles.[61] Rather, as Patel and several others have commented, the union tacitly acquiesced to (or even actively abetted) informalisation and industrial restructuring.[62]

The mid-1980s—a time of mill closures and rapid industrial restructuring—are marked out by Jan Breman as a crucial turning point in the city's industrial history. A distinction is thus posed between the period during which the textile industry was at its prime and that of its subsequent decline. Having argued persuasively against a dichotomy between formal and informal sector employment, he nevertheless draws attention to the very real, material experiences that distinguished the mill workers from the 'footloose labour' at the bottom of the economy. The industrial regime of millwork had introduced a perceptible shift in the patterns of work and employment. While factory work produced new modes of subjugation and discipline, the living conditions of most workers were marked by squalor and poverty and the early generation of mill workers did not experience a substantial improvement in their daily lives. There was, as Breman suggests, one key distinguishing factor between those who worked in the mills and the footloose army—'the fact that they were effectively guaranteed work every day'.[63] The 'nature, rhythm, duration and the terms of employment' in the formal and informal sectors varied and this differentiation between various categories of workers further deepened in the years that followed. The reasons for this growing differentiation included, among others: the enactment of industrial regulations, such as the legislations governing the length of the working day or the minimum age of employment; improvement in the terms of employment, which could include not just a material betterment of the work environment, but also greater dignity and status accorded to the mill workers; the changes in the structure of wages, which comprised the shift in methods of payment, from piece rate to time rate, standardisation of wages and wage increases; and greater employment security and protection against dismissals.[64] Thus, while the city's industrial labour *as a whole* or as a *homogenous* category was in a far better situation in the late 1970s than ever before, there was increasing differentiation within this body of workers—between the slim majority of permanent workers and the large proportion of *badli* and contract workers.[65] Some of the privileges afforded by mill employment applied to all groups of mill hands (thereby, enabling us to see the mill work as a category distinct from footloose labour), others were more selective (and thus, pointing to the gradations within this category).

The most significant contribution, to my mind, of Breman's corpus of writings on Ahmedabad is the scrutiny of the processes of urban dispossession and marginalisation that followed the demise of the textile industry. His powerful account traces the loss of dignity and social status and foregrounds the downward mobility and despair that accompanied this large-scale industrial restructuring.[66] The political isolation of the TLA and its consequent loss of leverage was manifested not just as a failure of the union's 'righteous struggle' and its inability to temper the processes of deregulation of labour and informalisation, but also contributed to changed structures of political authority in the mill districts. The changes in employment regimes were reflected in the shifts in property relations in the mill districts, in the decline in affordable health care, and in the transformation of forms of social insurance and security. The dynamic relationship between the urban political economy, increasing precarity and communal conflict, which Breman alludes to, can be productively deployed to trace the interaction of political and ideological forces with broader processes of spatial, social and economic marginalisation.

The sharp distinction that is posed in these writings between the 'making' and 'unmaking' of an industrial working class offers a useful frame with which to view the transformation of Ahmedabad's labour spaces. That said, this monograph stands somewhat askew of Breman's main thesis. Informality was built into work processes, housing arrangements and forms of regulation *during* the period of the mill industry's peak, rather than as something that emerged *after* its collapse. These various forms of informality were amplified and even coalesced, coeval with the socio-political, economic and spatial transformations that unfolded through the late 1980s.

The incidence of communal violence has been another strong focus of the academic literature on Ahmedabad. Prior to 2002, which was arguably the most gruesome episode of violence in post-colonial India, the city had long been a site of communal tensions. In 1941 and 1946, riots occurred in the walled city and the industrial districts and have been seen as a local reflection of national-level tensions.[67] In 1969, there was a severe outbreak of communal violence where again the worst hit were the mill areas. Through the 1980s, there were several episodes of tension—in 1981, between upper and lower castes; in 1985, caste violence turned into communal violence; and in 1986, between Hindus and Muslims. In the 1990s, recurrent communal conflict occurred alongside persistent Hindutva mobilisation. Many of these riots followed a certain spatial pattern. They moved from the walled city—where the pols, with their labyrinthine streets and gated entrances, offered protection from violence as well as possibilities to escape the police—towards the mill areas.[68] This dynamic appears to be so familiar in Ahmedabad that popular sayings have been constructed around it—in many of my conversations, I was often told that riots begin in Dariapur and end in Gomtipur.

Of the several complex and nuanced approaches, the following paragraphs outline some of the key works and perspectives on questions of Hindu–Muslim conflict in the city that are relevant here. A significant body of work argues, for instance, that the prevalence and escalation of communal tensions are linked to the decay in civic associations.[69] The question of electoral and political benefits in communal conflicts has been examined in some detail in the context of Ahmedabad. Engineer, for instance, writing about the rioting in 1985, suggests that the ongoing anti-reservation agitation was given a communal turn by political 'masterminds'.[70] Similarly, some accounts of the events of 2002 suggest that the violence was orchestrated to cement the Bharatiya Janata Party's electoral dominance.[71]

Shani, in her monograph on the rise of Hindu nationalism in the 1980s and 1990s, attempts to develop a relational framework for understanding communal violence—moving beyond analyses that view conflict as being strategised by political elites or those that place the role of peacekeeping to 'prominent' members and institutions of civil society.[72] Thus, she locates as her point of engagement the relation between caste tensions and communalism, arguing that 'caste conflicts fostered communalism'.[73] The crisis that had been generated in the Hindu caste order through an expansion of affirmative action policies and caste mobility was addressed by redrawing social fault lines between religious groups.[74] This possibility for reconfiguring social anxieties was offered by a 'unifying' discourse of political Hinduism. Shani provides a persuasive argument for the instability of caste and communal identities and calls for an understanding of the contingent dynamics of these categories in the context of struggles for political, social and material resources. There is, however, a tendency to view the communal violence itself as being generated by the designs of the upper castes—as a way of transferring growing caste antagonism onto religious conflict.[75]

Another compelling vein of arguments further links changes in the political economy with the incidence of violence. Breman, for instance, has seen in Ahmedabad a 'resurgence of Social Darwinism', whereby the dispossessed are in fierce competition for scarce resources.[76] Writing about the events of 2002, Mahadevia suggests that the 'institutionalisation of exclusion'—through the marginalisation of certain segments of the population from development programmes and from economic and residential security—has provided a fertile crucible for communal ideology.[77] Social exclusion has been viewed from a slightly different perspective in Renu Desai's as yet unpublished doctoral dissertation. She finds that the notions of exclusion and marginalisation that are at the centre of Hindutva discourse are reproduced in the remaking of Ahmedabad as a post-industrial city, thus suggesting an overlap between the globalising city and the communalised city.[78] In another recent publication, Bobbio argues that the roots of violent outbreaks can be seen to lie in the historically contentious interactions between political and administrative control that has sought to mould city space and the 'adaption, reaction and disruption' of that control by the urban poor.[79] The question of exclusion has been explored at considerable length by way of an expanding interest in the material processes of segregation and ghettoisation in Ahmedabad.[80]

The thickest cluster of scholarship has emerged around the events of 2002. Writing about this pogrom through a close study of three neighbourhoods in eastern Ahmedabad, Berenschot calls for a deeper look at riot networks, arguing that 'versatile patronage networks' underpin the performance and organisation of riots. The quotidian struggles over access to state institutions are mediated by networks of patronage, which involve a 'constant exchange of favours'.[81] The daily functioning of these networks of political mediation and patronage provides a context for the political and electoral repercussions of communal violence and can offer an understanding of why and how such a broad range of figures (politicians, Rashtriya Swayamsevak Sangh [RSS] activists, *goonda*s, social workers, and so on) are involved in the performance of violence.[82] In his reading of violence in eastern Ahmedabad, he argues that Hindu–Muslim violence is more likely in areas where the channels of political patronage could potentially gain from the occurrence of riots. Conversely, patronage channels that do not rely on communal violence for electoral rewards could mobilise support for maintaining peace. Similar to Berenschot, other recent work has privileged a focus on the local and neighbourhood dynamics of communal conflict. These attend more closely to the perspective of the perpetrators with an aim to understand *why* the carnage unfolded. Valiani emphasises the crucial role of the RSS *shakha*s in fostering and sustaining anti-Muslim sentiments through the everyday practices of physical culture.[83] Ghassem-Fachandi foregrounds the psychological dimensions of collective violence, suggesting that a logic of sacrificial cleansing was at play.[84] Dhattiwala stresses the significance of spatial configurations in understanding the geographical distribution of violence, arguing that the built environment and distribution of population in the targeted neighbourhoods influenced both the mobilisation of rioters as well as the specific outcomes of the attacks.[85]

PLAN OF THE BOOK

This monograph aims to bridge these two historiographies by focusing on the interrelations and intersections between the two processes and tracing in miniature how they unfurl in the labour spaces of Ahmedabad. I do so through three methodological and analytical choices. The first relates to the selection of field sites—Gomtipur and Vatva. Both of these areas grew around sites of industrial production and represent distinct phases of industrial urbanisation and spatial segregation in Ahmedabad. Second, the analytical focus of this monograph—practices of political mediation, social regulation and property relations—allows us to examine critical yet understudied dimensions of industrial transformation and communalisation. Through this, we can trace how shifts in industrial regulation and communal polarisation impact not only upon employment security and the incidence of violence but also shape housing arrangements, access to state institutions and structures of local politics. Third, in terms of research methods, the integration of archival research with ethnographic and oral historical explorations permits the writing of a granular history of Ahmedabad's working-class areas, following both macro-level transformations and those at the level of lived experiences and subjectivities. This methodological choice allows us to traverse a long span of the city's history, knitting concerns of quotidian life with the broader trajectories of historical change.

While this mode of research opened up new ways of viewing the histories of the industrial east, it came with its own limits. As a woman from Assam, I was quite clearly an outsider in both Gomtipur and Vatva. My name, despite all its Hindu mythological connotations, also puzzled many people I spoke to. Very often I was asked whether I was Hindu or Muslim, occasionally probed quite at length when I said that my family is Hindu. Soon after arriving in Ahmedabad in the early months of 2011, I realised that the archives were lopsided, offering much more for the history of the mill areas and not enough about the peripheries such as Vatva. My somewhat rosy-eyed idea of fieldwork was also promptly punctured. I had thought that I could hang around street corners and tea stalls, chatting, through which I could glean the histories of these neighbourhoods. It was terribly awkward for me to just 'hang around', as I had initially planned. Many of my interlocutors, particularly in Gomtipur, were older men and most of our meetings, at the street side. I was, without fail, attentive to my comportment, from what I wore to the way I sat pillion on a motorbike. So, my interactions were nearly always framed as an 'interview', even when they were casual, informal conversations. The research interview was something that residents in Gomtipur and Vatva were quite familiar with (having spoken to scholars and activists researching the violence of 2002 and earlier) and it gave me a legitimate cover to loiter in a structured sort of way. In Vatva, where my access was mainly through a women's self-help group, Umeed, my interactions took place more in private spaces. It was easier, in a sense, to linger long after formal interviews were concluded, to be a part of daily activities and to participate in and observe women's group meetings. In a way, my ethnographic research was conducted in conversation with documentary sources. I worked backwards from my fieldwork, beginning from the archive that I built from oral narratives and referencing and juxtaposing it against other sources.

Since I had set out to trace the historical transformation of workers' neighbourhoods and the social and material structures of quotidian life, I did not explicitly refer to the communal violence that both Gomtipur and Vatva had experienced over the years. However, quite early on, I realised that communal violence was not a question that could be skirted in Ahmedabad. When I began my fieldwork, the memories of violence and the anxieties of security continued to surface in the everyday lives of the residents, especially in Vatva. The residents of the Muslim parts of Vatva had borne witness to the carnage many times over and I was periodically told about how difficult and painful it was to revisit those memories in order to answer a researcher's questions. Yet, despite my caution in asking any specific questions about the events of 2002, the violence loomed large in many conversations that I had. It materialised during discussions about children's education, in conversations about employment opportunities and in neighbourhood gossip. Most strikingly, the violence structured the parables of settlement in the area. During the course of my fieldwork conducted over twelve months between 2010 and 2013, I realised that the violence was visible not only in the virulence of Hindutva ideology or in the unfolding of pogroms, but equally so in the everyday structures of politics, urban governance and regimes of property. It is these aspects that I focus on, drawing out the underlying dynamics of communalism and its often obscured ramifications as they impact and transform everyday life in Ahmedabad's workers' neighbourhoods.

This book begins with a broad overview of the city's political history, with a focus on the workers' neighbourhoods of the industrial east in Chapter 1. It provides a chronological narrative of key events that have shaped the urban fabric from the 1920s to the 2000s. The rest of the monograph is divided into two parts, the first focusing on the transformations of political practices and mediation and the second examining the built form and the legal regimes that underlie the material conditions and experiences of urban living.

The three chapters of Part I provide a long history of the practices and figures of political mediation, relating local dynamics to wider scales of urban politics. This focus opens up questions regarding the distinction posed between the realms of civil and political society. Following Partha Chatterjee, if we were to see civil society as the domain of constitutionally defined rights and law, and political society as defined by a set of unstable, contingent, political negotiations, there appear throughout this book several points of intersection between the two.[86] In other words, we see a constant and contested interaction between the formal and informal levels of social regulation, which cannot be reconciled to a dualistic construction of the Indian polity.

Chapter 2 examines the overlaps and intersections between two figures of everyday significance—the union representative and the neighbourhood *dada*. By focusing primarily on local municipal politics in the mill areas from the 1920s to the late 1960s, this chapter charts the electoral fortunes of the main union, the TLA and the techniques of political control they exercised. The third chapter traces the connections between the underground economy, local politics and state agencies. Through this, I try to show how the political economy of the city (and especially the industrial areas) from the 1970s to the 1990s opened up intersecting channels of patronage—for security of life and livelihoods, and for engaging with state agencies. Chapter 4 examines the forms of political practice in contemporary working-class neighbourhoods—primarily in Gomtipur and Vatva—in which I follow the question of mediation through the figure of the social worker. This draws attention to how the city's working poor deal with the forms of precarity that are produced both by industrial development and by a variegated political landscape. Thus, these three chapters allow us, in a broad sense, to trace the shifts in the forms of political mediation and outline the kinds of intermediary figures that inhabit the neighbourhoods of the city's labouring poor. Reading these chapters together, we can see that mediation followed its own intimate rhythm and opened up micro circuits of local power and authority, which were rebuilt and reproduced in different historical moments.

Part II focuses on property relations in these neighbourhoods and contends that the transformation of property regimes rest upon the shifts in political mediation, electoral and administrative calculations and the dynamics of industrial change. In Chapter 5, I discuss the transformations of the built form of the mill neighbourhoods and examine how changing work relations and urban policy impacted tenurial rights. This chapter explores the production of mill housing, as it was directed by the civic bodies, the industrialists and the TLA. It investigates the shifting terrain of residential legality in these areas and the forms of precarious tenancy that have emerged in recent decades. Chapter 6 explores the anxieties of housing in a time of increasing communal conflict and segregation. It addresses how legal regimes—of property transfers and ownership—result in a precarious security of residence. Drawing attention to more subterranean implications of communalism, this chapter demonstrates how the process of 'ghettoisation' is paradoxically buttressed by the very legal measures framed to prevent it—particularly by the implementation, extension and the circumvention of the Disturbed Areas Act of 1986. Chapter 7 further deepens the discussion of 'ghettoisation' by tracing the histories of the settlement of Vatva and examining its location at the intersection of the working-class city and the segregated city. The process of urban and industrial transformation that Breman alludes to—the 'exodus' of the city's working poor to the eastern margins motivated by both employment opportunities in the industrial estates and by the process of residential segregation[87]—is examined at length here. It foregrounds questions of material and legal precarity that have accompanied unauthorised development (which, in this case, often took the form of post-conflict rehabilitation and resettlement). I illustrate here a dual (and sometimes, simultaneous) movement of urban restructuring—on the one hand, as a rupturing of property relations (through communal violence, displacement propelled by infrastructural projects and through a re-ordering of tenurial rights) and, on the other, as a 'fixing' of these populations in space, through the process of 'ghettoisation'. The investigation of questions of tenancy and property ownership in these chapters reveal a complicated terrain that is layered with intersecting claims and entitlements of citizenship, labour and community.

The transformation of these areas was a fundamentally political process. Therefore, we cannot understand the geographies of industrial transformation in the city, of communal conflict, of segregation, precarity and dispossession unless we see them in relation to wider political shifts and practices. By locating the practices of mediation, we can link the production of these geographies with broader political developments. The socio-spatial connections that were formed—the links between the city and its suburbs, between housing markets and (often enforced) mobility, between the local leaders and party bosses, between arenas of informal control and those of formal authority—were recalibrated at different historical conjunctures, producing simultaneously a variegated political landscape and a hierarchised social space. As we will see, questions of informality and precarity emerge as fundamental concerns in the daily lives of the city's working poor. Thus, above all, this book attempts to provide a historical understanding of informalisation, exclusion and precarity in Ahmedabad and how these forms of insecurity are negotiated and tackled.

NOTES

1 Achyut Yagnik and Suchitra Sheth, *Ahmedabad: From Royal City to Megacity* (Delhi: Penguin, 2011), 275.

2 Harish Doshi, 'Traditional Neighbourhood in Modern', in *A Reader in Urban Sociology*, ed. M. S. A. Rao, C. Bhat and L. N. Kadekar (New Delhi: Orient Longman, 1991), 179–208, 180.

3 Kenneth L. Gillion, *Ahmedabad: A Study in Indian Urban History* (Berkeley: University of California Press, 1968), 26.

4 Siddhartha Raychaudhuri, 'Colonialism, Indigenous Elites and the Transformation of Cities in the Non-Western World: Ahmedabad (Western India), 1890–1947', *Modern Asian Studies* 35, no. 3 (2001): 677–726.

5 Ibid., 682–83.

6 Gillion, *Ahmedabad: A Study in Indian Urban History*, 91ff.

7 Natvarlal Nandlal Desai, *Directory of Ahmedabad Mill Industry, 1929 to 1933* (Ahmedabad, 1935), 26.

8 L. G. Sedgwick, *Census of India*, Vol. IX, Part I: *Cities of the Bombay Presidency* (Poona: Superintendent, Government Printing, 1922); J. H. Whitley, *Report of the Royal Commission on Labour in India* [hereafter *RCLI*], Vol. 1, Part 1 (London: H. M. Stationery Office, 1931), 4.

9 A total of 45 per cent of textile workers were from Ahmedabad city and Ahmedabad district, while another 45 per cent came from the Gujarat region; the remaining 10 per cent were from the Deccan and Konkan regions, as well as the United and Central Provinces. *RCLI*, Vol. 1, Part 1, 4.

10 Ibid., 7.

11 Anasuyaben Sarabhai was the sister of Ambalal Sarabhai, one of the city's most prominent mill owners. She began her work in the textile mill districts with an educational initiative in 1914. She remained the president of the TLA until her death in 1972. Ambalal Sarabhai was closely associated

with the Ahmedabad Millowners' Association (AMA) as well as the city municipality.

12 Shankarlal Banker, a close associate of Anasuyaben, was one of the original founders of the Majur Mitra Mandal, the social service organisation that predated the formation of the TLA. Jan Breman, *The Making and Unmaking of an Industrial Working Class: Sliding Down the Labour Hierarchy in Ahmedabad, India* (New Delhi: Oxford University Press, 2001), 40–93. For a more detailed exposition on the formation of the TLA, see also Sujata Patel, *The Making of Industrial Relations: The Ahmedabad Textile Industry, 1918–1939* (New Delhi: Oxford University Press, 1987); M. V. Kamath and V. B. Kher, *The Story of Militant but Non-Violent Trade Unionism: A Biographical and Historical Study* (Ahmedabad: Navajivan Mudranalaya, 1993) and Makrand Mehta, *The Ahmedabad Cotton Textile Industry: Genesis and Growth* (Ahmedabad: New Order Book Co., 1982).

13 Breman, *The Making and Unmaking of an Industrial Working Class*, 44–45.

14 Sujata Patel, 'Class Conflict and Workers' Movement in Ahmedabad Textile Industry, 1918–23', *Economic and Political Weekly* 19, nos 20–21 (1984): 853–64, 857.

15 Salim Lakha, 'Character of Wage Labour in Early Industrial Ahmedabad', *Journal of Contemporary Asia* 15, no. 4 (1985): 421–41.

16 Ibid.; see also *RCLI* Vol. 1. Part 1, 7.

17 Breman, *The Making and Unmaking of an Industrial Working Class*, 132ff.

18 Lakha, 'Character of Wage Labour in Early Industrial Ahmedabad'; Gillion, *Ahmedabad: A Study in Indian Urban History*.

19 Breman, *The Making and Unmaking of an Industrial Working Class*, 57.

20 *Times of India*, 18 November 1937.

21 Raychaudhuri, 'Colonialism, Indigenous Elites and the Transformation of Cities in the Non-Western World', 677–726. See also Howard Spodek, *Ahmedabad: Shock City of Twentieth-Century India* (Indiana University Press, 2011), 71–94.

22 Harish C. Doshi, 'Industrialization and Neighbourhood Communities in a Western Indian City—Challenge and Response', *Sociological Bulletin* 17, no. 1 (1968): 19–34.

23 The Bombay Presidency was a province of British India, which included the cities of Bombay and Ahmedabad. The struggle for separate statehood, which began in 1956, demanded three states: Gujarat, Maharashtra and Bombay.

24 The New Textiles Policy introduced in 1985 laid out guidelines for reviving sick mills and offered easier options for mill closures. There were three main ways in which the textile industry was restructured—some of the 'sick' mills were taken over by the National Textile Corporation (NTC) or the newly established Gujarat State Textile Corporation (GSTC), a rare few rationalised their workforce and weathered the industrial crisis, and the majority shut down. It must be noted, however, that many mills in Ahmedabad did not proceed with closures in a lawful manner. Instead, many mills closed down from one day to the next. Mill workers would arrive at the factory gates only to find them locked. Supriya Roy Chowdhury demonstrates the extra-legal manner in which many of these closures occurred and argues that this 'inherently anti-labour' process could not have unfolded in the way it did, without the implicit support of the state government. See Supriya Roy Chowdhury, 'Industrial Restructuring, Unions and the State: Textile Mill Workers in Ahmedabad', *Economic and Political Weekly* 31, no. 8 (1996): L7–L13.

25 Renana Jhabvala, *Closing Doors: A Study on the Decline of Women Workers in the Textile Mills of Ahmedabad* (Ahmedabad: SETU, 1985). In this report, the numbers of women workers in the informal sector were placed at over 50,000. This, however, is not to imply that employment relationships in the textile mills were always formal and secure. In fact, several scholars have commented on the increasingly porous boundaries between formal and informal work regimes in the mills. However, the textile mills with their somewhat reliable work rhythms afforded the possibility of regular albeit contractual work.

26 Literally, gentlemen's jobs.

27 B. B. Patel, *Workers of Closed Textile Mills: Patterns and Problems of Their Absorption in a Metropolitan Labour Market* (New Delhi: Oxford/IBH Publishing, 1988).

28 Jude Howell and Uma Kambhampati, 'Liberalization and Labour: The Fate of Retrenched Workers in the Cotton Textile Industry in India', *Oxford Development Studies* 27, no. 1 (1999): 109–27.

29 Roy Chowdhury, 'Industrial Restructuring, Unions and the State', L7–L13.

30 Spodek, *Ahmedabad: Shock City of Twentieth-Century India*, 229.

31 Interview with Manilal Patel, former editor, *Majoor Sandesh*, December 2012. See *Powerloom Factories and Workers Therein* (Ahmedabad: National Labour Organisation, 1986), 7.

32 Jan Breman and Parthiv Shah, *Working in the Mill No More* (New Delhi: Oxford University Press, 2004); Manishi Jani, *The Textile Workers: Jobless and Miserable* (Ahmedabad: SETU, 1984).

33 I use the term 'mill district' synonymously with mill areas or neighbourhoods to refer to those parts of (eastern) Ahmedabad that were the sites of the textile mill industry and the residences of mill workers.

34 In 2002, the state of Gujarat experienced large-scale, organised communal rioting, following the arson of coach S-6 of the Sabarmati Express. There is strong documentary evidence implicating the state machinery in instigating and enabling this genocidal violence against the minority Muslim community.

35 See, for instance, Rajnarayan Chandavarkar, 'Workers' Politics and the Mill Districts in Bombay between the Wars', *Modern Asian Studies* 15, no. 3 (1981): 603–47; Rajnarayan Chandavarkar, *The Origins of Industrial Capitalism in India: Business Strategies and the Working Classes in Bombay, 1900–1940* (Cambridge: Cambridge University Press, 1994); Rajnarayan Chandavarkar, 'The Perils of Proximity: Rivalries and Conflicts in the Making of a Neighbourhood in Bombay City in the Twentieth Century', *Modern Asian Studies* 52, no. 2 (2018): 351–93; Vanessa Caru, 'The Making of a Working-Class Area, the Worli BDD Chawls (1920–40)', in *The Chawls of Mumbai: Galleries of Life*, ed. Neera Adarkar (Delhi: ImprintOne, 2011), 26–36, and Chitra Joshi, *Lost Worlds: Indian Labour and its Forgotten Histories* (Delhi: Permanent Black, 2003).

36 Chandavarkar, *The Origins of Industrial Capitalism in India*, 237.

37 Chandavarkar, 'The Perils of Proximity'.

38 Sallie A. Marston, 'The Social Construction of Scale', *Progress in Human Geography* 24, no. 2 (2000): 219–42.

39 Neil Brenner, 'The Limits to Scale? Methodological Reflections on Scalar Structuration', *Progress in Human Geography* 25, no. 4 (2001): 591–614. See also Neil Brenner, 'The Urban Question: Reflections on Henri Lefebvre, Urban Theory and the Politics of Scale', *International Journal of Urban and Regional Research* 24, no. 2 (2000): 361–78, 366.

40 Kevin R. Cox, 'Spaces of Dependence, Spaces of Engagement and the Politics of Scale, or: Looking for Local Politics', *Political Geography* 17, no. 1 (1998): 1–23; Kevin R. Cox, 'Representation and Power in the Politics of Scale', *Political Geography* 17, no. 1 (1998): 41–44.

41 Katherine T. Jones, 'Scale as Epistemology', *Political Geography* 17, no. 1 (1998): 25–28.

42 Sallie A. Marston and Neil Smith, 'States, Scales and Households: Limits to Scale Thinking? A Response to Brenner', *Progress in Human Geography* 25, no. 4 (2001): 615–19.

43 Ibid.

44 Henri Lefebvre, 'Reflections on the Politics of Space', in *State, Space, World: Selected Essays* (Minneapolis: University of Minnesota Press, 2009), 169.

45 Henri Lefebvre, 'Space: Social Product and Use Value', in *State, Space, World: Selected Essays* (Minneapolis: University of Minnesota Press, 2009), 188.

46 Ravi Ahuja, *Pathways of Empire: Circulation, Public Works' and Social Space in Colonial Orissa (C. 1780–1914)* (Hyderabad: Orient Longman, 2009), 17.

47 For a comprehensive urban history, please see Gillion, *Ahmedabad: A Study in Indian Urban History*; Yagnik and Sheth, *Ahmedabad: From Royal City to Megacity* and Spodek, *Ahmedabad: Shock City of Twentieth-Century India.*

48 Gillion, *Ahmedabad: A Study in Indian Urban History*, 75.

49 Chandavarkar, *The Origins of Industrial Capitalism in India*, 26.

50 Raychaudhuri, 'Colonialism, Indigenous Elites and the Transformation of Cities in the Non-Western World', 716–17. Countering the view that colonial Indian cities have been restructured solely through the imposition of British dominance, Raychaudhuri argues that the spatial reorganisation of Ahmedabad in the early twentieth century was a contested process, in which the city's elite groups challenged colonial urban policy and appropriated it. The phenomenal growth of the textile mill industry in the early 1900s acted as a catalyst for urban restructuring, which was interlaced with the reconfiguration of social relations. In the mill neighbourhoods, this took the form of 'homogenising' the workforce, through interventions in the built form. While Raychaudhuri convincingly argues that the 'indigenous elites' resisted, negotiated and appropriated colonial urban practices, he seems to view the imposition of the strategies of the elite as much less contested and the city's workers as having a 'collective and relatively quiescent identity'.

51 Lakha, 'Character of Wage Labour in Early Industrial Ahmedabad', 421. Nevertheless, the significance of non-urban ties was borne out quite sharply in the episode of industrial action that precipitated the formation of the TLA. Apart from this incident, where the rural–urban connections are drawn out in very contentious ways, the fluidities of the urban existence have been sharply highlighted in the episodes of communal violence,

especially in the 1940s and in 1969, when large numbers of textile workers returned to the relative safety of their villages.

52 Spodek, *Ahmedabad: Shock City of Twentieth-Century India*, 5ff.

53 In a recent publication, this emphasis on the city's distinctiveness has been critiqued, suggesting instead that the city's urban trajectory was no different from many other urban centres. Rather, the specificities of Ahmedabad enable us to ask questions about the broader processes of urban transformations that have shaped Indian cities. Tommaso Bobbio, *Urbanisation, Citizenship and Conflict in India: Ahmedabad 1900–2000* (London and New York: Routledge, 2015), 6.

54 See, for instance, Howard Spodek, 'From Gandhi to Violence: Ahmedabad's 1985 Riots in Historical Perspective', *Modern Asian Studies* 23, no. 4 (1989): 765–95; Kamath and Kher, *The Story of Militant but Non-Violent Trade Unionism*; Ashutosh Varshney, *Civic Life and Ethnic Conflict: Hindus and Muslims in India* (New Haven: Yale University Press, 2002) and Subbiah Kannappan, 'The Gandhian Model of Unionism in a Developing Economy: The Tla in India', *Industrial and Labor Relations Review* 16, no. 1 (1962): 86–110.

55 Patel, *The Making of Industrial Relations*.

56 Ibid., 136. See also Arup Kumar Sen, 'The Gandhian Experiment in Ahmedabad: Towards a Gramscian Reading', *Economic and Political Weekly* 27, no. 37 (1992): 1987–89.

57 Patel, 'Class Conflict and Workers' Movement in Ahmedabad Textile Industry', 855.

58 Patel, *The Making of Industrial Relations*, 138.

59 Breman, *The Making and Unmaking of an Industrial Working Class*, 46.

60 Ibid., 115.

61 Partly, this was due to the representative status of the TLA under the Bombay Industrial Relations Act, 1946, though Patel connects it more strongly with the 'state of consciousness' of the mill workers, who, at that point, had been removed from militant struggles for several decades. Sujata Patel, 'Nationalisation, TLA and Textile Workers', *Economic and Political Weekly* 20, no. 49 (1985): 2154–55, 2155.

62 Sujata Patel, 'Contract Labour in Ahmedabad Textile Industry', *Economic and Political Weekly* 21, no. 41 (1986): 1813–20; Roy Chowdhury, 'Industrial Restructuring, Unions and the State', L7–L13 and Darryl D'Monte, 'Ahmedabad's Alienated Textile Workers', *India International Centre Quarterly* 29, no. 2 (2002): 129–40. There is, of course, another perspective

on this. Surya Mookherjee argues that in an economic situation where restructuring was inevitable, the TLA has played a laudable role, fighting for the retention of jobs, compensation and re-employment. See Surya Mookherjee, 'Unions in Industries in Downturn: A Study of Cotton Textile in Gujarat and Role of Tla', *Indian Journal of Industrial Relations* 40, no. 2 (2004): 213–41.

63 Breman, *The Making and Unmaking of an Industrial Working Class*, 28.

64 Ibid., 112–15.

65 Ibid., 114–22.

66 For an exposition on Breman's conceptualisation of informalisation in Ahmedabad. Please see ibid., 259ff.

67 Spodek, 'From Gandhi to Violence', 789.

68 Rubina Jasani, 'A Potted History of Neighbours and Neighbourliness in Ahmedabad', in *The Idea of Gujarat: History, Ethnography and Text*, ed. Edward Simpson and Aparna Kapadia (Orient Blackswan, 2010), 153–67, 158.

69 For instance, Varshney, *Civic Life and Ethnic Conflict*', 219ff and Neera Chandhoke, 'Civil Society in Conflict Cities: The Case of Ahmedabad', Crisis States Working Paper, LSE 64 (2009), 6.

70 Asghar Ali Engineer, 'Communal Fire Engulfs Ahmedabad Once Again', *Economic and Political Weekly* 20, no. 27 (1985): 1116–20, 1116. Elsewhere, Paul Brass, in his seminal work on violence in Aligarh, argues that riots are produced by 'institutionalised riot systems', which rely on a specialised division of labour. The process of riot production is marked by phases—rehearsal, enactment and interpretation—and by figures that perform specific roles in each phase. Through this, communal tensions are created, maintained and galvanised into violence. In sites of chronic conflict, Brass writes, the process of rehearsal is nearly continuous, while the enactment or activation of violence is precipitated by the possibility of specific gains, most notably by electoral or political ones. Paul R. Brass, *The Production of Hindu–Muslim Violence in Contemporary India* (Seattle and London: University of Washington Press, 2003), 15ff.

71 Howard Spodek, 'From Gandhi to Modi: Ahmedabad, 1915–2007', in *The Idea of Gujarat. History, Ethnography and Text*, ed. Edward Simpson and Aparna Kapadia (New Delhi: Orient Blackswan, 2010), 136–52.

72 Ornit Shani, *Communalism, Caste and Hindu Nationalism: The Violence in Gujarat* (New York: Cambridge University Press, 2007), 6–9.

73 Ibid., 12.

74 Ibid., 152ff.

75	Ornit Shani, 'The Rise of Hindu Nationalism in India: The Case Study of Ahmedabad in the 1980s', *Modern Asian Studies* 39, no. 4 (2005): 861–96, 894.

76	Jan Breman, 'Communal Upheaval as Resurgence of Social Darwinism', *Economic and Political Weekly* 37, no. 16 (2002): 1485–88.

77	Darshini Mahadevia, 'Communal Space over Life Space: Saga of Increasing Vulnerability in Ahmedabad', *Economic and Political Weekly* 37, no. 48 (2002): 4850–58.

78	Renu Desai, 'The Globalising City in the Time of Hindutva: The Politics of Urban Development and Citizenship in Ahmedabad', PhD thesis, University of Berkley, 2008, 2.

79	Bobbio, *Urbanisation, Citizenship and Conflict in India*, 8–10.

80	See, for instance, Christophe Jaffrelot and and Charlotte Thomas, 'Facing Ghettoisation in the "Riot City": Old Ahmedabad and Juhapura between Victimisation and Self-Help', in *Muslims in Indian Cities: Trajectories of Marginalisation*, ed. Laurent Gayer and Christophe Jaffrelot (London: Hurst and Co., 2012), 43–79, and Darshini Mahadevia, 'A City with Many Borders–Beyond Ghettoisation in Ahmedabad', in *Indian Cities in Transition*, ed. Annapura Shaw (Hyderabad: Orient Longman, 2007), 315–40.

81	Ward Berenschot, *Riot Politics: Hindu–Muslim Violence and the Indian State* (New Delhi: Rupa Publications, 2013), 96.

82	Ibid.

83	Arafaat Valiani, *Militant Publics in India: Physical Culture and Violence in the Making of a Modern Polity* (New York: Palgrave Macmillan, 2011).

84	Parvis Ghassem-Fachandi, *Pogrom in Gujarat: Hindu Nationalism and Anti-Muslim Violence in India* (Princeton: Princeton University Press, 2012).

85	Raheel Dhattiwala, 'The Ecology of Ethnic Violence: Attacks on Muslims of Ahmedabad in 2002', *Qualitative Sociology* 39, no. 1 (2015): 1–25; Raheel Dhattiwala, *Keeping the Peace: Spatial Differences in Hindu–Muslim Violence in Gujarat in 2002* (Delhi: Cambridge University Press, 2019).

86	Partha Chatterjee, *The Politics of the Governed: Reflections on Popular Politics in Most of the World* (New York: Columbia University Press, 2004), 57.

87	Jan Breman, *The Labouring Poor: Patterns of Exploitation, Subordination, and Exclusion* (New Delhi: Oxford University Press, 2003), 249.

1

SETTING THE STAGE

A Brief Political History of Ahmedabad, 1920s to 2000s

When Kacharabhai Bhagat, a Dalit spinner from Laxmi Cotton Mills, was elected as the TLA candidate to the city municipality in 1924, it set in motion a decades-long involvement of the union in municipal politics. One of the key intentions of this book is to understand the changing claims asserted by workers like Kacharabhai Bhagat upon the city. To do so, it is necessary to first outline the broad narrative of Ahmedabad's history through the twentieth and early twenty-first centuries. This serves as a frame on which to map the questions of political and spatial claims that we go on to address in greater detail. In the following sections, I lay out in a broadly chronological order the key events, movements and ideological shifts that have shaped the city's political field from the 1920s onwards. Paying particular attention to the dynamics of the workers' districts, I discuss the consolidation and disintegration of the Congress–TLA nexus, the arithmetic of caste politics, deindustrialisation and the emergence of Hindu nationalism.

THE CONGRESS AND THE TLA: COLLABORATIONS AND CONTESTATIONS

In the early years of the twentieth century, Ahmedabad assumed great prominence in the Indian freedom movement, helped in part by Gandhi's decision to make the city his base in 1915. At this point, Ahmedabad was the centre of a flourishing textile industry, fuelled largely by Indian capital as well as robust urban governance institutions that were being given a new direction by the Congress Party[1] and 'indigenous elites'.[2] The city's significance to the Congress Party is visible in the close relationship that Vallabhbhai Patel, one of the architects of the Indian National Congress, had with the civic body.

Sardar Patel's political career began in the Ahmedabad municipality, when he was elected councillor from Dariapur in 1917. It was under his leadership that the first urban planning schemes were enacted, the walled city opened up and westward expansion facilitated.[3]

British influence over Ahmedabad was limited—the city's commerce, industry and, to a large extent, administration remained with the traditional Indian elite.[4] Positions of customary influence, the *nagarseth*, the *sarafs*, and so on, allied with the colonial authorities. Urban reorganisation schemes—'decongesting' the urban core, laying down roads and pathways, and conversion of land-use patterns—emerged as a flashpoint around which tensions appeared between the colonial authorities and the local leadership of Ahmedabad. By the mid-nineteenth century, the Town Wall Committee, which was composed, in part, by the city's mercantile elite, segued into the municipal commission, carrying forward the agenda of civic works.[5] The reputation and authority of the Ahmedabad Municipal Commission, which had a primarily Indian leadership,[6] fluctuated—with the government assuming control over it after the death of its first chairman, Ranchhodlal Chhotalal, a prominent mill owner.[7] Opposition to colonial control was brewing. When, in the face of declining political and moral authority, the elective municipality was restored, a faction of Indian elites led by Sardar Patel wrested control of the municipality in 1917. Once in power, as Raychaudhuri argues, they embarked on their own vision of urban reorganisation. This group of Indian leaders that aligned with Patel deviated from the 'traditional' elite of the city, insofar as they came from more obscure lineages.[8] Prominent among these were mill owners Kasturbhai Lalbhai and Ambalal Sarabhai and trade unionist Shankarlal Banker. While the previously dominant group of Indians allied closely with the colonial administration, this newly formed group took a markedly antagonistic stand against the British.

Under Patel, the Ahmedabad Municipality remained hostile towards the colonial authorities and consolidated the agenda of the Indian National Congress. This resistance appeared in a range of policies and positions that the civic body adopted—demonstrations against the Rowlatt Acts and the Jallianwala Bagh incident, emphasis on *swadeshi* as a mode of consumption,[9] participation in the Swadeshi and Non-cooperation movements, support for the Salt March, and the boycott of the official census, among others. Patel raised funds and mobilised cadre for the Non-cooperation movement of the early 1920s. Though active repression of nationalist politics by the colonial authorities was somewhat limited, tensions between the government and the municipality simmered, coming to a head over the control of public schools.[10] The municipality was suspended for two years and when it was restored in 1924, Patel was elected as the chairman and Kacharabhai Bhagat as the first TLA candidate.

The composition of the elected leaders of the municipality underscored the political unity across the city's elites—which included at this point members of the Indian National Congress, the AMA and the higher ranks of the TLA. The interplay of tensions and alliances between the four central urban institutions—the Congress Party, the TLA, the AMA,[11] and the municipality—shaped the city's political landscape, until the middle of the twentieth century.[12] The role of workers' neighbourhoods in this political arrangement was particularly crucial. The TLA's close ties with the Congress Party, its involvement in municipal affairs and its phenomenal electoral success were seen by party leaders as a way of expanding the Congress's support base and incorporating the city's workers into the urban political body. This relationship, while mutually beneficial, was not uncontested by any means. The first hints of tension can be seen in the conflicting accounts over Kacharabhai Bhagat's candidacy for the municipal elections of 1924. Bhagat's entry into municipal politics was at once electorally fruitful and an occasion for the appearance of caste tensions. In Gulzarilal Nanda's[13] account, the 'kingmaker' of Ahmedabad, Sardar Patel, was reluctant to support a Dalit candidate for the municipal corporation:

> His initial reaction was hostile because he was unsure of the effect of this on the voters generally. We stood firm because of the principle involved. Our candidate was elected unopposed. This was the beginning of our effective work in the civic body and facilities being created in the workers' localities. This helped to boost the TLA's prestige.[14]

Other accounts contradict Nanda's, suggesting that it was Patel who introduced the idea of workers' participation in local governance, even in the face of opposition from fellow party members.[15] Mill workers' entry into the electoral fray, while contested, nevertheless signalled a moment of political and spatial integration through matters of urban governance.

Fissures surfaced in this alliance through the 1930s. However, the relationship between the Congress and the TLA remained fairly robust, while the party's electoral fortunes fluctuated in conjunction with their active confrontations with the British.[16] The tight connections between the Congress and the TLA set the stage for the circulation of power in the mill neighbourhoods. The attention that these areas received, in terms of civic amenities, infrastructure and educational institutions, was in part due to the significant presence of worker representatives in the civic bodies. Beginning in the late 1920s, the union instituted a practice of obtaining written pledges from their electoral candidates, declaring their intention to 'give special attention to working-class localities, and provide them with amenities such as lights, water taps and public latrines'. Only those candidates who endorsed these promises were then supported by the TLA.[17] The entire machinery of the TLA and its electoral fortunes were dependent on mill workers. Thus, the power that the union representatives (the *pratinidhi*s) were invested with was simultaneously constituted, at one level, by their position of dominance within the mill neighbourhoods and, at another level, by their connections to larger processes of urban governance. The TLA's publications, such as the one quoted below, no doubt self-aggrandising to an extent, routinely pointed out the union's own contributions to ameliorating the living conditions in the mill areas.

> The present day improvement of the labour localities in respect of the civic amenities like water, drainage, roads, lights, schools, maternity homes, dispensaries, etc., are all largely due to the persistent efforts of these representatives along with members of the Congress party in the Municipal Corporation.[18]

The spate of labour conflicts, strike activity and fractures within the mill workforce through the late 1930s manifested in tensions at the municipal level. As Muslim workers turned away from the TLA, more pronounced differences appeared between the Congress and Muslim League leadership in the civic body.[19] Through the 1940s, the city experienced overwhelming nationalist agitations as well as intermittent communal conflict. In the grip of the Quit India movement in the early 1940s, industrialists and the union joined forces and called for a political strike, during the course of which TLA secretaries Gulzarilal Nanda and Khandubhai Desai were jailed by the colonial authorities.[20] The municipality was superseded; mill hands struck work for over three months before Nanda called off the strike from prison. At the height of the independence movement, the four crucial institutions in the city—the Congress Party, the TLA, the AMA and the municipality—worked in close cooperation. The association of the Congress and the TLA, in particular, was fortified as increasingly large numbers of TLA candidates occupied elected positions in the municipality. From the solitary mill hand in 1924, TLA worker representation had grown to nineteen municipal councillors in the immediate post-independence years.[21] This impressive presence in the civic body ensured that the mill districts, so far categorised as suburban, grew to be seen as part of the city.

THE MAHA GUJARAT MOVEMENT AND THE MARGINALISATION OF THE CONGRESS PARTY

Agitations for the linguistic division of states gained momentum across India through the 1950s. With the start of the Maha Gujarat movement in 1956, which raised demands for the creation of a separate state of Gujarat, the Congress Party and, by association, the TLA began to be increasingly isolated in the city's politics. Indulal Yagnik, a one-time Gandhian, who had had his own tensions with the Congress Party, assumed leadership of the movement after the police fired upon demonstrators on 8 August 1956. A day earlier, it had been announced that the proposal for the formation of three separate states of Maharashtra, Gujarat and Bombay city had been rejected, and, instead, a larger bi-lingual Bombay state was to be carved out—a plan that was enthusiastically endorsed by Gujarati Congress leaders.[22] As protestors took to the streets, targeting the Congress House and the TLA building in particular, they were met with repressive force.[23] Although previously identified as the Congress's political ally, the secretary general of the TLA, Shyam Prasad Vasavada, tried to distance the union from the political fracas, declaring, 'This is a labourer's institution. It has nothing to do with politics.'[24] This statement was met with criticism. A letter to the editor of the *Times of India*, for instance, pointed out the inconsistency of Vasavada's claims:

> The office bearers of the TLA, including Shree Vasavada, have utilised Congress tickets to get a seat in the legislatures and the Municipal Corporation. During the last election the services of textile workers were utilised for election propaganda. A 'political fund' was collected from workers and by workers at the insistence of the Textile Labour Association.[25]

Ahmedabad ceased to be a loyal supporter of the Congress Party. The white Gandhi cap, previously the symbol of political activism in the city, now bore the brunt of its anger. Indulal Yagnik described the political situation in his memoirs: 'All over Gujarat, crowds shouting "Maha Gujarat" forced people to take off their white caps (the symbol of Congress membership). At times they took out effigies of Morarji[26] and burnt them.'[27] The violence rapidly spread through the city and to the mill districts. Unions other than the TLA called for strikes and closure of the mills. The political alliances that were forged during the early days of the agitation were formalised on 9 September 1956, with the formation of the Maha Gujarat Janata Parishad (MGJP). This was a multiparty coalition comprising members of the Praja Socialist Party, former Congress workers and communists, with Indulal Yagnik as its president.[28]

Between 1956 and 1960—between the initiation of the Maha Gujarat movement and the actualisation of statehood for Gujarat—the fortunes of the Congress Party waned. The party was held responsible for the denial of statehood to Gujarat and the repressive measures taken to quell protestors.[29] The TLA's control over the working-class areas, which had faced consistent, though largely unsuccessful, threats since its formation, was challenged yet again.[30] These regular incursions upon the TLA's dominant position notwithstanding, the union retained a tenacious hold over the mill districts.[31] Partly, this was due to the TLA's extensive organisational apparatus—its vast network of pratinidhis and representatives and its presence in the civic bodies and involvement in the quotidian affairs of the mill neighbourhoods. The TLA's status as the sole representative union further strengthened the influence it exercised over the city's workers.

THE (UN)STABLE REIGN OF THE TLA

By the 1961 municipal elections, the political atmosphere had changed considerably. The linguistic state of Gujarat had come into being, and the Congress had somewhat redeemed itself after the embarrassment of the Maha Gujarat movement. During these elections, the Congress Party's dependence on the TLA and the working-class areas was made even more stark. Out of a total of seventy seats, the Congress won fifty. Out of the thirty-one TLA candidates, twenty-nine won and the mill areas accounted for twenty-seven of them.[32] The TLA's institutional apparatus was mobilised to support the Congress campaign in 1961. The services of the Seva Dal[33] (volunteer corps) and the mill representatives' committees were marshalled for campaigning. A voters' fund was organised, through which the union was to reach the mill workers' constituencies.[34]

The Congress Party's dominance in Ahmedabad was, thus, clearly buttressed by TLA support. The linkages between the TLA and the Congress, which had been formed first in 1924, was at its peak at this point. The depth of this alliance is highlighted by the resolutions taken by the union in 1961:

> The Joint Representative Board ... welcomes the ideal of socialistic setting of society set before the nation, by the National Congress and appreciates its resolve to establish it. The Textile Labour Association will *always endorse everything* [emphasis mine] which the National Congress will do to reach this goal.... This Board believes that it is in the interest of labour to give support to all the Congress Candidates.[35]

The 1961 elections indicate one fundamental aspect of the city's political geography—that the textile mill areas were absolutely key to the control of the Ahmedabad Municipal Corporation (AMC). Despite Indulal Yagnik's personal appeal among the working classes, the Janata Samiti (the name under which the new MGJP contested elections) had not been able to mobilise the industrial workers.[36] After the dismal performance of the MGJP in the 1961 AMC elections, it became strategically important to sever the ties between the mill areas and the TLA–Congress combine.[37]

The crucial position of the mill neighbourhoods in the arrangement of local political power in this period was also echoed by Jigneshbhai, a communist activist and social worker from Gomtipur. Fiercely critical of the TLA, he blamed the union for the collapse of the textile industry and was quick to point out its callousness towards workers. While talking to me over tea one October morning, Jigneshbhai mentioned something that would keep resurfacing in our conversations over the next few months—his admiration for Indulal Yagnik and the key role of the mill areas in determining civic politics.

> The trade union movement has had great significance. Like for instance, there was Harikrishna Vallabhdas, the owner of Ambica mills and many others, who were defeated by the worker's leader, Indulal Yagnik. The same Indulal who would eat *channa* (chickpeas) here, who would live with the

workers, was elected to the municipal corporation. Dinkarbhai Mehta, who was associated with the Communist Party, was elected as the mayor. The mills and the mill workers used to play a very important role in these elections.

Resentment against the TLA had been festering in these areas. The union's hierarchical structure, paternalistic mode of engagement and allegations of corruption were damaging their support base. An article published in the *Janata* in 1950 discussed the collusion between the mill management, the TLA and the Congress Party and presented a scathing critique of the union's functioning. Rather sarcastically, the news report stated: 'The result of this employer-Mahajan-Government combination is that many a worker is without a job today. This is the Congress-cum-Mahajan board of democracy.'[38] By the early 1960s, there had already been several attempts to break away from the union—the Mill Kamdar Union led by Dinkar Mehta and the doffers' union founded by veteran republican Karsandas Parmar, and the anti-TLA alliance, the Kamdar Sangram Samiti. Forming such unions was fraught with difficulties since the TLA was the only representative union under the Bombay Industrial Relations Act.

Soon after the landslide Congress victory in the municipal elections, the political terrain of the industrial east was deeply contested as the TLA, the communist and the socialist parties wrestled for control. During the TLA Labour Day event on 4 December 1962, Yagnik convened a rival meeting and exhorted the city's workers to free themselves from the control of the TLA and chart a new future for themselves.

> Until now the worker of Ahmedabad was not on the map of India—he was in the pocket of the Majoor Mahajan Sangh. Today he has come out. Today is not the day of the founding of the Majoor Mahajan Sangh, it is the day of the liberation, of the revolution, of the worker. Now a united front of free workers of Bombay and Ahmedabad will be formed. For all of India a strategy will be formed, from it a brilliant future for the workers.[39]

The TLA, by now acutely threatened, expressed serious concerns about the increasing communist activity in the mill neighbourhoods.[40] Between 1963 and 1965, the communist and socialist alliances—most notably the Kamdar Sangram Samiti, led by Indulal Yagnik[41]—organised protests and called for strikes, rupturing the somewhat uneasy hold of the TLA. The tensions between the TLA and the other unions, particularly the Sangram Samiti, came to a head in 1964.

In the municipal elections in 1965, the year after the Sangram Samiti agitation, the Congress Party and the TLA lost its dominance over the AMC for the first time in the civic body's history.[42] This defeat was roundly lamented in the TLA reports, declaring, 'The representatives of the union especially in the suburban areas received a setback, with the result that after a long time, the voice of Ahmedabad labour ceased to be heard in civic councils.[43] At this moment, the deep interdependence between the city's four central institutions—the Congress, the TLA, the AMA and the municipal corporation—was irrevocably broken.

The violence of 1969, the first major communal riot in independent India, unfolded in its most brutal form in the industrial districts. The events of September 1969 lay bare the simmering tensions underlying the city's 'harmonious' façade and revealed the depth of the connections maintained between the police, state agencies and local strongmen.[44]

FRACTURES IN THE CONGRESS AND THE TLA'S FORTUNES

Within a few months after the communal unrest of 1969, the Congress Party officially split into two blocs—Indira Gandhi led the Congress (R), while many of the older party bosses remained with Congress (O) helmed by Morarji Desai. The Gujarat Congress (O) momentarily survived the turmoil and continued to hold power in the state assembly. Following Indira Gandhi's impressive victory at the national polls in 1971, alliances were shifting rapidly and defections and political bargaining governed the political scene in Gujarat.[45] The TLA, in the meantime, was undergoing a rather rapid decline. Having decided to remain with Morarji Desai's Congress (O), the TLA severed ties with Indira Gandhi's Congress and the Indian National Trade Union Congress (INTUC)[46] and formed an independent political party, the National Labour Party (NLP). Led by former INTUC president S. R. Vasavada, the party was poised to contest the state assembly elections of 1972.[47] Though no formal electoral alliance was forged, the Congress (O) offered tacit support to the newly formed party. Congress (R) performed spectacularly well at the state elections, led to victory by Chimanbhai Patel, whose strong connections to the Patidar[48] caste group proved to be electorally very useful.[49]

These changes were palpable in the mill neighbourhoods as the terrain of local politics fragmented with former TLA and Congress allies now contending against each other for higher stakes in political control. The TLA's political clout was fading so rapidly that even a home turf victory was no longer assured. The very connections—those between the mill workers, the pratinidhis and their representatives in local politics—that had ensured the union's control in the mill areas for decades were now being shredded, perhaps even by those who had buttressed them in the first place. The circuits of patronage and protection that had been established by the TLA in the mill neighbourhoods were now diversifying to accommodate a range of political intermediaries and allies. Not only did this period signal a transition from the Congress Party to other emerging electoral forces, but also marked the proliferation of mediatory figures—for instance, slum lords, 'baron bootleggers', and businessmen land grabbers—and an expansion of the instruments of power and control.

Despite the decline in the TLA's political influence, their union membership remained robust. Breman notes that even while factoring in the possibility that the union had somewhat exaggerated its membership figures, the TLA's organisational base still included nearly 75–80 per cent of textile workers.[50] The proportion of textile workers in the urban economy had, however, fallen dramatically—decreasing from 17 per cent in 1930 to 8 per cent in 1980.[51] Therefore, while the TLA continued to have large numbers of textile workers as members, its presence amongst the city's workers had weakened considerably. This was exacerbated by the union's dismal performance in the civic elections in the mid-1970s. From twenty-one elected members in the AMC in 1969, their numbers fell to just eight representatives in 1975.[52] Following this, the union too appeared to draw a distinction between their political activities and their continued presence as a mediator of industrial relations, rather churlishly stating, 'The workers were not as politically conscious as they are on the trade union front.'[53]

The two factors—the TLA's loss of political power and the decline in the numbers of textile workers (as a result of the mill closures beginning in the late 1970s)—contributed to the union's diminishing *social* importance. The reasonably tightly knit circuits of local power that emerged from the position that the TLA (and its representatives) occupied in the mills, in the neighbourhood and in the municipal corporation were fractured. Other competing networks of power and patronage grew in its place. Central to this, it would appear, were the practices of everyday corruption that were surfacing during this period.

POLITICAL CORRUPTION AND THE NAV NIRMAN MOVEMENT

Chimanbhai Patel, one of the key politicians in Indira Gandhi's Congress (R), was widely credited with having introduced this form of personal patronage and corruption that, as Spodek commented, 'would even sanction violence for personal gain'.[54] Despite Chimanbhai's contributions in securing the state elections of 1972, he had been overlooked for the chief minister's position, in favour of Ghanshyam Oza, a senior leader from Saurashtra. The group of Congress (R) leaders in the state assembly included politicians from different ideological positions and, as such, was a fairly unstable one. 'Calculations about power' engendered a rift between the two dominant factions in this group—the 'loyalists' led by Ratubhai Adani and the new party chief, Jinabhai Darji, supported Chief Minister Oza, while the 'dissidents' coalesced around Kantilal Ghia and Chimanbhai Patel, who managed to manoeuvre a somewhat strong-armed takeover of the state government in 1973.[55] Demonstrations and protests followed. Organised by groups across the political spectrum—the Nagrik Samiti (a group of students and teachers), Jan Sangh supporters, the Communist Party of India (Marxist)—these protests consistently used symbols and theatre to highlight and critique increasing political corruption. If at one such demonstration, a procession of sheep was organised to parody the ongoing political drama over the formation of the legislative assembly, at another, brooms were distributed to symbolically 'clean up' the Congress government, while in others, it was a performance showing ministerial positions being offered to the highest bidder.[56] The protests soon escalated into communal conflict—the targets, initially, were public properties and shops selling essential commodities and the rioters, local. The Jan Sangh, already having cut their teeth on the 1969 violence, descended upon the city as a primary vector in this episode of unrest. The party's membership had grown considerably, and they had established a network of shakhas and full-time volunteers.[57] Chimanbhai Patel was elected in this atmosphere of mounting tension, which grew progressively worse through 1974.

Apart from this, unrest in educational institutions over fee increases, job insecurity and increased interference from the state added to growing social tensions in the city. This amorphous middle-class movement was then given shape and direction by the teachers' and students' organisations that had sprouted across the state. The Jan Sangh was playing a careful game during this agitation—offering support to anti-price-rise demonstrations, but then skilfully withdrawing when Chimanbhai Patel (who as an ally) was made the chief target. The movement gained momentum across the state, accompanied by regular *bandh*s, intermittent rioting and mass demonstrations.[58]

The end of Chimanbhai's government appeared imminent, as protesters called for his dismissal while his own party members initiated attempts to depose him. By early February, Patel resigned as chief minister under orders from Delhi and President's rule was imposed in Gujarat.[59] The Nav Nirman agitation in Gujarat was seen as symbolically significant for Jayprakash Narayan's movement in Bihar, which provoked the imposition of the national Emergency in 1975.[60] From 1974 to 1990, Chimanbhai Patel was in the opposition, moving from one political alliance to another, while former fellow Congress member Madhavsinh Solanki transformed the rubrics of caste alliances in the state.[61]

THE KHAM ALLIANCE AND THE POLITICAL SIGNIFICANCE OF CASTE

The influential position of the three dominant castes—Patidars, Banias and Brahmins—which had historically played the most central roles in Gujarati politics,[62] began to be tentatively challenged with the formation of caste associations, the most significant of which was the Kshatriya Sabha. The Sabha was an initial attempt at forming formal political solidarities based on caste, knitting together various sub-castes through a collective claiming of Kshatriya identity. The 'spirit' rather than 'blood' was flagged as the true marker of Kshatriya identity, as all those 'who were willing to serve and die for his country' and 'those who are martial by nature' were included in this caste group.[63] This included the numerically dominant Koli sub-caste as well as the historically significant Rajputs, among others. Notwithstanding the vast social and ritual distance between these sub-castes, the Kshatriya Sabha enabled them to fashion a collective political identity that also held some promise for upward mobility.[64]

For most of the 1950s, the Kshatriya Sabha had supported the Congress Party, though their relationship had hardly been smooth. By the early 1960s, new political arrangements were formed, with the Kshatriya Sabha ending its relationship with the Congress and moving towards a more politically rewarding one with the Swatantra Party.[65] A major part of the Swatantra Party's support was drawn from the Patidar community, and with the numerically significant Kshatriyas allied with them, the party went on to make remarkable electoral gains by the 1967 elections.[66] This alliance, however, frayed steadily through the 1970s, primarily because of the changing political configurations of caste. As Patidars moved away from the Swatantra Party and towards the Janata Morcha, the 'Paksh' (Patel–Kshatriya) coalition fragmented. The Janata Morcha government, which was in power for a brief period before the imposition of the national Emergency, also included Chimanbhai Patel's newly formed Kissan Mazdoor Lok Parishad as a key coalition partner. Patel who had consistently displayed strong loyalties towards his caste group—to the extent that he was accused of wanting to 'usher in Patel raj'—was steadily consolidating his hold over the affluent land-owning Patidars.[67] The Janata government with its various allies, in the mid-1970s, represented, as the *Times of India* reported, 'the high watermark of Patel power'.[68]

The Congress Party in the meantime was forging political solidarities across castes and communities, with the winning KHAM coalition.[69] This alliance between Kshatriyas, Harijans, Adivasis and Muslims reaped remarkable electoral benefits, with 96 out of 111 candidates winning in the 1980 state assembly elections.[70] Not only did this victory destabilise the electoral prominence traditionally maintained by the Brahmins and Patels, it also signalled the rise of the Kshatriyas as a critical political force. The political ascent of the Kshatriyas was accompanied by a shift in the broader equations of power in state politics. Whereas the Kshatriya was the second element in the acronym for the 'Paksh' alliance, it was the leading term in the KHAM alliance that now emerged. By 1980, the Kshatriyas had emerged as the single-largest caste group in the Congress Party, while the powerful Patidar community as well as other traditional elites were entering and shaping other political constellations. The Bharatiya Janata Party (henceforth BJP), Janata Party and the Lok Dal, in particular, were led by Patel politicians and, consequently, drew a significant share of Patidar support.[71] Solanki's own tenure as the chief minister as well as the appointments to his cabinet revealed sharp cleavages within the Congress Party. As Gujarat's first non-upper-caste chief minister and without a single Patel minister in his cabinet, nor any key Patel leaders in the state Congress, Solanki's government was promptly branded as anti-upper caste.[72] With the powerful Patidar community excluded from positions of power, there emerged a strong anti-Solanki lobby within the party, which demanded for greater Patel representation in the government.[73]

Solanki began his second term by introducing reservations for postgraduate medical students—a move that was met with a severe backlash from upper-caste groups across the state. The anti-reservation agitation rapidly transformed into anti-Dalit violence across the state, with Ahmedabad and its neighbouring districts of Kheda and Mehsana being the worst affected. In Ahmedabad city, the conflict originated in B. J. Medical College, located in the mill neighbourhood of Asarwa. From there, the violence spread across the city, though much of it was concentrated on the mill areas where Dalit workers were routinely targeted. This episode of violence, which lasted three months in 1981, marks two significant transformations in the political landscape of the city. One, caste gained a new political currency. Through the Congress Party's electoral strategy, the opposition that it provoked and the movements of self-assertion, caste had acquired a political charge that could sustain or undermine governments. Two, the TLA's studied silence on the issue of caste violence brought the union's politics into sharp relief.[74] The union, the bulk of whose support was constituted by Dalit workers, no longer commanded any moral authority over the city's workforce. Its already feeble social control was further diminished.

Through the early 1980s, Solanki pushed a two-pronged agenda for Gujarat—on the one hand, the KHAM coalition was strengthened through political appointments; on the other, he drafted an industrial policy that envisioned the state as 'mini-Japan'.[75] As part of this new industrial policy, there was a heightened focus on electronics and chemical industries, as well as on campaigns for urban renewal. The KHAM strategy, though electorally very rewarding, was not built on a strong grassroots base. Without a mass base, Solanki relied on an urban and rural elite that emerged 'through manipulation, manoeuvring and breaking of earlier bourgeois-democratic traditions and norms'.[76] This new 'elite', Yagnik argued, was composed of 'lumpen elements', rooted in various economic activities that were carried out on the margins of legality—quasilegal small- and medium-scale industries, for instance, the real estate market, the bootlegging trade and the smuggling networks. [77]

We could, perhaps, sharpen this distinction further. By the 1980s, the traditional political elite had been displaced from positions of power, while the authority commanded by the traditional economic elite of the city, the mill owners, had diminished significantly. The AMA was no longer as deeply involved in city politics, and with the growing crisis of the textile mill industry, their clout was greatly depleted.[78] In the meantime, however, the city had grown tremendously, both spatially and demographically.[79] Newer and more informalised production regimes had emerged and access to urban land for housing grew to be even more contested. The forms and figures of mediation that appeared to facilitate transactions between the growing numbers of the working poor, the economy and the state went on to shape local political practices. As we shall discuss further in this book, they occupied a range of social positions and while I would hesitate to categorise this emerging social group as uniformly 'elite', they were no doubt politically influential in varying degrees.

Immediately before his re-election to a third term as chief minister, Solanki introduced new affirmative action policies. Nearly a month after its introduction, the first anti-reservation protests began in February 1985 and would continue for almost seven months, repeatedly spilling into communal violence. This long spell of violence not only produced a communalised social space, but also significantly shaped political cultures and allowed for the remaking of social and political identities. Two events in particular—the murders of two policemen, Laxman Desai and Mahendrasinh Rana, in April and May 1985 respectively—which triggered fresh communal violence, highlighted the involvement of two sets of figures. In the former, it was key BJP leaders who were allegedly involved in stoking the violence; in the latter incident, it was Abdul Latif who was the main suspect as the perpetrator of violence. These figures—Ashok Bhatt and Harin Pathak of the BJP and Abdul Latif—went on to position themselves in opposition to each other through the late 1980s and early 1990s.

Amarsinh Chaudhary, also of the Congress Party, eventually replaced Solanki as chief minister in July 1985. An immediate reshuffling of the ministerial cabinet followed, which somewhat restored the traditional caste order, with Patel and Bania ministers replacing some of the KHAM politicians. The violence abated within a few weeks and an agreement was reached between the state government and the anti-reservationists.

CASTE AND THE BJP'S POLITICS OF 'INCLUSION'

The Sangh Parivar had embarked on a nationwide effort to embrace Dalits into the greater Hindu fold in the early 1980s and their initiatives in Ahmedabad and in the mill areas in particular mirrored that. During the caste violence of the early 1980s, the official stand of the Sangh Parivar remained steady—both the BJP and the RSS issued statements declaring that they were 'committed to reservations'.[80] Other accounts of this prolonged period of caste and communal violence in the city, however, suggest otherwise, with the BJP consistently implicated in the anti-reservation protests.[81]

This appears nearly paradoxical. While the BJP had launched a grand mission to unify the Hindu social order, the party cadre was allegedly fuelling violence in Ahmedabad. A look at the party's early support base would indicate why it might have been politically expedient to be involved in the anti-reservation agitation. With the party's support centred on Patels and other upper-caste groups, this move would have helped to strengthen their political base. However, this powerful though numerically limited support was no match, at this historical moment, for the Congress Party's broad political alliance of lower castes, Muslims and tribals. The anti-BJP sentiment that had been growing among Dalits following the party's fairly open collusion with the anti-reservationists had to be corrected.[82] To damage Madhavsinh Solanki's popular electoral alliance, the BJP began to make a tentative bid for Dalit support, in tandem with a nationwide project to forge a Hindu nationalist consciousness. One of the more explicit strategies was the series of large-scale *yatras* orchestrated mainly by the Vishva Hindu Parishad (VHP) and the RSS.

According to the VHP high command, these were undertaken with the intention of unifying different castes, creeds and sects.[83] Attempts were made, as Jaffrelot highlights, to craft a unified social body through social inclusion. Furthermore, through spatial strategies employed during these pilgrimages that traversed the country, a Hindu social space was produced.[84] In Gujarat, Dalit leaders were involved in the yatras of the early 1980s—indeed, appeals from diverse groups such as Sikh Sampradaya, Bauddha Sampradaya and Bhartiya Dalit Vargha Sangh to join these political pilgrimages testified to the success of the BJP's project of inclusion.[85]

The Sangh Parivar intensified its attempts to consolidate Hindu identity as a cohesive whole that was placed in opposition to the Other (a category that has included, at various points, Muslims, Christians and any other social group deemed un-Indian by the Hindu Right). Gujarat was particularly receptive to this wave of militant Hinduism, which had acquired, as the *India Today* reported, 'a new legitimacy, a new belligerency'.[86] During the caste violence of 1985, VHP leaders along with upper-caste Hindus distributed relief material to Dalit families in Ambedkarnagar, Ahmedabad. Dalit leaders who threatened to convert to Islam if the anti-reservation violence continued were again counselled and dissuaded by RSS and VHP members.[87] By 1986, the VHP had made public appeals, on the one hand, to Hindu youth to work towards the abolition of untouchability and, on the other, to Dalits to unify in defence of Hinduism.[88] 'Re-conversion' of Dalits and tribals was highlighted as a crucial political and ideological strategy. Simultaneously, RSS shakhas in the state proliferated between 1983 and 1986, increasing from three hundred to more than a thousand. Elaborate outreach programmes were initiated, leading Narendra Modi, who was the head of the RSS in Ahmedabad at the time, to exult about 'public involvement'.[89]

The BJP's political strategy thus involved a careful balancing—of retaining its upper- and middle-caste support base, while at the same time, attempting to produce a unified Hindu identity by forging solidarities across castes. This play of contradictory political ambitions is visible even in some of the local political players in Ahmedabad. A BJP leader, once alleged to have placed a garland of shoes on a statue of Ambedkar during an anti-reservation rally, recast himself over the years as a 'superb Dalit' in the mill neighbourhoods.[90]

Through this volatile period, the Congress Party retained shaky control over the municipal corporation. The civic body polls of 1987 ended that control. The elections, which had been billed as the 'mini general elections',[91] were swept by the BJP.[92] The victories revealed the geographies of political influence. The western part of the city accounted, in a large part, for the BJP's electoral success.[93] The Congress, on the other hand, performed dismally in the walled city, the western suburbs as well as in its former stronghold of the labour belt,[94] and was to stay out of power in the civic body for the next thirteen years. The Muslim-majority constituencies of eastern Ahmedabad, another erstwhile Congress bastion, dealt the most damaging verdict to the party's credibility. Abdul Latif, contesting from five different wards as an independent candidate, won from them all. The BJP, experimenting for the first time with a 'Hinduite' strategy, had mounted an aggressive campaign during these local elections—relying extensively on 'the communal idiom', factoring, as this news report suggests, 'that a sharp polarisation cannot hurt its electoral chances'.[95]

Within two years of their landslide victory in the AMC, the BJP executed a coup of sorts in the national elections—it moved from just two seats in 1984 to securing the third-highest number of seats in 1989. The party's success was largely attributed to the hard-line Hindu image it cultivated under the leadership of L. K. Advani.[96] Not surprisingly, the massive gains made by the party came in the wake of another theatrical mass movement orchestrated by the Sangh Parivar. The Ram Shila Pujan, which was undertaken through most of 1989, was to consecrate bricks donated and collected from across India to lay the foundations for the Ram Mandir in Ayodhya. The bricks, inscribed with the name Ram, were produced from local earth, then sanctified through worship and finally joined the many processions that were streaming through the country to converge at Ayodhya.[97] The programme was met with great enthusiasm in Gujarat, including Dalit neighbourhoods in Ahmedabad and even remote tribal areas contributing sacred bricks and financial support.[98] Through the 1990s, the BJP stepped up its Hindutva propaganda, organising several *rathyatras*, the most violent of which culminated in the demolition of the Babri Masjid and resulted in horrific consequences that were felt across the nation.

In early 1990, an uneasy alliance was cobbled together in the Gujarat Assembly between the Janata Dal, headed by Chimanbhai Patel, and the BJP.[99] The coalition government that was formed indicated the reinstatement of Patel leadership in the state—Chimanbhai Patel of the Janata Dal, Keshubhai Patel of the BJP and Babubhai Patel of the Lokswaraj Manch had emerged as contenders for the chief minister's position. The social and economic alliances that were fashioned during the KHAM years were on the verge of being reversed, as the historically powerful Patidar community returned to political power.[100]

ETHNO-RELIGIOUS MOBILISATION AND THE GROWTH OF THE HINDU RIGHT

While these seismic changes were unfolding in the political landscape of the city, the textile industry in Ahmedabad entered its most serious crisis, engendering not only in a shift in production and employment regimes, but also precipitating a more pervasive transformation of life in the industrial east. The early 1990s thus marked a period of economic upheaval as well as social unrest—with the Mandal agitation[101] and episodic communal violence lacerating the state of Gujarat. The BJP had already made sizeable gains in local civic bodies through the 1980s and assumed a more significant role in both the state legislature and in the national government by the beginning of the decade. The alarmingly regular incidence of communal violence was, as some commentators observed, an enabler of the party's spectacular success in the Lok Sabha elections of 1991.[102] The initial base of the party was concentrated among the urban middle classes and through the 1970s and 1980s, the party had made sustained efforts to create a base among the urban working classes as well as in the rural constituencies. BJP-affiliated trade unions proliferated across the state, with a membership of about 20,000 workers.[103] Simultaneously, associations of slum dwellers were formed to allow greater access to the previously untapped urban constituencies. Following the long years of Congress rule in the state, the BJP fashioned itself in the 1990s as a 'value-based party with non-corrupt and devoted cadres who are committed to the betterment of society'.[104] If we recall, political corruption was the rallying point for mass movements in the 1970s, through which the Jan Sangh gained public legitimacy and visibility.

The demolition of the Babri Masjid in 1992 by Hindu nationalists triggered a wave of sectarian violence across the country. The scale of violence and displacement in Ahmedabad (and even more so in Surat) was horrific.[105] After the demolition of the Babri Masjid, the BJP returned even more forcefully to the Hindutva plank[106] while preparing for the Ahmedabad municipal elections.[107]

The BJP not only won control of the AMC but also of five other municipal corporations—Surat, Rajkot, Baroda, Jamnagar and Bhavnagar, and Una.[108] Soon after that, the party won a large majority of the *taluka* and district *panchayat* elections.[109] The fortunes of the AMC, which was practically bankrupt, had turned by the mid-1990s, and the civic body initiated investments in attractive public infrastructure projects with renewed enthusiasm.[110]

Internal conflicts within the BJP, however, continued simmering. The tensions between the chief minister, Keshubhai Patel, and dissident leader Shankarsinh Vaghela spilled on to the streets, as the two factions battled each other across the state.[111] Internecine strife continued for the next few years, with the state legislature undergoing several moments of crisis. The state government stabilised somewhat, when Keshubhai Patel gained the majority support in 1998. After a dismal performance in the civic elections of 2000, the party's central leadership replaced Keshubhai Patel with Narendra Modi as chief minister, who then retained control over the state assembly for the next fourteen years.

Consistent BJP control of both the state assembly and the AMC, until date, was interrupted when the Congress Party won the AMC elections in 2000. Commentaries on these elections emphasise surprise at the Congress victory, even within the party.[112] The *Times of India* reported that workers, 'the backward classes' and 'even the Muslims' had returned to the Congress.[113] In what almost appeared to be a momentary revival of old political ties, Himmatsinh Patel, the son of a former TLA member, was elected as the Congress mayor of the AMC.[114]

The rapid ascent of the BJP was accompanied by a far-reaching penetration of the Hindutva ideology into the state machinery.[115] This went beyond the actions of a few actors and was central in pushing forward the Hindu nationalist project. Activities of the Sangh Parivar permeated not only the state machinery, but also educational, professional and co-operative institutions.[116] The 1990s (which was the first decade of the BJP's rule in Gujarat) were marked by violence against minorities. In the anti-Christian attacks that took place in south Gujarat in late 1999, there was considerable evidence of police complicity and of state-sanctioned prior planning.[117] Other state initiatives that advanced the Hindutva agenda included establishing official units to protect Hindu women from men of 'other religions'.[118] Having decreed the state as the 'Hindutva laboratory', the Sangh Parivar conducted what Spodek calls a 'battle for the control of the culture of the state, and especially of Ahmedabad'.[119] The educational system was sought to be remoulded to fit the ideology of the Hindu Right, while critique of the Sangh Parivar and free cultural expression was curtailed.[120]

The machinery of the Sangh Parivar not only influenced state practices and policies but also shaped the organisation of relief and rehabilitation following the devastating earthquake in 2001. This revealed the extent to which Hindu right-wing political and socio-cultural organisations held sway over both local government institutions and civil society. Not only were the efforts of the state administration inadequate,[121] but some civil society interventions also reportedly privileged Hindu areas for reconstruction. For instance, India Development and Relief Fund, a non-profit organisation, channelled considerable funds through Sewa Bharati, an NGO with strong links to the Sangh Parivar. A Sabrang fact-finding report documented that the RSS not only excluded minority areas in dispensing relief, but also further impeded other 'non-Hindu' organisations from attending to aid and reconstruction.[122] The communal carnage of 2002 most convincingly documents the role of state agencies in planning, implementing and sustaining the violence against Muslims.[123] The 'normative' secular practices of the state were called into question during this episode of violence—the rejection of a public pretence of constitutional secularism was accompanied by an unprecedented involvement of state actors in the performance of violence.[124]

Despite the mass destruction and insecurity generated by the communal carnage of 2002, the state administration nevertheless proceeded with conducting assembly elections towards the end of the year. The BJP's campaign rhetoric was framed clearly in the language of militant Hindutva. Modi embarked on a *gaurav yatra* (literally translated as a march for pride) in September 2002, ostensibly to 'strengthen communal harmony and social unity'.[125] The gaurav yatra was a blatant display of Hindu pride, and Modi's speeches demonstrated an openly militant stance.[126] The BJP won these elections with a clear majority, especially in those areas that had been deeply affected by the violence. Violent communal politics proved to be useful for the BJP's electoral success. The city's ethos changed to one that, as Spodek argued, 'endorsed contestations for political power, even when they relied on the strategic use of violence'.[127]

The BJP led by Modi (who by now faced a threat from detractors within the Sangh Parivar) returned to campaign for the AMC elections of 2005. The campaigning for the AMC polls (and those that followed) moved away from the communal rhetoric and relied more strongly on that of development. However, as Renu Desai suggests, the development platform on which these elections were contested was strongly underscored by Hindutva ideology and was governed by the same 'vectors of marginalisation and exclusion' that are central to the politics of the Hindu Right.[128] The BJP's victory in the civic elections of 2005 was largely credited to Modi's personal involvement, and the party has remained in power in the AMC since.[129] By the early 2000s, then, we are presented with a city that is deeply divided, with a public sphere that is overwhelmingly Hindu and with increasingly limited space for minorities.[130] The broadly delineated political landscape that this chapter has presented offers a backdrop against which to plot two critical forms of urban claim making—political engagement and property relations—that are the focus of this book. The changing contours of the political field that we have addressed here are given empirical depth and texture in the chapters that follow.

NOTES

1 The Congress Party is a national-level political party founded in 1885 that played a significant role during the Indian independence movement and continues to play a crucial role in national and local politics.

2 Raychaudhuri, 'Colonialism, Indigenous Elites and the Transformation of Cities in the Non-Western World', 677–726.

3 Ibid.

4 Gillion, *Ahmedabad: A Study in Indian Urban History*, 58ff.

5 Ibid., 117.

6 The constitution of the Ahmedabad Municipal Commission was related to the Rippon local self-government reforms, by which local bodies were popularly elected and granted more autonomy. The first elections for the Ahmedabad Municipal Commission were held in 1883, organised by ward instead of caste. The civic body introduced a wider scheme of taxation (in the form of house tax, wheel tax, taxes on the cleaning of privies, and so on) which received criticism in the local press. Ibid., 141.

7 Ibid., 143.

8 Raychaudhuri, 'Colonialism, Indigenous Elites and the Transformation of Cities in the Non-Western World', 691.

9 The Swadeshi movement gave a boost to domestically produced goods, and in Gujarat, this political stand translated into an expansion of the textile industry and substantial economic profits. Howard Spodek, 'The Manchesterisation of Ahmedabad', *Economic Weekly* 13, no. 11 (1965): 483–90.

10 Spodek, *Ahmedabad: Shock City of Twentieth-Century India*, 72–75.

11 Though I will not be focusing on the AMA in detail, the millowners' association and municipal politics were also closely tied. Ambalal Sarabhai and Kasturbhai Lalbhai, both prominent members of the AMA, were members of the Ahmedabad Municipality in late 1920s. In 1942, another member of the Lalbhai family was elected to the city municipality as a Congress candidate. Chinubhai Chimanbhai went on to become the first mayor of the AMC, from 1950 to 1961. Until 1965, the triumvirate of the Congress Party, the TLA and the AMA reigned in city politics. After Chinubhai's term as the mayor of AMC, another prominent mill owner, Jaykrishna Harivallabhdas, from the Ambica Mills family, succeeded him and was mayor until 1965.

12 Spodek, *Ahmedabad: Shock City of Twentieth-Century India*, 139. I owe the notion that the city's political field was shaped by the tensions and collaborations between these four key institutions to Howard Spodek.

13 Gulzarilal Nanda was a member of the TLA and was later appointed as labour minister and served as the prime minister of India for two short terms.

14 Promilla Kalhan, *Gulzarilal Nanda: A Life in the Service of the People* (New Delhi: Allied Publishers, 1997), 186.

15 Spodek, *Ahmedabad: Shock City of Twentieth-Century India*; Ravindra Kumar, *Life and Work of Sardar Vallabhbhai Patel* (New Delhi: Atlantic Publishers & Distri, 1991), 94.

16 Spodek, *Ahmedabad: Shock City of Twentieth-Century India*.

17 Vasant Bhagwant Karnik, *Indian Trade Unions: A Survey* (Bombay: Popular Prakashan, 1966), 97.

18 'Six decades of the TLA: 1917–1977', 17, available at http://www.indialabourarchives.org, accessed on 13 September 2013.

19 Yagnik and Sheth, *Ahmedabad: From Royal City to Megacity*.

20 Breman, *Making and Unmaking of an Industrial Working Class*, 79.

21 TLA, *Annual Report of the Textile Labour Association (Ahmedabad)* [hereafter *TLA Annual Report*], 1949–50.

22 *Times of India*, 7 August 1956.

23 In the protests that followed, some student leaders threw stones and were fired upon by the police without any prior warning. Four people were killed and fifty injured in this incident.

24 Indulal Yagnik, *The Autobiography of Indulal Yagnik*, trans. Devavrat N. Pathak, Howard Spodek and John R. Wood, vol. 3 (New Delhi: Manohar Publishers & Distributors, 2011), 450.

25 *Times of India*, 28 August 1956.

26 Morarji Desai was the chief minister of Bombay state (1952–57) and later the prime minister of India.

27 Yagnik, *Autobiography of Indulal Yagnik*, 459.

28 From across the political and ideological spectrum, candidates came together to form a multiparty platform called the Nagrik Paksh (Citizens Party) to contest the Ahmedabad municipal elections in 1957. Chinubhai Chimanbhai, a prominent mill owner who was the Congress mayor at that time, resigned from the party and joined the Nagrik Paksh as its leader. Neither the Congress nor the TLA contested these elections, preferring

instead to 'go into wilderness to serve the people only by peacefully waiting and watching'. The central and state elections, which took place nearly simultaneously, revealed the continued dominance of the Congress Party and the skewed geography of MGJP influence. The Congress captured both the central and the state elections. The influence of the MGJP was concentrated around the city of Ahmedabad and its adjacent districts of Mehsana and Kheda. The southern parts of the state, historically more connected to Bombay, were less moved by the zeal of the Maha Gujarat agitation. Twenty-five of the twenty-nine seats won by the party in the state elections and all of the five Lok Sabha seats came from the districts of Ahmedabad, Mehsana and Kheda. In Ahmedabad, Indulal Yagnik defeated TLA leader Khandubhai Desai for the Lok Sabha seat. For the state assembly, there was a close fight between the TLA secretary and INTUC president at the time, S. R. Vasavada, and the Maha Gujarat Janata Parishad candidate, Dinkar Mehta, locally known as the 'surprise man'. For a detailed analysis of these elections, see Spodek, *Ahmedabad: Shock City of Twentieth-Century India*, 143–57. See also *Times of India*, 11 March 1957 and 12 March 1957, and *TLA Annual Report*, 1961–62, 2.

29 Papers relating to Ahmedabad Police Firing Inquiry Commission, 1958. File no. 76. Nehru Memorial Museum and Library.

30 The most visible challenge was posed by Karsandas Parmar—a leader of the Republican Party and a member of the MGJP—and the doffers' union. Despite the successful strike action of July 1958, the union could not survive and returned to the TLA fold within a few years.

31 Yagnik, who would go on to cement his image as a working-class leader, had not gained a strong presence in the mill districts until the mid-1960s. By his own admission, it was only during the Maha Gujarat agitation in the mid-1950s that he ventured into the working-class districts for the first time.

32 Spodek, *Ahmedabad: Shock City of Twentieth-Century India*, 137–39. The TLA figures for these elections are somewhat different. The 1961–62 annual report states that the Congress put forward candidates for all sixty seats. They won fifty of those, out of which twenty went to TLA candidates. Of these, seventeen were mill workers. *TLA Annual Report*, 1961–62, 2.

33 A voluntary organisation established in 1946 comprised of mainly male mill workers and their sons.

34 *TLA Annual Report*, 1961–62, 2.

35 Ibid., 30.

36 The Praja Socialist Party and the Janata Samiti won a total of nineteen seats in the municipal corporation, none of which were from the mill neighbourhoods. Until 1960, the MGJP had primarily been concentrated in the middle-class areas of Khadia, Kalupur, Maninanagar and Ellisbridge, and the working-class areas had received somewhat limited attention from Indulal Yagnik and other leaders.

37 Breman, *The Making and Unmaking of an Industrial Working Class*, 85.

38 *Janata*, 2 April 1950.

39 Yagnik, quoted in Spodek, *Ahmedabad: Shock City of Twentieth-Century India*, 158.

40 *TLA Annual Report*, 1962–63, 6.

41 The Sangram Samiti was formed in 1963. It grew into Mahagujarat Millworkers' Union with 50,000 dues-paying members and twenty-six full-time party workers. Yagnik and Mehta were elected president and vice president respectively. Spodek, *Ahmedabad: Shock City of Twentieth-Century India*, 159.

42 The Congress had contested all seventy-eight seats and won only thirteen of them while the Janata Parishad and the Sangram Samiti swept the elections, winning forty-two seats. The different factions within the MGJP, however, ensured that municipal governance was fraught with tensions. Each party sought to promote their own candidate as mayor, and, as a result, the position rotated each year. Matters were not helped by the fact that the Congress in power in the state assembly and the MGJP in the municipal corporation were often locked in an impasse.

43 *TLA Annual Report*, 1964–65, 7.

44 Ghanshyam Shah, 'Communal Riots in Gujarat: Report of a Preliminary Investigation', *Economic and Political Weekly* 5, nos. 3–4–5 (1970): 187–200.

45 Dawn E. Jones and Rodney W. Jones, 'Urban Upheaval in India: The 1974 Nav Nirman Riots in Gujarat', *Asian Survey* 16, no. 11 (1976): 1012–33.

46 Indian National Trade Union Congress was the umbrella trade union of the Congress Party, formed in 1947.

47 *Times of India*, 24 January 1972.

48 An affluent land-owning and farming caste.

49 Jones and Jones, 'Urban Upheaval in India.'

50 Breman, *The Making and Unmaking of an Industrial Working Class*, 94.

51 Ibid.

52 *TLA Annual Report*, 1974–75, 5.

53 Ibid.

54 Spodek, *Ahmedabad: Shock City of Twentieth-Century India*, 169. Part of Patel's early agenda was to expedite a favourable decision on the Narmada Dam project which had been caught in a stalemate for more than a decade. The foundations of the grand Narmada Valley Project had been laid in newly independent India. It was to include several dams along the course of the river, the most significant of which was the Sardar Sarovar Dam. The construction of the dam would affect nearly 4.7 million acres of land, the lives of up to half a million people and have severe ecological consequences. The question of resettlement and rehabilitation was at the centre of the social movements that had opposed the construction of this project. In exchange for support on the Narmada issue, Patel promised financial help to the Congress high command for the forthcoming electoral campaign in Uttar Pradesh. This financial assistance was reportedly procured through dubious means, thus bringing the issue of political corruption to the fore. For instance, it was alleged that the powerful groundnut farmers' lobby had extended monetary help, in return for relaxed state controls over prices and exports of oil. The price rise of cooking oil, then, emerged as a mobilising issue for the city's middle classes and remained a key reason for continuing tensions. Another cause for public displeasure was the alarming rise in the prices of food grains. This, too, was related circuitously to the Uttar Pradesh elections. For a longer discussion of these tensions, please see Jones and Jones, 'Urban Upheaval in India', 1012–33. For a detailed analysis of Narmada Dam project and the social activism around it, please see Amita Baviskar, *In the Belly of the River: Tribal Conflicts over Development in the Narmada Valley* (Delhi: Oxford University Press, 1999).

55 Jones and Jones, 'Urban Upheaval in India', 1015.

56 Ghanshyam Shah, 'Anatomy of Urban Riots: Ahmedabad 1973', *Economic and Political Weekly* 9, nos. 6–7–8 (1974): 233–40.

57 Ibid.

58 Jones and Jones, 'Urban Upheaval in India', 1023.

59 Patel, however, tenaciously refused to dissolve the state assembly, negotiating instead with the Congress high command to allow a new government under the leadership of Thakorbhai Desai, an ally. This plan did not succeed and Patel was expelled from the Congress Party for defying orders. He immediately formed the Kisan Mazdoor Lok Parishad (KMLP), which relied mainly on the support of Patel farmers and in a bizarre turn of political play, led the movement for dissolving the legislative assembly. This discussion of the chronology of the Nav Nirman movement has been drawn

extensively from Jones and Jones, 'Urban Upheaval in India', 1012–33; Shah, 'Anatomy of Urban Riots', 233–40 and Spodek, *Ahmedabad: Shock City of Twentieth-Century India*, 181–94.

60 For comparative accounts of the Gujarat and Bihar agitations, please see John R. Wood, 'Extra-Parliamentary Opposition in India: An Analysis of Populist Agitations in Gujarat and Bihar', *Pacific Affairs* 48, no. 3 (1975): 313–34 and Ghanshyam Shah, *Protest Movements in Two Indian States: A Study of the Gujarat and Bihar Movements* (Ajanta Publications, 1977).

61 Patel began his time away from the Congress Party with the formation of the KMLP, following that with joining the Janata Party in 1977, against the opposition of many party members, such as Harin Pathak and Ashok Bhatt. See *Times of India*, 4 December 1977 and 23 December 1977. By the early 1990s, Patel had founded the Janata Dal (Gujarat), which immediately entered into an alliance and thereafter merged with the Congress. See Ghanshyam Shah, 'BJP's Rise to Power', *Economic and Political Weekly* 31, no. 2–3 (1996): 165–70.

62 Ghanshyam Shah, 'Polarised Communities', *Seminar* 470 (1998): 33.

63 Narendrasinh Mahida, one of the founders of the Kshatriya Sabha, cited in *Times of India*, 22 July 1985.

64 Rajni Kothari and Rushikesh Maru, 'Caste and Secularism in India: Case Study of a Caste Federation', *Journal of Asian Studies* 25, no. 1 (1965): 33–50.

65 The Swatantra Party was established in 1959 with the intention of providing a 'non-leftist' opposition to the Congress Party. For a history of the party, please see Howard L. Erdman, *The Swatantra Party and Indian Conservatism* (New York: Cambridge University Press, 1967). See also Kiran Desai and Ghanshyam Shah, *Gujarat: When Patels Resist the Kshatriyas* (New Delhi: Routledge, 2009).

66 *Times of India*, 22 July 1985.

67 *Times of India*, 2 February 1994.

68 *Times of India*, 14 July 1985.

69 Similar mobilisations had taken place a decade earlier in north India, for instance, Charan Singh's Bharatiya Kranti Dal (BKD), which was organised around peasant identity rather than caste identity. The BKD went on to become one of the key coalition partners in the Janata government that toppled the Congress in 1977. Caste, until this point, at least in Gujarat, had not emerged as a potent political force.

70 *Times of India*, 14 July 1985.

71 Between 1967 and 1980, the membership of Patidars within the Congress Party fell from 21.5 per cent to 10.7 per cent, while their representation in other parties more than doubled—from 21.3 per cent to 52.4 per cent—during the same period. *Times of India*, 22 July 1985.

72 Achyut Yagnik, 'Spectre of Caste War', *Economic and Political Weekly* 16, no. 13 (1981): 553–55.

73 Ibid.

74 Spodek, *Ahmedabad: Shock City of Twentieth-Century India*, 209–11.

75 Achyut Yagnik, 'Paradoxes of Populism', *Economic and Political Weekly* 18, no. 35 (1983): 1505–07, 1507. See also *BusinessLine*, 18 September 2011.

76 Ibid., 1505.

77 Ibid.

78 Harish Khare, 'Social Tensions in Ahmedabad', paper presented at the Ahmedabad 2001—Imperatives Now Towards a New Metropolitan Management Strategy, 1988. This, of course, refers to the position of the AMA as an institution, and not to the industrialists per se. Industrial investments had since diversified—channelled into chemicals, real estate and other ventures.

79 The city's population had grown from 1,149,918 in 1961 to 2,876,710 in 1991. *Census of India*, 2001.

80 *Times of India*, 28 February 1981. The RSS resolutions stated: 'The RSS considers it necessary that reservation be continued for the present with a view to bringing all these brethren of ours who have remained backward in educational, social and economic fields over the centuries at par with the rest of society.' *R.S.S. Resolves 1950–2007: Resolutions Passed by A.B.P.S and A.B.K.M. of R.S.S. from 1950 to 2007* (New Delhi: Suchi Prakashan, 2007), 100.

81 In 1981, R. S. Gavai, president of the Republican Party of India, alleged that the BJP's 'rank and file was actively taking part in the agitation'. *Times of India*, 8 March 1981. Similar allegations were made by the Congress Party, whose leaders implied that 'BJP workers and anti-social elements having links with the RSS were trying to instigate people and spread violence in Ahmedabad'. *Times of India*, 4 February 1981 and 11 February 1981. Likewise, police testimonies to the Dave Commission investigating the violence of 1985 recorded that the Akhil Bharatiya Vidyarthi Parishad (ABVP), the student wing of the BJP, assumed command over the anti-reservation agitation by February 1985, 'master-minding the planning and execution' of the movement. Justice V. S. Dave, *Report of the Commission*

of Inquiry: Into the Incidents of Violence and Disturbances which Took Place in Various Places in the State of Gujarat since February, 1985 to 18th July, 1985, Vol. I (Ahmedabad: Government of India, 1990), 269. See also Engineer, 'Communal Fire Engulfs Ahmedabad Once Again', 1116–20, and *Illustrated Weekly,* 19 May 1985.

82 Ashis Nandy, Shikha Trivedy, Shail Mayaram and Achyut Yagnik, *Creating a Nationality: The Ramjanmabhumi Movement and Fear of the Self* (Delhi: Oxford University Press, 1998).

83 *Times of India,* 21 November 1983.

84 Christophe Jaffrelot, 'The Hindu Nationalist Reinterpretation of Pilgrimage in India: The Limits of Yatra Politics', *Nations and Nationalism* 15, no. 1 (2009): 9–11.

85 Nandy et al., *Creating a Nationality.* The involvement of these groups signified Sikh, Buddhist and Dalit participation.

86 *India Today,* 31 May 1986.

87 Ibid.

88 Nandy et al., *Creating a Nationality.*

89 *India Today,* 31 May 1986.

90 Berenschot, *Riot Politics: Hindu–Muslim Violence and the Indian State,* 143–45.

91 *Times of India,* 25 January 1987.

92 Incidentally, Narendra Modi joined the BJP as the general secretary in 1987, and it was reported that his 'first test' were the AMC elections the same year. Available at www.narendramodi.in, accessed on 23 June 2015.

93 *Times of India,* 29 January 1987.

94 *Times of India,* 31 January 1987.

95 *Times of India,* 6 January 1987 and 9 February 1987.

96 *India Today,* 15 December 1989. The party secured eighty-five seats in the 1989 general elections.

97 Christophe Jaffrelot, *Religion, Caste, and Politics in India* (Delhi: Primus Books, 2010), 359.

98 Nandy et al., *Creating a Nationality.*

99 Shah, 'Bjp's Rise to Power'.

100 *Times of India,* 27 February 1990.

101 In 1990, the then prime minister, V. P. Singh, accepted the recommendations of the Mandal Commission, which advocated an extension of caste-based reservations in government jobs. This led to protests by upper-caste groups across the country.

102 Ghanshyam Shah, 'Tenth Lok Sabha Elections: BJP's Victory in Gujarat', *Economic and Political Weekly* 26, no. 51 (1991): 2921–24, 2924.

103 Ibid.

104 Ibid., 2922.

105 The techniques and tactics of rioting in Surat and the presentation of the riot as a televised spectacle, in a sense, foreshadowed the pogrom of 2002. This episode of violence also prompted mass displacement as nearly 200,000 Oriya workers employed in the power-looms migrated back to their villages. See, for instance, *Times of India*, 18 December 1992 and 25 December 1992. See also Jan Breman, 'Anti-Muslim Pogrom in Surat', *Economic and Political Weekly* 28, no. 16 (1993): 737–41.

106 *Times of India*, 25 December 1992.

107 These elections were repeatedly postponed and were finally held in June 1995. By this time, Chimanbhai Patel had passed away, and the BJP had come to power in the state assembly. The BJP's win in Gujarat was accompanied by electoral gains elsewhere in the country, most significantly in neighbouring Maharashtra, where the Shiv Sena–BJP combine came to power in 1995. The AMC elections were then bracketed by the BJP's first majority win in the state assembly and the forthcoming Lok Sabha elections. As such, these elections were expected to have 'far reaching political repercussions in the state'. See *Times of India*, 9 June 1995.

108 *Times of India*, 15 June 1995.

109 *Times of India*, 19 June 1995.

110 Howard Spodek, 'Crises and Response: Ahmedabad 2000', *Economic and Political Weekly* (2001): 1627–38. Some of these infrastructure and municipal projects find mention through this book, for instance, the Sabarmati Riverfront Development Project and the Slum Networking Project.

111 *Times of India*, 3 October 1995.

112 Spodek, 'Crises and Response', 1627–38.

113 *Times of India*, 4 October 2000.

114 *Indian Express*, 18 October 2000.

115 Nikita Sud, 'Secularism and the Gujarat State: 1960–2005', *Modern Asian Studies* 42, no. 6 (2008): 1251–81.

116 Sanjeevini Badigar Lokhande, *Communal Violence, Forced Migration and the State: Gujarat since 2002* (Delhi: Cambridge University Press, 2015), 43–44.

117 Previously, the state government had sanctioned a survey of the churches and Christians in Dangs district (where much of the violence took place), and observers averred that these surveys provided a road map for the systematic

attacks that followed. See 'Human Rights Watch', available at https://www.hrw.org/legacy/reports/1999/indiachr/christians8-04.htm#P393_83982, accessed on 20 October 2015. See also Sud, 'Secularism and the Gujarat State'.

118 Sud, 'Secularism and the Gujarat State'.

119 Howard Spodek, 'In the Hindutva Laboratory: Pogroms and Politics in Gujarat, 2002', *Modern Asian Studies* 44, no. 2 (2010): 349–99, 381.

120 Ibid. Especially significant here are the routine attacks and acts of vandalism by members of the Hindu Right directed at art shows, film screenings and other cultural events.

121 Lokhande, *Communal Violence, Forced Migration and the State*, 44.

122 Sabrang, 'Foreign Exchange of Hate', available at http://www.sacw.net/2002/FEHi/FEH/appendixe.html, accessed on 13 May 2020.

123 An extensive body of literature exists on various aspects of this episode of violence. For a wide-angled and empirically detailed account of the events of 2002, please see the Concerned Citizens' Tribunal, 'Crime against Humanity', Vols. 1, 2 and 3 (2002), available at http://www.sabrang.com/tribunal/index.html, accessed on 13 May 2020. See also Siddharth Varadarajan, *Gujarat: The Making of a Tragedy* (New Delhi: Penguin Books, 2002).

124 Sud, 'Secularism and the Gujarat State', 1276.

125 *Times of India*, 22 August 2002.

126 *Outlook*, 22 November 2002.

127 Spodek, 'From Gandhi to Modi', 149.

128 Desai, 'The Globalising City in the Time of Hindutva', 118.

129 *BusinessLine*, 17 October 2005.

130 A study on the BJP's Muslim supporters suggests that while public support for the party may have increased amongst the city's Muslims, this has not translated into an electoral mandate. One explanation that the author presents for this contradiction between support and votes is in terms of expressive dissonance that is engendered by the absence of a space of dissent. Raheel Dhattiwala, 'The Puzzle of the BJP's Muslim Supporters in Gujarat', The Hindu Centre for Politics and Public Policy, Policy Report 5 (2014).

PART I

INCARNATIONS OF THE POLITICAL INTERMEDIARY

An interesting place to begin our discussions on local political practices would be through an account of the daily routines of two municipal councillors[1] from Gomtipur, a former mill area in eastern Ahmedabad. Imdad Sheikh (name changed), the Congress Party corporator from Gomtipur, was serving his third term in the AMC when I met him for the first time in 2011. On most days, he attends to his constituents from his residence-office in Ameen Society. One of the more affluent housing societies in the Rajpur–Gomtipur area, Ameen Society was located along the broad road that connects the neighbourhood to Amraiwadi, another large mill area, and the New Cotton Mills Circle. Surrounding these slightly more upscale residences were rows upon rows of chawls, interspersed with small workshops, the vast expanse of the closed Topi Mills compound, the impressive Bibiji's mosque and the shaking minarets, one of the city's minor tourist attractions. The single- and double-storeyed houses in the society were fronted by an enclosed verandah, usually left curtained to keep out the unbearable Ahmedabad heat or the prying eyes of one's neighbours. It is on the enclosed verandah of his house that Imdad Sheikh has his audience with his constituents from 9 a.m. to 11 a.m. every morning.

Imdadbhai,[2] like most other residents of the neighbourhood, has strong ties to the textile mill industry. The son of migrant mill workers from Andhra Pradesh, he grew up in the neighbouring Nagpur Bohra ki Chaali before moving to the more gentrified environs of Ameen Society. In his political affairs, he is assisted by Shekharbhai. If Imdadbhai is busy during this daily 'public time', disposing of complaints and petitions with alarming speed, barely pausing in the face of a steady stream of supplicants, Shekharbhai is even busier, keeping track of the various complaints, attending to those waiting at the gates, while simultaneously fielding calls on two cell phones and one cordless phone. The complaints and appeals ranged from broken water connections to seeking permission to hold festivals to assistance with legal matters. Some he would brush aside with a curt 'Aap ka kaam ho jayega';[3] with others he would write out letters of recommendation or supplication. Apart from this designated 'public time' and his office hours at the AMC in the afternoons, people would drop in to see him throughout the day.

Imdad Sheikh's manner of attending to his constituents was rather akin to holding court—there was usually an extended period of waiting before he would emerge from his house to meet his audience. Most of those who came to see him would wait patiently on the street rather than stepping up to the shaded and somewhat cooler verandah, which was furnished with divans to receive visitors. This meeting space displayed artefacts of his success—both as a social and a political leader. In a glass cabinet prominently placed in front of the visitors were arrayed several awards from the Congress Party and Islamic social organisations. These are both connections that he flaunts, having repeatedly offered to channel *zakaat*[4] funds and mobilise support from fellow Congress leaders to finance NGOs working in predominantly Muslim areas such as Vatva.

Imdadbhai's personal style was impressive and one that was visible in his mannerisms, in his dress and his oratory. For instance, he would answer the phone with a 'yes, boss' instead of a more conventional greeting. Included among his various artefacts of success was a laminated (and obviously photoshopped) headshot of himself, wearing aviator sunglasses and posing against a sunny sky. At public events, this style and flair are reinforced. Of the three Congress municipal corporators from the area, Imdadbhai was the most prominent during the state assembly election campaign of 2012. At almost all the public events organised by the Congress Party in the neighbourhood, he was assigned the role of master of ceremonies and shared space most closely with the Member of Legislative Assembly (MLA).

Imdad Sheikh has been the municipal corporator of Gomtipur since 2000, having served his first term as an independent and the later two terms as a Congress candidate. He and Jeevanbhai Parmar, the other Congress councillor from Gomtipur, formed an independent panel in the 2000 municipal corporation elections and had contested elections together ever since. In 2005, they were rewarded for their close associations with the Congress Party with electoral nominations. I first met Jeevanbhai through a reference from his daughter-in-law, a grassroots worker with Self Employed Women's Association (SEWA).[5] His manner of engagement with his constituents was markedly more plebeian as he conducted his daily meetings at the Gomtipur post office crossroads.

This particular *char rasta* is of some significance in the neighbourhood, as it is the site of Congress power in the area and forms a 'border' of sorts between the 'Hindu' and 'Muslim' parts of the neighbourhood. Its symbolic significance is attested to by the fact that Narendra Modi's 2012 state election rally[6] was held here. The crossroads (officially named Maganbhai Mithabhai Chowk after a former mill worker and municipal corporator) has a warren of streets radiating from it, each with rows of chawls. On either side of the char rasta are small shops—a photocopy shop–garment processing workshop owned by Jeevanbhai, a photography studio owned by his nephew and a Muslim-owned tailor's shop that has since then relocated to Vatva. The fourth side was dominated by the eerily vacant Sarangpur No. 2 Mill compound.

On most days, this char rasta bears witness to the workings of Jeevanbhai's municipal offices. In his third term as the local Congress Party corporator from Gomtipur, he attends to complaints, supplications and appeals from his constituents. Despite his advanced age, he keeps regular office hours—sitting on a tin chair at the curb from 11 a.m. to 1 p.m. and then from 4 p.m. to 8 p.m.—and conducts his business in an intimidatingly brusque manner.

Both Jeevanbhai and Imdadbhai had various other demands on their time beyond their political commitments. Jeevanbhai was involved in bootlegging and ran a registered cultural organisation, while Imdadbhai dabbled in the real estate business and was active in several Muslim charitable organisations. The electoral calculations between the two proved to be very successful. They won as independent candidates in a Congress stronghold, no doubt supported by their long histories of engagement in neighbourhood life. Part of the logic behind this alliance was the sharing of a deeply communally divided constituency. The social divisions, in this case, were reflected quite starkly in the spatial arrangement of the neighbourhood, with entire pockets being uniformly Hindu or Muslim. With Jeevanbhai's hold over the Dalit areas and Imdadbhai's influence in the Muslim parts of the neighbourhood, they managed to forge an effective partnership.

'Communal harmony' became an important platform through which they positioned themselves as formal politicians in Gomtipur. News reports have also mentioned their contributions in maintaining peace during the violence of 2002. An article in the *Indian Express*, for instance, noted that their 'firm resolve to maintain peace meant that no untoward incident took place'.[7] By

Jeevanbhai's own accounts, their close relationship has managed to diffuse many potentially tense communal situations—at any point when there is an indication of conflict, he would make a phone call to Imdadbhai asking him to keep peace in his area, while reciprocating with equal commitment in his own locality. At other times, however, his deep suspicion of Muslims and fleeting references to his own involvement in episodes of rioting would surface.

Alternative sources also point to the fragility of this 'harmony'. Fact-finding reports suggest that in 2002, he along with Jitu Vaghela, a former BJP corporator and MLA, instigated and led about 700 Dalit residents to attack Muslims in the neighbouring Mariam Bibi ki Chaali.[8] Imdadbhai, similarly, has been embroiled in judicial proceedings as an accused in a riot case of 2002.[9] Harmony,[10] then, perhaps remains a feint, obscuring the negotiations and contestations that play out in the everyday political rhythms of the industrial east.

While the notion of harmony retains a strong emotive charge (and is often posed as a powerful political plank) for a city as sharply divided as Ahmedabad, it does not adequately capture the alliances, the strategies and the conflicts that govern the micro-level politics of the working-class neighbourhoods. An examination from the top—through an analysis of city-level political calibrations or the shift of electoral powers—while providing a bird's-eye view of the political field also does not reveal the richness of local political engagement. How, then, could we make an attempt to understand the transforming terrain of politics in working-class Ahmedabad? Through what devices could we trace political practice, while retaining a view of both the broader historical shifts and the texture of quotidian politics? How could we analyse the beat and the cadence of everyday social practice as it interacted with, responded to and, in turn, shaped wider political and economic processes?

An incident in Imdadbhai's office provided a pointer. On one regular day, when I was awaiting my turn to speak to him, an elderly Muslim gentleman approached him with a request. It was a fairly routine matter—his young grandson needed admission in a local private school. Imdadbhai assured him that he would reason with the school principal and that his work will be done. On taking his leave, the older man turned to Imdadbhai and said, by way of appreciation and gratitude, 'You are a dada, Imdadbhai.' *Dada*, a term commonly used to describe those operating at the margins of the law, with an easy reliance on violence or the threat of it, was being used as a complimentary one.

A second encounter furnished further insights into the workings of contemporary political practices in the mill areas and provided a lens through which to examine the historical transformation of local political figures and forms of political engagement. Even during our very first meeting, Jeevanbhai dropped hints about his violent past, proudly displaying battle scars from his days at the *akhada*. A 75-year-old great grandfather as well as a bootlegger of some serious repute,[11] he had been actively involved in local politics for several decades. Over months of interaction with him, I learned more concrete details of his career—as a political intermediary, a TLA representative and a formidable dada.

In writing about working-class neighbourhoods in colonial Bombay, Chandavarkar points out that '*dada* is properly a reputation rather than a status or profession—a reputation for physical prowess or for getting things done'.[12] The association of the figure of a dada with that of a fairly respectable politician opens up ways of addressing questions of local political practices. It points to, for instance, the multiplicity of roles that local influential figures may occupy. It emphasises the centrality of reputation in the making of local leadership and it allows us to interrogate the historical processes that produce spheres of neighbourhood control and authority. It alludes to how formal and informal registers of authority could coexist and bolster each other. In a sense, the three chapters that follow examine the interfaces between formal and informal realms of politics. In this, I locate the figure of the intermediary, in its various forms, at the centre of my explorations. This line of inquiry helps us make a broader comment on the distinctions posited between 'civil' and 'political' society, foregrounding the interpenetration and intersection between the two realms, the points of which were historically dynamic and shifting.

The figure of the intermediary, in its various configurations, then, emerges as a central element in the production of social space of the neighbourhood. It embodies in some measure the authority of the dada, the goonda and the local leader as well as that of the elected political representative, party member or the trade unionist. Or in other words, they operate at the intersection between the 'formal' and 'informal' registers of social regulation. Without understanding the intermediary, and the rhythms of political practice that she or he is enmeshed in, we cannot understand the changing socio-spatial form. While this figure is a necessary one, it is, by no means, a fixed one. It is inherently unstable—transforming and being transformed by the networks of politics and the circuits of local power.

The three chapters in Part I map changes at the neighbourhood level, tracking the circulation of power, the modes of political engagements and the constitution of local forms of leadership. They discuss the making of a variegated political landscape, exploring questions of civic, spatial and political marginalisation. Reading the three chapters together will allow us to outline the plebeian city's political history for nearly a century and also glean insights into some of the practices and figures that animate this landscape. The broadly chronological arrangement of these chapters is not intended to signify transition or evolution from one form of mediation to another but rather serves as a frame on which to plot the thickening or diffusion of certain forms of political practice at particular historical moments. Through an examination of the circulation of local power, I trace how formal and informal modes of authority are imbricated in working-class Ahmedabad.

NOTES

1　A councillor is an elected member of the AMC. The term 'councillor' is often colloquially referred to as a 'corporator'. In this book, as in colloquial speech, these terms have been used interchangeably.

2　*Bhai* and *ben* are common honorifics used in everyday Gujarati speech.

3　'Your work will be done.'

4　A form of alms-giving in Islam.

5　SEWA was founded in 1972 by Ela Bhatt. It emerged from the TLA, the city's dominant trade union, and continues to command a certain presence in the mill neighbourhoods. Many of the organisation's grassroots workers are former mill workers and continue to live in the mill districts.

6　Narendra Modi, currently the prime minister of India, was then the chief minister of Gujarat.

7　*Indian Express*, 8 March 2002.

8　Memoranda in Asghar Ali Engineer, *The Gujarat Carnage* (Hyderabad: Orient Blackswan, 2003), 466.

9　*Times of India*, 15 September 2003.

10　Ward Berenschot has discussed in considerable detail the links between communal violence and the practices of political mediation. He argues that one motivation for keeping peace during situations of communal conflict would be if the local patronage channels do not accrue electoral gains from rioting. For a more detailed exposition of this argument, please see Ward Berenschot, 'The Spatial Distribution of Riots: Patronage and the Instigation of Communal Violence in Gujarat, India', *World Development* 39, no. 2 (2011): 221–30. Raheel Dhattiwala further complicates the understanding of harmony in situations of conflict. Peacekeeping and inter-community cooperation, she argues, is underpinned by mechanisms of enforcement that draw upon the authority of both legitimate and illegitimate institutions. See Raheel Dhattiwala, 'Cooperation and Protection in a Peaceful Neighbourhood', paper presented at conference on Re-visiting the Working-Class Neighbourhood in South Asia, University of Göttingen, Göttingen, 11–12 July 2014.

11 Alternatively, he has been described by many others in the locality as an 'anti-social element'.

12 Chandavarkar, *The Origins of Industrial Capitalism in India*, 201.

2

THE TLA AND *DADAGIRI*

Mediation in the Mill Neighbourhoods

Present-day mill neighbourhoods in Ahmedabad still retain traces of their previous incarnations. The vast emptiness of the former textile mill compounds is a material reminder of the city's earlier prominence as an industrial centre rivalling Bombay. Contemporary styles of everyday political functioning similarly owe their origins to the historic position of these localities as sites of prosperous industrial activity and as spaces of vibrant working-class politics. A close reading of the local politics of the mill neighbourhoods of Ahmedabad reveals the layers of mediation that existed between the dominant trade union, the TLA, the Congress Party and the city municipality. It offers us crucial insights into the textures of worker politics in an industrial city and leads us towards a more complex understanding of the multi-scalar dynamics of local political practices.

I discuss two figures of local importance, both considerably invested in matters of everyday political mediation—the union representative (the pratinidhi) and the local strongman (or dadas, as they were colloquially referred to)—and focus particular attention on the ways in which their power was constituted and on the points of intersection between their seemingly discrete realms. These two figures—the morally upright TLA pratinidhi constructed, for all discursive purposes, in the image of the model worker and the dada, the 'anti-social element', operating on the fringes of respectable society—appeared to inhabit two very different worlds. Literally meaning 'elder brother', the term *dada* is often used to signify a neighbourhood tough. In Ahmedabad, as elsewhere, they carry a reputation of being *mathabhari*, which, roughly translated, means hot-headed and dangerous. In more concrete terms, a mathabhari person would be defiant of established structures of authority and would have a penchant for violence while being able to extend a hand of patronage and protection in their domain of influence. Yet, as this chapter will show, the worlds of the dada and the pratinidhi coincided and converged at various points and it was through these intersections that the power of both of these political intermediaries was constituted during the period under study.

Though the dada has been widely represented in popular culture, a staple of Hindi cinema, there has been limited scholarly inquiry into this figure.[1] In Bollywood films, the figure of the dada has had multiple portrayals, from a small-time crook to a thug with a heart of gold, sometimes growing in influence to assume the position of 'don' or a gangster.[2] Usually posed against the 'hero', or protagonist, such figures operate on the margins of the law, though often within certain codes of honour. Historically, the figure of the dada, the local tough, the hoodlum, or the goonda, has had a wide presence across South Asia and is often seen as part of a 'rough', urban underbelly and neatly distinguished from the 'respectable' working classes. Much of these categories emerged as social and legal entities through modes of colonial governance.[3] The aim of these strategies of categorisation was to group a broad spectrum of 'deviant' activities and to separate this group from the 'rest of society'. As Das notes in the case of colonial Calcutta, there was a remarkable heterogeneity to this group.[4] Part of the exercise undertaken in this section of the book is an attempt to pixelate this category.

I place this figure within the broader narrative of the TLA's political, civic and electoral engagements from the early 1920s to the late 1960s and trace his political lineage, his modes of forming social and political relationships, and the consolidation and contestations of his power.[5] TLA gained a foothold in the mill districts through its impressive network of grassroots institutions and intermediaries, maintaining what could be called a 'parallel government'.[6] As within the textile mills, the TLA's civic and political activities needed the active participation of certain dominant neighbourhood figures. These figures, the pratinidhi and the dada, were key players within the TLA's institutional apparatus. Their authority, in some part, stemmed from their ability to provide services and mobilise connections in higher places in the union offices and in the municipal corporation. The union's grassroots presence, on the other hand, was dependent upon these intermediaries. The actual functioning of union representatives served as an interface between the formal and informal registers of control in the mill districts.

The significant overlaps between the two figures of local leadership—the dada and the TLA representative, the pratinidhi,[7] as they were called in Gujarati, or 'member', as they were colloquially referred to—manifested not only in the scope of their functioning but also in the performative styles that they embodied. And it was a very particular form of masculinity, that of *dadagiri*,[8] that tied together the seemingly separate realms of the dada and the pratinidhi. The TLA, as I show in this chapter, reinforced its presence over the mill districts through the figure of the dada and his performance of masculinity. This is particularly striking since one of the TLA's primary objectives was to create the model worker and to sanitise what was seen as an unruly one.

THE INSTITUTIONAL APPARATUS OF THE TLA

Beginning with the 1924 elections when the first mill worker candidate was elected to the city municipality, certain mechanisms and institutions were established in the mill areas to strengthen the union's electoral prospects. These were expanded and consolidated over the years and were given great legitimacy by the TLA's prominence in municipal politics. In part, this attention to workers' living spaces was prompted by the growing influence of rival unions and the challenges they posed on the TLA's hegemony. Through the late 1920s and the 1930s, the declining profits of the industry and the wage reductions that followed were met with a wave of strikes and industrial action.[9] The Delhi Agreement of 1935 between the TLA and the AMA, which sanctioned wage cuts and rationalisation further exacerbated the situation—protests and strikes escalated while state authorities came down heavily on workers' militancy.

There are clear indications at this point that the TLA's authority was waning in the mill areas. Two tendencies are worthy of note: old TLA hands, like Kacharabhai, for instance, the union's first mill worker municipal councillor, were defecting to the Congress socialists.[10] Accompanying this shift was an overwhelming support for the strike activity led by the Mill Kamdar Union.[11] This spate of strikes in the late 1930s was a reaction against the 25 per cent wage cut of weavers. Predominantly Muslim, weavers were already alienated within the TLA's dominant Hindu style of functioning and came out en masse in support of the strike.[12] The Mill Kamdar Union concentrated on building networks within the neighbourhoods, forming chawl committees as crucial strategies of industrial action.[13] The strike of 1937 and the techniques devised by the rival trade unions further alerted the TLA to the importance of securing a hold upon the working-class areas.

The union began deepening its involvement in neighbourhood affairs.[14] Substantive changes in the union's constitution in 1930 included an amendment that called for the 'promotion of civic and political interests of the workpeople'.[15] This, in Ahmedabad, converged in the union's participation in municipal politics. Similar to developments elsewhere in the subcontinent, the civic body began making increasingly greater interventions in the social reproduction of labour.[16] As Shankarlal Banker, one of the union's founders, stated in an interview:

> With Kacharabhai in the Municipality, it became easier to call the attention of both the Congress Party and the municipal officers to the needs of the workers' neighbourhoods for roads, lights, water, toilets and other facilities.... The working classes had been unaware of the responsibilities and the activities of the Municipality, on their behalf, and they had suffered from feelings of inferiority.[17]

The TLA's neighbourhood-level associations—the ward unions,[18] the voters' association, the Seva Dal and the *latta mahajans*—thus formed one powerful flank through which the union retained its control over the mill neighbourhoods. The other equally robust strategy was centred on the workplace—that is, the legislation of the Bombay Industrial Disputes Act in 1938, shepherded into existence by Labour Minister Gulzarilal Nanda, which enshrined arbitration as the model of industrial negotiation. Under this Act, the TLA acquired the position of the sole representative union for dispute settlements.

In order to examine the TLA's dominance and its eventual decline in the city's local government, it is important to understand the peculiarly hierarchical structure of the union. The TLA retained its top-down, Gandhian structure until the end. The union comprised of twelve occupational unions, each with their own representatives (one for every fifty to seventy workers) on the Joint Board of Representatives. Occupational representative boards were formed in the mills, and elections were conducted every two years. The representative board had committees that dealt with neighbourhood issues, including one specifically dedicated to municipal affairs.[19] Out of these pratinidhis on the joint board, 115 were appointed to the Central Executive Committee on the basis of the numerical strength of the subsidiary unions. The Central Executive Committee was composed of these pratinidhis as well as twenty-eight honorary members 'who operated independently of the rank and file', as did the nominees to the Advisory Council.[20] The president and the secretaries assumed office for an indefinite period, through appointment rather than election, resulting in a distinctly hierarchical structure. The higher echelons of the union were largely composed of non-worker trade unionists.[21] Workers' participation in the union's functioning was limited to electing their pratinidhis. The pratinidhi's position, meant specifically for mill workers, was usually a very profitable one and, therefore, in such great demand that it was often, as Jan Breman writes, 'lucrative enough to be auctioned off in advance'.[22] The pratinidhis were the ones who collected the members' contributions and negotiated employment relations among the workers, the management and the union. For these services—addressing workers' complaints, mediating recruitment, extending contracts for temporary workers, and securing loans and other benefits—the pratinidhis would expect to be paid. On payday, it was the pratinidhis who would collect the union membership fees from the workers under them, out of which they were entitled to a 5 per cent commission.[23] TLA representatives occupied a range of roles—they doubled up as contractors and small-time money lenders—and lubricated the channels of patronage for the payment of a fee.[24] Recruitment remained one of the key mechanisms through which the pratinidhi exerted his influence, dispensing employment to relatives or members of the same village or community.[25]

A short note on the early forms of recruitment in the Ahmedabad textile industry is perhaps necessary to situate the pratinidhi's institutional lineage. The jobber system, which was the main channel of recruitment through the late nineteenth century, relied extensively on social connections (including, to a large extent, caste, community and regional networks).[26] While providing a certain level of employment security, it was also deeply exploitative. The labour shortage that beleaguered the Ahmedabad mills until 1923 had allowed workers some control in negotiating the terms of their employment.[27] As labour supply progressively increased, the relationship between the jobber and the mill workers gradually changed. Evidence presented to the Royal Commission on Labour suggests that, by the late 1920s, 'jobbers and mukkadams were notoriously corrupt and [did] not hesitate to extract bribes. Something has to be paid at the time of entering service and on the first and very subsequent pay day to keep the jobber in good humor'.[28]

The transformation of the terms of this relationship also signalled the greater control that the jobber was beginning to exercise over the mill worker's life.[29] Drawing upon the combined authority of the caste leader and the goonda, the excesses of the jobber were well documented for the early years of the twentieth century.[30] The murder of jobber Ebrahim of Bharatkhand Mills, by an eighteen-year-old mill hand, prompted a sessions judge to declare that there are jobbers who 'desire to unduly extend the period of harsh apprenticeship … live on the earnings of their workers or victimize those, who after 18 years, desire to be free'.[31] One of the TLA's early (and frequently publicised) goals and one of its most cherished successes was curtailing the power wielded by the jobber.[32] The *Majoor Sandesh*, the union's mouthpiece, regularly carried reports of threats of violence by jobbers. These threats made on the shop floor sometimes spilled over to the neighbourhood, as in the case of Lala Dana, the head jobber of the throstle[33] department of the Vivekanand Mills. Not only did Lala Dana, a mathabhari character, abuse workers within the mill, his relatives also did so, on the strength of his name, outside the mill.[34] The union set up a victimisation fund, which protected workers unfairly dismissed from their jobs; they organised institutional channels through which workers' complaints and grievances could be recorded and addressed, and as a culmination of these efforts of protecting union members from harassment and persecution, also formed a union of jobbers.[35] By the late 1920s, through this newly formed union, the TLA incorporated the jobber within the union's functioning, thereby regulating and managing their authority. The union then was poised to take on some of the responsibilities of recruitment: on the one hand, through an absorption of the jobber into the union's institutional apparatus and, on the other, through the union representatives, the pratinidhis, who began playing an increasingly significant role in the recruitment of labour. As the pratinidhi became ever more influential in the mill neighbourhoods, he drew from the jobber's styles of functioning—both in terms of a public persona of hot-headedness and in the acts of dispensing favours.

The centrality of the pratinidhi in negotiating the world of work (through mediating the process of recruitment and industrial settlement) and the home (through involvement in civic and neighbourhood affairs) reminds us just how crucial it was for workers to cultivate relationships with union representatives.[36] Operating in the interstices between formal and informal regulatory mechanisms, the partinidhi occupied an ambivalent position—as a formally elected representative, while also drawing upon and displaying the informal authority of a contractor. This figure was then staged to occupy both worlds, his authority relying as much on his formal position as a

TLA representative as well as on his command over informal processes of recruitment, disciplining and patronage.

CIRCULATION OF POWER: THE PRATINIDHI, THE TLA AND THE AMC

Within the neighbourhood, the TLA's *latta khatta* or the latta mahajan, the department that focused on local problems, was one of the most crucial elements in the union's functioning—precisely because it served an essential role in maintaining the TLA's presence in the working-class areas. A product of Gandhian ideas of *seva* or social service, the latta mahajan was formed with the specific intention of doing civic work in the working-class areas.[37] Gulzarilal Nanda explained the rationale behind its creation: 'We in the TLA felt that we should do some work of civic significance in the localities where the workers stayed…. This helped us to improve our membership in the mills where the employer's agents created difficulties in enlisting members.'[38] The first latta mahajans were established in 1924 in the neighbourhoods of Gomitpur, Saraspur and Asarwa, with an eye to enhancing the TLA's reach—both numerically as well as politically.[39]

The latta mahajan was involved in a wide range of neighbourhood activities—providing assistance during social or personal events, negotiating with the civic bodies over the supply of services, running libraries and social welfare centres, keeping a watch on immoral activities such as gambling or drinking.[40] Regular meetings would be organised by the *latta* department, usually in association with municipal officials, in order to discuss problems of sewage, sanitation, cleanliness and temperance.[41] A pratinidhi was put in charge of forty to fifty households and was entrusted with the task of attending to their social and moral well-being.

Not only did institutions like the latta mahajan, ward unions and voters' associations (which were accountable to both the Congress and the TLA) ensure that the union was firmly anchored within the mill areas, they also worked as party mobilisers for the elections. 'Apart from enlisting voters to the civic body,' explained Gulzarilal Nanda, 'the work of these *mandals* was to understand local problems; may it be cleanliness in localities, water supply, lighting in lanes and by-lanes etc.'[42] The relationships between these units of the TLA, the pratinidhis and the workers were formed and consolidated at various levels—within the mills, in the neighbourhood, during social and cultural events and, especially, during elections. 'The activities of the Association,' it was declared, 'therefore, include not merely a machinery for disposal of industrial disputes but cover all aspects of a workman's life both inside the factory and at home.'[43] This focus on the home and the prosaic concerns of mill workers was part of the vision of a 'comprehensive' development of the industrial working classes, which involved social uplift as well as heightened political engagement. In the years immediately following independence, the TLA's political presence was phenomenal—in the municipal elections of 1949, the union contributed about a third of the Congress Party's successful candidates, seventeen of them mill workers.[44] The TLA's representation in the civic body continued peaking through the 1960s, while other union members went on to hold positions in state and central government and in national-level trade union federations. Gulzarilal Nanda, for instance, was labour minister in the Bombay state assembly, moving on to the Lok Sabha, and later appointed as member of the Planning Commission and served as India's prime minister briefly in 1964 and 1966,[45] while Khandubhai Desai of the union went on to become the general secretary of the INTUC. The Ahmedabad Congress Party, in the meantime, had come under scrutiny for their reliance on 'goondas and anti-social elements' for winning elections.[46]

The TLA's political participation was vigorous, as was the discourse surrounding it, which signals, to an extent, the pride taken in this civic involvement. Official publications routinely celebrated the civic and municipal work carried out by the union. Electoral politics was seen as part of a broader project of workers' mobilisation; the union's political participation was crucial to the worker's 'happiness' and 'satisfaction'.[47] The result of the TLA's dominance in the municipality was reflected in the public services that were provided to the mill areas during this period, though it must be noted that they were far from adequate. Through their municipal complaints' sections, the TLA created institutional channels for negotiating issues relating to tenancy rights, health, urban planning and other quotidian 'nuisances'. It was the TLA that prepared lists of roads to be asphalted, pressed the municipality for schools in the mill districts, demanded that water connections be installed and wastewater plants constructed.[48] Some of the TLA's reportage would be undoubtedly self-congratulatory, as suggested by this extract from the *Annual Report of 1965*, describing the collapse of the close association between the municipal corporation and the TLA after the Congress Party's municipal defeat: 'Those matters [civic complaints] which were formerly dealt with expeditiously were retarded and obstructions in obtaining required facilities were noticed. Workers felt convinced about the obvious delay occurring in getting their complaints redressed.'[49]

The process of spatially integrating the working-class neighbourhoods into the broader city space began at the time when the TLA was most dominant in the municipal corporation.[50] Krantikbhai, a social worker and former resident of Gomtipur, remarked upon the central position occupied by the TLA representative in easing access to civic services:

> The same TLA member [representative] would either be elected to the Municipality or the State Assembly.... They could influence voting since all our necessary work would be done by them.... If you needed better water supply or needed a new water tap installed, you would tell them [the pratinidhis] and they would facilitate matters with the municipal corporators.[51]

According to the TLA, these everyday mediations were conducted through 'personal contact and talk' as union officials tended to complaints, big and small.[52] The personal relationships emphasised in the union's institutional dealings in civic matters were enhanced by the pratinidhi's connections to the 'formal' political and electoral field. If we look closer, the union representative's authority was shaped by other more informal forms of 'personal contact', such as those manifest in the practice of dadagiri.

THE PRATINIDHI AND DADAGIRI

Akhadas and gymnasiums were prime sites of recruitment for other neighbourhood-level institutions such as the Majoor Seva Dal.[53] These spaces were known as the haunts of the local dadas and strongmen and offered an arena where a dominant masculine self could be fashioned.[54] These young men, who were presumably recruited for their display of masculine aggression (given that akhadas were the very spaces where masculinities took on deeply aggressive forms), were then deployed for TLA's social and political work, which included, among other things, enforcing prohibition.[55] The Seva Dal's role as primarily a regulatory and disciplining force or, for that matter, the placing of dadas in supervisory positions of jobbers and *mukadam*s suggests that a certain propensity for unpredictable violence (or bearing a mathabhari character) was valued in the lower levels of the TLA.[56]

That masculine idioms honed in akhadas and on street corners shaped the practices of grassroots-level TLA functionaries was hardly unique to Ahmedabad—trade union practices and shop-floor control across industries have long relied on muscular tactics and a performative display of aggression.[57] What makes these figures and practices particularly striking in the case of Ahmedabad is the contradiction they pose to the official stand of the union. The Gandhian orientation of the TLA ensured that much of the union's focus was on producing docile, prudent and obedient workers who zealously guarded their morality from the onslaught of any anti-social element. The existence of highly volatile union representatives—who, while involved in union activities, also performed a range of other functions—presents an ambivalent picture. These representatives, whose influence took the form of dadagiri—the ability to command respect, inflict violence and extend patronage—also moonlighted as contractors, bootleggers and strong-arm supporters during elections. As I argue through the following section, it was the practice of dadagiri that, in a sense, allowed the TLA to establish an impressive apparatus of local control.

The official discourse of the TLA posed a clear distinction between the model worker (illustrated by the pratinidhi) and the 'anti-social element', the goonda or dada: a humble servant, the representative was to prevent workers from going on the wrong path, be committed to observing all union resolutions, behave humbly and sweetly with workers and refrain from addictions.[58] While advocating frugality, temperance, cleanliness and other such desirable habits, the union's civilising mission also targeted the unruly worker.[59] Militancy and violence was not something that was officially sanctioned or even tolerated by the TLA. However, as Jan Breman observes, every neighbourhood had its fair share of dadas, leaders of their own gangs and jostling for deference and fear in local akhadas, betting shops and drinking booths.[60] Contrary to previous scholarship, which has tended to view dadagiri in terms of the failure of the TLA's civilising project, I suggest that it was inherent to the union's very mode of functioning. They needed precisely this kind of worker in order to retain their control over the working-class areas.

The union bosses relied on the pratinidhis to maintain and consolidate grassroots support, while the very authority that the pratinidhi commanded was, in turn, dependent on their everyday presence in the mill neighbourhoods, on their ability to get things done, as well as on their closeness to those in higher positions of power. To be a pratinidhi, the most crucial element was *pakkad* (literally translated as 'hold'), and *dadagiri* is a term specifically used to describe exactly what kind of hold the pratinidhi exercised.[61]

So valued was the pratinidhi's position that once a worker 'manoeuvres' himself into the post, as one news report mentioned, 'he sees to it that he retains it'.[62] Unless the pratinidhi in question was 'foolish' enough to criticise the TLA, he could continue in this position for years. Indeed, as one study shows, an overwhelming majority continued their tenure for over fifteen years.[63] The union's hold over its functionaries was such that 'the smallest criticism is enough to entitle the dismissal of a *pratinidhi* from his post and sometimes, even his job'.[64] If the union bosses exercised such control over the lower-level representatives, how then did this authority play out in the neighbourhood? One point of view suggested that 'while the *pratinidhis* dare not criticise the leaders, the workers dare not criticise the *pratinidhis*'.[65] The pratinidhis were seen by some as exercising 'absolute control' or operating on a principle of 'indirect terror'.[66] The often routine display and abuse of power (which possibly accounted for the 'terror' in some part) can be traced in other sources as well. The *Janata*, in early 1950, reported that the pratinidhis had wide powers to dismiss workers, collect subscriptions at gunpoint, and rally the management's support against rival unions.[67] While such statements, upon closer examination, often unveil a much more contested landscape of power than that which appears at first glance, they are nevertheless revealing of the perception of the TLA representatives and their performative practices in the mill neighbourhoods. The appearance of unidirectional control—of power flowing downwards—that these accounts suggest is complicated by Masihi's observation of a certain reciprocity between these varying scales of authority. Considerable strain was placed on the union representative as they faced informal pressures from workers in dealings with the management.[68] In other words, the praitinidhi's hold, authority or even dadagiri was predicated upon his ability to deliver.

This dual dynamic of control and patronage can also be traced in the persistence of certain labour practices, such as contract labour. For instance, despite the TLA's official struggle for regularising contract labour, workers were often employed in contractual positions through the mediation of the pratinidhis. Contractors, often in collusion with TLA representatives, operated through finely calibrated practices of bribery and concealment. Gelabhai, a contractor who ran an operation with his brother, a TLA pratinidhi, describes how his entire family was kept on the muster rolls of the Swadeshi Mills when, in reality, he oversaw a team of five women and two boys:

> That way, I would make Rs. 1,000 per month. It was my brother's job to see that we had no trouble from the union or the mill management.... The labour official would always warn me when he was coming, and when he came I used to fold Rs. 200 into an empty cigarette box and give it to him.[69]

The TLA's control over the workforce and local politics from the late 1950s onwards began to slacken, in the wake of the Maha Gujarat agitation (with the notable exception of the municipal elections of 1961). Other contenders for power emerged on the scene—the most powerful of which were the Kamdar Sangram Samiti (workers' battle committee), the anti-TLA alliance and the MGJP, both led by Indulal Yagnik. There were palpable upheavals in the TLA's support base and concerted efforts to contest the union's hegemony, or, more precisely, its dadagiri.[70] The pratinidhi, at this point, rivalled 'old time jobbers' in their control and corruption.[71] 'Workers turned away from the TLA,' Sanjaybhai Parmar recounted to me. 'Partly, this was to counter the kind of dadagiri exercised by the TLA pratinidhi. So Indulal Yagnik formed the Sangram Samiti.' He repeats himself, emphasising the phrase Sangram Samiti with a certain theatrical air, investing his retelling with the same dramatic charge that the moment might have carried for him as a young man. 'This spelt an end to the stranglehold of fear that the Mahajan had.'[72]

The TLA's membership dwindled in the early 1960s, as the Sangram Samiti organised workers around issues of price rise, dearness allowances and bonuses.[73] Among these demands was also one that centred on more quotidian matters—that workers should not be forced to get their leave requests endorsed by TLA representatives.[74] The year-long mobilisation was punctuated by strikes, fasts and state repression. Indulal Yagnik charged the TLA of utilising their connections with mill owners to harass and intimidate Sangram Samiti members.[75] The agitation peaked on 5 August 1964 when the MGJP and Sangram Samiti gave a statewide bandh call. Thousands of workers participated, with Dalit workers joining non-Dalit workers, for the first time, crippling the textile mills.[76] The reaction of the government was brutal; the police fired into the crowd and five people were killed. In an appeal to the fact-finding commission appointed to investigate the police firing, the Sangram Samiti rather bluntly stated that the TLA–Congress combine oriented the state's violent response against the demonstrators.[77]

Oral accounts from Gomtipur suggest that TLA dadas and pratinidhis worked hard during this period, disturbing meetings, breaking up demonstrations and threatening and intimidating communist and socialist supporters. Ajay Singh, a TLA pratinidhi from Sarangpur Mill No. 2, was a formidable dada during the height of the communist and socialist mobilisation of the 1960s. 'Wherever there was a trade union movement and struggles for workers' rights, then they [the TLA] would send goondas to break it up, to threaten workers, to physically intimidate them. Mostly, they would bother lone workers cycling or walking to work.'[78] Competing political interests were reflected in the production of the social space of the neighbourhood, especially as the sphere of working-class leisure grew to be increasingly fragmented. With young communist supporters frequenting akhadas, admittedly to fortify themselves and build 'muscle tuschle', the sites of leisure were shaped by, and in turn were shaping, these countervailing political forces.[79]

Dadagiri as a form of social practice and regulation was certainly not solely the preserve of the TLA. Many dadas operated outside of the union's institutional framework; others, such as Jigneshbhai, were part of competing political networks. Jigneshbhai, a worker in the now closed Jay Bharat Mills, was a small-time bootlegger, a self-confessed former goonda turned Ambedkarite and Communist Party worker. In the retelling of his political trajectory, Jigneshbhai's association with the Communist Party of India emerges as a key moment of transformation; in his own words, a point of reform.[80] He gave up the life of crime and bootlegging and concentrated his energies on social activism. His life history suggests the possibility that the figure of the dada and the performance of dadagiri may have constituted a significant element in various political configurations. That said, I am not suggesting that all TLA pratinidhis were dadas or vice versa. However, there seems to be an indication that the qualities required of a pratinidhi, such as having a hold on the area, possessing the ability to mobilise workers and issue favours, being able to perform a kind of muscular politics and utilise personal networks of patronage, were the same as those of the local tough.

THE MAKING OF A DADA

Characters such as Jeevanbhai or Ajay Singh point to the fact that these figures occupied a whole range of positions and performed several functions in the neighbourhood. Ajay Singh, for instance, was one of the reigning dadas of the 1960s, a mill worker and a TLA representative. Among other things, he also ran a brothel, a betting outfit and an akhada. Ajay Singh not only dabbled in petty acts of defiance, such as stealing cloth from the mill, but was also allegedly involved in the massacre of Muslims in neighbouring Amraiwadi in 1969.[81] Referring to Ajay Singh and Vijay Singh, two TLA representatives and notable toughs, Jeevanbhai once said, 'These people were like my brothers,' thus, establishing kinship with the most dangerous of the dadas in Gomtipur. 'There is nobody left now ... just me.' Speaking about his youth, he describes himself as mathabhari. The image of being mathabhari appears to have been crucial in the self-presentation of the dada. The term encompasses the styles of behaviour necessary to be a dada—the reputation of hot-headedness, the ability to inflict violence as well as extend protection, defiance of established structures of authority and, always, just a hint of disrepute. Often colloquially referred to as an 'antisocial element', there was nothing a mathabhari person could not do. Respect, however, was not garnered merely through the performance of violence but also by the accompanying capacity to dispense favours and some form of justice in quotidian matters. A dada of this period, thus, seemed to straddle two kinds of imaginaries—one, as a person who possessed an ability to intimidate. As Jeevanbhai recounts, 'Nobody would have the guts to even speak in front of me, I could beat up anyone.' The other imaginary, as a keeper of peace and order in the neighbourhood, the dada was someone who was invested with the moral authority to declare to the police and the trade unions, as well as the politicians that 'there should not be any trouble in our territory'.

Jeevanbhai's career as a dada-turned-politician presents us with a lens through which we can map these practices of dadagiri and explore the links between the aggressive masculinity that the dada embodied and the practices through which the TLA established its control. In retelling his life story, Jeevanbhai initially avoided any references to his youth, brushing away questions with one trademark curt sentence, 'I was very naughty.... I made a lot of trouble, used to create a lot of disturbances.'[82] With the details that trickled in over months of conversation, one can draw an arc between the rebellion of his youth and the styles of public behaviour that he later employed.

As a young boy he was brazen, resistant to authority. By the end of 1952, at the age of fifteen, he joined Sarangpur Mill No. 2 in the spinning department. During his early days in the mill, Jeevanbhai was already established as a local tough. So great was his clout that as a worker in the last shift, he could go off to sleep whenever he pleased and receive no censure or punishment. The supervisors and the managers would, instead, go out of their way to avoid rather than confront him. His heavy drinking and excessive cigarette smoking marked him as someone with 'vices', a necessary attribute for a dada. He was soon dismissed and shuttled between textile mills, helped by his father and brother-in-law, both TLA representatives, to find new work. He returned to Sarganpur Mill No. 2 in 1956 and remained there until the mill closed down in 1996—these forty years allowed him to establish himself as a TLA pratinidhi, climb the ranks of the union leadership and fashion an impressive political career for himself.

Jeevanbhai had taken pains to craft a certain image of himself, one that was predicated on the practice of dadagiri. The aesthetics and style of dadagiri construct a masculinity that was opposed to that of the TLA's model worker. Here, the dada is 'virile' and manly, bullying his wife, threatening violence on figures of authority, ensuring that no romantic or sexual transgressions take place in the neighbourhood, while being fairly predatory towards women himself. The average male mill worker, on the other hand, was being urged to be prudent, nonviolent and respectable. A person such as Jeevanbhai, in his time as a Congress Party mobiliser, would also be entrusted with making key electoral calculations on the ground. He explained:

> The candidates would come to me and ask me to take care of the neighbourhood votes ... they would just fill the forms and we would take care of the rest.... Those who liked to drink, we gave them alcohol.... Those who liked to eat, we fed them.... That's how votes are won.... Nobody wins just like that.[83]

The TLA pratinidhi remained an ambivalent figure, simultaneously an enforcer of a model code of conduct and its challenger.[84]

The public persona of an Ahmedabad dada was no different from other hyper-masculine figures. From Chitra Joshi's compelling narrative of masculinities in de-industrialised Kanpur to contemporary accounts of the Shiv Sena activist, aggression and self-assertion appear as key markers in the making of a dada.[85] The construction of a dada retained, at its heart, a fundamental anxiety—the perpetual threat of emasculation—and the dada armed himself against this by relentlessly honing his mathabhari image.[86] Jeevanbhai coming home drunk, his wife mute despite her annoyance, his alcohol supplied by a close friend who was part of a prohibition committee, his fondness for cheroots, cigarettes that 'foreigners smoked', his easy cursing— as he replayed his life story for me, he fashioned himself carefully as a man possessed of a short temper, impressive connections and love for the good life.

What Jeevanbhai recounted to me could very well be coloured by nostalgia and a manufactured sense of glory attributed to his dada days. However, the representation of himself as a tough, violent person who defies established structures of authority is resonant of contemporary dadas as well.[87] Jeevanbhai equates the dada culture of the mill neighbourhoods with the *daku*s of Chambal,[88] both marked by a similar structure of hierarchy and command. The skills of street fighting, the capacity to command a gang and the ability to pose a challenge to an established dada were all necessary attributes in the making of such a figure.[89] The contours of a dada's authority in the mill areas were shaped by several forces. On the one hand, the contradictions between the TLA's public position on such figures and the actual practice of the union's functioning significantly forged his spheres of influences. The union relied on the techniques of control perfected by the dada, even though the figures of the dada and the pratinidhi were placed on opposite ends of the union's moral spectrum. In the actual practices of local power, the worlds of these two figures often overlapped. Even if the pratinidhi was not, in real terms, the commander of a gang of local strongmen or practiced in the art of street fighting, his mode of control was distinctly that of dadagiri. On the other hand, the dada's authority was often territorially defined, with each one protecting and controlling a particular turf. As Chandavarkar demonstrates, this turf could be anything from a street corner to a neighbourhood.[90] The tensions between dadas and their entanglements with broader structures of power, such as the TLA, the police or the municipality, defined and limited their scales of influence to a certain extent.

Notions of masculinity, respect and reputation were operationalised in Jeevanbhai's initiation into the world of the dada. What began as a minor scuffle with Nur Ahmad, a fellow mill worker and a famous dada from a neighbouring area in Gomtipur, escalated into a months-long conflict. Eventually, peace was brokered by local Pathan money lenders, and Jeevanbhai and Nur Miyan became associates of sorts, controlling adjacent areas of Gomtipur. The public posturing of masculinity and the easy performance of violence spilled over into the cultural life of the neighbourhood, as dadas organised dance performances across the mill districts, inviting dancers and musicians from Bombay. Beginning at 11 p.m. and ending at dawn, these dos were attended by dadas from across the city; each one of them armed and accompanied by his gang of mathabhari men. Jeevanbhai would organise these performances at the same char rasta where he would meet me: 'I am the dada of the Gomtipur post office area, so if I attend these functions then I should have twenty to twenty-five men with me, because at any time a fight could break out. And we have to be ready to face death.... Some would take hockey sticks, some knives. A person should have enough strength to crush another.' The geography of local dominance could be mapped at these social affairs. These were not solely occasions of leisure but were contested sites where dadagiri was displayed and performed. Each dada and his gang, and their associates, would sit separately; the immediate spatial constellations thus formed during the event pointing to enmities and alliances. For every such grand occasion, there was an effort to keep peace—smaller fry, allies and even rival dadas were allowed entry with a warning that there should be no violence. However, only very eminent dadas could ensure peace at these extremely charged gatherings. The alliances that were forged between dadas of different territories served to both secure and expand their own spheres of influence. Jeevanbhai's associates ranged from Manga Bhoot, a Dalit dada from Calico Mills (who offered refuge during his confrontation with Nur Miyan), Mai Baap, a goonda so fierce that he carried not one but two revolvers upon his person at all times, to Ajay Singh and Vijay Singh, both fellow union representatives. *Bhaipanti* and *dosti* are the terms that he uses to describe these relationships, which were based on mutual help and support.

Jeevanbhai's career within the union and beyond complicates the understanding that dadas and goondas emerged in the vacuum left by the dissolution of the TLA. He was a TLA pratinidhi, a representative to the joint board of the labour union, a Congress Party worker who dealt not only with everyday issues of neighbourhood life but also as a strong-arm supporter during elections and, later, a politician. Later in his political career, he capitalised on these very networks—of patronage and dadagiri—to gain electoral support for himself. His ascent and, indeed, his importance in the neighbourhood reveal that dadas and other 'anti-social' and 'criminal' characters did not appear in the mill neighbourhoods after the collapse of the TLA. The 'righteous struggle' of the TLA, which was directed partly at creating a docile and non-confrontational worker, was buttressed by those who were seen as 'unruly elements'.

We have already seen that the union kept its command over the neighbourhood through its massive institutional networks of pratinidhis and through its well-oiled channels of patronage. It was these institutions and figures, which operated in the interstices between formal and informal modes of regulation, that were crucial in the everyday rhythms of mediation between the residents of these neighbourhoods, the mills and the state agencies. In Jeevanbhai, we have a pratinidhi who was also a well-respected and feared dada in Gomtipur. His authority in the mill was largely dependent on the respect he commanded in the neighbourhood, while his hold over the neighbourhood was in part constituted by his closeness to other important figures to whom he had easier access through the TLA and the Congress Party. These relationships of power that Jeevanbhai was enmeshed in were marked by a certain reciprocity of obligations in the neighbourhood—the dada's dominance depended, to a large extent, on his ability to do things for his constituents. Through the routine operations of the TLA representative's dadagiri, informality was crystallised as a mode of political practice that tied the union with formal registers of politics and state activity. Thus, the social authority of these dadas, who are often thought of as criminal elements that emerged after the collapse of the TLA, appear instead to have been constituted by the union's very structure of power.

This chapter has focused on one crucial form of political mediation in the textile mill neighbourhoods.[91] In the following chapters, we explore other historically contingent mediatory practices. The period after the late 1960s has been marked by a series of communal and caste riots as well as a rapidly changing political field, which drew on emergent caste alliances. With the TLA–Congress alliance broken and their traditional support base denuded, the political landscape of the mill neighbourhoods transformed. In the changed socio-economic climate that followed the rationalisation of the textile mill industry and its eventual collapse in the mid-1980s, local power was reconfigured and entered new orbits of patronage. Drawing on the vestiges of the TLA's mode of functioning, dadas, bootleggers and social workers of various kinds grew in significance as mediating agents between state institutions and citizens. The political economy of bootlegging, while never of inconsiderable importance in the neighbourhood, appeared to have grown in scale.[92] As the links between dadas, politicians and the police were being consolidated, the role of the local dada was also being diversified. He was now called upon also as a general mathabhari type, who could be sent out to riot. Political parties had taken to rewarding local leaders for their involvement in riots. From 1985, when many accused rioters were elected to the AMC, especially from Muslim-minority mixed areas, to Jitu Vaghela's Legislative Assembly candidacy after he embellished his reputation for violence during 2002, this signified a disturbing yet very powerful form of political practice.[93]

NOTES

1 Notable exceptions remain Chandavarkar's magisterial work on Bombay, *The Origins of Industrial Capitalism in India*, 200–18, and Joshi's examination of masculinities in working-class Kanpur, *Lost Worlds*, 116–20. For more contemporary work on the figures of the dada and the goonda, see also Ward Berenschot, 'On the Usefulness of Goondas in Indian Politics: "Moneypower" and "Musclepower" in a Gujarati Locality', *South Asia: Journal of South Asian Studies* 34, no. 2 (2011): 255–75 and Ornit Shani, 'Bootlegging, Politics and Corruption: State Violence and the Routine Practices of Public Power in Gujarat (1985–2002)', *South Asian History and Culture* 1, no. 4 (2010): 494–508. See also other contemporary accounts such as Lucia Michelutti, 'Wrestling with (Body) Politics: Understanding "Goonda" Political Styles in North India', in *Power and Influence in India: Bosses, Lords and Captains* ed. Pamela Price and Arild Engelsen Ruud (2010): 44–69, which discusses the significance of the figure of the dada in electoral machinations, and Hansen's exploration of popular politics in Bombay, Thomas Blom Hansen, *Violence in Urban India: Identity Politics, 'Mumbai', and the Postcolonial City* (Delhi: Permanent Black, 2005).

2 Ranjani Mazumdar, *Bombay Cinema: Archive of the City* (Minneapolis: University of Minnesota Press, 2007), 149ff.

3 See, for instance, Suranjan Das, 'The "Goondas": Towards a Reconstruction of the Calcutta Underworld through Police Records', *Economic and Political Weekly* 29, no. 44 (1994): 2877–83.

4 Ibid.

5 I use 'his' since the figure of the dada in my sources from this period was almost uniformly male. However, during my fieldwork in 2011–12, I did come across women leaders whose public image and styles of functioning echoed those of the earlier dadas.

6 The relationship between the union and its members has been explored in some detail in Breman, *The Making and Unmaking of an Industrial Working Class*, and Spodek, *Ahmedabad: Shock City of Twentieth-Century India*. See

also Patel, *The Making of Industrial Relations*, and Spodek, 'From Gandhi to Violence', 765–95.

7 The existing literature shows that there was a significant under-representation of women workers. Furthermore, in the *TLA Annual Reports*, 1950–69, there is no mention of any female pratinidhis. A study conducted in the early 1970s found a miniscule number of women leaders at the higher levels of the TLA, one of whom was in charge of the women's wing of the union. Edwin Masihi, 'Trade Union Leadership in Textile Industry of Ahmedabad', unpublished PhD thesis, Gujarat University, 1976, 103.

8 A term used to imply a dada's power and his particular performative style. This would include his bravado, his aggression, his ability to inflict violence as well as his ability to offer patronage and protection.

9 The mill owners retaliated by dismissing gangs of workers and employing new jobbers to keep the mills running. For instance, in Rajnagar Mills No. 3, Shamsher Khan, a jobber, joined work with 200 new mill hands, breaking picket lines. See *Times of India*, 20 June 1933. Elsewhere, the Commercial Mills dismissed striking weavers and employed new workers. See *Times of India*, 20 June 1933.

10 Spodek, *Ahmedabad: Shock City of Twentieth-Century India*, 109–10.

11 The Mill Kamdar Union was formed by a collaboration between the communists and the Congress socialists. In an earlier form, it was the Mill Mazdoor Union, banned in 1934. The union continued much of its activity underground; it was rehabilitated as the Mill Kamdar Union (or Lal Vavta) in 1935, as the Congress socialists and the communists joined forces in Ahmedabad. For a more detailed analysis of this period, see also ibid.; Patel, *The Making of Industrial Relations*; and Manju Parikh, 'Labor–Capital Relations in the Indian Textile Industry: A Comparative Study of Ahmedabad and Coimbatore', PhD thesis, University of Chicago, Department of Political Science, 1988.

12 Yagnik and Sheth, *Ahmedabad: From Royal City to Megacity*, 135–37.

13 *Times of India*, 22 November 1937.

14 Shyam Prasad Vasavada, *Majoor Charwal* (Ahmedabad: Textile Labour Association, 1968), Vol. 1, 18–22.

15 Shiv Kumar Goel, *Gandhian Perspective on Industrial Relations: A Study of Textile Labour Association, Ahmedabad, 1918–48* (Delhi: Shipra Publications, 2002), 126.

16 The establishment of the Bombay Improvement Trust in 1898, for instance, sought to both reorder the city as well as regulate working-class housing.

These interventions were partly shaped by the needs of capital and partly by policies of social improvement. By the early twentieth century, cities like Kanpur and Calcutta saw tentative measures being made in social housing through the formation of city improvement trusts and other civic bodies. See, for instance, Prashant Kidambi, *The Making of an Indian Metropolis: Colonial Governance and Public Culture in Bombay, 1890–1920* (Aldershot, UK: Ashgate Publishing Ltd., 2007); Sita Ram Sharma, *Municipal Administration and Education*, Vol. 2 (New Delhi: Mittal Publications, 1994); and Nandini Gooptu, *The Politics of the Urban Poor in Early Twentieth-Century India* (Cambridge: Cambridge University Press, 2001).

17 Shankarlal Banker quoted in Spodek, *Ahmedabad: Shock City of Twentieth-Century India*, 101.

18 The ward unions began as parallel unions, composed of workers from a chawl or *mohalla* (neighbourhood), until they were subsumed within the formal structure of the TLA in 1936. Goel, *Gandhian Perspective on Industrial Relations*, 140.

19 *TLA Annual Report*, 1950.

20 Breman, *The Making and Unmaking of an Industrial Working Class*, 100.

21 Masihi, 'Trade Union Leadership in Textile Industry of Ahmedabad', 101.

22 Breman, *The Making and Unmaking of an Industrial Working Class*, 101; Masihi, 'Trade Union Leadership in Textile Industry of Ahmedabad', 170.

23 Ibid.

24 Patel, 'Contract Labour in Ahmedabad Textile Industry', 1813–20. Interview with Manilal Patel, former editor of *Majoor Sandesh*, Ahmedabad, 6 December 2012.

25 Interview with Jigneshbhai Waghela, Ahmedabad, 15 December 2012.

26 A rich body of literature exists on the figure of the jobber. This key intermediary was central not just in the textile mills of Ahmedabad and Bombay, but in a range of production regimes. Scholarly accounts of the jobber have focused on its role as a supplier of labour as well as its supervisory and disciplinary functions. Of particular note, for instance, is Rajnarayan Chandavarkar, 'The Decline and Fall of the Jobber System in the Bombay Cotton Textile Industry, 1870–1955', *Modern Asian Studies* 42, no. 1 (2008): 117–210. Chandavarkar traces the transformation of the jobber system in Bombay, arguing that the jobber's authority rested upon a fine balance of forces. It was this recognition of the jobber's concealed

vulnerabilities by industrialists and the state alike that precipitated its decline. Other discussions of the jobber's significance, such as Tirthankar Roy's for instance, imbue the figure with the authority of a headman and suggest that they represented the incorporation of traditional authority in a modern setting. Other academic works have explored the significance of the intermediary in diverse labour regimes, such as Samita Sen's analysis of the *sardari* system in the Assam tea plantations and Ravi Ahuja's examination of maritime labour, among others. Please see Tirthankar Roy, 'Sardars, Jobbers, Kanganies: The Labour Contractor and Indian Economic History', *Modern Asian Studies* 42, no. 5 (2008): 971–98; Lakha, 'Character of Wage Labour in Early Industrial Ahmedabad', 421–41; Samita Sen, 'Commercial Recruiting and Informal Intermediation: Debate over the Sardari System in Assam Tea Plantations, 1860–1900', *Modern Asian Studies* 44, no. 1 (2010): 3–28; and Ravi Ahuja, 'Mobility and Containment: The Voyages of South Asian Seamen, C. 1900–1960', *International Review of Social History* 51 (2006): 111–41.

27 Patel, *The Making of Industrial Relations*, 28–29.

28 *RCLI*, Vol. 1, Part 1, 10.

29 Patel, *The Making of Industrial Relations*, 29.

30 Lakha, 'Character of Wage Labour in Early Industrial Ahmedabad', 428; *RCLI*, Vol. 1, Part 1,10.

31 *Times of India*, 12 January 1927.

32 See *Majoor Sandesh*, 28 December 1985. Evidence presented to Royal Commission—ranging from the AMA, to workers, to civic officials—testifies to the excesses of the jobber and the attempts to curb it.

33 A mechanical frame used for spinning cotton.

34 *Majoor Sandesh*, 28 June 1950.

35 Patel, *The Making of Industrial Relations*, 8464; *TLA Annual Report*, 1928.

36 Many other scholarly works on labour have argued the significance of these lower-level intermediaries. See, for instance, Chandavarkar, *The Origins of Industrial Capitalism in India*; Rajnarayan Chandavarkar, 'The Decline and Fall of the Jobber System in the Bombay Cotton Textile Industry, 1870–1955', *Modern Asian Studies* 42, no. 1 (2008): 117–210; and Joshi, *Lost Worlds*. For ethnographic studies of labour mediation, please see Geert De Neve, *The Everyday Politics of Labour: Working Lives in India's Informal Economy* (New Delhi: Social Science Press, 2005), among others.

37 Kalhan, *Gulzarilal Nanda*, 185. The notion of social service remains fairly instrumental in solidifying local authority in these areas in contemporary

Ahmedabad. For a longer analysis of this aspect of political engagement, please see Chapter 4.

38 Ibid.

39 *TLA Annual Report*, 1924.

40 *Majoor Sandesh*, 23 April 1977. I thank Siddhi Shah for the Gujarati translations.

41 Select issues of *Majoor Sandesh*, 1950–64.

42 Kalhan, *Gulzarilal Nanda*, 185.

43 *TLA Annual Report*, 1951, 2.

44 *TLA Annual Report*, 1950.

45 'Shri Gulzari Lal Nanda', available at https://www.pmindia.gov.in/en/former_pm/shri-gulzari-lal-nanda-3/, accessed on 20 June 2020.

46 *Times of India*, 29 July 1954.

47 Rukmini Barua, 'The Textile Labour Association and Dadagiri: Power and Politics in the Working-Class Neighborhoods of Ahmedabad', *International Labor and Working Class History* 87, Spring (2015): 67–91. S. R. Vasavada quoted in Spodek, *Ahmedabad Shock City of Twentieth-Century India*, 138.

48 *TLA Annual Report*, 1950, 58–61.

49 *TLA Annual Report*, 1965, 24.

50 Interviews with Jeevanbhai Parmar and Jigneshbhai Waghela, Ahmedabad, 2011–12.

51 Interview with Krantikbhai, Ahmedabad, 15 December 2012.

52 *TLA Annual Report*, 1967, 29.

53 A labour volunteer corps, the Seva Dal was maintained as a reserve for civic and electoral duties. This very masculine institution enlisted young men between eighteen and forty years of age. *TLA Annual Report*, 1962–63, 22.

54 For a more detailed analysis of the akhada as a site of masculine self-fashioning, see also Joseph S. Alter, *The Wrestler's Body: Identity and Ideology in North India* (Berkeley: University of California Press, 1992) and Gooptu, *The Politics of the Urban Poor in Early Twentieth-Century India*, 215ff.

55 *TLA Annual Report*, 1963–64, 25–26.

56 *TLA Annual Report*, 1949–50, 55. Interview with Jigneshbhai Waghela, Ahmedabad, 2011–12.

57 Shaheed's analysis of labour leaders in Pakistan details the qualities that were valued in these intermediary figures—physical prowess, courage and 'hot-headedness'. This attribute of 'hot-headedness' finds a certain resonance in the mathabhari figures of the Ahmedabad textile industry.

Ahuja's study of maritime labour similarly comments on the significance of 'hot-headedness' in the constitution of leadership. Please see Zafar Shaheed, *The Labour Movement in Pakistan: Organization and Leadership in Karachi in the 1970s* (New York: Oxford University Press, 2007); Ravi Ahuja, 'A Freedom Still Enmeshed in Servitude: The Unruly "Lascars" of *Ss City of Manila* or, a Micro-History of the "Free Labour Problem" ', in *Working Lives and Worker Militancy: The Politics of Labour in Colonial India*, ed. Ravi Ahuja (New Delhi: Tulika Books, 2013), 97–133.

58 *TLA Annual Report*, 1967, 15.

59 *Majoor Sandesh*, 10 March 1951, 17 March 1951, 8 September 1951, 10 February 1968, 6 April 1968, 5 May 1976 and 15 May 1976.

60 Breman, *The Making and Unmaking of an Industrial Working Class*, 103.

61 Interviews with Sanjaybhai Parmar and Jigneshbhai Waghela, Ahmedabad, 2011–12.

62 *Janata*, 2 April 1950.

63 Masihi, 'Trade Union Leadership in Textile Industry of Ahmedabad', 170.

64 *Janata*, 2 April 1950.

65 Ibid.

66 Interviews with Sanjaybhai Parmar and Jigneshbhai Waghela, Ahmedabad, December 2012.

67 *Janata*, 2 April 1950.

68 Masihi, 'Trade Union Leadership in the Textile Industry of Ahmedabad', 175–78.

69 Renana Jhabvala, *Closing Doors: A Study on the Decline of Women Workers in the Textile Mills of Ahmedabad* (Ahmedabad: SETU, 1985), 23.

70 Interview with Sanjaybhai Parmar, Ahmedabad, 2012.

71 Bharti P. Kansara, 'Business, Labour and Opposition Movements in the Politics of Ahmedabad City, 1960–72', unpublished thesis, SOAS University of London, 1975.

72 Interview with Sanjaybhai Parmar, Ahmedabad, 2012.

73 *TLA Annual Reports*, 1960–70. The TLA membership dropped from 101,315 in 1961 to 82,287 in 1964 before rising marginally in the mid-1960s. It is possible that these figures were indicative of the growing attraction of communist and socialist ideologies among mill workers in the early years of the 1960s—an appeal that did not really translate into electoral success for the MGJP, except during the municipal elections of 1965. We can perhaps speculate that the rise of TLA membership after 1965 shows a dissatisfaction with the Sangram Samiti and other unions that were in

opposition to the TLA. Workers returned to the TLA fold, though this does not necessarily imply that there was great faith in the union or in its functioning. *Times of India*, 13 December 1963.

74 *Times of India*, 7 February 1964.

75 Ibid.

76 Spodek, *Ahmedabad: Shock City of Twentieth-Century India*.

77 File No. 104, Police Firing Inquiry Commission, Indulal Yagnik Papers, Nehru Memorial Museum and Library.

78 Interview with Jigneshbhai Waghela, Ahmedabad, 2011–12.

79 A colloquial formulation that often uses rhyming though meaningless words as a narrative device.

80 *Sudhar gaya* is the phrase that he used.

81 Interview with Jeevanbhai Parmar, Ahmedabad, 2011–12.

82 *Main bahut badmash tha. Bahut toofan karta tha. Bahut dhamal karta tha.* The words *dhamal* and *toofan* are both used colloquially to describe riots and disturbances.

83 Interview with Jeevanbhai Parmar, Ahmedabad, 2011–12.

84 The oral narratives that I have collected, unfortunately, do not reveal much about the dada's way of engaging with the women of the mill neighbourhoods. This remains a lacuna in my understanding of this figure.

85 Chitra Joshi, 'On "De-Industrialization" and the Crisis of Male Identities', *International Review of Social History* 47, no. S10 (2002): 159–75; Gérard Heuzé-Brigant, 'Populism and the Workers Movement: Shiv Sena and Labor in Mumbai', *South Asia: Journal of South Asian Studies* 22, no. 2 (1999): 119–48.

86 The threat of emasculation took on a different form as Ahmedabad grew to be increasingly communalised. Reclamation of Hindu masculinity against the Muslim 'other' is a common trope employed by Hindu fundamentalism. I encountered this narrative several times during discussions of the communal violence of the 1990s and 2002. An extensive body of work exists on this subject, including Thomas Blom Hansen, 'Recuperating Masculinity: Hindu Nationalism, Violence and the Exorcism of the Muslim "Other" ', *Critique of Anthropology* 16, no. 2 (1996): 137–72; Tanika Sarkar, 'Semiotics of Terror: Muslim Children and Women in Hindu Rashtra', *Economic and Political Weekly* 37, no. 28 (2002): 2872–76; and Dipankar Gupta, *Justice before Reconciliation: Negotiating a 'New Normal' in Post-Riot Mumbai and Ahmedabad* (New Delhi: Routledge, 2013).

87 For a detailed account of these practices, see Berenschot, 'On the Usefulness of Goondas in Indian Politics', 255–75.

88 Literally meaning the bandits of the Chambal region, an area in central India that is topographically marked by ravines and scrubland. Historically, this area has seen competing gangs of outlaws. These figures and their exploits have been powerfully represented in popular cinema.

89 Interview with Jigneshbhai Waghela, Ahmedabad, 2012.

90 Rajnarayan Chandavarkar, *Imperial Power and Popular Politics: Class, Resistance and the State in India, 1850–1950* (Cambridge: Cambridge University Press, 1998), 112.

91 No doubt there were other equally important forms of mediation—such as those relating to labour practices—that shaped the everyday lives of Ahmedabad's mill hands. See, for instance, Patel, *The Making of Industrial Relations.*

92 N. M. Miyabhoy, *Report of the Laththa Commission of Inquiry* (Ahmedabad: Government of Gujarat, 1978); N. M. Miyabhoy, *Report of the Commission of Inquiry into the Prohibition Policy in Gujarat* (Ahmedabad: Government of Gujarat, 1983); Asghar Ali Engineer, 'Communal Riots in Ahmedabad', *Economic and Political Weekly* 27, nos. 31–32 (1992): 1641–43.

93 A politician from Gomtipur who was given a BJP ticket to contest the legislative assembly elections in 2002. Jaffrelot and Thomas, 'Facing Ghettoisation in the "Riot City"', 56.

3

THE UNDERGROUND ECONOMY, THE STATE AND THE POLITICAL INTERMEDIARY

The 1970s witnessed a veritable explosion in public conversations about the underground economy in Ahmedabad. Part of this concern stemmed from an increasing visibility of the hooch trade, of smuggling networks and of the rising influence of slumlords.[1] To a great extent, this anxiety was centred around the figure of the 'anti-social element' who was alleged to play a key role not only in local politics, but also in the episodes of communal violence that occurred with alarming regularity during this period. Scholarly work on Ahmedabad has remarked upon the growth of the underground economy during this period in the city's history, suggesting that the criminalisation of politics was one of the consequences of the collapse of the textile industry.[2] The disintegration of the industry and the TLA (especially the union's political clout) undoubtedly contributed to crucial transformations in the modes and mechanisms of mediation. The previous chapter adds to this analysis in arguing that a reliance on the 'anti-social' and 'criminal' elements formed a crucial part of the TLA's political tactics and that the worlds of the union representatives and that of the local thug often overlapped. The 1970s (and Chimanbhai Patel's tenure as chief minister, in particular) is often regarded as having introduced new forms of political corruption and economic crime, so routine that they could be considered 'a way of life in Ahmedabad'.[3] While it is difficult to ascertain whether there was an *actual* increase in the number of people involved in the underground economy, one can certainly identify heightened anxiety over 'anti-social' elements and activities. This took two main forms—on the one hand, there was an intensification of official interest in these matters—several judicial inquiry commissions were established, for instance, and the 'Anti-Goondas Act' was framed; on the other, public (and predominantly middle-class) discourse over everyday acts of criminalisation was amplified.

The institutional recalibrations of this period, the shifts in the urban political economy—in the contestations in the land market and the continued imposition (and contravention) of prohibition—had led to deep connections being forged between the city's underworld, politicians and the police. Practices of everyday corruption grew to be increasingly regulated, as other modes of social and political control operated parallel to and in conjunction with practices of state power.[4] This chapter connects the changing political landscape of Ahmedabad, the transforming urban economy and the emergence of a new intermediary figure. More specifically, I follow the shifts in the forms of political practice by drawing upon the intersections and interfaces between various scales of political practice, from national-level power play to the more intimate landscape of the local dada. The political actors that I refer to straddle a wide range—from local leaders, bootleggers, slumlords to the neighbourhood tough. I examine the poles between which these actors moved—from the arena of formal politics to the nebulous terrain of the underground economy to the field of politicised religion. At the centre of my explorations here is the figure of the 'anti-social element' and his[5] location in the practices of political mediation.

It was the caste and communal violence of 1985 that prompted scholarly attention on questions of crime and criminality in the city. In his commentary on this prolonged period of rioting, Spodek argues that 'criminal activity flourished as civic order declined'.[6] Civic order, in this analytical framework, was seen as being maintained by a complex of social forces, which included the Congress Party, the TLA and the city's business elite, among others. As we examine similar questions located in the same historical milieu, it is perhaps necessary to somewhat complicate Spodek's understanding. Spodek convincingly argues that with the TLA's isolation from formal politics, its political and electoral clout declined rapidly. However, although he suggests that the TLA ran a 'parallel government' of sorts, he does not focus on the forms that this 'parallel government' may have acquired in the years following the union's decline. He tends to view the TLA as a 'unifying' force—a 'legitimate institution' upon which bootleggers, working in collusion with the police and government officials, posed consistent challenges.[7] Instead, this research contends, the existing networks of local power and patronage in the industrial east (that had been forged to a large degree by the TLA) adjusted to accommodate the changed political and economic realities of the city. The TLA's waning social and political influence and the transformation of the urban economy gave rise to a set of political actors, who entered new orbits of political influence in the industrial areas of eastern Ahmedabad. While the practices of mediation and the figure of the political intermediary continued to represent the interface between the formal and informal realms of politics, with the decline of the union as a political institution, the intermediary grew to be less integrated in larger formal structures. In this particular historical context, corruption and criminality—especially around electoral politics and material dynamics of urban living—emerged as key aspects of political practice in the neighbourhoods of the urban labouring poor. This is not to imply that the bootlegger or the slumlord or other such figures that facilitated urban living for the working poor were 'free agents', operating at will and unconnected to larger structures and processes. The figure of the 'anti-social element', the embodiment of the world of crime and notoriety and the practices of dadagiri, in this case, however, presented not only a point of engagement, but also, often, an overlap with the state agencies. Instead, as I show, the vast and shadowy underground economy was rather significantly imbricated in the practice of urban governance. The 'anti-social element' was meanwhile being defined in very specific ways. The contours of these figures, I suggest, were defined by two critical processes—one was an increasing interaction between the state agencies and officials and the city's burgeoning underground economy; the other, the rise of political mobilisation along religious lines.

PRACTICES AND POLITICS OF BOOTLEGGING

On 27 February 1977, 200 litres of hooch were produced and stored at Harji Rabari's *adda* in Sarangpur. By that evening, the liquor had made its way to various vending spots in the neighbourhood and to other areas in eastern Ahmedabad. Over a hundred people died of alcohol poisoning over the next few days and two government inquiry commissions were immediately instituted to investigate the incident and the routinely obscured practices of bootlegging.[8] These reports contain not only the first official acknowledgement of bootlegging, but also the first tentative official documentation of the links between the underground economy and practices of state power.[9]

The network of distribution, as outlined in the Lattha Commission report, appeared to have been fairly well organised. In Sarangpur Daulatkhana, where the most vigorous sales seem to have been carried out, the term *adda* would appear to refer not just to the open plot near Rabari's house, but to the entire range of vending spots that dotted the locality.[10] Employees of the main accused, Harji Rabari—boys, the commission noted—circulated between the adda and certain designated vending spots. When contact was made with a prospective buyer, the liquor was procured from where it was stocked and delivered to the vending spots, which, the report detailed, were furnished with some rudimentary equipment for drinking—glasses and a water tap. Should the customer be unwilling to take the liquor home, they could partake of it right there. As such, evidence presented to the commission disclosed that on the evening of the 27th, groups of people could be seen surrounding the liquor vendors and some 'were drinking liquor on the open road'.[11]

Engaged in the bootlegging business since 1968, Rabari had had several externment orders passed against him. Alleged to enjoy considerable political patronage, he emerged as one of the city's most prominent bootleggers in the 1970s.[12] He was described in legal records as 'a dangerous and desperate man and constantly indulg[ing] in acts involving force and violence'.[13] In the late 1960s, the charges brought against him included 'terrorising people', extorting money, assaulting and beating 'innocent persons' living around Sarangpur, and threatening witnesses from giving testimonies against his bootlegger friends.[14] By 1977, the charges were even more grave—he was the main accused in the hooch poisoning case which resulted in the death of more than a hundred people, most of them mill workers.[15]

The practices of bootlegging and the figures involved in it were deeply enmeshed in the quotidian rhythms of the industrial areas. Gujarat has had a historically ambiguous relationship with prohibition, first imposed in 1938. At one level, the continuing ban on the sale and consumption of liquor in the state has been little more than political posturing, complying with Gandhian notions of self-denial. This was particularly visible in the mill areas, where temperance remained a key element in the TLA's agenda. At another, they have produced thriving spaces of illicit economic activity as well as generated imaginaries of paranoia.[16] Given the clandestine nature of these activities, it is difficult to judge the extent of the bootlegging economy, though some sources suggest that there has been a phenomenal increase in the trade since the 1960s.[17]

The official evidence on the subject (mostly in the form of government inquiries) sheds some light on the manner in which prohibition was routinely circumvented, and highlights the deep connections forged between the state agencies, political parties and the bootleggers. Contemporary journalistic accounts draw attention to the discourses of paranoia over the 'anti-social element' at large and the bootlegger in particular—two figures that were easily collapsed together, as Simpson and Heitmeyer point out, both in popular imagination and in the perception of the state.[18] Oral narratives of bootleggers and other residents of the mill neighbourhoods present other more locally rooted dimensions of these practices.

In the investigations into the hooch poisoning case of February 1977, a wide network of Harji Rabari's accomplices was identified, including one Chhagan Ala. Accounts from the contemporary mill areas indicate that Chhagan Ala was another fairly accomplished dada from Gita Mandir, a rival of Jeevanbhai's associate Manga Bhoot. Manga Bhoot, a dada, a worker at the Calico Mills and an occasional rioter, was reportedly involved in a long-standing turf war with Chhagan Ala. As Jeevanbhai, former TLA pratinidhi and strongman from Gomtipur, recounted, Manga's very name was meant to inspire fear:

When his name was already Manga Bhoot, it was because he was like a demon. If he caught hold of someone, he would not let them go easily. If he had to kill someone, he would only rest after finishing the job. So, Chhagan and he would meet with their respective gangs of 50–60 men each. Blood would be shed, bones would be broken.[19]

This aside allows us to connect a horrific public incident with the intimate workings of local dadas. In particular, through this narrative, we can etch out the web of relationships that existed between big bootleggers such as Harji Rabari and smaller operators such as Jeevanbhai in Gomtipur. Jeevanbhai's career followed one particular trajectory—from a TLA pratinidhi to a municipal corporator, ably supported by his many allegedly 'anti-social' activities. However, in this period, other paths were opening up for this intermediary figure. The collapse of the TLA and the closure of the mills had a significant role to play in this, as earlier circuits of local power were fragmenting and reconfiguring.

Returning to the hooch incident of February 1977—a parallel inquiry commission had been constituted to investigate whether the police stationed in these areas had been 'negligent in discharge of their duties' or were 'guilty of corruption'.[20] One of the allegations that had been put forward to the inquiry commission was against police sub-inspector Jenumiya, suggesting his involvement in bootlegging in the area. While this charge was not investigated further, the commission report concluded that despite several applications detailing the illegal activities carried out at the Daulatkhana, such complaints were treated as 'routine' and no action was taken either to further probe the said illicit activities or to control them.[21]

The illegal transactions on the day of the hooch deaths, the report stated, were 'carried on in broad daylight', drawing crowds from across the city.[22] On the day of the incident as well as the days preceding it, copious quantities of prohibited items were bought, liquor was produced and its sale organised. The sale was 'open, continuous and brash', and the easy knowledge that appeared to have circulated amongst the consumers regarding the sites of sale suggests that this may have been a fairly routine practice that largely went unnoticed, unless there was a major tragedy.

The loose and fluctuating coalition governments of the mid-1970s, led largely by the Janata Party, remained publicly committed to enforcing total prohibition. Following strong Gandhian principles, the Janata Party required its candidates to pledge a commitment to prohibition, among other things.[23] The stringent measures introduced by the government included a complete curb on individual liquor permits, restrictions on toddy tapping, imposition of regulations on the sale of molasses, a key ingredient in liquor production, as well as the particularly zealous actions undertaken by the prohibition minister, Harisinh Chavda, in combing out illegal liquor operations.[24] The tightening of prohibition and the interruption of supply chains coincided with burgeoning production of 'country liquor' or *laththa*.[25] Methyl alcohol, present in substances such as French Polish and varnish, were unregulated by the prohibition laws and were easier to acquire, though more expensive than rectified spirits or denatured alcohol, for brewing hooch.[26]

A few months later, in November 1977, another incident of mass alcohol poisoning further intensified the public debate around police collusion with bootleggers, drawing attention to these shrouded practices. Five police officers were charged with taking *hafta*s from the bootlegger and suspended; Congress leader Chablidas Mehta announced that 'it was an open secret that from top to bottom all police officers were taking *hafta*s from anti-social elements and if any honest police officers made efforts to check the evil, they were being maligned and harassed'.[27] The TLA, in the meantime, stepped up its efforts at enforcing prohibition, appealing to the government to place even stricter controls on alcohol. These incidents were held up as cautionary tales as the union issued pleas to their members to abstain.[28]

The investigative exercises of the state government attempted to document not only the modes of operation that bootleggers of the time would employ but also the means by which they would accumulate social and political clout. In the official representations, there appear to be four crucial dimensions to the bootlegger's functioning—secrecy and subterfuge, as the 'bootlegger operated behind the curtain'; ruthlessness, for he was identified as a 'tough character', who had in his employ 'hoodlums who can create an atmosphere of terror in the locality for those who may think of obstructing him in his nefarious activities'; charity and social work, through which 'he is able to build up a social and economic position for himself in the locality'; and political influence, which 'enable him to establish contacts with the high echelons whose shield can be invoked in times of difficulties'.[29] Part of their activities, these reports imply, were covert, while others were conducted in the open, geared specifically towards building a favourable public image. The clandestine, illegal aspects of their operations were given license and supported by the networks that had been forged in the lawful and 'open' spheres of politics and social work.

Information on bootlegging was proliferating rapidly—if not in the detailed reports compiled by the enquiry commissions, then in the records maintained in the local police stations.[30] The police station under whose jurisdiction they operate would be aware of their activities, their modes of functioning, their names would be documented in a 'register' and often, these bootleggers would be required to present themselves at the police station at regular intervals. Despite this seemingly strict surveillance maintained over the bootleggers, the operation of the actual business—the production, circulation and consumption of alcohol—was often remarkably transparent. These activities, as the government and news reports suggest, not only 'assumed patent forms' and were carried out 'openly and continuously', but also enjoyed some form of political patronage and, as such, had the wherewithal to negotiate the disciplinary and regulatory procedures of the state.[31]

The liquor business, scholarly and local accounts suggest, were financed by Patel and Bania sponsors, close to circles of formal political power and hidden from the everyday operations. The quotidian affairs of managing the drinking dens and the coordination of supply and delivery were largely undertaken by Dalits and Muslims, who were invariably more vulnerable when it came to police scrutiny. In particular, local dadas were crucial in this arrangement of overseeing daily functions and keeping channels with the police well lubricated with haftas.[32] The system of haftas, for instance, indicates a regularity, a rhythm within which such activities unfolded.

The chain of command employed in most bootlegging operations likewise suggests a well-calibrated and considerably regulated system which allowed these practices to exist and even flourish at the margins of the economy.

The social unrest of the 1980s and the episodes of caste and communal rioting were punctuated by repeated incidents of hooch poisoning in the industrial areas.[33] The bootlegger, as a manifestation of the 'anti-social element' and a key actor or inciter, loomed large, though shadowy in state and public narratives of violence. Communal violence in several cases appeared as a feint for articulating local tensions and competitions around the control of the underground economy. The first two incidents of communal rioting in the long violence of 1985 were centred around turf wars and the non-payment of haftas.[34] Bootlegging, with its nebulous contours and figures, lent itself fruitfully to the production of social myths and fears.[35] The easy assumption of the bootlegger as 'Muslim',[36] focalised on the figure of Abdul Latif, the city's most prominent gangster, allowed for social paranoia to coalesce around religious lines. Latif, a small-time bootlegger operating out of the walled city, grew in prominence through the 1970s and 1980s, establishing links with the Bombay underworld as well as with powerful political figures.

With the dense and thick networks between what was commonly considered 'formal' politics and the 'illicit' world of crime becoming visible during this period—in the form of the networks of patronage that were built during Chimanbhai Patel's tenure (for instance, with groundnut traders, oil merchants and with notable gangsters), Madhavsinh Solanki's reliance on what Yagnik called the 'lumpen elements', as well as Amarsinh Chaudhury's entanglements in the land grab scandals[37]—new pathways opened for locally influential figures to accumulate social and political clout. The bootlegger, along with other such figures of what Thomas Blom Hansen has elsewhere termed the 'urban specialist', was invested with quasi-magical properties of navigating urban life. At this point in Ahmedabad's history, the 'urban specialist' was proliferating on the basis of their specialised knowledge, networks, connectedness and daring that allowed a performative and often mythologised claiming of 'hidden and dangerous abilities and powers' to stake a claim on the city.[38]

NEW PATHS FOR TLA PRATINIDHIS

The earlier channels of patronage, especially in the mill districts, relied on the institutional structure of the TLA. The social or political authority exercised by the bootlegger or the local strongman, as we have seen in the previous chapter, was often mediated by the union's vast institutional apparatus. Among the many repercussions of the TLA's decline, two are of critical importance to our analysis. The first occurred at the level of political alliances and positions. The union's association with the Congress (O), its subsequent electoral marginalisation and the indifference to the caste violence of the 1980s had eroded its political and moral authority. When the textile mills closed, the union was ill-equipped to contest the closures or bargain with the government. By the early 1980s, though the TLA had mended its relationship with the INTUC,[39] it was increasingly isolated, without the formidable political connections of its early years. By the time large-scale retrenchment occurred in the 1980s, the TLA was fast losing its status as 'real representative of the workers', as its leaders had developed a reputation of having 'vested interests in the union'.[40] The second repercussion of the TLA's disintegration can be traced in the material conditions of life in the working-class neighbourhoods. The union had been intensively involved in social and civic life. With its marginalisation in municipal politics, the TLA as an *institution* could no longer intervene in questions of housing and civic services with the same degree of competence.

The union's extensive network of local units and figures was overwritten by emerging sets of political actors and by new conduits of patronage. Slumlords and builders, for instance, not only became increasingly important in the supply and management of housing but also forged powerful political connections. Bootleggers similarly formed a formidable force in the political landscape of the state, offering financial and strong-arm support during elections. They emerged as influential figures not only in the world of the underground economy but also in the everyday life of the neighbourhood— their social position bolstered by their investments in education, social welfare and charity.[41]

Other sources substantiate this observation. According to news reports, bootleggers contributed generously during religious festivals like 'Ganpati Mahotsav and Navratris' and supported educational and personal expenses in the neighbourhoods of their operation.[42] 'By meeting the material needs of the common people', such figures acquired a certain legitimacy.[43] Equally significant in the accumulation of social influence was the provision of aid and assistance following the riots. Assuming positions of responsibility in relief committees, this 'new faceless mafia', as Harish Khare termed it, oversaw reconstruction in areas affected by violence.[44]

Bootleggers in Ahmedabad, like the ambiguously termed 'anti-social element', were hardly a homogenous category. There were those who operated on an impressive scale—the 'baron bootleggers', as identified by the Justice Miyabhoy Commission.[45] Perhaps, the most striking example of such a figure would be Abdul Latif, whose political career we discuss later in the chapter. There were others, like Manga Bhoot, Jeevanbhai and Ajay Singh, who commanded smaller territories. In the following paragraphs, through a discussion of Ajay Singh and Jeevanbhai's career, we can trace the ways in which their roles as TLA pratinidhis and local big men allowed them to enter new networks of power and politics.

The readjustments of local political alliances were visible in the state assembly elections in 1972 following the Congress Party's split in 1969. The election campaign in the labour constituency of Rakhiyal between the Congress (R) candidate, Kantilal Ghia, and Navinchandra Barot of the TLA was tense, with several clashes erupting between the two camps.[46] Ghia won, allegedly with the support of local dadas.[47] Alternative accounts also highlight Ghia's close association with local strongmen in the mill districts, Ajay Singh, in particular. A TLA representative, Singh ran an akhada, a brothel and betting shops. Widely acknowledged as a dual 'agent' of both the TLA and of the mill management, Singh was said to be instrumental in curtailing the rising communist influence in the mill neighbourhoods through the early 1960s. He had built his credibility partly through his position in the TLA and partly by honing his reputation for violence. With the TLA's electoral prowess enfeebled, Singh sought out other more powerful patrons. His turn towards respectability came when Kantilal Ghia won the state assembly elections and took him under his wing. Ajay Singh transformed himself under Ghia's patronage and support—shifting from a reputation for petty crime and violence to one of respectability. Ghia helped Ajay Singh obtain a loan to open a hotel and he ostensibly turned away from his life of 'anti-social activities' and refashioned himself into a person who kept more august company, such as the likes of senior Congress Party leaders. Ajay Singh's assets and lifestyle became ever more upwardly mobile—he constructed a multi-storeyed residence at a time, I was told, when it was uncommon for even politicians to do so.[48]

Jeevanbhai, the TLA pratinidhi, local dada of Gomtipur and bootlegger, whose political trajectory we had discussed in the previous chapter, had in the meantime tied his fortunes to Manubhai Parmar of Indira Gandhi's Congress Party. Parmar, the son of a mill worker, who would go to hold a ministerial position, was, in the 1970s, a secretary of the Gujarat Pradesh Congress Committee (GPCC). Having held reasonably important administrative posts within the party bureaucracy through most of the 1970s,[49] Parmar won the state assembly elections from Shaherkotda in 1980. At the heart of this electoral constituency was the erstwhile TLA stronghold of Rajpur–Gomtipur, populated predominantly by Muslim and Dalit mill workers. The assembly seat was reserved for Scheduled Caste candidates; Manubhai's appeal seemed to extend to both dominant communities in the area.[50] His electoral performance was certainly impressive. He retained the Shaherkotda seat until he died in 2000, with the exception of 1995, when he lost to Girishbhai Parmar of the BJP.[51]

Jeevanbhai forged a strong relationship with Manubhai Parmar based on political and civic activity, through this period. For instance, not only was Jeevanbhai crucial in garnering electoral support but he also provided a conduit for residents to approach the MLA with complaints and grievances of service provision in the neighbourhood. These ties were given greater solidity by the relationships of fictive kinship that were established between Jeevanbhai and Manubhai. Sailesh Parmar, Manubhai's son and the current MLA of the area, has always addressed Jeevanbhai as *kaka*. If Jeevanbhai had at this point confirmed allegiance to Manubhai, his contributions were recognised, at one level, by this public show of respect. At another level, Jeevanbhai nurtured this connection for more concrete political gains. After years of association with Manubhai Parmar, he approached him for a Congress nomination for the AMC elections of 1995. Through his association with Manubhai, Jeevanbhai had entered an orbit of patronage that was distinct from, though clearly built on, the TLA's networks of local power. Jeevanbhai continued as both a TLA pratinidhi (occupying important posts by the 1980s), a mobiliser for a rival political party and an important dada.

He established a stronger hold on the bootlegging business, moving his operations from less attractive sites to one stable location at the corner of the Sarangpur Mill No. 2 compound. His reputation and prestige grew in the neighbourhood through his political connections, his dadagiri and his social and community work. He was appointed a leader of the Vankar[52] community in the area, a position that involved, to a great degree, arbitrating personal disputes, brokering marital alliances and mediating ritual observances. He acted with impunity—before beating up anyone in the neighbourhood, he would first apprise the police and yet faced neither penalty nor discipline.

The techniques of his dadagiri too appear to have taken on more flamboyant forms. One incident, in particular, deserves attention. Jeevanbhai and Nur Ahmad, the dadas of neighbouring territories in Gomtipur, had become allies. The two of them, along with their respective gangs, went to watch a film, *Nagin*, Jeevanbhai recollects.[53] The cinema happened to be very crowded that day, and the dadas were made to suffer the ignominy of having to stand in a queue. Public order at the cinema was being maintained by Pathans. Jeevanbhai recounts that Nur Miyan repeatedly goaded him into breaking the queue. He resisted this heckling, more out of fear of the Pathans, until Nur called him a *hijra*.[54] Incensed that his masculinity was being questioned, he dove right into the middle of the queue. He was shoved and pushed, and in the ensuing melee, he stabbed a man to death. In different versions of this incident, Jeevanbhai has alternatively identified himself as the perpetrator and, at other times, placed himself as part of the gang that committed this murder. Thus, this dramatic spectacle may have been significantly less charged in reality—there is no way of knowing for certain. However, it presents two poles in Jeevanbhai's imagination—his emasculation at being mocked as a hijra and the reclaiming of his masculinity by being part of a very public murder.

It was this very kind of dadagiri coupled with his growing political clout that allowed Jeevanbhai to build and continuously expand a temple at the site of his bootlegging operations, in the Sarangpur Mill compound. When the AMC threatened to demolish this unauthorised structure, he convinced other residents (both Hindus and Muslims) to testify to its historical existence. The petition presented to the civic authorities also carried a coded threat of violence, as it implied that razing a place of worship could potentially lead to trouble. A temple at his bootlegging adda not only lent his operations some sort of cover, for large groups of people could gather in the evenings without attracting undue attention, but also offered some degree of protection.

For some of these actors, the everyday connections maintained with formal institutions may have remained veiled, only to surface during critical moments—elections, public scandals, riots.[55] Others, like Jeevanbhai, embodied routine and regular interactions between the formal and informal registers of political control. While the world of the bootlegger of this period was undoubtedly just as regulated as the world of the TLA pratinidhi, his links with formal political processes, however, were being forged through different techniques of mediation. As these networks reconfigured during this period, they remained amorphous to an extent, often without being rooted in any particular institutional structure (or being part of opposing institutional frameworks). At a time when personal circuits of patronage could no longer be pinned to the institutional frame of the TLA, these figures emerged as some key points through which to approach the state agencies. Simultaneously, practices of political corruption gained public visibility and invoked strong (and often violent) responses, such as during the Nav Nirman movement.

SLUMLORDS AND THE URBAN LAND MARKET

Living arrangements in the industrial belt of the city had been historically contentious. Chawls, slums, hutments and shanties jostled for space. The TLA's influence over the broader realm of housing and urban service provision, cemented in the years of the union's robust presence in municipal and state government, began waning by the late 1960s. As the city was straining to accommodate its ever-increasing population, the AMC withdrew from the provision of housing and increasingly focused on surveying and regulating slums. The material distinctions between chawls (as the emblematic form of industrial housing in the city) and slums (as sites of deprivation) blurred, while the legal boundaries between them deepened. Slums, according to official discourse, were unauthorised settlements, devoid of basic amenities, built in contravention of municipal regulations.[56] These 'quasi-legal' structures were often built with consent from the legal landlord, with an intermediary organising the logistics of renting.[57] Between 1961 and 1981, there was a steady growth in the share of informal housing in the eastern zone of the municipal corporation, accompanied by a decline of chawls in the urban housing market.[58] Much of the slum settlements, concentrated in the textile areas of eastern Ahmedabad, were built on private land.[59] Through this brisk growth of informal housing, land was steadily withdrawn from the formal market—either public vacant land was appropriated by slumlords, or private land was 'sold' off in parcels to the new occupiers.[60]

A slew of land legislations introduced through the 1970s shaped the supply and dynamics of workers' housing in Ahmedabad. The Slum Areas Act of 1973 empowered the state to declare any area that it saw as 'a source of danger to the health, safety or morals of the inhabitants' as a slum area, which, in turn, opened up the land and the dwellings upon it to a range of bureaucratic and regulatory practices.[61] It required slum residences to be registered and granted the Slum Clearance Board fairly wide-ranging powers in matters of eviction and upgradation.

The Urban Land Ceiling and Regulation Act (ULCRA) in 1976 introduced another layer of mediation on the already fraught domain of working-class housing. The law imposed a limit on ownership of vacant urban land at 1,000 square metres.[62] The surplus land acquired by the state under the Act was to be used for housing the economically weak.[63] Prior to its implementation, plots of land larger than the ceiling limit were changing hands at a 'dizzying rate'.[64] Land acquisition and residential development were pushed to areas like Vatva, Naroda, Narol—localities which lay beyond the municipal limits of Ahmedabad and, therefore, outside of the purview of the Act.[65] Simultaneously, speculation, so far restrained to land, was now shifting to real estate, which offered substantial and steady returns.[66] There was one exception to state appropriation of vacant land—under section 21 (1), exemptions could be granted for 'the construction of dwelling units for the accommodation for the weaker sections of society'.[67] While only 0.3 per cent of the estimated surplus land had been acquired until the mid-1980s,[68] Gujarat granted more than 60 per cent of the total exceptions to the Act.[69] Most of the properties built as part of these exceptions were entirely unaffordable for their ostensible market and were targeted instead at the middle and upper-middle classes.

Ownership patterns and tenurial relationships on private lands changed dramatically. On the one hand, as the supply of private land diminished for low-income housing, encroachments on municipal lands increased.[70] On the other hand, informal transactions and settlements mushroomed on remaining private tracts, with landowners encouraging squatting to circumvent acquisition under ULCRA.[71] 'The Act became a boon to racketeers,' *India Today* reported, 'Those who had excess land divided it and sold to squatters. The omnipotent slumlords ensured that nobody dared to evict them.'[72] Urban land, either by virtue of the constructions made on it or the grey transactions surrounding it, entered the informal market and a new 'petty-capitalist class' emerged, which 'had strong links to local political processes'.[73]

Two crucial figures emerged to supply housing and to navigate the changed political economy of urban land—the 'promoter-developer' of the corporate real estate sector and the 'slumlord'.[74] 'Specialists' surfaced who eased access to permits and licences, as well as the 'land grabber' turned slumlord, who cultivated relationships with government officials and politicians.[75] In 1976, the *Majoor Sandesh* estimated nearly 300,000 inhabitants of such slum settlements—mill operatives, those who toiled in small factories, and those who worked as hawkers and vendors. The landlords of such settlements were influential people with the ability to collect rent by force.[76] The use of violence in rent collection was fairly routine, surfacing occasionally to attract the attention of state authorities in particularly severe instances.[77] The figure of the slumlord itself was not a new player in working-class housing. Chawls in the early years of the twentieth century were built with a similar logic— abysmally serviced, overcrowded and unsanitary tenements rented out for maximum profits. Chawl owners often allowed for informal settlements to grow around the more legally authorised space of the chawl, and significant links had been forged between local landlords and politicians.[78] However, what appears to have been recalibrated was the *access* to security and stability of housing. Where the TLA pratinidhi would mediate rental disputes, negotiate the provision of civic services, it was now the landlord (and perhaps, to some extent, civil society organisations) that would provide a way of approaching state agencies and also offer the possibility of evading coercive state measures such as eviction.

The uneasy coalition government formed after the national Emergency was lifted in 1977 proved to be ineffective in curbing exceptions granted under the ULCRA.[79] Within a few years, Congress Chief Minister Madhavsinh Solanki's vision of transforming the state into 'mini Japan' saw slum clearance drives initiated and street hawkers displaced as access to land and housing for the urban working class grew ever more meagre.[80] Solanki, it was argued, had been particularly lax in implementing land redistribution policies, both in urban and rural Gujarat, instead forging relationships of patronage with 'industrialists and real estate dealers' across the state.[81] Thus, new forms of industrial development, which strongly favoured investments in chemicals and electronics, also generated immense struggles over urban land, as precariously placed residents were displaced to make way for factories and workshops.[82] Control over urban land in the state, in turn, became a politically sensitive issue—government officials were being reportedly transferred to please powerful politicians (or to limit obstructions to the involvement of these politicians in extra-legal activities).[83] With urban land in short supply, and the access to it heavily contested, the episodic communal violence that Ahmedabad experienced could have also been directed towards freeing up urban land. The violence of 1985–86 made the otherwise slippery links between these figures and their connections with state agencies more explicit, as slum landlords with political positions were incriminated in communally oriented displacement of slum residents.[84]

The slumlord appears to have simultaneously assumed a number of roles, often complementary and sometimes contradictory. Invested in both settling and unsettling urban land, the slumlord, in part, controlled the degree of security of the settlement. By offering access to politicians and municipal officials, the slumlord could ease the process of acquiring government documentation (ration cards, voter identity cards and the like) and thus ensure a form of tentative security.[85] Conversely, by denying this access or by actively demolishing slums and displacing residents, the slumlord undermined residential security. As we have seen, strong links were maintained between these figures operating at the margins of legality and formal political structures and state institutions. Furthermore, there was also considerable diversification in terms of their actual practice within the underground economy. The connections forged in one domain of informal and quasi-legal activity proved to be useful in expanding their field of operations.[86] Thus, not only were there considerable overlaps between enterprises, but also between the formal and informal realms of politics. These porous borders ensured that the figure of 'a slumlord turned builder who at the same time is a municipal councilor or office bearer of a national political party' was not out of the ordinary in Ahmedabad.[87]

The increasing significance of landlords and slumlords as intermediaries in the provision of housing and official documentation, and in securing (or destabilising) tenurial rights, grew stronger in the light of the three historical processes that began in the mid-1980s and have escalated since. One was the collapse of the textile industry, the reconfiguration of tenancy in the mill districts and the gradual but steady undermining of property rights. The second was the process of religious segregation, supported by the enactment of the 'Disturbed Areas Act',[88] which, as we discuss in a later chapter, produced two distinct property markets in the city. And the third was the expansion of the city's boundaries as outlying agricultural lands were acquired for urban development.

For instance, Congress municipal corporator Kishansinh Tomar's acquisition of a factory and his attempts to evict nearly 350 chawls in Saraspur signal, on the one hand, the involvement of politicians in the real estate business and, on the other, a drive to forcibly transform the built environment of eastern Ahmedabad. The transformation of the mill areas is often met with pessimism. Jigneshbhai Vaghela, a former mill worker and social activist from Gomtipur, outlined his view on the situation:

> Now by 2013–14, all *chawl*s, *basti*s, *jhuggi jhopri*s, will be demolished. Agricultural land is easily seized, but it is difficult to capture mill workers' *chawl*s. People here are aware, they are political, so they [state agencies in collusion with builders] have adopted a new plan … that they would use muscle power, the landlord would be bribed, and through *dadagiri* they will attempt to evict *chawl*s…. If there is resistance, they employ another technique…. They [the state agencies] would approach you and say, 'this is a slum area. If you vacate it, you will be resettled in a proper well-serviced apartment.' And in this scheme, there would be the government (*sarkar*) and builders involved.

Jigneshbhai's worries are trained upon two sets of actors—builders (which included big corporations such as Safal and smaller ones such as Kishansinh Tomar) and state agencies (in this case, primarily, the AMC and the Slum Clearance Board). The two ways, described by Jigneshbhai, of destabilising claims on working-class housing highlight the points of intersection between state agencies and key figures in the real estate market and allude to the importance of the intermediary (in this specific case, the 'builder') in both offering the promise of secure housing and in denying it.

The extension of the municipal limits, the repeated episodes of communal violence and the strategic use of the Disturbed Areas Act has produced a communalised social geography, which, in a sense, amplifies the significance of these intermediaries. Take, for instance, the case of Nawab builders. A family business, run from the Shah Alam locality in eastern Ahmedabad, Nawab builders—through social work, relief work (in the violence of 2002), political involvement (through Shehzad Khan Pathan's[89] successes in the AMC elections), their investments in real estate in Muslim-majority areas of the city and allegations of 'criminal activity'[90]— has acquired a position of great prominence.[91] Or for that matter, the rise of a particular kind of 'property magnate' who (often without possessing real legal claims on the land) provided housing for the Muslim working poor, facilitated interactions with the civic bodies and established networks of patronage.[92]

THE ANTI-SOCIAL ELEMENT AND THE LAW

The nebulous figure of the 'anti-social element', the goonda thus emerged not only in discourses of urban crime or in judicial readings of episodes of violence but also in the everyday negotiations in the workers' neighbourhoods. In Ahmedabad, as elsewhere, the figure of the 'anti-social' itself was notoriously difficult to define. As a legal distinction, the term can be traced to colonial legislations governing surveillance and preventive detention. The implementation of these colonial laws, which legislated surveillance of 'habitual criminals' or 'criminal tribes', enhanced the sense of danger embodied in this figure rather than diminishing it. As Singha argues, a certain dynamic of 'illegality' was built into the formulation and practice of such laws; the discretionary powers invested in the lower functionaries of the police and the judiciary generated an entire spectrum of practices that ranged from the informal to the illegal.[93] Gujarat Prevention of Anti-Social Activities Act drew from earlier preventive detention laws. The Bengal Goondas Act of 1923, where the provenance of the Gujarat legislation lay, was aimed at particular segments of urban society, with a specific emphasis on the single male migrant.[94] The legal category of the 'goonda' under colonial law contained a wide variety of figures from diverse social worlds, and who could assume multiple identities at different historical moments.[95] The figure operated as a social imaginary, embodying elite and middle-class anxieties. The legislation, in turn, was the mechanism through which the distinction between the respectable and the disreputable was reinforced.[96] The category of the 'goonda' emerged as a particularly potent one during the Non-cooperation movement of the early 1920s, and scholarship on Calcutta has demonstrated how fears of nationalist agitators and labour leaders were collapsed together in the enactment of the law.[97] The Calcutta Goondas Act of 1923 became the template for similar legislations across urban India—in Kanpur in 1930, Delhi in 1937 and Berar in 1946. Echoing the discourse around 'criminal tribes' in the nineteenth century, the 'goonda' continued to be collapsed with the 'migrant' as state authorities debated the legislation in colonial Kanpur.[98]

In Gujarat in the mid-1980s, another legislative exercise was initiated with the intention of delineating the figure of the 'anti-social element' and its fields of operation. The Prevention of Anti-Social Activities Act (henceforth PASA) was aimed at trying to outline these figures, to legally define and, in turn, curtail the scope of their activity. The ordinance (which was replaced by a legislation within a few months) was introduced in May 1985, in order to 'deal with the deteriorating law and order situation in the state'.[99] Commonly known as the anti-goonda law, it empowered the state to detain a suspect for up to a year without trial, 'on his or her past record of anti-social activity, without the necessity of a witness'.[100] The National Security Act of 1980, another preventive detention legislation, which extended to nearly all parts of the country, was already in practice in Gujarat. While the National Security Act sanctioned detention for those who were seen by the state as compromising national security or posing a threat to public order,[101] the new legislation pre-emptively identified a range of 'anti-social' figures as those whose activities were 'prejudicial to the maintenance of public order'.[102] The 'anti-social' elements that were clearly outlined in the act included bootleggers, drug offenders, immoral traffic offenders, property grabbers and the somewhat vague category of 'dangerous persons'.[103]

The Gujarat legislation joined a series of anti-goonda laws that were enacted across India, from the 1970s onwards. Unlike its colonial predecessors, this law shifted its attention away from the mobile figure of the 'migrant' to a clearly defined set of (largely) urban economic activities. The implementation of the PASA was predictably uneven and coded with notions of respectability. The promulgation of the act was accompanied by a promise from the then Home Minister Amarsinh Chaudhury (who would soon take over as the chief minister) that the legislation would not be deployed to target any political activity.[104] Nevertheless, charges were levied against the state government that the 'Anti-Goonda' ordinance was being used to harass anti-reservation leaders[105] and the political opposition, while not 'a single notorious goonda or bootlegger had been held under these measures'.[106] In this view, a distinction is posed between 'legitimate' political workers and 'real' goondas. These boundaries, as we have seen in the discussion above, however, were far more blurred and porous in practice.

The first sensational case that caught the attention of the news media involved a land grab scandal in BJP-controlled Rajkot. Popatlal Patel, an industrialist, was detained under the Goondas Act and accused of encroaching upon 10,000 square yards of government land for setting up a factory manufacturing oil engines.[107] Key ministers in Amarsinh Chaudhury's cabinet rallied around Patel, demanding for his release and for strict action to be taken against the Rajkot district collector who had sanctioned the detention.[108] Most vocal among Patel's supporters was the health minister, Vallabhbhai Patel, who described Popatlal Patel in no uncertain terms as a 'gentleman businessman'.[109] Following considerable political pressure, Patel was released from detention within twenty-four hours. This incident revealed some dramatic fault lines in state politics as well as in the implementation and intent of this legislation.[110] The government's quick capitulation to the demands for Popatlal Patel's release was seen as being anti-poor.[111]

The Gujarat government, not only in this more prominent case but in others as well, had been reluctant to impose the anti-goonda legislation against land sharks, despite a specific clause that listed land grabbing as a key 'anti-social activity'. The reason for this, Chief Minister Amarsinh Chaudhury explained, was because the legislation was intended for 'hardened criminals' and 'habitual offenders'. 'Businessmen', by this logic, came with somewhat more respectable credentials and were, according to Chaudhury, not to be clubbed with goondas.[112] Respectability and networks of caste and class privilege appeared to be central in the practice of this law, as Vallabhbhai Patel, Popatlal Patel's defender, remarked, 'It is true that we would not have been upset over the arrest of a slum dweller for a similar offence, but isn't there a difference between a slum dweller and a man of stature, like Popatbhai?'[113] While the letter of the law suggested a far more imprecise definition of the 'anti-social' figure, its practice was tentatively sharpening the contours of this figure.

Another reading of the law could be offered by examining the way in which the Anti-Goondas Act was employed against Abdul Latif, a fairly well-established bootlegger by the mid-1980s and, more recently, a subject of a film starring Shahrukh Khan as the lead. Accused of the murder of a police officer during the riots of 1985, Latif was in jail from November 1985 to May 1986, when he was acquitted.[114] On the day of his release, he was taken back into preventive custody under PASA, 1985. Successive detention orders kept him in custody for over four months in contravention of the constitutional protection offered under Article 22 (4), which offered relief against detentions longer than three months, unless approved by a special advisory board.[115] Latif's case generated some debate about the constitutionality of the Gujarat PASA.[116] Exploiting certain loopholes in the Act, a fresh detention order could be issued every eighty-ninth day, thereby, making the submission of a report from the advisory board unnecessary. In its usage, the law then produced its own regime of 'extra-legality'. Based as it was on suspicion rather than on proof, the law offered greater license to the police force while limiting the space for judicial procedure.[117] The wide administrative latitude granted and the repeated extensions of the order, as we see in Abdul Latif's case, allowed for an extraordinary measure to become normalised.

PASA was deployed in both the cases mentioned above—one, on the charges of land grab and, the other, on grounds of being a 'dangerous person'. These two cases represent, in a sense, the selective ways in which this law was implemented. The fact that the law's usage was not entirely uniform is not unique. However, it does allow us to reflect on how the state, at this historical moment, was attempting to construct the image of the 'anti-social element'. In constituting this figure as a legal category, the 'anti-social element' was rendered ever more vague. At the same time, it served to criminalise a wide range of urban activities, drawing suspected 'anti-socials' into tighter webs of police surveillance and action. The slippages between the ambiguity of the law and its increasingly focused application allowed for a more sharply defined figure to emerge in state practices and in public discourse. Reading the enforcement of the law against the ways in which this figure operated on the ground, we get a sense of how certain parameters of defining criminal activity were being hardened and how the contours of the 'anti-social element' were gradually sharpened. One, it seemed to be predicated on a notion of social respectability and privilege. Indeed, much of the criticism of Popatlal Patel's arrest was centred around the reportedly 'biased' application of the law—an argument was thus extended that the Rajkot collector had 'discriminated by moving against industrialists but sparing slum lords who had similarly grabbed land'.[118] The second was a move to attribute certain religious markers to the 'anti-social element'. Over the next few decades, the implementation of the law acquired even sharper communal markers. PASA was amended in March 2000 to include cow slaughter as an 'anti-social activity'.[119] In the state assembly elections following the violence of 2002, the BJP's election manifesto threatened to deal with anti-nationals and anti-socials alike through PASA and the Prevention of Terrorist Activities Act.[120]

THE EMERGENCE OF A POLARISED LOCAL POLITICS

I employ Harin Pathak and Abdul Latif as exemplars of the sorts of local political leaders that were emerging at this point, drawing on their political trajectories to gain insights into the communally divided political landscape that was forming at the end of the 1980s. Pathak, a key BJP leader, and Latif, a bootlegger turned municipal corporator, were two figures intimately involved in the world of local politics. Latif's political trajectory pushed him from the margins where he operated, like many other shadowy figures. For a brief moment, it was possible for someone like Abdul Latif to occupy a 'formal' role in local political processes. Pathak's career, in particular, shows how the BJP penetrated the industrial districts, while the broader electoral strategies pursued by his party demonstrate how a politico-religious polarisation was being produced.

Pathak, like Ashok Bhatt before him, began his electoral career with the Ahmedabad Municipal Corporation in the 1970s.[121] The charges of his involvement in the murder of policeman Laxman Desai during the violence of 1985 did not hinder his political career; instead, in 1989, he was granted a ticket to contest the Lok Sabha elections from the Ahmedabad constituency, which he won for the first of his seven consecutive terms.[122] This parliamentary constituency included the BJP stronghold Khadia, Muslim majority areas in the walled city and the mill areas of eastern Ahmedabad, which housed large numbers of Dalit and Muslim workers in close proximity. Pathak was an RSS worker and his early influence in the mill areas stemmed from his position as a teacher at a local school. Krantikbhai, a human rights activist who grew up in Gomtipur, explained to me, 'He mobilised many of his students ... and if there was ever a fight, he would always be able to get hold of about 10–15 students.... Now, if your guru has decreed, one must follow, right?' In the later years, especially after the mill closures and the BJP's victory in the civic elections of 1987, the mobilisation became even more intense. Beginning with widely established techniques of gaining neighbourhood support—they organised health camps, distributed school supplies and books to students— the party moved on to incorporating young Dalit men into the lower rungs of their leadership.[123] At a time when the first shock of the mill closures had sent the industrial districts into a crisis—of livelihoods, social identity, reputation and social honour—this move could have offered a space in which young working-class men could make an attempt to reclaim some degree of social respectability.

Krantikbhai, explaining the techniques of mobilisation amongst working-class youth, detailed:

For boys [young men] who are jobless at the moment, say for instance, they are designated the leader of a *prakhand* [party division] ... he will have a sense of power then. In this way, many boys who were associated with the Dalit movement, even with the Dalit panthers, joined either the BJP, or the Durga Vahini or the RSS. The mass [base] was made up of these boys.... You will find a number of Dalit boys, who, on April 14th would be shouting Ambedkarite slogans ... these same boys could be found in a BJP or VHP [Vishwa Hindu Parishad] programme.[124]

Once the BJP entered the civic body, the party corporators opened local offices in every neighbourhood. These spaces became points of access to state services—an adda, a site of male sociality which also opened up the channels for approaching the state. While possibly drawing from the TLA's mode of functioning, the party also transformed it, especially since the BJP's socio-political activities in the neighbourhood introduced spaces where senior party members could directly interact with the local youth. Simultaneously, the party penetrated existing arenas of urban sociality. For instance, Gomtipur has what was described to me as a 'pan shop culture'. This suggests a public life, primarily masculine, centred around local *pan* shops. These shops, usually equipped with a radio, would sell pan and cigarettes (and, sometimes, bootleg alcohol). With a running supply of tea sourced from a nearby *kitli*, large numbers of men would linger for hours around the pan shops, chatting, playing board games and discussing the state of the world. Harin Pathak, in particular, was deeply enmeshed in this world, interacting regularly with men assembled on the streets of Gomtipur.

In Ahmedabad, one way in which the BJP had been able to accumulate grassroots support was by promising proximity of sorts to politicians in power. While this may have replicated the older Congress–TLA strategy for garnering support, the BJP introduced a new element—offering closeness to important political figures—and thereby, reconfigured the existing channels of patronage.[125] Krantikbhai recollected that during the communal violence of the early 1990s, he would notice young BJP leaders from his chawl in Gomtipur, calling L. K. Advani, the then president of the BJP. 'Directly to Advani,' he added for emphasis, 'this is how it worked. A direct connection was established between supporters and the leadership, and that's how people were recruited to participate in the yatras, the Ram Shila pujan, etc.'

Between 1989 and 1993, Hindutva politics took on ever more militant forms and the BJP's self-assertion in the mill neighbourhoods was also reflected in the kinds of local skirmishes that broke out. In April 1990, for instance, soon after the BJP had cobbled together an alliance with the Janata Party, riots broke out in Gomtipur. The violence in Gomtipur soon bled into communal clashes, with local BJP and VHP leaders acquiring license to flex their political muscle and adopt an aggressive public posture.[126] The belligerent public personas of local BJP leaders in areas such as Gomtipur were then contributing to and being constituted by the changing discourse of militant Hindutva.

Pathak in the meantime had moved from local to national-level politics. Though his political arena had expanded, he was nevertheless seen a local man. When he was denied a Lok Sabha ticket in 2014, presumably in a move to eliminate Advani loyalists from Narendra Modi's BJP, he declared that the 'Ashok-Harin' era of BJP politics had come to an end.[127] Media reports cloyingly described his tenure as an MP—the *Times of India* anointed him a 'trusted friend', 'more like a family member' for the people of east Ahmedabad. The report continued:

> Pathak's mass appeal stems from his active contact with his electorate since 1971. Be it a *besna*, a dog's burial or any exigency—Harinbhai as he is popularly known—has always been there for the people of his constituency. He even once ensured a memorial for a 'martyr' sparrow that died in a police firing.[128]

Another report gushed,

> Since 1974, when Pathak fought the municipal elections, he has pampered his voters relentlessly and politically. Pathak helps his voter's children get school admission; he attends to complaints to replace covers of gutters in lanes and bylanes; he gives character certificates to voters' sons in the hundreds; he attends more than 100 marriages round the year; makes his presence felt in an equal number of *uthammas* (condolence meetings for the dead); and it is not a joke to say that Pathak many a time goes to the police station to register a missing complaint for his voter's teenage daughters in order to fix the rowdies of the area.[129]

So effusive in their praise, one could perhaps speculate that these journalistic pieces were written by admirers of Harin Pathak. However, they do offer certain clues to understanding the political persona that Pathak had constructed over four decades. He was, as other accounts also suggest, accessible—someone who nurtured his grassroots connections.[130] He managed his parliamentary constituency with the attention of a local-level leader, as someone who was invested in the social world of his constituents. He not only tended to everyday concerns but also displayed a certain zeal in containing what he considered the 'rowdies'.

This image of Pathak as a crusader against crime and the 'anti-social element' was carefully crafted. In 2000, both Pathak, then the minister of state for defence production and supplies, and Ashok Bhatt, the Gujarat health minister, were charged with instigating the murder of police constable Laxman Desai during the anti-reservation violence of 1985. Pathak maintained that the charges brought against him were false and a part of a vendetta against him for having exposed the links between the Congress Party, the police force and Abdul Latif.[131] Pathak consistently tried to make his allegations against the Congress Party's links with the underground economy even more explicit. For instance, in the 10th Lok Sabha session, he argued, 'For the past 10–15 years, some Congress leaders in connivance with anti-social and anti-national elements have been creating a vicious atmosphere in Ahmedabad…. They ran authorised pubs, gambling dens and accumulate foreign arms and ammunition.'[132]

Admittedly, the trope of the 'anti-social element' was employed by nearly all commentators on the city's violent history. This took on a range of representations—from newspaper reports, which would often present the anti-social figure as a free-floating agent of violence and mayhem, to fact-finding reports, which addressed the forms that the figure was taking, to judicial enquiry commissions, whose findings while leaving the figure ambiguous and shadowy, nevertheless, added a certain amount of credulity to its existence. Political parties, too, accused each other of having entire armies of 'anti-social elements' at their disposal.[133]

However, by the late 1980s, with the BJP in power in the city municipality, the contours of this figure became increasingly more defined. The anti-national character of the 'anti-social element', which had been alluded to in the violence of 1969, was further reinforced during this period. Infiltration and arms smuggling were flagged as critical concerns by the Gujarat BJP in the early 1990s.[134] In this general atmosphere of suspicion, there was one particular character who would be invoked persistently by the BJP to highlight, on the one hand, the supposedly anti-social and anti-national behaviour of the Gujarati Muslim, and on the other, the alleged links maintained by the Congress Party with the underworld.

Abdul Latif—small-time bootlegger in the 1970s, established gangster by the early 1980s and a politician by the late 1980s—was, as this news report suggests, 'the state BJP's first whipping boy'.[135] Latif's prominence must be seen in connection to two processes that were occurring through the 1970s and 1980s—one, the emerging forms of caste and community alliances that were gaining a new political currency and the other, the phenomenal expansion of smuggling in Gujarat[136] as well as the links formed with the Bombay underworld, which not only brought more attention to the underground operators in Gujarat, but also raised the stakes somewhat. Latif's rise as a politician coincided with the BJP's first electoral victory in Ahmedabad. In the municipal elections of 1987, which crystallised the political polarisation that had been brewing, the Congress Party lost miserably and was to stay out of power for the next thirteen years.[137] The mixed areas of the walled city, traditionally strongholds of the Congress Party, voted instead for Abdul Latif, who was contesting as an independent candidate.

Latif began his career as a delivery boy for established bootlegger Manjur Ali, operating out of Saraspur, a mill neighbourhood.[138] By 1980, he had branched out independently setting up his own adda in the walled city. His business flourished, his networks expanded and soon he was dabbling in the extortion and protection racket and, later, in the real estate market.[139] Latif's gang had increased threefold by 1984, when internecine conflict in Bombay's gang world spilled over to Gujarat.[140] Turf war ensued in Ahmedabad, compounded by the caste and communal violence that broke out in the city in 1985–86. The communal violence of this period allowed Latif to remake himself as a stalwart member of the city's Muslim community. Inner-city Muslims, who were more dependent on daily wages, were severely affected by the protracted periods of curfew in 1985 and 1986. Through his interventions during this period of crisis, Latif had positioned himself as a Robin Hood–like figure and as the 'defender and protector' of the Muslim community in the city.[141] Having 'actively nurtured' the Muslim electorate through his relief work during this spate of violence, his appeal amongst Muslims in eastern Ahmedabad was enhanced by the Congress government's ineptitude in providing either security or immediate aid.[142] Already established as a patron whose 'blessings' were crucial for electoral success, the relief work that he performed during the violence enabled him to remake his reputation—from one of notoriety to acquiring a veneer of respectability. This news article presented one view of his campaign for the 1987 AMC elections:

> His critics and the police authorities categorise him as a bootlegger, his admirers regard and respect him as a social worker.... By all accounts, the

Muslim community in the entire walled area converted his candidate [*sic*] into a people's campaign…. Latif emerged as a defender of his community against a partisan and communalised police force.[143]

He had been arrested prior to the municipal elections, on suspicions of having incited communal violence (as were many local leaders, including Ashok Bhatt and Harin Pathak of the BJP), but this widespread appeal would indicate that he was perceived as a heroic figure. Interestingly, both Latif and Pathak were valourised as people's leaders who were deeply committed to their constituencies. In the municipal elections of 1987, he won as an independent candidate from five wards across the mill districts and the walled city, despite being in preventive custody at the time.[144] Latif remained in jail until he was released on bail in January 1987 to contest the municipal elections.[145] Reportage on his candidacy indicates that support for him was overwhelming—'Waves of humanity cheered him wherever he went. A throng of about 40,000 people marched with his mother's funeral procession.'[146] On the day of polling, it was reported 'that even in areas he did not contest, voters struck off other names on the ballot paper and scribbled his name on it'.[147]

Soon after his victory, Latif was re-arrested for violating a previous externment order.[148] Violence broke out following his arrest—news reports commented that police action in this case was unnecessarily provocative, 'arresting Latif as if he just another ordinary pickpocket'.[149] The unrest that followed reaffirmed Latif's public appeal. He was externed from the city for two years, though he managed to retain his municipal seat with well-timed appearances.[150] He continued attending crucial meetings, either escorted by security personnel or by slipping through the police watch. By the early 1990s, Latif's empire grew tremendously.[151] His links with powerful political figures—Chimanbhai Patel, in particular—became even more visible with the assassination of Rauf Valliulah, the Gujarat Congress general secretary, in October 1992.[152]

Though Latif distanced himself from active electoral politics, he remained the BJP's favourite bogeyman. BJP electoral campaigns in 1993 urged voters to remember Latif when they went out to cast their ballot.[153] Again in 1995, when the BJP won the state assembly elections with a majority, Latif resurfaced as a symbolic target—'No election speech of a BJP leader was complete without the mention of Latif and his connections with Dawood Ibrahim and the Congress.'[154] The BJP's campaign consistently pitted 'Rama Raj', as a vision for their model of governance, against that of 'Latif Raj'.[155]

Having escaped from Ahmedabad to various other cities—Dubai, Karachi—Latif was captured in Delhi, in October 1995. With his arrest, Keshubhai Patel, the BJP chief minister, was popularly celebrated as 'Hindu Hriday Samrat'[56]—a title that has been periodically conferred to particularly successful soldiers of the Hindu Right, Bal Thackeray and Narendra Modi, among others. After just over a year in prison, Latif was shot dead in a dubious police encounter in Ahmedabad.

Latif was never a serious politician. However, his electoral victory offers us a lens through which to examine the changing forms of political mediation, to map the transforming social and political geography of the city, and to reflect on the limits that seem to have been placed on Muslim political leadership. The changing socio-political dynamics invested religion with a new political currency, allowing Pathak and Latif, for instance, to present themselves as leaders of politicised religion. This period also marked the end of Congress domination and signalled the beginnings of Hindutva politics, which was to shape the city through social and spatial segregation, and violence, in the following decades.

We can identify at this point two distinct but closely related processes occurring. New rhythms of political patronage as well as political corruption emerged as the Congress Party splintered and various factions jostled for higher stakes in the state government. Related to this was a second process in which the ever-expanding underground economy was attracting more attention and social tensions emerging from its operation were becoming progressively more controversial. Significantly, during this period, the intersections between these two processes became increasingly more visible. Whether it was through strong-arm support during elections, financial assistance, a wilful blindness to the illegal, the realms of the political figure and the 'anti-social' one coincided with great regularity. We have seen in the previous chapter that this overlap (both in terms of practice as well as social identity) was often visible in the figure of the union representative. It was this *institutional* interface that the TLA presented that was fundamentally transformed during this period—not only did multiple, competing channels for accessing urban resources open up, but there was also a corresponding shift in the dynamics of local political interactions. This indicated the formation of a new political configuration that linked the working-class neighbourhoods to the state. In a sense, this signalled the retreat of formal politics from certain spheres of urban governance, a tendency that was to intensify in the following decades.

NOTES

1 For instance, the several hooch poisoning cases of the 1970s and 1980s and the land grab scandals of the 1980s.

2 Breman, *The Making and Unmaking of an Industrial Working Class*, 211; Spodek, *Ahmedabad: Shock City of Twentieth-Century India*, 214–26; Yagnik and Sheth, *Ahmedabad: From Royal City to Megacity*. See also Shani, 'Bootlegging, Politics and Corruption', 494–508. For different perspectives on questions of crime and corruption in other South Asian contexts, please see, for instance, Andrew Sanchez, 'Capitalism, Violence and the State: Crime, Corruption and Entrepreneurship in an Indian Company Town', *Journal of Legal Anthropology* 2, no. 1 (2010): 165–88; Akhil Gupta, 'Blurred Boundaries: The Discourse of Corruption, the Culture of Politics, and the Imagined State', *American Ethnologist* 22, no. 2 (1995): 375–402; Jonathan Parry, '"The Crisis of Corruption" and "the Idea of India"', in *Morals of Legitimacy: Between Agency and System* (New York: Berghann Books, 2000), 27–56; and Michelutti, 'Wrestling with (Body) Politics.'

3 Spodek, 'Crises and Response.'

4 See, for instance, Shani, 'Bootlegging, Politics and Corruption', 494–508; Berenschot, 'On the Usefulness of Goondas in Indian Politics', 255–75. This process finds echoes at the national level as well. For instance, Sanchez notes that this period may have witnessed the rise of a new model of political leadership—a shift from the earlier 'statesman' of the Congress Party to a new 'charismatic' political leader. The more explicit connections between politics and criminality, he argues, can be dated to the Emergency. These networks seem to have been enhanced, with nearly 29 per cent of elected parliamentarians bearing some kind of criminal charges. Andrew Sanchez, 'India: The Next Superpower? Corruption in India', *IDEAS Reports—Special Reports*, Nicholas Kitchen (ed.) *LSE IDEAS*. SR010 (2012): 50–53.

5 I use 'his' primarily because much of the conversations (and my archival and ethnographic material) centre around significant male figures in the underground economy. It is important to note, however, that there were possibly many powerful women operating in these fields. A case in point is Santokben Jadeja, who was said to play an important role in the liquor and gold smuggling business of Porbandar-Rajkot region. See *Outlook*, 8 March 1999. Moreover, newspaper reportage suggests the involvement of women

in the lower rungs of the bootlegging business. See also *Times of India*, 23 March 1977.

6   Spodek, 'From Gandhi to Violence', 785.

7   Ibid., 791.

8   This incident, as horrific as it was, was certainly not the first case of mass alcohol poisoning. The *Times of India* reported that several hooch-related deaths had occurred earlier in the industrial areas of Ahmedabad and Surat. *Times of India*, 10 January 1976.

9   Harald Fischer-Tiné and Jana Tschurenev, *A History of Alcohol and Drugs in Modern South Asia: Intoxicating Affairs* (London: Routledge, 2014), 205. Here, Edward Simpson and Carolyn Heitmeyer posit a distinction between the 1977 commission report and later governmental inquiries, suggesting that the former displayed an 'institutional uncertainty', that is an inability to admit either the commerce or the consumption of alcohol, while the later investigations make clear the limits of prohibition policies.

10 Miyabhoy, *Report of the Laththa Commission of Inquiry*, 25.

11 Ibid., 30.

12 *Times of India*, 13 March 1989.

13 *Harji Hira Rabari v. E. N. Renison, Dy. Commissioner of Police*, Gujarat High Court, 25 April 1968.

14 Ibid.

15 *Times of India*, 13 March 1977.

16 Carolyn Heitmeyer and Edward Simpson, 'The Culture of Prohibition in Gujarat, India', in *A History of Drugs and Alcohol in Modern South Asia: Intoxicating Affairs*, ed. Jana Tschurenev and Harald Fischer-Tiné (London: Routledge, 2014), 203–17.

17 Sujata Patel, *City Conflicts and Communal Politics: Ahmedabad 1985–86* (Delhi: Oxford University Press, 2006), 335. *Times of India*, 10 January 1976.

18 Heitmeyer and Simpson, 'The Culture of Prohibition in Gujarat, India', 207–08.

19 Interview with Jeevanbhai Parmar. One Mangaji was incidentally also named as co-accused in the case, who was later acquitted. It would be difficult to establish, however, whether this was the same Manga Bhoot.

20 Miyabhoy, *Report of the Laththa Commission of Inquiry*, 13.

21 Ibid., 30.

22 Ibid.

23 The Janata Front and, later, the Janata Party was a somewhat tenuous political coalition that included the Congress (O) headed by Morarji Desai, among others. See *Times of India*, 7 May 1975.

24 *Times of India*, 25 July 1978; *Times of India*, 30 October 1975; *India Today*, 15 August 1987.

25 See *Times of India*, 10 January 1976.

26 Miyabhoy, *Report of the Laththa Commission of Inquiry*, 33–36.

27 *Times of India*, Ahmedabad edition, 4 November 1977.

28 *Majoor Sandesh*, 2 March 1977 and 9 November 1977.

29 Miyabhoy, *Report of the Laththa Commission of Inquiry*, 34.

30 See also *Report of the Laththa (Hooch) Commission of Inquiry*, Ahmedabad, 2008.

31 Miyabhoy, *Report of the Laththa Commission of Inquiry*, 34; *Report of the Laththa (Hooch) Commission of Inquiry*; *Times of India*, 13 March 1977.

32 Engineer, 'Communal Fire Engulfs Ahmedabad Once Again', 1118. Interview with Krantikbhai, Ahmedabad, 17 January 2013.

33 *Times of India*, Ahmedabad edition, 15 March 1985.

34 Sujata Patel, 'Debacle of Populist Politics', *Economic and Political Weekly* 20, no. 16 (1985): 681–82; Engineer, 'Communal Fire Engulfs Ahmedabad Once Again.'

35 Heitmeyer and Simpson, 'The Culture of Prohibition in Gujarat, India', 403.

36 Ibid., 215.

37 See also Asghar Ali Engineer, 'Communal Violence and Police Terror', *Economic and Political Weekly* 21, no. 9 (1986): 382–83; and Asghar Ali Engineer, 'Gujarat Burns Again', *Economic and Political Weekly* 21, no. 31 (1986): 1343–46.

38 Thomas Blom Hansen and Oskar Verkaaik, 'Introduction—Urban Charisma: On Everyday Mythologies in the City', *Critique of Anthropology* 29, no. 1 (2009): 5–26.

39 *Times of India*, 6 December 1980. Until the break up of the Congress Party, the TLA was central to the INTUC. In 1971, when the TLA withdrew, INTUC, it was reported, was left 'virtually orphaned'. Late 1980 saw a rapprochement between the two organisations.

40 Patel, 'Nationalisation, TLA and Textile Workers', 2155.

41 Miyabhoy, *Report of the Laththa Commission of Inquiry*.

42 *Times of India*, 10 March 1989.

43 *Times of India*, 15 September 1986.

44 Ibid.

45 N. M. Miyabhoy, *Report of the Commission of Inquiry into the Prohibition Policy in Gujarat*, (Ahmedabad: Government of Gujarat, 1983).

46 *Times of India*, 1 March 1972 and 5 March 1972.

47 *Times of India*, 10 May 1991.

48 Interviews with Jeevanbhai Parmar, Jigneshbhai Waghela and Krantikbhai, Gomtipur, 2011–12.

49 *Times of India*, 2 November 1973 and 18 April 1976.

50 Residents of Gomtipur recount how Manubhai was always referred to as Manu Miyan, as an acknowledgement of his influence amongst the Muslims of the area. Interview with Sanjaybhai Parmar, 2012.

51 *Statistical Report on General Elections to the Legislative Assembly of Gujarat, 1975–1998* (New Delhi: Election Commission of India).

52 A Dalit weaving caste.

53 *Nagin* released in 1976.

54 Eunuch, a term mostly used as a slur.

55 For instance, Abdul Latif's connections with Chimanbhai Patel were most widely speculated in the discussions of Congress leader Raoof Valilullah's murder.

56 A methodological distinction was posed between slums and chawls, even though public amenities in many chawls might be similarly inadequate. AMC, *A Report on the Census of Slums in Ahmedabad* (Ahmedabad: Ahmedabad Municipal Corporation, 1976), 3.

57 Meera Mehta and Dinesh Mehta, 'Metropolitan Housing Markets: A Case Study of Ahmedabad', *Economic and Political Weekly* 22, no. 40 (1987): 1701–09.

58 Informal housing increased from nearly 23 per cent in 1961 to 34.4 per cent in 1981, while chawls declined from 45 per cent to 24 per cent. Ibid.

59 AMC, *A Report on the Census of Slums in Ahmedabad*, 5–6.

60 Mehta and Mehta, 'Metropolitan Housing Markets', 1701–09.

61 The Gujarat Slum Areas (Improvement, Clearance and Redevelopment) Act, 1973 (henceforth, Slum Areas Act).

62 *Times of India*, 4 February 1976 and 9 April 1976. As part of the social and economic reforms introduced during the national Emergency, the Act aimed at state acquisition of land with the intention of redistribution to benefit the urban poor. Lakshmi Srinivas, 'Land and Politics in India: Working of Urban Land Ceiling Act, 1976', *Economic and Political Weekly* 26, no. 43 (1991): 2482–84.

63 Mehta and Mehta, 'Metropolitan Housing Markets', 1701–09.

64 *Times of India*, 4 February 1976 and 4 March 1976.

65 *India Today*, 15 June 1982.

66 Dinesh Mehta and Meera Mehta, 'Housing in Ahmedabad Metropolitan Area by 2001 AD—Certain Policy Imperitives', in *Ahmedabad 2001* (Ahmedabad: The Times Research Foundation, 1988), 24-01–24-20, 24-11.

67 The Urban Land (Ceiling and Regulation) Act, 1976.

68 Mehta and Mehta, 'Metropolitan Housing Markets', 1701–09.

69 *Times of India*, 4 June 1989.

70 *Illustrated Weekly of India*, 30 June 1985.

71 Darshini Mahadevia, 'Urban Land Market and Access of the Poor', in *India: Urban Poverty Report 2009*, ed. Ministry of Housing and Urban Poverty Alleviation (Delhi: Oxford University Press, 2009), 199–221.

72 *India Today*, 31 January 1988.

73 Mehta and Mehta, 'Metropolitan Housing Markets', 1706.

74 Kiran Wadhva, *Role of Private Sector in Urban Housing: Case Study of Ahmedabad*, Vol. 2 (New Delhi: Human Settlement Management Institute (HUDCO), 1989); Mehta and Mehta, 'Housing in Ahmedabad Metropolitan Area by 2001 AD', 24–11.

75 Shani, *Communalism, Caste and Hindu Nationalism*, 50; Srinivas, 'Land and Politics in India.'

76 *Majoor Sandesh*, 29 May 1976.

77 See, for instance, *Ajit Singh Thakur and Anr. v. The State of Gujarat*, Supreme Court of India, 9 January 1981, where hostilities around the issue of rent collection and ownership of property led to the murder of one tenant by the landlord.

78 Bobbio, *Urbanisation, Citizenship and Conflict in India*, 118.

79 Mehta and Mehta, 'Metropolitan Housing Markets', 1701–09.

80 Yagnik, 'Paradoxes of Populism', 1505–07.

81 Ibid., 1507.

82 *Illustrated Weekly of India*, 30 June 1985.

83 *Times of India*, 11 April 1989.

84 The *Times of India*, for instance, mentioned the involvement of one Megh Singh, a youth Congress leader and the son of a local slumlord in Chamanpura, in the violence of 1986. *Times of India*, 27 July 1986. See also Shani, *Communalism, Caste and Hindu Nationalism*; Bobbio, *Urbanisation, Citizenship and Conflict in India*, 77.

85 Shani, *Communalism, Caste and Hindu Nationalism*, 126.

86 Shani's research comments on the entry of bootleggers into the real estate business. Ibid., 127. This process is also documented in some of the reportage on the violence of 1986. Also worthy of note is the case of Dhirajlal Jaiswal, an influential bootlegger from Baroda, who was elected MLA in 1972. See *Times of India*, 10 March 1989.

87 Nandy et al., *Creating a Nationality*, 113.

88 The Prohibition of Transfer of Immovable Properties and Provision for Protection of Tenants from Eviction from Premises in Disturbed Areas (colloquially known as the Disturbed Areas Act, or Ashant Dhara in Gujarati) was enacted in view of curtailing the rising distress sales of property in eastern Ahmedabad, following the communal violence of 1985. The Act imposed stricter controls of property transfers in designated disturbed areas of the city.

89 Shehzad Khan Pathan, one of the Congress corporators from the Dani Limda constituency, is one of the scions of Nawab builders.

90 The current partners of the firm have through the 1980s and 1990s faced detention orders under the Goondas Act, on charges of bootlegging and on accusation of being 'dangerous persons'. *Mehboob Khan Nawab Khan Pathan v. Police Commissioner, Ahmedabad*, Gujarat High Court, 25 July 1989; *Ayub alias Pappukhan Nawab Khan Pathan v. S.N. Sinha and Another*, Gujarat High Court, 7 August 1990.

91 See *DNA India*, 16 May 2011, 9 November 2015 and 2 July 2015. See also *Mohammed Yunus Khan Pathan v. AMC, Municipal Commissioner*, Gujarat High Court, 10 May 2000.

92 For a longer discussion on the figure of the 'property magnate', please see Chapter 7.

93 Radhika Singha, 'Punished by Surveillance: Policing "Dangerousness" in Colonial India, 1872–1918', *Modern Asian Studies* 49, no. 2 (2015): 241–69.

94 Sugata Nandi, 'Respectable Anxiety, Plebeian Criminality: Politics of the Goondas Act (1923) of Colonial Calcutta', *Crime, Histoire et Sociétés/Crime, History and Societies* 20, no. 2 (2016): 77–99.

95 Das, 'The "Goondas"'.

96 Sugata Nandi, 'Constructing the Criminal: Politics of Social Imaginary of the "Goonda" ', *Social Scientist* 38, nos. 3–4 (2010): 37–54.

97 Debraj Bhattacharya, 'Kolkata "Underworld" in the Early 20th Century', *Economic and Political Weekly* 39, no. 38 (2004): 4276–82.

98 Joshi, *Lost Worlds*.

99 *Times of India*, 27 May 1985.

100 Ibid. and 28 May 1985.

101 National Security Act, 1980.

102 Gujarat Prevention of Anti-Social Activities Act, 1985.

103 Ibid.

104 *Times of India*, 27 May 1985.

105 *Times of India*, 15 June 1985.

106 Opposition leader Chimanbhai Patel's discussion in the Gujarat Assembly cited in *Times of India*, 26 June 1985.

107 *Times of India*, 8 August 1985. See also *India Today*, 31 August 1985.

108 *Times of India*, 8 August 1985 and 12 August 1985.

109 *Times of India*, 8 August 1985.

110 The health minister's involvement in staving off the anti-reservation agitation in Rajkot had allowed him to emerge as a powerful new political figure. His own caste background and the impassioned and successful plea he made in the defence of Popatlal Patel, also perhaps, indicated the crystallisation of a political rift in the Congress Party's caste order. The upper-caste Patels, historically politically dominant but at this moment marginalised by the Congress Party's KHAM (Khastriya, Harijan, Adivasi and Muslim) alliance, were reasserting themselves through this incident. *India Today*, 31 August 1985.

111 All Congress Party municipal councillors of Rajkot threatened to resign and collectively sent a telegram to Prime Minister Rajiv Gandhi stating that 'by releasing the industrialist, the Chaudhury government has exposed itself to the criticism that it is discriminating against the poor since slums are demolished without any regrets'. *Times of India*, 11 August 1985.

112 *Times of India*, 9 August 1985.

113 *India Today*, 31 August 1985.

114 *Abdul Latif Abdul Wahab Sheikh v. B.K. Jha and Others*, Gujarat High Court, 9 February 1987.

115 Article 22 (4), Constitution of India, 1949.

116 The real question, the judgment put forth, was 'whether a law meant for providing successive orders for detention in a manner as to render the protection of Art. 22 (4) of the Constitution ineffective'. *Abdul Latif Abdul Wahab Sheikh v. B.K. Jha and Others*, Gujarat High Court, 9 February 1987.

117 Parmjit S. Jaswal, 'India-Judicial Review', in *Preventive Detention and Security Law: A Commparative Survey*, ed. Andrew Harding and John Hatchard (Dordrecht: Martinus Nijhoff Publishers, 1993), 71–104.

118 *India Today*, 31 August 1985.
119 Parvis Ghassem-Fachandi, 'Ahimsa, Identification and Sacrifice in the Gujarat Pogrom', *Social Anthropology* 18, no. 2 (2010): 155–75.
120 Human Rights Watch, *India: Compounding Injustice: The Government's Failure to Redress Massacres in Gujarat*, (2003), available at https://www.hrw. org/reports/2003/india0703/India0703full.pdf, accessed on 18 June 2021.
121 *Indian Express*, 30 September 2010; *Economic Times*, 26 March 2014.
122 Member bio, Lok Sabha, available at http://164.100.47.132/LssNew/ Members/Biography.aspx?mpsno=310, accessed on 6 April 2015.
123 In other contexts, organisations of the Hindu Right have deployed similar techniques of mobilisation. For instance, in Bombay, the Shiv Sena entered mill neighbourhoods through an engagement with social and community work. See, for instance, Meena Menon, *One Hundred Years One Hundred Voices: The Millworkers of Girangaon: An Oral History* (Kolkata: Seagull Books Pvt Ltd, 2004); and Thomas Blom Hansen, *Wages of Violence: Naming and Identity in Postcolonial Bombay* (Princeton: Princeton University Press, 2001), 53–57.
124 The Vishwa Hindu Parishad is a Hindu Right organisation.
125 Berenschot reflects on this transformation, arguing that this opening up of patronage channels swayed 'young Dalits as they realized that this support could help solve local problems and boost their political careers'. Berenschot, *Riot Politics: Hindu–Muslim Violence and the Indian State*, 143.
126 *Times of India*, 6 April 1990 and 7 April 1990.
127 Sheela Bhatt, 'Why Modi Had to Get Rid of Harin Pathak', Rediff.com, 24 March 2014, available at http://www.rediff.com/news/column/ls-elections-why-modi-had-to-get-rid-of-harin-pathak/20140324.htm, accessed on 6 April 2015. This was perhaps a culmination of the political style that Modi had honed in his time as chief minister, building as Jaffrelot has suggested a 'personality cult'. See, for instance, Christophe Jaffrelot, 'Gujarat: The Meaning of Modi's Victory', *Economic and Political Weekly* 43, no. 15 (2008): 12–17.
128 *Times of India*, 25 March 2014.
129 Bhatt, 'Why Modi Had to Get Rid of Harin Pathak'.
130 *Economic Times*, 14 December 2014.
131 'The Rediff Interview/Harin Pathak', Rediff.com, available at http://www. rediff.com/news/2000/nov/12inter.htm, accessed on 6 April 2015.
132 Lok Sabha debates, available at http://parliamentofindia.nic.in/ls/lsdeb/ ls10/ses4/0409079202.htm, accessed on 13 April 2015.

133 In 1981, BJP party workers and anti-social elements with links to the RSS were accused of fomenting violence; in 1992, it was implied that the Congress was in league with anti-social elements. See *Times of India*, 11 February 1981 and 10 July 1992.

134 *Times of India*, 8 September 1992.

135 *Times of India*, 12 June 2008.

136 *Times of India*, 8 August 1974.

137 The BJP retained control of the AMC for thirteen years at a stretch, its control breaking only during the municipal elections of 2000. It returned to power in 2005 and has remained in the majority since.

138 Spodek, *Ahmedabad: Shock City of Twentieth-Century India*, 222–25.

139 Ibid.; *Times of India*, 1 February 2011.

140 Alamzeb, who was on the run from Dawood Ibrahim's gang in Bombay, sought refuge with Latif in Ahmedabad. An aborted assassination attempt later, Dawood entered into an alliance with another bootlegger in Ahmedabad, Pappukhan of Shah Alam. See also S. Hussain Zaidi, *Dongri to Dubai: Six Decades of Mumbai Mafia* (New Delhi: Roli Books, 2012).

141 *Times of India*, 9 February 1987.

142 'Gujarat: Communal Divide', *Economic and Political Weekly* 22, no. 8 (1987): 298.

143 *Times of India*, 9 February 1987.

144 *Times of India*, 1 February 1987.

145 *Abdul Razak Abdul Wahab Sheikh v. S.N. Sinha*, Commissioner of Police, Gujarat High Court, 3 March 1989.

146 *India Today*, 28 February 1987; *Times of India*, 10 March 1989 and 26 July 1990. It was during this funeral that his relationship with senior Congress leaders was displayed publicly. Janata Dal leaders, including Narhari Amin, were reported to have relied on Latif during the AMC by-elections.

147 *India Today*, 28 February 1987.

148 *Times of India*, Ahmedabad edition, 15 February 1987.

149 *Times of India*, 17 February 1987.

150 *Times of India*, 12 July 1987. The municipal regulations state that any member abstaining from the general board meeting ceases to be a member.

151 Asghar Ali Engineer, 'Gujarat Riots in the Light of the History of Communal Violence', *Economic and Political Weekly* 37, no. 50 (2002): 5047–54.

152 Valliulah, who was at that time preparing a dossier on Patel's alleged links with the underworld, was shot at point-blank range reportedly by Rasool

Party, one of Latif's gang members. *India Today*, 31 July 1994; Spodek, *Ahmedabad: Shock City of Twentieth-Century India*, 222–25.

153 *Times of India*, 12 June 2008.

154 Ibid.

155 Spodek, *Ahmedabad: Shock City of Twentieth-Century India*, 224.

156 *Times of India*, 18 May 2009.

4

CIVIL SOCIETY, 'SOCIAL WORK' AND POLITICAL MEDIATION

Underlying many of the previously discussed practices of mediation was the notion of social work or 'seva'—the TLA's struggle for social uplift of the working class or, for that matter, the investments made by bootleggers and other 'anti-social' elements in social and cultural affairs of the industrial neighbourhoods. *Seva* as an ethical and moral tool for building associational cultures was of course not unique to Ahmedabad.[1] What was interesting, however, was the ways in which seva in this case was imbricated in political and electoral scales and rhythms. Built into this notion of 'seva' was a certain idea of reciprocity—social service played a crucial role in building constituencies, in terms of both electoral and social support.

Ahmedabad has historically had a rich tradition of voluntary associations. The city's civil society has included, at various points in history, the once powerful traders' mahajans, or guilds, pol panchs (neighbourhood organisations), Gandhian social service organisations, influential trade unions and, presently, the large array of non-governmental organisations (NGOs) of varying degrees of influence and of diverse political persuasions. Social service in contemporary Ahmedabad, like elsewhere, spans a wide range—from bigger NGOs with a national presence and substantial foreign funding, to organisations governed by religious trusts, and still others who operate at a very modest scale. Discussions on civil society in Ahmedabad have followed certain key thematic thrusts. One focuses on the narrative of empowerment and social change.[2] This details, for instance, the successes of civil society organisations in offering possibilities for organising the working poor. Another significant strand of literature identifies civic engagement as a means through which 'communal passions' could be contained.[3] The writings on SEWA, for example, highlight the potential that civil society offers as both a way of providing security for a largely casualised workforce as well as for maintaining peace in a conflict city.[4] Furthermore, other critical works on the subject have focused on the complicity and the silence that was maintained by the civil society during the violence of 2002.[5] This has been understood alternatively as a 'politicisation' of civil society, of the significant appeal of Hindutva ideology to certain segments of the civil society or in terms of coercion and intimidation by the BJP-led state government, which effectively silenced any serious critique of its role in the violence.

This chapter places the performance of social work at the centre of the narrative. Focusing on one key dimension of local influence—that which is produced through an involvement or association with social service—I investigate the repertoires of local leadership and the transforming channels of political patronage in the making of a variegated political landscape. From the focus on the mill districts, we now shift our attention to a broader canvas, including within our explorations the industrial neighbourhood of Vatva, located in the south-eastern periphery of the city. The following sections focus on four related lines of inquiry to critically interrogate the relationship between civil and political society—the conceptual bifurcation of Indian politics posed by Partha Chatterjee. First, a consideration of new paradigms of urban governance, which rested on linkages between the urban poor, industrial capital, civil society and state agencies. Then, we move to an examination of Vatva to outline how new forms of industrial activity introduced an additional layer of precarity into working lives. I argue that a particular constellation of forces of marginalisation—at the level of ethnic exclusion, living conditions and employment security—contribute to the production of a variegated political landscape. Finally, we investigate the idiom of 'social work' in building local leadership and examine the ways in which this engaged with state agencies and formal electoral practices. Based on ethnographic accounts, mainly of smaller NGOs and 'social workers', functioning largely without any significant international linkages, and with paltry amounts of external funding, this chapter interrogates the dichotomous understanding of post-colonial Indian polity and suggest that they straddle—to use Partha Chatterjee's conceptualisation—the realms of civil and political society.

PUBLIC–PRIVATE PARTNERSHIP: DIFFUSING STATE POWER?

What has the intensification of civil society interventions in matters of civic, economic and social life over the last few decades meant for Ahmedabad's labouring poor? Or rather, at what different registers and scales did the involvement of NGOs in service delivery, in civic affairs and social issues play out? I begin the discussion of the growing significance of NGOs in addressing and mediating urban concerns through an example of an emerging mode of civic engagement—that of the public–private partnership model. By the 1990s, a global and national discourse emerged that sought to locate and encourage entrepreneurship among the otherwise dispossessed.[6] Questions of housing, sanitation, access to civic amenities and informal finance, among others formed key areas of focus. The public-private partnership model, much lauded as a vehicle of inclusive development, was one mechanism through which such projects were launched in Ahmedabad. The AMC's slum networking project, for instance, was planned as a 'unique partnership between Ahmedabad Municipal Corporation and NGOs' in 1995.[7] The pilot project under this scheme was located at the Sanjay Nagar slum in the working-class area of Bapunagar. Its execution was to be undertaken by six key partners, with varying degrees of responsibility—Arvind Mills; the AMC; SAATH, an NGO; the residents of Sanjay Nagar; the SEWA Bank; and an engineer.[8] Named Pandit Deendayal Upadhyaya Antyodaya Slum Networking Project by the BJP government, the initiative was formally launched in September 1995.[9]

Sanjay Nagar had been settled in the early 1970s on AMC land, and its inhabitants included, among others, present and former workers in Arvind Mills.[10] Services and amenities in the settlement were abysmal—there were no water connections, sewage and toilet facilities, power connections or paved roads.[11] The objectives of this project included in-site upgradation of facilities, community development and the formation of a city-level organisation for slum networking.[12] The collaboration between the key partners was not cemented through a legal agreement, but was instead based on a set of 'ground rules' that were outlined in a municipal resolution. The AMC was to take a 'back seat' and play 'the role of a facilitator', while the primary responsibility for managing and executing the project lay with Arvind Mills.[13] The textile company then registered a charitable trust for this purpose. The newly established trust, SHARDA (Strategic Help Alliance for Relief to Distressed Areas), did not have the organisational capacity to implement the project and, in turn, involved another partner NGO, SAATH. SAATH had been working in the slums of Ahmedabad since 1989 and, as such, was already 'known to the AMC authorities'.[14] The physical upgradation of the site was completed by April 1997, and the alliance between the six partners (which had not been very smooth, by many accounts) was dissolved. Many of the organisations, however, continued their independent involvement in Sanjay Nagar.[15]

Though the actual impact of this model was debatable, it was nevertheless replicated in other urban improvement endeavours. 'Inspired' by the Sanjay Nagar project, the World Bank and the United Nations Development Programme (UNDP) designed Ahmedabad Parivartan (Slum Networking Project).[16] This initiative, which was to take under its ambit nearly 500 slums, further highlighted the shift in the municipal body's role from that of provider to facilitator and coordinator.[17] The recognition and the emulation of this model hint at one critical emerging aspect of political practices. The role of the municipal body was being gradually shifted from that of the sole provider to that of an enabler, with many of their obligations of providing civic service being diffused through the model of public–private partnership. What this scheme and several other contemporary social welfare schemes have entailed is the introduction, in a formal capacity (and also often, in informal ways), of agencies and figures that negotiate between government departments and the urban poor.

Explicitly underscoring this scheme was the practice of mediation, with the NGO being the point of contact between the slum dwellers and the AMC. In order to participate in this programme, the slums were required to form a 'community-based organisation', which would then deal with the AMC, the financial institutions and other partners.[18] According to the AMC's statement, community development was to comprise forming neighbourhood groups, mobilising community savings, initiating educational activities, health services and livelihoods development.[19] In turn, all the residents were to be registered with the AMC to avoid any illegitimate claims that could be potentially made through this scheme. The implementation of the project, however, was not entirely smooth, with news reports alleging corruption.[20] In particular, the numbers of beneficiaries fluctuated—a discrepancy that could possibly point towards interference and dispensation of favours and patronage while preparing such lists.

This project was spearheaded by a collaboration between corporate capital, the state and 'civil society' and was implemented through a variety of practices of mediation and negotiation. As such, these practices, then, neither bypass the state nor could they be placed neatly within the categories of 'civil' and 'political' society. These organisations (NGOs, 'community-based organisations', Residents Welfare Associations) that emerge as intermediaries are connected (often quite directly and sometimes obliquely) to the organisations and associations that constitute the city's civil society. While they do appear, as Partha Chatterjee argues, as 'convenient instruments of administration of welfare to marginal and underprivileged groups', they also provide a base for acquiring formal political power.[21] These organisations operate both as bodies of citizens and as a crucial part of the apparatus of governmentality, thereby obscuring much of the analytical and empirical segmentation that Chatterjee poses with regard to Indian polity.

VATVA: URBAN EXPANSION, POLLUTION AND CIVIC NEGLECT

Vatva in the early 1970s housed the industrial estate as well as several large plants such as Ambica Tubes, Nirma and SLM Maneklal, which produced steel tubes, detergents and pumps.[22] With the growth of the industrial estates, the city's borders expanded to accommodate the large clusters of workers' settlements that had sprouted in the eastern peripheries. This zone accounted for not only the highest proportion of Ahmedabad's population, but also contained the densest concentration of chawls, hutments and slums.[23] To plan and oversee this growth, a new administrative body was constituted in 1978. The Ahmedabad Urban Development Authority was to execute planning policies for the entire urban area that fell outside of the municipal limits.[24] The transformation of these areas—from villages and open fields to part of the metropolitan region—has been rapid. The civic administration of the area shifted from the *gram panchayat* in 1987, when Vatva, along with two other large industrial estates, were included within the AMC limits. We can identify three vectors of demographic and spatial change in the area. The first was the establishment of the GIDC industrial estate; the second, the repeated episodes of sectarian conflict that pushed inner-city Muslims to more homogenous neighbourhoods such as Vatva; and third, the area's inclusion within the AMC limits, which transformed both land use and land value in the neighbourhood.[25]

Archival material and official statistics on Vatva remain patchy. However, we can tentatively trace broad demographic trends by collating census data and voting statistics. The total population of Vatva increased from 52,816 in 1991 to 121,725 in 2001 and then to 164,730 in 2011.[26] The documented growth of population from 2001 to 2011 does not correspond to local estimates, which claim at least a twofold increase.[27] The voters' lists, on the other hand, provide an alternative picture. Between 2001 and 2002, the number of voters in Vatva increased from 65,598 to 101,006.[28] There could, of course, be various reasons for this massive increase. Perhaps, the exercise of counting voters was far more rigorous than in other years; or perhaps, several thousand new voters came of age or registered in the list of 2002. Such a phenomenal increase could also be accounted for by the large-scale migration that occurred after the violence of 2002, which several testimonies allude to.[29]

The oral testimonies of older residents of Vatva have been remarkably silent on the early years of the AMC's involvement in the area.[30] All that these accounts indicate is the transformation of what was once seen as a 'jungle' to a reasonably well-connected industrial suburb. The growth of the area was seen as linked not to the administrative expansion of 1987, but to the bouts of communal violence that the city experienced in the 1990s.[31] As the tangled, unauthorised and often illegal growth of the area began, the most pressing concern faced by the residents was pollution from the adjacent industrial estate. Oral accounts, then, stress upon the anxieties of everyday life; and unlike in the mill areas, these anxieties were not sought to be resolved through formal electoral participation. Vatva, having been settled later and having grown without the same kinds of organised trade union activity, did not follow the same trajectory of political practice as the mill neighbourhoods.

The Vatva industrial estate specialised in chemicals, dyes and pharmaceuticals and the pollution caused by the effluents grew to be a matter of great worry. With immense investments being made in the chemical industries in Gujarat—INR 160 billion between 1990 and 1995—the central government repeatedly warned of the possibility of many 'mini-Bhopals'.[32] Not only environmentally damaging, these industries also paid scant attention to existing labour laws—instead, as the *Times of India* reported, workers employed in these hazardous industries were compelled to labour with meagre wages and without any training or protection against the bodily dangers involved.[33] Labouring under these conditions was undeniably precarious and accidents, illnesses and even casualties were commonplace. Across Vatva, workers bear the marks of their labour on their bodies. The factory, in their narratives, appears as a site of danger—in several cases inflicting lifelong damage.[34] The risks associated with this kind of industrial activity were made clear rather early on. From 1978 onwards, ten years after the establishment of the industrial estates at Vatva, Naroda and Odhav, complaints were filed alleging excessive discharge of pollutants by the units.[35]

Inquiries uncovered that the industries located at these three sites disgorged its untreated wastes into the Khari River (and the Kharicut canal which snakes through the residential areas of Vatva), rendering the canal water unsuitable for irrigation.[36]

In 1995, two farmers from villages in the neighbouring Kheda district filed a public interest litigation (PIL) stating that industrial pollution from Vatva had contaminated the groundwater, leaving their lands unfit for agriculture.[37] The court-appointed inquiry committees reported that not only was there large-scale pollution in the Kharicut canal, but also that the industries had studiedly circumvented regulations and made rather obvious attempts to evade monitoring. The court ordered the closure of 756 units and placed ceilings on further expansion of 'polluting' industries.[38] In a scathing critique of the state government's position, the High Court noted:

All that the Government has done, till the start of the present litigation, has been to have discussions, to set up Committees and to give assurances that the needful will be done. In effect, however, the Government has failed to discharge its legal obligations of enforcing the law ... the continued inaction of the Government can lead to only one conclusion, viz., that it has abetted or collaborated with the Industry in the breaking of the law resulting in large scale pollution of water, air and land, which has affected not only the vast multitude of people living in the villages along the Kharicut but even the workers who are working in these industrial units are reported to be suffering from skin and other diseases.[39]

The shift from rural to urban life was propelled by an enmeshed complex of factors—the expansion of industries, the gradual settlements of migrant workers, the subsequent spatial planning measures undertaken by the state authorities and equally by the disruption of the agrarian base of the area. This led to two significant consequences—one, it precipitated a shift in work rhythms and relations, in that smaller farmers in particular moved to factory employment. Two, the slide in agricultural activity also unsettled local property relations. Most of the land in the area continued to be administratively marked for agricultural use, while in practice, it was being developed for residential or industrial use. Changes in land usage and property ownership thus rested uneasily with the bureaucratic systems of land regulations. With the underlying structures and relations of property thus destabilised, life and access to space in Vatva grew to be infused with greater precarity. Vatva, as an industrial space, was constituted not just by what was being built *on* the land, but equally by what was happening to the land.

Pollution and environmental hazards, in a way, marked life in Vatva. It has remained a key area of concern and a constant site of civic negotiation. The court-ordered closures in 1995 were met with opposition.[40] Several rounds of petitions and appeals challenged the High Court judgment, and the closures were regularly postponed.[41] The common effluent treatment plant that was long years in the making was finally functional in 1999, financed by the World Bank.[42]

Irrespective of the area's inclusion within the civic limits, the provision of amenities remained dismal. Till the late 1990s, adequate drinking water in the urban peripheries was not provided by the state agencies. More than 150 private suppliers armed with about 300 tankers were catering to the increasing demand for drinking water in outlying areas.[43] Much of the water supply in the working-class neighbourhoods of Vatva continues to be drawn from bore wells, and the construction and management of bore wells have grown to be an important business and a source of employment for many in the area.

As contaminated water rolls through every monsoon, low-lying Vatva floods. The waterlogging in these neighbourhoods became a severe problem, and remains a critical issue around which residents mobilise. For settlements around the Bibi Talab—a lake which, for the better part of the year, remains semi-arid and littered with plastic refuse—monsoons were particularly dire. In the early years of the settlement, for instance, when the dwellings were predominantly *kutcha* and the overflowing lake entered and damaged these fragile constructions, the residents collectively approached the municipal authorities. They demanded immediate assistance for dealing with the inundation, as well as compensation for the damage and the provision of improved drainage facilities. After long negotiations at the local AMC office, the residents of Bibi Talab were sent back with a compensation amount of INR 21 per family and a warning that if they were to build their homes on the edges of the lake, they should be ready to face the consequences.[44] Such incidents were not uncommon—every year, bands of residents would approach the civic authorities with appeals, supplications or even threats.

Environmental degradation had not only exacerbated the vulnerability of life in these areas, but also formed a crucial point of engagement with state institutions and industrial capital. There is, for instance, an ongoing tussle between the residents of Vatva, the municipal corporation and the Vatva

Industries Association over issues of pollution. The periodic monitoring and regulation of industries (which rarely translate into any punitive measures) is occasionally prompted by protests and mobilisations in the area. During one particularly harsh monsoon around 2009, when chemically contaminated water flooded the Navapura locality of Vatva and gave rise to a great number of ailments, Amnaben and Shehnazben of Umeed, a local NGO, accompanied by ten other neighbourhood 'leaders' set out for the Vatva police station to register a complaint. Unsuccessful, they marched on the AMC zonal office. Armed with proof of several bottles of contaminated water, the residents of Navapura demanded immediate assistance with the waterlogging as well as adequate provision of sewage and sanitation facilities that would somewhat contain the threats posed by industrial pollution. The point of the protest, however, was not to demand industrial closures, but rather regular and effective civic amenities. According to the *Ahmedabad City Development Plan 2006–12*, sanitation and solid waste management were included as part of 'basic environment services' that were to be offered to the urban poor.[45] Through this moment of interaction with the AMC officials, the social workers of Umeed were mobilising residents of Navapura and collectively struggling for the civic rights that were due to them as citizens, rather than relying on negotiations, informal deals and personal and political connections to make do at the margins of the city.

The notion of civic neglect was one crucial way in which the residents of the predominantly Muslim and poor areas of Vatva experienced the state. This is not dissimilar to other Muslim 'ghettoes' in Ahmedabad. Reports from Juhapura—academic and otherwise—routinely flag the lack of civic amenities in the area as a key marker.[46] The contrast between bordering Hindu and Muslim areas at the edges of the city are particularly worthy of note. Journalistic accounts align with personal observations in Vatva. One news report, for instance, highlights the disparate conditions of neighbouring areas of Vatva, writing:

> Sajid Row Houses, that has about 150 houses, and Qutub-e-Alam nagar with around 500, present a picture of filth, slush and puddles of dirty water. They swarm with flies and mosquitoes. There are no sewage lines. A foul smell permeates the air. There is no water supply, and whatever is drawn is not always potable. The garbage van from the BJP controlled AMC is erratic. In contrast ... Dharambhoomi Society looks quite different. It has all the facilities that this neighbourhood lacks.[47]

Sajid Row House is located in Makdoom Nagar, perched at one edge of Vatva. As with many 'ghettoes', there is growing class differentiation in Vatva as well, though not to the same extent as Juhapura. The relative affluence of Makdoom Nagar is marked by its built structures, the concentration of private schools and the profusion of butchers and meat shops. Aside from the double-storeyed, tiled constructions of the few lower-middle-class housing societies—such as Sajid Row House, Taslim Society, Jehangir Nagar Society, Silicon City—and the newly built high-rise structures of Aman Residency, a large proportion of the population of Vatva are accommodated in unauthorised ramshackle tenements and shanties. As is the case with many residential structures in Vatva, both Sajid Row House and Dharambhoomi Society were unauthorised constructions. The crucial point here, however, is not the legal status of these buildings, but the civic services offered. In this unevenness of public amenities, we can trace one dimension of marginalisation of Vatva.

As a matter of almost routine engagement with the state authorities, yearly treks were undertaken by the residents of Vatva to the offices of the AMC, led by influential people from the neighbourhood, notably social workers from the local NGO, Umeed. In 2011, when chemically polluted waters again flooded the areas closest to the GIDC industries—Jain Ashram, Navapura and Jafar Row House—groups of people waded through knee-deep water to reach the AMC offices. The media coverage of this protest featured long-time Vatva resident Rashidbhai's wife and daughter-in-law—a photograph of them indignantly marching towards the civic offices illustrated the *Gujarat Samachar* article that covered the incident. A cutting of this newspaper article is folded away in a plastic bag, kept in a trunk, with the rest of their precious documents. Such care is invested in this newspaper cutting because, as Rashidbhai remarked, 'One must keep proof of such things.' For urban dwellers at the margins of the city, such proof was often invaluable in establishing a claim to the spaces they inhabit. This fragment of the newspaper could be used later to establish that Rashidbhai did indeed protest against the lack of services or to prove that civic amenities have been historically dismal or even to demonstrate a claim that he was, in fact, a resident of Navapura.

Social work and community service, as we have seen in the earlier chapters, were a way of acquiring social and political clout. Certainly, these constellations of local authority and influence, as they emerged over the course of the twentieth century, cannot be seen as temporally discrete categories, for there are considerable overlaps between them. What is significant and distinct, however, are the different abilities that these figures acquire to manoeuvre in the world of formal politics and also, occasionally, to either make some pecuniary gains or to secure electoral ambitions through these negotiations. In the following section, we trace how social workers of various kinds negotiate local bureaucracies, electoral structures and networks of political patronage.

Social work in Vatva is oriented along three main strategies of operation which address both quotidian issues as well as those that emerge during situations of 'exception'. The first centres around questions of service provision—civic neglect, quality of life and environmental pollution. The second is focused on acquiring the necessary documentation that allows a certain access to state schemes, especially those for the economically depressed—ration cards, BPL (below poverty line) cards, election cards, and so on. The third deals with compensation and rehabilitation after riots and violence.

'SOCIAL WORK' AND ACCESS TO STATE INSTITUTIONS

Several civil society organisations currently present in Vatva began working in the area following the carnage of 2002. In Gomtipur as well, which has historically had a stronger presence of voluntary associations, a marked increase of civil society interventions was reported post 2002.[48] In Vatva, this involvement can be traced to the relief camps that were established to shelter those fleeing the violence. When, on 28 February 2002, mobs of rioters, assisted by the police, began attacking the 'border' areas of Vatva, many people escaped to an open field at the heart of the neighbourhood. Amnaben was one of those who fled from Jafar Row House to the field bordering Jehangir Nagar Society. By nightfall, the numbers of those gathered there had increased and the slightly better-off residents of this part of Vatva came forward to organise some immediate relief.[49] This field was soon formalised as one of the several relief camps established in Vatva.

State-organised aid and compensation were abysmal, and the primary source of support for these camps came from Islamic charitable associations and other civil society organisations.[50] Reconstruction of affected neighbourhoods and rehabilitation of survivors of the violence were, again, primarily realised through the efforts of civil society organisations.[51] Many of the organisations currently working in Vatva—Islami Relief Committee, SAATH, Samarth, Sahyog and Himmat, among others—established their presence through a sustained involvement in the relief camps. At present, such organisations are engaged in a range of activities—from addressing questions of livelihoods, to assisting with compensation and legal aid, to mobilising support for better civic services. We trace the trajectory of these processes through a discussion of one such civil society organisation.

Umeed, a community-based organisation, was carved out of a bigger, more established NGO, and continues to be a part of several networks that include human rights groups, activists, national and international funders and other civil society organisations. Beginning with informal educational classes with children in the relief camps, the organisation moved into the neighbourhoods, organising women into a self-help group. The group, which made a modest start in 2004 with forty-seven women, is now a registered cooperative trust with more than 2,000 members. Run by a small team of staff—a founder manager and three fieldworkers—their operations now extend to nearly all parts of the working-class areas of Vatva. The organisation is run from a small two-room office located near the area's most significant monument, the Qutub-e-Alam dargah.

One of their main activities is the organisation of a micro-credit and savings group. On weekdays, the three main members of the field staff—Josephbhai, Shehnazben and Amnaben—would spend a part of the day collecting members' contributions. Often, Amnaben and Josephbhai would set off on his motorcycle to further reaches of the neighbourhood, while Shehnazben and whoever else was at hand (a part-time staff, in most cases) would visit the nearby homes. Josephbhai, the son of a former mill worker from Gomtipur, lives in a small Christian colony attached to the local Catholic church. The most educated of the three, Josephbhai was somewhat proficient in English and had some computer skills. His wife was employed as a grassroots worker with another organisation. Amnaben and Shehnazben live in Jafar Row House—an area that is caught in the cross hairs of the various strands of insecurity that were trained on Vatva. Both Amnaben and Shehnazben, while literate, had not completed their schooling, a fact that also limited their options of seeking work in other NGOs. Amnaben began her association with Umeed when she was housed in the Jehangir Nagar relief camp, while Shehnazben joined a few months later. Both Shehnazben and Amnaben's husbands previously worked at the GIDC estate and now drive autorickshaws.

The everyday rhythms of their work involved visits to the homes of their members to collect monthly contributions, trips to government offices to submit applications or complaints, and holding meetings in their localities on a range of issues. On most mornings, a plan would be drawn up and each of the three field workers would be assigned a locality to visit. There were, of course, other temporal rhythms that influenced their professional engagements. For instance, during the month of Ramzaan, field visits as well as collections would be rather subdued; similarly, during the marriage season, the payments came in fits and starts. On the whole, the reason for the staggered period of 'collections' was attributed to the delays of most of their members in paying their contributions on time. These routine lags in payment were the cause of many demonstrative complaints by the staff. While the official period of collection is concentrated between the 10th and 15th of every month (and indeed, the work is far more intense during this period), contributions trickle in throughout the month. The deferrals in payment also entail repeated visits to their members. Ostensibly, this irked both Shehnazben and Amnaben, and loud threats were often issued that they would not be making the rounds again the next day and whoever needed to deposit their money should come to the office. However, these official field visits often lapsed into an easy social interaction, fuelled by a brisk supply of tea and a speedy exchange of gossip.

The details of each member of the savings group were consigned to individual account books—a *khatta*. These details included not only their personal information, but also a rigorous account of their deposits and their withdrawals. Members' monthly contributions range on average between INR 50 and INR 150 and, in rare cases, even INR 200. If the collections made during the day did not total to a very large amount, the cash was locked away in the Godrej safe in the office. When a more sizeable amount was collected, exceeding a few thousand rupees, it was deposited in the local bank in the Vatva village. Against their deposits, and on the guarantees of two other group members, loans could be acquired. Monetary savings and especially liquidity remain a key concern in such areas of precarious living. The violence of 2002 drove home this point in a powerful way. Many residents had suffered extensive damage to their fixed assets—homes were burnt down, means of livelihoods, autos, carts and the like, destroyed. Providing access to some form of financial stability and easy liquidity, then, emerged as a central focus of many NGOs working in post-2002 Vatva, with several self-help groups established across the locality.[52]

Not all of them were successful, however. A few groups folded, some branched out into other activities and yet others, fleeced their members and disappeared. It is, as Shehnazben and Amnaben explained to me, work that is strongly based on trust and that would bear heavy consequences should it go wrong. In money matters, I was told, one needed to tread very carefully, for one wrong step could unleash accusations of fraud.[53] Their personal relationships with the group members, the daily interactions that went beyond just the professional, and the fact that they lived and worked in these same neighbourhoods formed the basis of this trust. Like Shehnazben and Amnaben, there were several other social workers (primarily women) who were involved in various aspects of 'development' work.

Unlike in Gomtipur, where the local municipal corporator was an important neighbourhood figure, residents of 'Muslim' Vatva preferred instead to keep their distance from their elected representatives. Only in rare and absolutely essential cases would anyone make the trip to the local corporator's office. In 2013–14, Sejalben Patel (name changed), the BJP councillor from Vatva, was the only one of the three elected municipal representatives who actually lived in the area. The other two, also BJP candidates—Gauravbhai and Hansalbhai (names changed)—lived at some distance from the area. Sejalben lived in one of the middle-class Hindu housing societies at the edge of the Vatva village and ran an office adjacent to the Vatva police station. By most accounts from the Muslim parts of Vatva, she was not an agreeable municipal councillor— rarely ever found in her office and unhelpful even when she could be located. Atul Patel, on the other hand, a Congress corporator from neighbouring Hathijan and a dogged, though still unsuccessful, contender for the Vatva legislative assembly seat, was considered to be far more cooperative and dependable.

The Vatva legislative assembly constituency had been carved out by the delimitation order of 2008 and was to include the Vatva municipal ward and some areas from the neighbouring Daskroi taluka, including Hathijan.[54] This newly created constituency saw an impressive number of candidates filing their nominations in the elections of 2012—most of them were contesting as independents and many, including Atul Patel, had disclosed their occupation as 'social workers'.[55] But the real contest, as one newspaper reported, was between the 'two strongmen'—Atul Patel of the Congress and Pradeepsinh Jadeja of the BJP.[56] At the time of the campaigning, Jadeja was the law minister and his close connections with both Amit Shah[57] and Narendra Modi were highlighted as his electoral 'strengths' by the city newspapers.[58]

Atul Patel, on the other hand, was seen as a 'local' and his electoral prospects were linked to the work he had done in Vatva so far.[59]

Amnaben and her colleagues saw Atulbhai as someone who had helped them over the years and they were, in their own opinion, the 'leaders' who could assist him in his campaign. For Atul Patel, nurturing political contacts in the settlements of Vatva could have been a way of securing a promise of support in future elections. Reaching him was not very difficult, but meeting him, however, was logistically complicated. Vatva was not his municipal constituency, and his visits to the area were infrequent. 'Leaders' from Vatva, such as Shehnazben and Amnaben, would maintain direct contact with him on the phone and, in exceptional circumstances, make the trek to his office in Hathijan. Patel had acquired a reputation of great efficiency—disposing of applications from his constituents with one trademark phrase, 'Aap ka kaam ho jayega' (and one that forms a crucial part of the performative repertoires of most 'efficient' local leaders). For most residents of Vatva, access to politicians like Atul Patel was mediated by neighbourhood 'leaders'. It would be Shehnazben and Amnaben and others like them who would apply pressure on politicians and government officials to secure access to civic services and social welfare programmes. And in turn, it would be such neighbourhood 'leaders' that politicians would rely on for assistance during elections. This relationship of reciprocity was demonstrated quite clearly when, during the state assembly elections of 2012, Atul Patel solicited support from Amnaben and Shehnazben to help canvass for votes. They made the journey to his campaign office in Hathijan to offer their allegiance, and gathered supporters to attend the few pre-election meetings that were held in Vatva. Besides this, they also began a cell phone messaging drive to mobilise support for 'their' candidate.

While certain links had been established between politicians and social workers in Vatva, and they did, as we have seen, help open up access to state agencies and processes, they were visibly less entrenched than in the erstwhile mill neighbourhoods. The contact, first of all, was limited, and interactions with the local municipal corporator became an event of sorts, rather than a routine engagement. The mediation, then, was even more deeply layered, with the residents' first point of engagement being the social worker, the slumlord, the local 'leader' and other such figures. Local influence in Vatva was generated through various means, which often interacted and reinforced each other—for instance, age, experience, local connections, money were some markers of status and prestige. There were, for instance, powerful builders and slum landlords who not only provided housing, but also offered a means of approaching the civic authorities. Similarly, lawyers involved in property transfers had built impressive channels of contact with the revenue department and the collectors' office.[60]

The networks of political patronage for working-class Muslims in Vatva, while helpful, were also somewhat frail. Atul Patel, in this case, could dispense favours with regard to finalising official documentation—helping to acquire BPL cards and ration cards, ensuring that his constituents entered the voters' lists, and so on. But his interventions in the daily negotiations of life in Vatva were limited. Another circuit of local authority—that of social workers and the low-level bureaucracy—was more firmly embedded in neighbourhood life.

To explore this aspect of local authority, we follow one incident centred around the Chiranjeevi Yojana scheme. This social welfare measure launched in 2005 was to provide maternity care through the public–private partnership model. On possession of a BPL card, women could access private medical practitioners enrolled in the government scheme.[61] The scheme was managed by a sizeable apparatus of field workers, administrative staff and government officials. It was the several rungs of field workers (called 'link workers') who provided crucial contact between the headquarters of the project and the beneficiaries.[62] In the implementation of this scheme in Vatva, the social workers from Umeed have emerged as important 'middle men', even though they were not formally (even tangentially) associated with the programme. For instance, they would help prepare the documentation with which to benefit from the scheme, and refer patients to the nearby private hospitals. Through this, they built contacts in the local offices of the health department and in the private medical enterprises (networks which, in the absence of government dispensaries in the area, were a very valuable asset) and acquired credibility in the neighbourhood as resourceful people.

When Fizzaben, a Chiranjeevi link worker, reportedly charged INR 8,000 from a patient for a caesarean delivery, Amnaben and Shehnazben were informed at once. They marched down to the local office of the health department located in the Vatva village. A heated discussion followed when some of the office staff refused to allow them to meet Sonalben, the officer-in-charge of the Vatva health centre. Having built up a relationship with Sonalben over the years, the women from Umeed freely brandished their connections with her, threatened the office peons and demanded to be shown into her office. In their retelling of this incident, the office staff had, by now, begun apologising and promised that the INR 8,000 wrongfully charged would be returned. Within a few hours, the absconding link worker called Amnaben to clarify her 'mistake' in charging fees for what was to be a free medical service.

Amnaben and Shehnazben's leadership was constituted at several intersecting levels. The first was reputational—the fact that they were seen as resourceful enough to intervene in a local scandal and conduct a negotiation that they had no formal role in. The second aspect were the personal contacts they had built through referrals to the hospital, on the one hand, and through assisting with the required documentation for the patients, on the other. The third was the mild dadagiri they displayed in their interactions with the lower functionaries of the health office in Vatva. Their ability to command respect through verbal aggression and a fair bit of combative posturing augmented the social esteem that they acquired in the area through their role as formal workers of Umeed. The successful resolution of episodes such as this reinforced their influential position in facilitating and monitoring service delivery to the area. Their ability to perform services thus reaffirmed would only enhance their reputation for resourcefulness.

'CIVIL SOCIETY', 'POLITICAL SOCIETY' AND POST-CONFLICT RESETTLEMENT

Resettlement and rehabilitation efforts in Vatva, following the carnage of 2002, introduced two related dimensions of social work. First, civil society organisations entered the property market, acquiring land, building homes and providing water and electricity connections. Second, builders and property dealers branched out into social work and relief operations. The involvement of Alam builders in resettlement efforts is an obvious example. The building firm constructed Afzal Park in Vatva and organised the rehabilitation of riot-affected persons from Naroda Patiya.[63] In the absence of any support from the state, mainly Muslim social organisations began organising the process of resettlement. These efforts were not coordinated by a centralised body, and, as Badigar points out, there were often allegations of unfair allotments, based on the exchange of monetary favours.[64] The Islami Relief Committee (henceforth IRC), the social wing of Jamaat-e-Islami, stepped in to reconstruct damaged property in Vatva as well as constructing resettlement housing for those displaced from Naroda Patiya.[65] Called Ekta Nagar, this colony contained over 100 homes and took over two years to complete. The IRC had to counter persistent obstructions to this project—the building permissions were perpetually delayed, they received several notices and warnings for illegal construction, and the struggle for acquiring public amenities had continued up to late 2012. Far from offering aid and assistance, the Gujarat government was unwilling to even authorise these constructions. According to an office bearer of the IRC, Ekta Nagar was finally regularised around 2010–11.

By 2012, there were increasing demands for better services and property rights in the resettlement colonies across Ahmedabad, including Ekta Nagar. Salim Sheikh of Ekta Nagar had begun a hunger fast in order to pressurise the IRC to transfer the property titles to the residents.[66] Except for a few houses that had been allotted for free, most residents had had to pay a certain amount to acquire resettlement quarters. This transaction had been effected through documentation on stamp papers, and though the residents paid municipal and property taxes, their ownership status remained ambiguous.[67] While the IRC had displayed intent of eventually transferring the property to the occupiers, no concrete action had been taken to that effect.[68]

The land on which the relief colony stood was owned by the IRC and the rationale offered by the organisation for their reluctance to issue property deeds found mention in the *Times of India*: 'The moment we transfer the property to their name, we fear they will sell the houses. Even when they have been given houses to live in, many try to sell them off.'[69] Those from Ekta Nagar were not the only ones demanding documentary evidence of residence—nearly 100 protestors from fifteen resettlement colonies gathered at the collectors' office in 2014, appealing for official papers.[70] Mobilised to a large extent by another influential NGO, Jan Vikas, this struggle was centred around the acquisition of legal proof of residence—without which these dwellings would remain in ambiguous tenurial zones, and access to government social welfare schemes, deferred. These local appeals tied up with a broader protest launched by Citizens for Justice and Peace, demanding dignified rehabilitation, regulation of relief colonies, and provision of sanitation and public health facilities.[71]

The question of whether the IRC was deliberately withholding the transfers of property to the residents, as was implied in the newspapers, or whether the construction itself had a dubious legal status (and, therefore, could not be transferred) cannot be resolved with the evidence that we have. However, the process of resettlement and the subsequent tensions over ownership point to two key aspects of civil and political society practices. First, it was the disinterest of the state in ensuring the safety and security of its citizens that produced a situation of illegality and informality. Therefore, the failure of the state authorities in first providing security and arranging rehabilitation resulted in other aspects of state regulations being breached (in this case, legal property rights). Second, the residents of Ekta Nagar made their claims on the state agencies not so much through contingent, unstable, legally ambiguous political negotiations, characteristic of 'political society' practices, but rather through a mediated struggle to acquire the legal recognition and entitlements due to them. The structural oppositions between 'civil and political society' as posited by Chatterjee remain untenable in practice. Rather, what we see is an interpenetration, an intercalation of the two domains in the ways in which political struggles, mobilisations and even everyday claim making are effected.

THE SOCIAL WORKER AND POLITICAL AMBITIONS

While several forms of civil society activism (the slum networking project, for instance) can be seen as processes that enabled the state's authority to be 'pluralised', the social workers in both Gomtipur and Vatva functioned, to a large degree, as agents through which state services could be accessed, as entry points into channels of patronage. Local leadership in this situation was constituted, in part, by the ability to offer nodes of interaction with state practices. And conversely, this engagement often constituted the basis of electoral ambitions. The forms of engagement varied. In some cases, the social worker functioned as a broker, charging a fee for lubricating access to state agencies; in others, the social worker acted as an enabler, accumulating clout in the process of easing access to public services, though not necessarily in return for monetary gains. The social workers and the organisations that they were part of, thus, presented an interface between the formal authority of the state and the informal authority of the local leader.

The career and political aspirations of Radhaben Babubhai of Gomtipur help illustrate how local leadership drew from the repertoire of social work.

I first met Radhaben on the day that Sailesh Parmar, the standing MLA from the Dani Limda assembly constituency, was going to file his nomination papers for the 2012 state elections. Jeevanbhai, the municipal corporator from Gomtipur, had been looking forward to this day, and his changed attire reflected the significance accorded to the occasion—instead of his usual *kurta pyjama*, he was wearing a starched safari suit—as did the excitement of the motley crowd that had gathered near Sarangpur Mill No. 2 awaiting Saileshbhai's arrival. Jeevanbhai was seated with Radhaben on the pavement, whom he introduced as a 'main man' of Gomtipur, later adding, 'she is *toofani*.'[72]

Jeevanbhai, whose trajectory we have followed in the previous chapters, was then serving his third term as corporator.[73] Saileshbhai inherited the Shaher Kotda assembly seat from his father, Manubhai Parmar, who passed away mid-term in 2000. Though its geographical limits had changed several times with every delimitation order, the core of this constituency had remained Rajpur-Gomtipur. Shaileshbhai's electoral debut in the assembly by-elections of 2000 was supported by Jeevanbhai, who boasted that this victory too was his handiwork. As political power shifted from father to son, Jeevanbhai's relationship with the local MLA was also changing. During Shailesh Parmar's first electoral campaign, Jeevanbhai tried to bargain for a Congress ticket to contest the forthcoming municipal polls. Unsuccessful, he contested as an independent candidate until 2005, when he was finally allotted a Congress ticket.

When Saileshbhai arrived in an open jeep, he was accompanied by Imdad Sheikh and Bharatiben, the two other corporators from Gomtipur. His motorcade—a few jeeps stuffed with supporters and about fifty odd young men on motorcycles bedecked with Congress flags—was allowed a brief rest; as he was greeted at the crossroads, where Jeevanbhai was one of the first to garland him. The motorcade sped off to the fading sounds of firecrackers, and Jeevanbhai followed it on his newly purchased moped to the AMC office in western Ahmedabad. Radhaben had other 'matters' to tend to. She had to, as she often did, go to the pigeonholed government offices in the multi-storeyed complex known as Apna Bazar. Her work in the neighbourhood made her a frequent visitor at these offices, for she dealt with a whole range of issues—from facilitating the making of identity (ID) cards to securing gas connections to helping with acquiring financial assistance.

Both Jeevanbhai and Imdadbhai have a few trusted assistants, supporting them in their civic and social works. For Jeevanbhai, Radhaben was one such person. A former mill worker, Radhaben was a long-time resident of Gomtipur. She was a contract worker in the Mankeklal Harilal Mills in Saraspur when, in 1997, her entire unit of twenty-two women workers was dismissed. Operating outside of the TLA's ambit, she and the other workers filed an application for reinstatement at the labour court. The many appeals, the long judicial process and expenses related to the process added to their already precarious situation. Other members of the group, Radhaben insisted, were anxious about their financial predicament and agreed to settle with the mill management. Each worker was given compensation of INR 35,000 and their employment in the mill terminated. When recounting this incident, which was one of her first interactions with the larger machinery of the state, she repeatedly emphasised her status as a single woman. She was not bound by the kinds of social pressures and obligations that, for instance, some of her workmates experienced. The dissolution of her marriage, her divorce and her return to her natal home in Gomtipur had, by her own admission, allowed her to refashion herself as a local leader.

In the making of her political clout, we can identify several vectors of influence. Her divorce, which was finalised soon after her negotiations with the Mankeklal Harilal Mill management, seemed to have been another way for her to gain experience in dealing with state agencies. Having managed to secure her own alimony through a prolonged judicial process, she began helping other women from Gomtipur claim theirs. As her engagements with neighbourhood life intensified, she caught the attention of Manubhai Parmar, the Congress Party representative to the Gujarat legislative assembly. Their first interactions took place at the local party office, when she would approach the elected officials with complaints from the neighbourhood—of overflowing toilets, non-existent gutters and sparse water supply. During these interactions, she was identified as someone with promise, as Manubhai complimented her and offered support and encouragement in her social works. He had said, she recollected, 'You have a lot of knowledge, little girl. I will show you the ropes. What do you do now? he asked…. I am divorced, I replied…. Well, finalise your divorce papers, and I will get you some work.'

The work in this case was primarily what was considered social work, or *samajik kaam*, as she explained. Her influence in the neighbourhood gradually expanded, as she began taking on 'cases' not just related to service provision, but also extended to helping residents in accessing their entitlements from the state. Her activities in the neighbourhood, which had so far been limited to questions of civic interest, soon turned to the sphere of formal politics, as she registered as a member of the Congress Party. Explaining her political turn, she remarked:

> I developed an interest in politics since I achieved success in my social work. I thought I could help people, and I was also making a name for myself in the community.... And I don't have children, I am all on my own, so why shouldn't I be able to do this work for people?

Her 'social' work and her political work, for the last decade or so, have been interlaced, with each bolstering the other. Her closeness, of varying degrees, to key local politicians—ranging from the municipal corporator to the MLA—has marked her as someone who can get work done. Similarly, her reach in the neighbourhood is exceptionally useful for electoral campaigning and voting.

On a typical day, Radhaben would set out from home at 9 a.m. 'And I go everywhere.... If Jeevankaka has some work for me, then I go to him. If someone needs to be taken to the hospital, I take them there. If someone needs to get a marriage certificate, I go to Lal Darwaja to get it done.' After dinner from about 8 p.m. to 10 p.m., she takes her spot at the corner of Nagri Mills, where she attends to everyday complaints. During elections, her work schedule is heavier and she is often still at the street corner until well after midnight.

Underscoring her public persona and self-presentation is a distinct notion of morality. The neighbourhoods in which she works—the former mill areas—are frequently referred to as spaces of vice and notoriety. 'It is difficult work, but I still do it,' she explained to me. 'If a fight breaks out somewhere, I still stand steady ... if someone is picked up by the police, then I have to deal with the police officials.... This is a very dangerous area. See, there is a lot of bootlegging.... And then ganja and other drugs are also sold....' At another time, she further expounded on how she negotiates the 'dangers' involved in her work: 'I have never had any trouble in my work. I go everywhere, even to the Muslim areas. They also treat me with a lot of respect.... I am not going to do any such work ... you know, wrong work....' Before taking on cases, she would judge both the task and the client, asking herself one critical question: 'Does this person need or deserve my help?'

One can identify two strong tendencies in the ways in which her work is presented. On the one hand, her social work bears an air of righteousness, as she maintains that she avoids undertaking any work that may be morally or legally tainted. She does not, in other words, do anything that is 'do numberi' (illegal or quasi-legal) and, in the course of our conversations, has been quick to point out others who do such disreputable work. On the other hand, her own character and the respect and social honour that she commands emerge as significant. The two strands of her public persona seem to be inextricably tied. The distance she maintains from all manner of wrongdoing then appears to be reflected in the kind of respect accorded to her. The reason why she can hold court on the main road late in the evening (a space that is otherwise, heavily male) is, according to her, because of her unimpeachable moral character. Nobody would harass her, she contends, and everybody would behave respectfully towards her when she is attending to business at the corner of Nagri Mills. In this, Radhaben presents a divergence from the sorts of local women leaders that populate Ward Berenschot's exceptional ethnography of the mill neighbourhoods of Ahmedabad.[74] The threat of being labelled a 'loose character' is, nevertheless, quite evident, as she carefully constructs both her morality and modesty through explicit references to the righteousness and respectability of work. That said, Radhaben occupied public spaces, associated with men of all political persuasions and engaged in loud debates in street corners until late at night. Her social work also marks a departure from the kinds of activities typically undertaken by such social and political actors. Her work studiedly avoids any engagement with the intimate spaces of domestic life, as she baldly stated: 'I don't involve myself in private problems.' As Berenschot points out, women's participation in local politics or their ability to build concrete networks of support is limited by the notion of social respectability, and it is rather rare to see a woman like Radhaben, who occupies the local political realm with such ease.[75] One way in which the norms governing women's public conduct could be circumvented, as seems to be the case with Radhaben, is through a liberal deployment of kinship as a means of establishing non-transgressive relationships with the opposite gender. Many men in her circle of neighbourhood contacts were introduced as brothers and other relatives. Whether they all were related to her or not, we cannot ascertain, but this form of naming does, to some extent, diffuse the potential stigma of 'characterlessness'.

On a closer look, we can perhaps trace another relationship of local power that enabled Radhaben to command such respect. From other accounts and personal observations, it gradually became clear that not only was she a social worker and a party worker, but also a fairly well-established bootlegger. On the day of the state assembly elections in December 2012, Radhaben had placed herself at the Congress stall outside of her chawl. While she meticulously went through the electoral rolls, directing residents to their polling booths, exhorting passers-by to exercise their franchise, arranging tea and snacks for her underlings, there was another set of transactions happening in the narrow streets nearby. Several vats of bootleg alcohol had been stored at her friend's chawl, and young men at various stages of drunkenness were periodically dispatched to refill bottles and pouches and distribute it amongst voters and party workers.

Through all three dimensions of her public works, Radhaben had acquired contacts in the state agencies, at the higher levels of the Congress Party and within the neighbourhood. It is difficult to systematically trace which of her operations constituted or enabled the others; and it is, perhaps, not particularly necessary for our analysis to disentangle the chronology. What is important, however, is that this constellation of social, political and (technically) anti-social activities seems to have provided her with a launching pad for her involvement in formal electoral politics.

Already in the municipal elections of 2010, Radhaben had made her political aspirations clear, as she tried to bargain for a Congress ticket. Unsuccessful, she trained her hopes on the 2015 elections.[76] 'Political success was a possibility,' she commented, 'if I do everybody's work.... In any case, I am already amongst the people.' In anticipation of being granted a Congress nomination, she had registered a social organisation by the name of Ma Kali Seva Trust. Should she manage to enter active electoral politics, she could continue her social work through the trust.

During elections, she is sought out for all manner of functions—from door-to-door campaigning, to mobilising audiences for public meetings, to bribe (and possibly coerce) voters on election eve. This peak period requires her to assemble all her associates and muster a fair bit of her own resources. In the weeks preceding the assembly elections of 2012, party offices (mainly of the BJP and the Congress) jostled for space on the crowded streets of Gomtipur. These offices that sprouted in the empty *godowns* and vacant rooms that faced the streets were opened by supporters and well-wishers and hosted night-long games of cards; Radhaben along with a few others had rented a room to open an election office for the Congress Party in the Nagri Mills areas.

Contrasting with this nearly festive atmosphere was the lacklustre campaigning in most parts of Vatva. There were very few public meetings, and certainly none as spectacular as those in Gomtipur, which included, among others, a meeting with Modi. The most striking evidence of any electoral activity in the Muslim areas of Vatva was the change in the orders for production—for a few weeks in early December 2012, workers laboured over their sewing machines producing party banners and flags instead of hemming petticoats, *salwar*s and *dupatta*s. As the day of the elections drew closer, the other strategic calculations made by the residents of the 'border' areas of Vatva were to identify a safe house in the heart of the neighbourhood, to which to flee should there be violence.

However, despite the sharp differences in the levels of political engagement in the two areas, there is a certain coincidence of ambitions and aspirations. Like Radhaben, Amnaben and Shehnazben too harbour some hope for an electoral ticket. Their networks are nascent, and their political contacts less entrenched than those in Gomtipur; nevertheless, there were gentle boasts about other residents appealing appealing to them to contest elections, and their considerations of which political party to contest for. Whether any of them will launch successful electoral bids remains to be seen, but what is significant is the ways in which social work (especially those related to NGOs) is used as a way of building a political career. The interventions made by civil society organisations are enabled, to a large degree, by the contacts maintained with the formal realm of electoral politics and with the vast and fragmented state machinery. Furthermore, these very activities in the field of social work helped prepare for (and gain access to) a future in electoral politics. However, the discussions up to this point have dealt primarily with those organisations and figures that could loosely be seen as operating within a 'secular' (and not overtly religious) framework. We briefly address other dimensions of social work, and its connections with the politico-religious ideology of the Sangh Parivar. This complicates the understanding of civil society, both as the space of elite associations governed by constitutional law and as that of a benign space of goodwill.

Take, for instance, Sameer Barot, an RSS member, a BJP party worker and a social worker from Gomtipur. Arrested in 2010 for posing as a Crime Branch official and conducting raids to seize illicit alcohol and intimidate bootleggers,[77] Barot is well known in the area as an established dada. One of his operations were services offered to bootleggers—he negotiated haftas with the local police and brokered deals between bootleggers and the police to evade prohibition-related arrests on the payment of fees. In my conversations around questions of local politics and social work, one of my interlocutors, Jigneshbhai, described such figures with a particularly striking term. Jigneshbhai portrays himself as an erstwhile goonda—a former bootlegger turned Ambedkarite, who then joined the Communist Party and is now an established social worker in the area. He called the practice of such forms of local authority *dharmik dadagiri* (religious dadagiri). When in the early 1990s, Jitu Vaghela and his band of VHP foot soldiers marched through the streets of Gomtipur armed with swords, this was seen as an act so brazen that only a dada could have performed it. Vaghela rose through the ranks of the Sangh Parivar to be elected to the AMC in 1995. During the violence of 2002, he was arrested for rioting and murder.[78] While the criminal cases against him were still ongoing, he was granted a BJP election ticket and won the legislative assembly seat from the Sheherkotda constituency in the elections of 2002. While social workers affiliated to the Hindu Right continued to mediate access to state institutions and civic services, they also monitored social transgressions in the neighbourhood. Inter-religious romances, for instance, were one critical site upon which Hindutva ideology was played out. As such, the everyday performance of violence became a part of the repertoire of such social workers. Consider, for instance, the case of Rinku, another such social worker from Gomtipur, who spent part of his time helping people acquire water and sewage connections and part of his time in readiness 'to attack'.[79] He was to be found at every public function that the Hindu Right deemed offensive and monitoring potentially transgressive behaviour in the neighbourhood. Several animal protection societies that have been established in Gomtipur and other mill areas, particularly around the issue of cow protection,[80] also point to the formation of NGOs and social organisations that are closely linked to the Sangh Parivar's ideology.

REVISITING CIVIL SOCIETY/POLITICAL SOCIETY

The set of practices that are visible in these areas of the city's urban poor allow us to empirically and analytically delineate modes of political engagement, as they have been shaped by historical processes. The 1990s signalled a transformation in the institutional, ideological and operational paradigms of such social service organisations. This shift was marked in terms of the liberalisation of the Indian economy, the shrinking of state intervention and 'clear NGOisation of the voluntary sector'.[81] In a period that has ushered in pervasive vulnerability for the city's workers and, in particular, for the Muslim working poor, the sorts of 'civil society' organisations and actors discussed in this chapter have emerged often in the absence of the state as well as crucial conduits for accessing state authorities.

'Civil society' has been commonly understood as the domain between the state and the private sphere of the family. Alternatively conceived of as the 'watchdog' of the state, as a substitute for formal politics or as the means through which the state came to be pluralised,[82] the concept of civil society has remained slippery. It has been seen as a 'hold-all' used both as an explanatory category and as a normative one—to understand both the management of democratic processes as well as to establish it as a normative goal.[83] In part, criticism has been directed at the 'foreignness' of this concept, its inadequacy in explaining processes, practices and institutions in societies like India.[84] Arguing for a more inclusive understanding of civil society, Varshney brings together both 'informal group activities and ascriptive associations … so long as they connect individuals, build trust, encourage reciprocity, and facilitate an exchange of views on matters of public concern—economic, political and cultural'.[85] Associational and everyday forms of civic networks, in his reading, form a 'bulwark of peace' against the incidence of communal violence.[86] Institutions such the Ahmedabad Mill Owners Association and the TLA were instrumental in establishing 'civic contact between Hindus and Muslims', and hence the disintegration of the city's formerly 'harmonious' social fabric can be dated to the collapse of the textile industry.[87]

While the industrial restructuring that the city experienced in the mid-1980s undoubtedly transformed the social texture of Ahmedabad and left pervasive traces in the industrial areas, it is perhaps too easy to collate the violence beginning in this period merely with the decline of these associational civic institutions. As Breman argues, the social divisions that existed in Ahmedabad earlier were deepened by the 'segmentary' strategies deployed by the Congress Party.[88] Key to Breman's analysis is the changing form of the city's political economy, the attendant socio-economic precarity and the emergence of what he calls 'Social Darwinism' by which the urban poor compete for social and economic security.[89] The TLA did, in many cases, forge relationships across castes and communities. They also launched peace initiatives during episodes of violence (particularly in the 1940s and during 1969). However, other accounts suggest that the relationship of the union members with communal violence remained ambivalent.[90]

To conceive of the realm of civil society as a uniformly democratic space, of 'self-help, solidarity and goodwill' would be problematic.[91] Chandhoke presents her concerns in the context of the violence of 2002 and the silence maintained by nearly all civil society organisations in the city.[92] In arguing that the necessary preconditions for a democratic civil society had been left inadequately institutionalised, there is a similar tendency to view civil society as a front against communal violence, rather than as a realm composed of disparate, often conflicting and competing interests.[93] The linkages maintained by the Hindu Right with civil society have been highlighted by other scholarship. Amrita Basu argues that the close relationship between the Hindu Right and civil society is most visible in Gujarat. Sangh Parivar–affiliated organisations have both wide-reaching international links and a strong grassroots presence. Governed by 'a single set of ideological principles' and performing everyday acts of violence to impose this ideology, such organisations provided ready networks through which collective communal violence could be orchestrated.[94] Tanika Sarkar similarly suggests that the scale and form of violence that Gujarat witnessed in 2002 was possible precisely because of relentless activity within 'the very pores of civil society'.[95] That said, it should also be noted that much of the relief and rehabilitation work after the violence of 2002 was carried out by civil society organisations. This involved not only immediate relief but also legal assistance in acquiring compensation, financial support in rebuilding homes and also a continued engagement with the violence-affected areas.

A critical if not provocative intervention in the theorisation of civil society came from Partha Chatterjee. He argued for a theoretical separation in the domain of the political—civil society, as 'the closed association of modern elite groups, sequestered from the wider popular life of the communities, walled up within enclaves of civic freedom and rational law',[96] and political society, as the 'domain of mediating institutions between the state and civil society'.[97] Chatterjee sees political society as 'emerging out of the developmental policies of government aimed at specific population groups'.[98] These groups, which often live and labour on the borders of legality, then have to negotiate with state agencies, government functionaries, political parties as well as 'civil society'.[99] Franchise was one mode of negotiation; however, the terms on which members of 'political society' engaged with the state varied greatly.[100] The state, thus, governed this vast segment of the population 'not within the framework of stable constitutionally defined rights and laws, but rather through temporary, contextual and unstable arrangements arrived at through direct political negotiations'.[101] The 1980s, Chatterjee argues, proved to be particularly productive for the consolidation of these sets of practices which are seen as integral to 'political society'. On the one hand, this was due to the acknowledgement of governmental responsibilities towards its populations. The gaps in the state's fulfilment of its obligations were then filled by 'non-governmental' (and sometimes international) organisations. On the other, electoral competition facilitated the emergence of modes of political mobilisation and association that would be placed outside of what is conventionally thought of as 'political'.[102]

In further elaborations of his conceptualisation of civil and political society, Chatterjee related the domain of civil society to corporate capital, and political society with non-corporate capital.[103] This distinction was perhaps too neat, as other critics suggest, and is not reflective of the interlinkages between the two domains.[104] While there has been considerable debate around the conceptualisation of the spheres of civil and political society, it remains significant that Chatterjee's intervention has opened up new ways of locating and understanding forms of political practice.[105]

The conceptual distinction between the notions of civil and political society marks a separation in the ways in which the state and state practices are approached. Therefore, it allows us to locate a set of negotiations by the poor and the marginalised that rely on relationships of political patronage, personal connections and contingent conduits of power, in order to access the state agencies. However, it is perhaps not conceptually very productive to impute a distinction between the two categories—of civil and political society. We have seen in the earlier chapters that many aspects of political mediation were effected through 'political society' practices—the significance of the TLA pratinidhi in regulating access to employment and civic services, for instance, or the influence of the slumlord in providing or denying housing. At the same time, it is especially clear in the case of the TLA's circuits of patronage that the formal authority of the union (which would be squarely located in the realm of civil society) and the informal authority of the local dada (a figure that, in a sense, was an embodiment of political society practices) were mutually constituted. To draw on another example of the blurred boundaries between the two categories—the extent of the authority and patronage of the bootlegger or the slumlord drew from the existing structures of local power (mainly the TLA) and from connections with state agencies and political parties (which again is reflective of the negotiations of political society). The linkages between formal and informal registers of local authority were further diversified with the proliferation of NGOs and various other civil society organisations, as detailed in this chapter. Political mediation through civil society organisations allowed state practices to become ever more diffuse. At one level, this signalled a shrinking of the state's role in the provision of services, especially to the working poor, and at another level, social workers emerged as key 'agents' through which the urban working class accessed state services and civic amenities. Examining interactions between NGOs, social workers and the formal structures of the state, this chapter has highlighted the porous boundaries between the realm of 'civil society' practices and those termed as 'political society' practices. Social work (both in terms of everyday services as well as relief and rehabilitation during periods of communal violence) assumed multiple forms, drew on divergent agendas and appeared as increasingly significant in constituting local authority. The practices through which the working poor strive to become visible and legitimate city dwellers and establish enduring claims and rights over urban space further points to the overlap and intersections between the domains of political and civil society, blurring the distinction between them, perhaps to the point of irrelevance.

To conclude this discussion on the historical transformation of political practices and intermediary figures, we can draw our attention to the ambivalences, hybridities and contradictions that are written in them. In the longer history of Gomtipur, these characters are made ambiguous by the fact that they have played several roles over a lifetime, shifting back and forth from union leaders to dadas to goondas to local leaders and politicians, while never really shedding any of their previous incarnations. In the ethnographic study of Vatva, we are presented with a set of characters that straddle different roles and inhabit multiple registers of functioning, while at the same time, engaged with the possibility of an expanding arena of influence.

NOTES

1 See, for instance, Watt's discussion of transforming practices of service and its place in public life. In many urban centres, notions of seva were systemised and institutionalised in the form of social service bodies and

societies, contributing significantly to ideas of nationalism and practices of nation building. Carey Anthony Watt, *Serving the Nation: Cultures of Service, Association, and Citizenship* (New York: Oxford University Press, 2005).

2 See, for instance, Bijal Bhatt, 'Mobilizing Women for Change: Case Study of Sanjaynagar, Ahmedabad', Working Paper 7, Centre for Urban Equity, CEPT University, Ahmedabad, 2010) and Rajendra Joshi, Pooja Shah, Keren Nazareth and Darshini Mahadevia, 'From Basic Service Delivery to Policy Advocacy: Community Mobilisation in Pravinnagar-Guptanagar, Ahmedabad', CEPT Working Paper 6, Centre for Urban Equity, CEPT University, Ahmedabad, 2010); for other contexts, please see, for instance, Colin McFarlane, 'The Entrepreneurial Slum: Civil Society, Mobility and the Co-Production of Urban Development', *Urban Studies* 49, no. 13 (2012): 2795–816.

3 Varshney, 'Civic Life and Ethnic Conflict', 226.

4 Howard Spodek, 'The Self-Employed Women's Association (Sewa) in India: Feminist, Gandhian Power in Development', *Economic Development and Cultural Change* 43, no. 1 (1994): 193–202.

5 Sarkar, 'Semiotics of Terror', 2872–76; Breman, 'Communal Upheaval as Resurgence of Social Darwinism', 1485–88.

6 See, for instance, McFarlane, 'The Entrepreneurial Slum.'

7 Slum Networking Project, Urban Management Centre, available at http:// mirror.unhabitat.org/bp/bp.list.details.aspx?bp_id=1762, accessed on 24 December 2015.

8 Dwijendra Tripathi, 'Slum Networking in Ahmedabad: The Sanjay Nagar Pilot Project', University College London (UCL), Development Planning Unit (DPU), 1999.

9 Uttara Chauhan and Niraj Lal, 'Public–Private Partnerships for Urban Poor in Ahmedabad: A Slum Project', *Economic and Political Weekly* 34, nos 10–11 (1999): 636–42.

10 Tripathi, *Slum Networking in Ahmedabad.*

11 Ibid.

12 Chauhan and Lal, 'Public–Private Partnerships for Urban Poor in Ahmedabad.'

13 Ibid., 637.

14 Tripathi, *Slum Networking in Ahmedabad*, 6.

15 Ibid.

16 World Bank, 'Ahmedabad Parivartan', Water and Sanitation Program field note, South Asia, World Bank, Washington, DC, 1999), 5, available at

http://documents.worldbank.org/curated/en/1999/03/2148260/ahmedabad-parivartan, accessed on 25 December 2015.

17 See https://www.mahilahousingtrust.org/wp-content/uploads/Parivartan-Impact-Study_Final.pdf, accessed on 22 June 2021.

18 A similar process was visible in the mega Sabarmati riverfront development relocation sites. For every resettlement colony, it was required that a Residents' Welfare Association be formed, which would not only supervise the upkeep and maintenance of the buildings, but also carry out 'community mobilisation' to increase awareness of the government's welfare schemes in the area. There is a rich body of field studies and sociological surveys on these aspects of resettlement. For example, please see Darshini Mahadevia, Neha Bhatia and Bijal Bhatt, 'Decentralized Governance or Passing the Buck: The Case of Resident Welfare Associations at Resettlement Sites, Ahmedabad, India', *Environment and Urbanization* 28, no. 1 (2015): 294–307; Renu Desai, 'Municipal Politics, Court Sympathy and Housing Rights: A Post-Mortem of Displacement and Resettlement under the Sabarmati Riverfront Project, Ahmedabad', Working Paper 24, Centre for Urban Equity, CEPT University, Ahmedabad, May 2014, and Darshini Mahadevia, Bijal Bhatt and Neha Bhatia, 'Resident Welfare Associations in BSUP Sites of Ahmedabad: Experiences of Mahila Housing SEWA Trust (MHT)', Working Paper 25, Centre for Urban Equity, CEPT University, Ahmedabad, September 2014.

19 AMC Proactive Disclosure on the Slum Networking Project under RTI Act, 2005.

20 *DNA India*, 5 October 2012.

21 Chatterjee, *The Politics of the Governed*, 40.

22 *Times of India*, 24 June 1970.

23 In the 1980s, the price of urban land in the eastern peripheries increased by nearly 400 per cent. D. G. Pandya, 'Land Markets in Ahmedabad Metropolitan Region: The Demand, Supply and Pricing Scenario, 2001 AD', in *Ahmedabad 2001* (Ahmedabad: Times Research Foundation, 1988), 27-01–27-35, 27-10. Population in 1981, Eastern Sector: 1,153,045, of which nearly 50 per cent lived in sub-standard housing.

24 Tommaso Bobbio, 'Collective Violence, Urban Change and Social Exclusion: Ahmedabad 1930–2000', PhD thesis, University of London, 2010, 117.

25 Pandya, 'Land Markets in Ahmedabad Metropolitan Region', 27–32. Simultaneously, the city's western boundaries were expanding, and there

was an even greater corresponding increase in the value of urban land. The westward expansion was focused more on commercial and residential growth.

26 AMC Statistical Outline 2006–07, Census data, Ahmedabad, ward level, 2011.

27 The 2011 census was criticised for alleged oversights in Vatva. The *Indian Express* reported that several colonies along the Kharicut canal were overlooked in the enumerative exercise. *Indian Express*, 19 March 2011.

28 AMC Statistical Outline 2003–04, 9–10.

29 Until 2002, violence in Vatva was restricted to certain pockets—the railway station, for instance, or the sheds in the GIDC. The living spaces of these industrial areas were largely spared in the almost routine communal violence that the city experienced—until 2002, when the neighbourhood was a site of some of the worst atrocities. Vatva interviews, 2011–12; see also *Times of India*, March 1974 and 17 January 1993.

30 Vatva's first entry into civic politics was slated for the municipal elections of December 1992, which were finally held in 1995.

31 Interviews, Vatva. For a longer history of the settlement of the area, please see Chapter 7.

32 *Times of India*, 8 May 1995.

33 *Times of India*, 8 May 1992.

34 Interview with Gulab Khan, Vatva, 2010–12.

35 *Pravinbhai Jashbhai Patel v. The State of Gujarat*, Gujarat High Court, 5 August 1995.

36 Letter dated 24 June 1981 and report dated 19 July 1980 cited in *Pravinbhai Jashbhai Patel v. The State of Gujarat*, Gujarat High Court, 5 August 1995.

37 *Pravinbhai Jashbhai Patel v. The State of Gujarat*, Gujarat High Court, 5 August 1995, 2.

38 This mirrored other similar forms of judicial interventions that were being made across the country. Delhi, in particular, experienced mass industrial closures during the mid-1990s. Environmental considerations as well as a move towards a 'bourgeois aesthetic' marked the Delhi closures. In Ahmedabad, at this point, the factory closures appear more motivated by concerns of agricultural impoverishment, rather than what Baviskar terms 'bourgeois environmentalism'. See Amita Baviskar, 'Between Violence and Desire: Space, Power, and Identity in the Making of Metropolitan Delhi', *International Social Science Journal* 55, no. 175 (2003): 89–98.

39 *Pravinbhai Jasbhai Patel v. The state of Gujarat*, Gujarat High Court, 5 August 1995, 17.

40 For instance, the president of the Gujarat Dyestuffs Manufacturers' Association argued that with most of the units being small scale, it would be difficult not only to sustain losses for a long period, but also to pay wages to their employees, many of whom were casual workers. The TLA had, in the meantime, made some efforts to organise chemical workers—their efforts were lacklustre at best and they did not ever gain much presence in Vatva. See *Times of India*, 19 September 1995.

41 *Times of India*, 24 December 1995.

42 Industrial Pollution Control Project, World Bank, 'Implementation Completion Report (1999)', Report No. 19678.

43 *Times of India*, 19 May 1999.

44 Interview with Hamidaben, Vatva, 8 March 2011.

45 *Ahmedabad City Development Plan 2006–2012*, (AMC, Ahmedabad Urban Development Authority, CEPT University), 140.

46 See Zahir Janmohamed, 'Muslim Education in Ahmedabad in the Aftermath of the 2002 Gujarat Riots', *Studies in Ethnicity and Nationalism* 13, no. 3 (2013): 466–76, and Rubina Jasani, 'Violence, Reconstruction and Islamic Reform—Stories from the Muslim "Ghetto"', *Modern Asian Studies* 42, nos 2–3 (2008): 431–56.

47 *The Hindu*, 28 October 2013.

48 Interview with Sister Rose, Gomtipur, 20 September 2011.

49 Interview with Amnaben, Vatva, 4 October 2011. See also Lokhande, *Communal Violence, Forced Migration and the State*, 72–73.

50 *Frontline*, vol. 19, issue 10, 24 May 2002; *Communalism Combat*, July 2002; Lokhande, *Communal Violence, Forced Migration and the State*, 72–73.

51 Varadarajan, *Gujarat, the Making of a Tragedy*.

52 It is not within the remit of this book to explore the problems with microfinance. The politics and practices of micro-credit groups in Ahmedabad would entail further research.

53 One Safiaben from Navapura, who was associated with one such micro-savings organisation, was hounded from her home, ostracised by her neighbours and threatened with violence when it was discovered that the funds collected by her micro-credit group had disappeared along with the bosses of the outfit.

54 Previously, this particular geographical territory had been electorally fragmented to form parts of Sarkhej and Daskroi constituencies. The delimitation order changed the electoral arithmetic considerably. The primary intention of the reorganisation was to re-calculate the Scheduled Castes (SC) and Scheduled Tribes (ST) representation according to the 2001 census. In Ahmedabad, this meant not only a remaking of the constituencies, but also a reassignment of their reservation status. For instance, Asarwa, a general seat (located in a former mill workers' constituency), was reclassified as an SC reserved seat in the 2012 assembly elections. Pradeepsinh Jadega, the sitting MLA from Asarwa, was then nominated as the BJP candidate from Vatva. See 'Delimitation Order 2008', Government of India, and 'Delimitation, Guidelines and Methodology', Government of India, accessed from the website of the Delimitation Commission, https://eci.gov.in/files/file/3931-delimitation-of-parliamentary-assembly-constituencies-order-2008/, on 24 June 2021.

55 'Association for Democratic Reforms', available at www.adrindia.org.

56 *DNA India*, 6 December 2012.

57 Amit Shah was the BJP MLA from Sarkhej and is presently serving as the home minister in the central government in New Delhi.

58 *Desh Gujarat*, 21 August 2010; *Ahmedabad Mirror*, 15 December 2015.

59 *Ahmedabad Mirror*, 15 December 2015.

60 Property arrangements in the area were legally ambiguous and were made even more so by the fact that most parts of Vatva were designated as 'disturbed areas' and did not have the requisite municipal clearances. Interview with Dilawar Sayyid, Vatva, 16 November 2012.

61 Chiranjeevi Yojana Scheme, 2005.

62 Family-centred safe motherhood and new-born care, SEWA Rural, 2011.

63 Interviews with Salmaben, Faridaben and Hammadbhai, Vatva, 2011–12.

64 Lokhande, *Communal Violence, Forced Migration and the State*, 140–41.

65 *IRC Report* 2004, 28–29. Interviews, Ahmedabad, 13 February 2013.

66 *Times of India*, 9 October 2012.

67 Lokhande, *Communal Violence, Forced Migration and the State*, 140–41.

68 Ibid.

69 *Times of India*, 9 October 2012.

70 *DNA India*, 5 March 2014.

71 Citizens for Justice and Peace, press release, 13 March 2013. See also *Indian Express*, 28 February 2013.

72 *Toofani* in this case could be loosely translated as feisty, a force of nature.

73 After a long career assisting others to victory, Jeevanbhai decided to enter formal electoral politics in 1995. Contesting as an independent candidate in the municipal elections of 1995, he lost by 500 votes.

74 Berenschot, *Riot Politics*, 111–13.

75 Ibid.

76 So far, she has been unable to secure a Congress ticket.

77 *Indian Express*, 1 January 2010.

78 In 2014, he was acquitted of these charges. *Indian Express*, 4 September 2014.

79 'Hamla karna' was the term used. Interviews with Rajeshbhai and Jigneshbahi, Ahmedabad, 10 December 2012.

80 Over the last decade, 'cow protection' has emerged as a significant mode of Hindutva politics across India and has resulted in several cases of vigilante violence against Muslim minorities. See https://www.hrw.org/report/2019/02/18/violent-cow-protection-india/vigilante-groups-attack-minorities, accessed 15 April 2022.

81 *Times of India*, 2 September 1995; Spodek, *Ahmedabad: Shock City of Twentieth-Century India*, 227.

82 Neera Chandhoke, 'Civil Society', *Development in Practice* 17, nos 4–5 (2007): 607–14; Ernest Gellner, 'Civil Society in Historical Context', *International Social Science Journal* 43, no. 3 (1991): 495–510.

83 Ajay Gudavarthy, *Re-Framing Democracy and Agency in India: Interrogating Political Society* (London: Anthem Press, 2012), 1.

84 Ibid.; see also Gupta's analysis, which calls for an investigation of the modalities by which the state (and the non-state) is discursively constructed, rather than a focus on the separation of the state and civil society. Gupta, 'Blurred Boundaries', 375–402.

85 Ashutosh Varshney, 'Ethnic Conflict and Civil Society: India and Beyond', *World Politics* 53, no. 3 (2001): 362–98, 370.

86 Associational in this case would refer to formal, institutional modes of interaction that take place within, say, business associations, trade unions or cadre-based political parties. Everyday forms of civic networks rely on, Varshney suggests, 'simple, routine interactions of life as Hindu and Muslim families visiting each other, eating together'. See Varshney, 'Civic Life and Ethnic Conflict', 3, 375.

87 Varshney, 'Civic Life and Ethnic Conflict', 231.

88 Breman, *The Making and Unmaking of an Industrial Working Class*, 287. Of particular importance here is the KHAM alliance of the 1980s.

89 Breman, 'Communal Upheaval as Resurgence of Social Darwinism', 1485–88.

90 Oral narratives from Gomtipur and other mill areas suggest that during the violence of 1969, TLA members were leading the charge against fellow mill workers. TLA members and grassroots union representatives were involved in the violence while, at the same time, being part of the union's peace keeping efforts. Interview, Gomtipur, 2011–12.

91 Neera Chandhoke, then, argues for a project of a 'democratic civil society', one that is Janus faced—one face trained on the state and the other on itself. Implicit in this is the notion of vigilance, both towards the excesses of the state and towards lapses within the realm of civil society. Chandhoke, 'Civil Society', 608; see also Chandhoke, 'Civil Society in Conflict Cities', 26.

92 Breman, *The Making and Unmaking of an Industrial Working Class*, 292; Chandhoke, 'Civil Society in Conflict Cities'; T. K. Oommen, *Reconciliation in Post-Godhra Gujarat: The Role of Civil Society* (New Delhi: Pearson Education India, 2008), 252.

93 Chandhoke, 'Civil Society in Conflict Cities', 28.

94 Amrita Basu, 'The Long March from Ayodhya: Democracy and Violence in India', in *Pluralism and Democracy in India: Debating the Hindu Right*, ed. Wendy Doniger and Martha C. Nussbaum (Oxford: Oxford University Press, 2015), 153–73.

95 Sarkar, 'Semiotics of Terror', 2874.

96 Chatterjee, *The Politics of the Governed*, 4.

97 Partha Chatterjee, 'Beyond the Nation? Or Within?' *Social Text* 56, Autumn (1998): 57–69, 60.

98 Chatterjee, *The Politics of the Governed*, 40.

99 Ibid.

100 Partha Chatterjee, 'Democracy and Economic Transformation in India', *Economic and Political Weekly* 46, no. 16 (2008): 53–62.

101 Ibid., 57.

102 Chatterjee, *The Politics of the Governed*, 47. Chatterjee draws on examples of festivals, religious gatherings and even cinema clubs to illustrate this point.

103 Chatterjee, 'Democracy and Economic Transformation in India', 53–62.

104 Sundar and Baviskar point to the inadequacy of the terminology, arguing that Chatterjee has used 'non-corporate' as synonymous with forms of mercantile exchange. Amita Baviskar and Nandini Sundar, 'Democracy

Versus Economic Transformation?' *Economic and Political Weekly* 43, no. 46 (2008): 87–89.

105 This distinction has been used rather productively in a variety of empirical studies. To highlight a few, Ward Berenschot, for instance, in his ethnography of 'riots networks' in Ahmedabad, understands 'civil' and 'political' society as different modes of engaging with the state. Stuart Corbridge and others, in their study of developmental schemes in West Bengal, suggest that political society is a 'set of institutions, actors and cultural norms that is often constructively engaged in providing links between the "government" and the "public", as well as in brokering deals and forming patterns of authority that hold these deals in place'. See Berenschot, 'Riot Politics: Communal Violence and State-Society Mediation in Gujarat, India.'; Gudavarthy, *Re-Framing Democracy and Agency in India*, 174.

PART II

PROPERTY AND PRECARITY

In speaking of housing arrangements and property claims of Ahmedabad's working poor, it would be interesting to take the Sabarmati riverfront relocation housing projects as a starting point. The on-going Sabarmati Riverfront Development Project, which appears to be one of Ahmedabad's 'proudest' achievements, was sanctioned in 1997. Work began along the riverfront around the mid-2000s, during the course of which tens of thousands were evicted from their residences on the banks of the river to relocation sites scattered across the city, one of which is Vatva.[1]

From the late 1990s onwards, the urgency with which projects of urban renewal were planned and executed was linked to certain global trends, as cities worldwide were being remade to attract capital investments.[2] The Sabarmati Riverfront Development Project, widely acknowledged as Narendra Modi's 'pet project', was one such, involving state acquisition of urban land, large-scale displacement of worker settlements and real estate development. The AMC established a special purpose vehicle, the Sabarmati Riverfront Development Corporation Limited (SRFDCL), in 1997 to execute the project. Within a year, a private planning outfit headed by architect and urban planner Bimal Patel, the Environment and Planning Collaborative (EPC), produced a proposal for the project, which also included plans for rehabilitation. As construction began, the initial plans for resettling displaced households within 2–3 kilometres of their original residences[3] were largely abandoned, as 'entrepreneurial politics' increasingly governed the orientation of the project.[4]

The riverfront slums were demolished between 2006 and 2011 and a fraction of those were resettled under the Basic Services for the Urban Poor scheme (BSUP) of the Jawarharlal Nehru National Urban Renewal Mission (JNNURM). The evictions began without a concrete plan for resettlement, which was then ordered by the Gujarat High Court in view of the PIL filed by the Sabarmati Nagrik Adhikar Manch and Girish Patel.[5] The resettlement sites were spread across the city, a few in vacant mill lands in eastern Ahmedabad and the bulk concentrated in outlying industrial areas such as Vatva and Odhav. Resettlement would then effectively splinter employment and social ties, pushing most residents to the outskirts of the city.

The process of acquiring rights to resettlement was long and arduous, mediated by civil society organisations and local politicians. For many riverfront dwellers, the shift from slum housing along the Sabarmati to the high-rise resettlement quarters was a staggered one. The evictions began without the alternative residences already in place, and many of the displaced were first moved to a transit camp in Ganeshnagar, located near the city's largest garbage dump. The more fortunate ones were assigned flats with two rooms and a kitchen in the resettlement sites; those who did not have the required documentary evidence to qualify as 'project affected persons' remained at various inhospitable temporary sites and shanties that grew (often by state design and support) to accommodate the thousands of workers displaced from the river banks.[6]

In Vatva, which has the largest proportion of BSUP housing, hulking concrete blocks that loom over the otherwise flat terrain of this area were built to house roughly 5,500 families displaced from the riverfront as well as in the course of other development projects in the city.[7] The process of resettlement began sometime around 2010 and this latest addition to Vatva's landscape is as deeply tied to practices of violence as those before it. Recent studies of the Vatva resettlement sites document the ruptures in employment relations, as those who have been displaced from the inner city have had difficulties in maintaining their livelihoods. Employment options available in Vatva are significantly different from the sort that they were previously engaged in.[8] As with many other Muslim workers in Vatva, those from the resettlement flats similarly indicated discrimination with regard to employment opportunities in the adjacent GIDC estate.

The computer-generated allotments were meant to be arbitrary, by which Hindus and Muslims could be assigned resettlement facilities together or be placed in localities where they may be the minority community. For instance, nearly 500 Muslim families were evicted from Khanpur Darwaza along the riverbank and relocated to newly built quarters in the Vivekananda Mill Compound and Isanpur, both predominantly Hindu areas.[9] When some of the 140 Muslim families assigned housing in Vivekananda Mills went to the relocation site, they were met with hostility and intimidation from Hindu residents of the area.[10] They appealed for resettlement in Vatva, a Muslim-majority neighbourhood. Similarly, Hindu evictees from the riverfront who were allotted flats in Ajit Mills, situated in a largely Muslim neighbourhood, demanded for relocation in the Hindu-majority areas of Vadaj and Isanpur.[11] The argument presented here was one of security, as both communities requested to be rehabilitated in communally homogenous areas. There are, of course, historic reasons for the persistence of insecurities in a city such as Ahmedabad, and cohabiting amongst one's own could be a way of negotiating that anxiety.

As the location of housing grew to be an increasingly significant concern amongst the city's working poor, the judiciary offered some directives with which to negotiate the processes of resettlement. The Gujarat High Court in *Rajubhai v. Sabarmati Riverfront Development Corporation Ltd.* decreed:

> It will be open to one or the other allottee to exchange units from one place to another place or one block to another block, after prior permission of the Corporation. If any such application is filed, with the consent of another party for exchange, the Corporation will look into it sympathetically and my [*sic*] reallocate units on such exchange.[12]

The municipal corporation, however, refused to reassign the flats and instead suggested that two communities could exchange the properties among themselves, should they so wish.[13] These transfers of property, then, were to be concluded informally (and in most cases, illegally), while at the same time, endorsed by state authorities. It would appear that such exchanges have indeed taken place in the resettlement flats in Vatva, for there are visible signs of segregation between blocks, with entire towers of flats being uniformly Hindu or Muslim. A recent publication confirms my fieldwork impressions—two out of the three early resettlement blocks are communally homogenous.[14] These spaces, with their disturbingly neat religious slotting, are exemplars for real estate in contemporary Ahmedabad. They bear testimony to the continuous and simultaneous processes of settling, dismantling and recalibrating neighbourhood spaces. While my research does not explicitly address the process or the politics of eviction and resettlement, this moment of displacement offers a productive entry point into the discussions of the historical transformations of property in eastern Ahmedabad.

In this brief excursion into the Sabarmati Riverfront Development Project, we can identify a central tension between the precarity of settlements and the limits of choice that the city's labouring poor had recourse to. This is the fundamental problematic that I attempt to explore in the next three chapters. Drawing on archival material on the city's urban and industrial history, and ethnographic research conducted in two neighbourhoods—Gomtipur and Vatva—I map the histories of settlement in the industrial east from the early years of the twentieth century to the 2000s, tracing the transformation of tenancy regimes, urban planning and housing security.

A key objective of this book is to grasp how working people make a home in the city. A thicket of social relations undergirds housing options and choices. The focus on housing and property relations, particularly on the everyday politics of securing a home, present another critical lens with which to approach the broader transformations of twentieth-century Ahmedabad. It allows us to reflect on the changing modalities of working-class housing and the fluctuating relationship between employment and property rights. It offers a way of connecting the changing topographies of the city's workers' neighbourhoods with the wider social, industrial and political shifts. The far-reaching processes of communalisation of city space and the stealthier subterranean structures of ghettoisation governed the orientation of housing arrangements; the informality that surfaced as a routine feature of the property market, itself, is a consequence of the state's inability to provide a certain security of life to its citizens.

NOTES

1 See   http://www.sabarmatiriverfront.com/rehabilitation-resettlement, accessed on 20 June 2015.

2 See, for instance, Saskia Sassen, *The Mobility of Labor and Capital: A Study in International Investment and Labor Flow* (Cambridge: Cambridge University Press, 1990). For an empirical exposition on the investment flows in Ahmedabad, please see Desai, 'The Globalising City in the Time of Hindutva.'

3 Proposal for Sabarmati Riverfront Development, 1998, 44.

4 Desai, 'Municipal Politics, Court Sympathy and Housing Rights', 13.

5 The AMC policy on rehabilitation and resettlement, finalised in 2008, indicated that funds from the BSUP programme were to be diverted to provide housing for those displaced under the riverfront project. This was contrary to the claims so far that the project was to be entirely self-

financed—raising funds for construction as well as resettlement from the sale of riverfront land for commercial and residential purposes. This rerouting of finances implied that the costs of the Sabarmati Riverfront Development Project were being subsidised by other government funds. Desai, 'Municipal Politics, Court Sympathy and Housing Rights', 13.

6 *LA Times*, 3 August 2014, available at http://www.latimes.com/world/asia/la-fg-india-river-20140803-story.html, accessed on 15 September 2015.

7 See http://www.crdf.org.in/cue/saic/?page_id=238, accessed on 8 March 2015.

8 Darshini Mahadevia, Renu Desai, Shachi Sanghvi and Suchita Vyas, 'Vatwa Resettlements Sites: Basic Services and Amenities; Deprivations and Infrastructural Conflicts', Ahmedabad policy brief 2, Centre for Urban Equity, CEPT University, Ahmedabad, 2015; Darshini Mahadevia, Renu Desai, Shachi Sanghvi and Suchita Vyas, 'Vatwa Resettlements Sites: Thefts, Robberies and Burglaries', Ahmedabad policy brief 3, Centre for Urban Equity, CEPT University, Ahmedabad, 2016; Darshini Mahadevia, Renu Desai, Shachi Sanghvi, Suchita Vyas and Vaishali Parmar, 'Vatwa Resettlements Sites: Constrained Mobility and Stressed Livelihoods', Ahmedabad policy brief 1, Centre for Urban Equity, CEPT University, Ahmedabad, 2015.

9 *Hindustan Times*, 28 February 2010.

10 NDTV 15 March 2010, available at http://www.ndtv.com/news/blogs/a_fine_balance/riverside_story.php, accessed on 6 April 2015.

11 *Indian Express*, 19 February 2010.

12 *Rajubhai Kumavati Marwadi v. Sabarmati River Front Development Corporation Limitation*, Gujarat Hight Court, 13 June 2012.

13 *Financial Express*, 19 February 2010.

14 Darshini Mahadevia, 'Unsmart Outcomes of the Smart City Initiatives: Displacement and Peripheralisation in Indian Cities', in *The New Companion to Urban Design*, ed. Tridib Banerjee and Anastasia Loukaitou-Sideris (Abingdon: Routledge, 2019), 310–24.

5

CHAWLS WITHOUT CHIMNEYS

As mill chimneys were beginning to sprout across the city at the turn of the previous century, workers' neighbourhoods bloomed in a crescent along the railway line connecting Ahmedabad and Bombay. The phenomenal demographic growth of the early twentieth century, largely propelled by the expansion of the textile industry, was accompanied by a host of civic and urban issues—of housing, sanitation, urban transport and overcrowding.[1] The city municipality, led largely by the local elite, launched a set of initiatives to tackle the changed urban situation. The urban body 'opened up' the overcrowded heart of the city, restructured the pols, marked distinctions between public and private space, conducted a city survey, documented property rights and revised valuations of private property.[2] Land within the walled city became increasingly profitable and landlords, eager to invest in real estate and immovable property.[3] The 'mud and straw hovels' of the urban poor and industrial workers were gradually shunted beyond the city limits. The process of incorporating the outlying, suburban areas into the municipal limits was staggered and uneven. In 1858, Hathipura, Madhavpur and Rajpur (which includes parts of present-day Rajpur-Gomtipur) were included within the city boundaries, before being excluded two years later. In 1881, the civic limits expanded again to absorb some textile mills and the railway station. Over the next twenty years, new residential settlements on the western banks as well as industrial localities towards the east of the Sabarmati were brought within the ambit of municipal regulations and taxation. This expansion and reorganisation of the city were not without resistance and protest.[4] The opposition to spatial reorganisation and increased taxation precipitated a crisis of authority within the municipality, which was, at one level, mobilised by the Congress Party, led by Vallabhai Patel to wrest control of the civic body in 1919.

SETTLING THE MILL NEIGHBOURHOODS

As early as 1890, the municipality recognised the need for organised chawl housing for the burgeoning population.[5] After building some model chawls, their enthusiasm petered out. The housing question remained a pressing concern, acquiring greater urgency through the politically turbulent decade of the 1920s. This attention to workers' accommodation and social welfare was propelled, in part, by an unsuccessful strike in 1923 (which led to a 15 per cent reduction in wages) and the TLA's entry into municipal politics in 1924. With the failure of the strike in 1923, the TLA retreated from struggles over wages and focused instead, in the following years, on workers' social welfare.[6] The city's working classes emerged as a visible political force, attracting the attention of mill owners and urban reformers alike.[7] As McGowan observes, a wide range of institutions and actors—civic bodies, social reformers, mill owners, trade unions—came together to articulate a 'shared vision of the city'. Central to this vision was housing for the working poor, which was seen to have implications on the 'happiness', 'health' and 'wealth' of the entire urban population. Unsuitable housing arrangements for the urban workforce were regarded as 'responsible for the low vitality', ill-health, the 'horrible drink habit' as well as a 'considerable lowering of the moral tone in relation to the sexes'.[8] Though the tangible gains made through this project of inclusion and (often righteous) reform were inadequate, housing and other social concerns of the urban poor were acknowledged as part of a 'public duty'. This overarching project gradually eroded as narrower, more exclusivist concerns oriented the production of housing from the late 1930s onwards, thereby reinforcing social distinctions.[9]

Underlying the public commitment to a sanitary and inclusive city were considerable tensions over financial responsibility and the logistics of housing and service provision. Accountability volleyed between the mill owners and the municipality. The floods of 1927, for instance, which damaged large swathes of workers' settlements, received no attention from the municipality. Vallabhai Patel, the mayor at the time, maintained that the mill owners were responsible for relief and reconstruction in the working-class areas and that the municipality did not have any obligations towards them.[10] A TLA appeal following the floods, remarked: 'Better housing in Ahmedabad will not be a reality unless the Millowners' Association, the Municipality and other organisations interested in and responsible for the welfare of the work-people combine and carry out a large programme.'[11] Notwithstanding the template laid out by the TLA for collaborative investments in workers' housing, the mill owners maintained that it was the 'primary duty of the Municipality and the State to provide good sanitary accommodation to the workmen in general'.[12] The few chawls that had been built by the mills were 'in no way, an improvement on the other private chawls'.[13] The grim conditions of workers' housing arrangements were well documented. The *Times of India* entered the public conversation on the housing question with vivid descriptions of these settlements:

> There are some hovels, the roofs of which are on a level with the road and there are others into which one cannot get admittance except by squatting on the ground and crawling. Light and air scarcely enter these habitations, and in most centres sanitary conveniences are woefully defective, if not altogether absent. Huts lie scattered about here and there and everywhere, and, where the land or tenement belongs to a private landlord, heavy rents are exacted.[14]

By the end of the 1920s, more than half of the city's population lived under these distinctly trying conditions. Out of a total of 314,093 residents, 185,490 were workers—a majority of whom, as the TLA recorded, were crammed into 'long rows of tenements facing each other across a narrow passage sometimes not more than 6 ft in width'.[15] Windowless, and without any drainage or facilities, these dwellings did not conform even to the very low standards of sanitation required by the civic bodies.[16]

Private enterprise, beyond the investments made by industrialists and the AMA, as an institution, was central to the production of the mill neighbourhoods. The provision of amenities was borne almost equally by the municipality and private landlords. Forty-seven per cent of privies were constructed by state authorities, while landlords built another 48 per cent. The city municipality provided 28 per cent of the water supply and nearly 60 per cent was private, with a majority of residents sharing one tap between eight to sixteen tenements.[17] The bulk of workers found accommodation in private tenements, while only 16 per cent of mill hands resided in chawls built by the mill owners.[18] Apart from certain segments of the workforce—such as gatekeepers and watchmen—who, in some mills, were housed free of charge, mill owners charged rent. In some cases, the rents were slightly concessional—a majority charged roughly at 70 to 90 per cent of the market rate. Some others charged full economic rent.[19] Mill owners' chawls, even at a time of housing shortage, were not always fully occupied. Employers commonly let out chawls to tenants other than workers in their own mills.[20] In fact, employers' disciplinary control and surveillance over living quarters was a flashpoint around which labour mobilised. The TLA, having faced difficulties in organising workers in mill-owned chawls—where they could be forced to work during strikes, evicted if involved in industrial activity or whose mobility and freedom of association could be curtailed—counselled workers for a brief while to boycott mill chawls.[21] These early attempts at providing housing are remembered by contemporary chawl dwellers, as being motivated partly by the philanthropic spirit of the Gujarati industrialists of the early twentieth century and in part as a form of labour control.[22]

Private chawls were thus the most densely populated and private landlords were seen as those most acutely responsible for the squalid conditions in the mill areas. Jobbers and mukadams often operated as essential conduits in securing private accommodation for workers.[23] Testimonies to the Royal Commission on Labour suggested that the civic body allowed for the persistence of settlements deemed 'unfit for human habitation' and was negligent in enforcing the laws enacted for the orderly growth of the city,[24] while the TLA reported that 'private enterprise ... has permitted the growth of slums and the accumulation of a heavy proportion of uninhabitable tenements'.[25] Ambalal Sarabhai pointed out that much of the municipality's lacklustre commitment to drafting and enforcing building bye-laws was, in part, due to a strong representation of landed interests on the municipal board.[26] A range of private actors was operational at this moment. Influential figures such as Parvati Bai, a voter and a chawl owner, sued the municipality when directed to provide privies to her tenants. This was not a solitary occurrence; the *Times of India*, in 1927, reported ten similar cases where the municipality ultimately compromised the suit.[27] Elsewhere, religious property belonging to Pir Mushayak Roza was used and leased out for building chawls for mill hands by the Pirzada.[28] These chawls soon began to be known popularly by the names of the landlords, local landmarks or the mills they were attached to.

To counter the 'avaricious policy pursued by private landlords', the TLA appealed for greater state involvement, through the establishment of a Housing Board, which was to undertake direct constructions as well as subsidise private and cooperative investments.[29] This called for an engagement with the housing question, intensified beyond the routine matters of urban governance conducted by the Municipal Standing or Sanitary Committee.[30] In drawing attention to workers unattached to the textile industry and terming 'the City as a whole' as the employer, the union relieved the mill owners of the sole responsibility of providing workers' housing and attempted to speak on behalf of the entirety of the urban working classes.[31]

The rhetoric of 'public duty'—shared by the civic authorities, the mill owners and the labour union—did translate into limited but concrete interventions. The AMA finalised a cooperative housing scheme supported by most of the city's textile mills, and acquired land for the project by early 1934.[32] By the end of the 1930s, the AMA had constructed 435 tenements through the Ahmedabad Mills Housing Society Limited; the TLA built another 125 two-room tenements and the municipality, a 100 more.[33]

The urban landscape was transformed by the 'property boom' of the 1930s.[34] While the affluent moved westwards of the walled city and beyond the Sabarmati to build bungalows and cooperative housing, the industrial east was marked by land speculation, increasing rents and overcrowding.[35] The municipal limits were periodically expanded—to include new development in the west and to incorporate large tracts of mill land in the east.[36] While private landlords continued to control the housing market, providing nearly 79 per cent of rental properties, and the one-roomed tenement remained the dominant architectural form of workers' housing, there were other investments underway in the mill areas.[37]

Mill workers were also coming together to form housing cooperative societies. The first of these, Vankar Co-operative Housing Society, was established by Dalit textile workers with the support of Pritamrai Desai, a pioneer of cooperative housing in the city.[38] The formation of cooperative societies was actively encouraged by the TLA. Trade unionism and the cooperative movement were seen as mutually beneficial and complementary in their aims and objectives.[39] 'Self-reliance', the union advised, was the 'best remedy' to address the housing shortage, marking a shift from their earlier position holding mill owners and the municipality responsible for the housing of industrial workers.[40] By 1950, there were twelve housing societies of mill workers, financed by the Workers Co-operative Bank.[41] The TLA was entrenched in the property market of the industrial districts—as a mediator between state authorities, mill owners and private landlords and as a builder and financer of housing.

In 1937, the Congress Party won the Bombay legislative assembly elections. Two secretaries of the TLA, Gulzarilal Nanda and Khandubhai Desai, were elected as Congress representatives. Social welfare for industrial workers was high on the party's election agenda and over the late colonial and early post-colonial period, the Bombay government emerged as the fulcrum for advancing a nationalist labour policy.[42] As labour minister in the Bombay government, Nanda headed the Housing Board, which designed an ambitious plan of providing industrial housing as part of the post-war reconstruction plan.[43] The Bombay Housing Board acquired 'large' and 'unprecedented' powers for the drafting of housing policy and acquisition of land.[44]

Greater state involvement followed—in the provision of public housing and in the regulation of the property market through rent control. The municipality intensified their housing initiatives through the 1940s—about 900 tenements were slated for construction by the civic body in Jamalpur and Shahpur, and a model three-storey building planned for Sarsapur, possibly the first experiment in Ahmedabad, in high-rise housing for workers.[45] The newer residential structures in Ahmedabad's labour spaces, built through government's, mill owners' or the TLA's interventions, did mark a perceptible shift in the quality of working-class housing. For one, many of these new dwellings were two-roomed structures, already an improvement over the 'hovels' of the earlier decades. They were 'sanitary' and 'accommodating', with plenty of light and ventilation and increasingly positioned against the insanitary conditions of the chawls.[46] The few tenements built by the TLA were even more well appointed, with 'two living rooms, a kitchen, a verandah and a courtyard'.[47] The introduction of subsidised industrial housing by the Bombay government in 1952 further encouraged the formation of workers' housing cooperatives, of which thirty-six were established immediately following the scheme.[48]

The bulk of public housing built by the Bombay and, later, the Gujarat Housing Board was made available to workers on a hire-purchase scheme, on the evidence of employment in a textile mill. The TLA sustained a close relationship with the Housing Board, with Nanda and then, later, union secretary Noor Mohammad Sheikh, as its chairperson. The relationship between employment and residence was given a new heft by these housing options. Access to better housing as well as the slew of social security measures introduced during this period were predicated on permanent employment, widening the gap between 'formal' and casual workers in the textile mills.

The overcrowding of workers' settlements, which was seen as a vector of 'inefficiency' and 'immorality', was arrested through the remaking of housing in the industrial east. This fit with a wider vision of domesticity that encompassed work and the home. The category of the 'natural family', as outlined in the Family Budget Surveys of the Bombay Presidency—members who have a right to be fed, housed and clothed by the head of the family, that is, the wife and unmarried children of an individual—made the notion of a 'family wage' explicit and enshrined the male breadwinner model.[49] As early as 1924, the representatives of the throstle union passed a resolution to pare down women's employment.[50] Recommending that married women be retrenched over men, the union explained, 'If in a family a man and wife are both working and the man is retrenched, then how bad will it look.'[51] Going beyond retrenchment, the TLA also aimed at curbing new employment of women.[52] In arguing that women's work in the mills bore unhappy consequences for children's and family well-being, sexual propriety and male wages, the union foregrounded gendered ideologies of domesticity and respectability.[53] Statistics, however, show that the 'natural family' was hardly as prominent in practice—between 1928 and 1937, the declining numbers of the 'natural family' were accompanied by an increase in 'joint households', which referred to any group of people living together in one household.[54] Two rationalisation drives, mediated by the TLA, were particularly critical for women's exclusion from secure mill work—that of 1935, which allowed for the dismissal of married women, and of 1955, which used technological innovation as a rationale for pruning women's employment.[55] Between 1921 and 1951, the proportion of women workers fell from 20 per cent to 5 per cent.[56] This gendered exclusion from stable employment was central to the TLA's template of the working-class family. As Ratanben, who worked as a spinner in the 1940s, recalled one of S. P. Vasavada's speeches: 'Why are you women working in the mills. You should be at home looking after the children. Your men will come home tired and you are not there to serve them. My advice to you is that you should all leave the mills.'[57]

Investments and involvements in shaping the materiality of housing was a strand of this broader agenda. The new built form, along with the individual property rights that came with it, was a way to tackle the formation of joint households, where 'a worker, in addition to his own family [would] take in to live with him his relations and their families'.[58] The TLA's investments in 'creating physical conditions where [workers] would live healthily and happily' were equally directed towards refining the aesthetics of workers' housing.[59] New centres were established in the mill districts, through which the union executed their programmes of 'social betterment'—which involved a focus on prohibition and temperance, inculcation of thrift and savings habits, and sanitation and social hygiene, among others.[60] A women's wing was started to spread 'the message of creating happy homes for workers'.[61] Cleanliness, housekeeping and home decoration emerged as key areas of engagement. Advice on 'proper elegant arrangement of household articles in rooms' and 'simple methods of decorating rooms and tenements', and directives towards 'reform of harmful social customs', eradication of superstitions and other unsavoury habits such as 'indiscriminate spitting' were offered.[62] Underwritten with a broader comment on citizenship, this mode of homemaking and shaping of working-class lifestyles was centred around acquiring dignity and respectability and was presented as a way of reforming the city's workers into responsible citizens of a newly independent India.[63]

CHANGING CONNOTATIONS OF THE CHAWL AND THE SLUM

Around the same time that the TLA was actively promoting and facilitating organised housing schemes, the union was also formulating a stand on the hierarchies of housing and shelter, which was strongly coded with notions of moral and social respectability. In an article published in 1951, the *Majoor Sandesh* reported on the housing conditions through descriptive accounts of the types of housing available in the industrial areas. The first was a one-room structure measuring 8 x 10 feet. One corner of this space was the kitchen area—with a *chulha* and around it, some piles of firewood and blackened utensils. In other parts of this small room, shrouded with cobwebs, lay a child's cradle, mattresses and clothes strung across a wall. The second kind was slightly bigger, with a room and a separate kitchen. The first room contained a few *matka*s (presumably for storing water) and trunks and bags. The kitchen, dark and coated with ash, dust and cobwebs, was equipped with a kerosene stove. A heap of things were scattered around—dirty utensils, uncovered food, empty bottles and a *hukkah* lay in disarray, for there was no space for storage. The third had a room, a kitchen and a courtyard. This account of the material conditions of housing also included a little tableau that appears to have been intended to provide a glimpse of everyday life of the mill districts: An old lady is sitting outside her chawl on a *charpai* smoking a hukkah, when a young man smoking a *bidi* joins her. Children, noisy, snotty and nonchalantly aggressive, play around them. One of the little children playing in the vicinity soils himself; his mother, yelling, slaps him a few times and then carelessly cleans him up, dumping the pile of excreta a few steps from their house. The impression of coarseness, indolence and an incessant clamour permeates this scene.

Reviewing the types of housing available in the industrial districts, the article uniformly regarded local housing arrangements as sites of deprivation, disrepair and dirt. This piece of reportage appears to not have been intended merely as a documentation of the living conditions but also as a judgement on life in these neighbourhoods. Laziness, carelessness, illiteracy and negligence were identified as the reasons for the unsanitary conditions of worker's localities—that workers themselves were responsible for the unsanitary conditions of their habitat. By inculcating a disgust for dirt, workers could, as the union suggested, be motivated to improve their residential conditions.[64] The push towards sanitary, sensory and aesthetic reform was undergirded by the union's rhetoric of blaming and shaming, bring into sharp relief the emerging hierarchies of housing and their social connotations.

Rent restrictions, intermittently in place through the war years, were formalised through the Bombay Rent Control Act of 1947. The legislation placed certain ceilings on rents and protected tenants from eviction, and chawl housing was accorded some degree of legal stability. The rent receipt was a key piece of evidence around which the legislation operated, and on the basis of which tenancy was secured. The feverish pace of chawl constructions abated and the enforcement of this law changed the landscapes of the neighbourhoods significantly. With rent restrictions in place, the construction of chawls was no longer lucrative and landlords began skimping on maintenance and repair costs. Questions of service provision then grew to be ever more contentious as neither the municipality nor the chawl owners were willing to assume responsibility for it. The greater tenurial security now enjoyed by the chawl residents was accompanied by rapidly deteriorating material conditions.

The Rent Act did not ease the relationship between landlords and tenants. Rental rights emerged as a major point of conflict in the industrial neighbourhoods. Landlords made continued attempts to increase rents and evict tenants, while neglecting to provide basic facilities and residential upkeep. A 'black market' rent was put in practice, with landlords issuing rental receipts for amounts lower than what they actually charged.[65] Violence became increasingly visible and coercion common in practices of rent collection.[66] With jobbers, pratinidhis, landlords and hotelkeepers involved in money lending, the realm of housing often overlapped with the local informal credit market, both of which relied on the use of force for the collection of dues.[67] The complaints submitted to the TLA over rent issues boomed in this period, followed closely by police matters. The union through its pratinidhis positioned itself at the centre of everyday life, leveraging their connections with the municipal bodies for civic amenities, squaring off against landlords and mediating with the police. Every Saturday, elected TLA pratinidhis of the latta khatta would visit the chawls, often accompanied by civic officials.[68] During these visits, grievances were aired, formal and informal negotiations conducted and instructions issued on clean and healthy living. In this way, the TLA intervened in a dispute in Musa Suleman ki Chaali, when tenants refused to pay rent unless water connections were installed. Municipal water connections were laid and new toilets built across the mill areas through the TLA's everyday involvement.[69] Workers were counselled to keep the union involved in discussions with chawl owners, as in the case of a chawl in Jamalpur, where the landlord was demanding payment with interest for the loan that he would have to take to install toilets and water taps.[70] The union's formal electoral participation was at its peak through the 1950s, and much of their support was secured through this deep involvement in the social life of the mill districts. Special units were constituted to look into the various dimensions of local affairs, with the singular goal of maintaining sustained close contact with the city's mill workers. The union ran libraries, gymnasiums, dispensaries, social and cultural centres and, most crucially, set in place institutions through which to approach the state.

Alongside the tensions around tenancy and rents, questions centring on the legality of residential structures appeared. Despite the new investments in public housing, shelter had to be arranged in the interstices of planned settlements and at the margins—through squatting or renting more precarious habitat. It became increasingly lucrative to informally rent out vacant plots of land to workers, who then built physically and legally unstable dwellings on their own expense.[71] Landowners would let out plots measuring 6 x 6 feet or 10 x 10 feet, often at the borders of the more established chawls, which allowed for easier access to water and sanitation.[72] Thus, by the early 1950s, when the population of the city had already grown to more than a million, semi-permanent residential structures of less than 25 square metres formed an important part of the city's landscape.[73]

These structures were not clearly separate from the existing chawls, nor was their administrative problematising a particularly new development. Present in earlier government and union documentation was a similar rhetoric of dirt and sanitation. The introduction of town planning in Bombay and Ahmedabad in 1915 was, in a sense, seen as 'preventive', to thwart the growth of 'slums'.[74] Similarly, the housing question of the late 1920s and early 1930s was framed through an emphasis on the 'notoriety of slums' and of the 'hovels unfit for human habitation'.[75] The concern with slums as a site of disease, overcrowding and disrepair (more broadly, as imperilling public health) shifted to one where aspects of their legality, their impermanence and (the lack of) rights of tenure were underlined. This mode of engaging with shelter, as Haynes and Rao have pointed out, had become increasingly common across the subcontinent.[76]

In the 1950s, slums in Ahmedabad attracted the attention of the state and the TLA, as encroachments and unplanned settlements, producing a discursive and administrative distinction between them and chawls. Mill workers and large sections of the labouring poor found shelter in these settlements, and slum clearance emerged as a well-endorsed strategy for dealing with what municipal officials termed 'haphazard' constructions.[77] In the debates in the Bombay legislative assembly, over the creation of municipal corporations in the province, Khandubhai Desai, elected representative of the TLA, argued that 'Ahmedabad had been clamouring for a Corporation' in order to 'execute schemes for slum clearance and sanitation speedily'.[78] The civic body's enthusiasm was given an added boost with the introduction of slum clearance and improvement schemes in the Second Five Year Plan of 1952. The AMC regularly appealed to the Bombay government for funds for slum clearance, as the TLA urged the municipal corporation to evict and resettle slum dwellers.[79] By the time town plans were drafted for many of the mill neighbourhoods, with the professed hope that these suburban areas will develop on orderly lines, these localities had already grown in rather disorderly ways.[80] The town planning map envisioned the neighbourhood as a strikingly neat formation, ironing out and obscuring much of the tangled growth that had already taken place (Figure 5.1).

The mill neighbourhoods of the early 1950s then had two dominant architectural forms—the chawls and the slums. In material terms, the distinctions between these two forms were almost negligible. A spatial blurring of the two categories of housing was manifested in the partition and sub-division of chawls. For instance, tenants of Bakar Ali ni Pol in the walled city reported a proliferation of new hutments around their residences.[81] Or the case of Foujdar ki Chaali in Gomtipur, where in December 1957, during the discussion of a rent dispute, it was discovered that the landlord had constructed twenty-eight illegal hutments within the chawl premises. This complaint came from the 'lawful tenants' of the

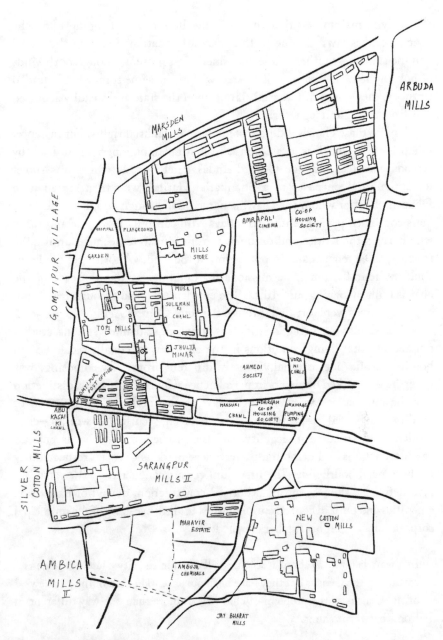

Figure 5.1 Map of Rajpur-Gomtipur

Source: Prepared from Town Planning Map for Rajpur-Gomtipur, administrative map, Ahmedabad Municipal Corporation, and 'City Map', SETU, Ahmedabad, 1989.

chawl, who maintained that the slum dwellers were infringing upon the civic resources lawfully due to them.[82] The gradations between the chawl and the slum were rather subtle but nonetheless present. Though both kinds of housing may have very well existed within the same somewhat bounded territory, they posed differential claims upon the state and steadily acquired a distinct social and legal form.

Many of these chawls did hold some form of tenurial rights. For instance, Dhupsingh ki Chaali is located on land first taken on a permanent lease by Aryodaya Mills from one Govardhandas Patel in 1918, which was sublet for agricultural purposes to a Shankarlal Harilal, who then rented it to Dhupsingh, after whom the chawl is named. Dhupsingh and, later, his legal heirs continued paying rent to Aryodaya Mills until it closed. He and those who derived their titles and occupancy from him were deemed, until quite recently, to be tenants and in possession of the land.[83] Another set of claims could be found through permissions for building, as was the case of the chawls built by Sarangpur Mills.[84] The entitlements held through leases and consent decrees were fortified through the Rent Control Act.

While slums were being identified as targets of state interventions, studies pointed out that living conditions in the chawls were equally bleak.[85] Slum housing, while not materially greatly different from chawl housing, was nevertheless marked out by its impermanence. Underpinning this distinction (for the built structures were not always so distinct) was the question of legality and social respectability. The tenurial security of working-class residences was tied to its legality, and the protection that chawls enjoyed against evictions and demolitions were clear markers of social respectability in these neighbourhoods. The first slum census conducted by the AMC in 1976 defined a slum as an unauthorised construction, devoid of basic civic amenities and built in contravention of the building bye-laws of the municipal corporation. The report further clarified:

> In a way, as many as about 1500 chawls located in the city could have been covered in the Census but they have been purposely kept out of the purview of the Census as the problem of chawls is in more than one way different from that of the slums.[86]

As chawls acquired a modest amount of tenurial stability, slums continued to be materially and legally precarious. Distinctions between the two were marked out through everyday negotiations with the municipal authorities, landlords and the union officials, as the space of the chawl and the slum was being gradually delineated.

While the city witnessed a prodigious expansion of slum dwellings through the 1960s—a 329 per cent increase between 1961 and 1971—property relations in the chawls were solidifying. The ownership of chawls began shifting at a time when the construction of rent-protected low-income housing was no longer lucrative for landlords, while land in the high-density industrial areas was still very profitable.[87] Studies on working-class housing recorded rents as having stagnated at a uniformly low rate.[88] Landlords and rent collectors, thus, no longer found it worth their while to make the monthly visit to the chawls. Jeevanbhai, who was born in and continues to live in Kundawali Chaali in Gomtipur, recalled these regular visits from the landlord. Named after a *kund*, a tanning pit nearby, this chawl, like many others in Gomtipur, expanded gradually over the years. From fifty-two tenements in the 1940s, it is now a cluster of sixty-two dwellings. As the landlord's visits gradually petered out, many tenants began buying out their chawls, as did Jeevanbhai in 1965–66 for INR 1,251. The transfer of chawls was not necessarily a straightforward process. They were bought individually from the landlord, as Jeevanbhai did, or from the rent collector, who in many cases acquired possession of the land. In other cases, some tenants bought over the rest of the units in the chawls. With already occupied properties being sold off, tenants experienced a moment of vulnerability when the new chawl owners attempted to evict them. These new owners were in many cases fellow mill workers who, recently upwardly mobile, began acquiring property. Much of these transactions were (and continue to be) effected through a legal instrument known as the Power of Attorney. The rights conferred through this process were shaky to begin with and have grown to be increasingly feeble over the years. The TLA issued repeated warnings against the purchase of individual or multiple units, arguing that difficulties would arise in gaining possession of these new investments.[89]

These transfers, however, continued and the Rent Control Act was amended in 1963 (according to the TLA, through direct intervention of the union) to assign even greater tenurial security.[90] The changes to the Act further buttressed the control exercised by the tenants. First, the legal connotations of the 'landlord' were reformulated, in that a landlord would be recognised legally only if they had acquired the premises before the tenancy was established or on 1 January 1964.[91] While tenants acquired a new level of security of residence, as landlords who purchased properties after 1964 could not, by law, compel them to leave, this also diffused the landlord–tenant relationship.[92] Second, through the amendments, tenants were entitled to perform repairs and construct additional structures such as walls, doors, adding kitchen shelves, and so on. While the original Act ensured that *any* constructions made on the premises could be grounds for eviction, the modified law permitted cosmetic and substantial changes to be made, assigning a degree of ownership that was previously absent. Third, tenants were also empowered to directly approach the collector to acquire electricity connections. These changes allowed for newer, stronger claims that tenants could stake on chawl properties. Through these claims there was far greater protection from eviction while the aesthetic and practical changes that were now authorised by law invested the chawls with a greater degree of material solidity.

During Indira Gandhi's tenure as prime minister, through the late 1960s to the mid-1970s, poverty was increasingly identified as a central target of state action, gaining traction through the period of the national Emergency, with its programmes of forced sterilisations and slum evictions. In Ahmedabad, the local civic bodies and state agencies accelerated their efforts in tackling urban poverty, with slum improvement, in particular, emerging as a key intervention in the housing question.[93]

Public bodies, most notably the AMC, ended its involvement in the provision of housing by 1974[94] and changed its strategy from the *construction* of residences to *acquisition*. In the meantime, as with chawls, tenements constructed by state agencies, such as those by the Gujarat Housing Board in Bapunagar, were sold (or handed over in accordance to the hire-purchase scheme) to tenants.[95] New legislations simultaneously transformed the terrain of workers' settlements in the city. Slums, which had so far been targets of social reform and administrative concern, acquired a sharper legal currency with the introduction of the Gujarat Slum Areas Act in 1973. The Act added to the regulatory frame governing land use, providing measures for the improvement, clearance and redevelopment, and requiring permissions to be acquired for all constructions in notified slum areas.[96] The legislation also invested greater powers in the local bodies—now empowered to declare any slum area a 'slum clearance' area as well as authorised to demolish any building considered 'unfit for human habitation'. International aid, led by the World Bank, was pooled towards slum rehabilitation and clearance.[97]

The Urban Land Ceiling Act was introduced in 1976 with the intention of a more equitable redistribution of land; in effect, the law tightened the supply of urban land. In connection with the broader transformations occurring in the political field of Gujarat, the TLA's electoral activities, by this time, had diminished considerably. With their historically close association with the municipal corporation broken, the union's intermediary role also changed somewhat. The institutional apparatus of the union, which had so far mediated between working-class citizens and the state, was replaced by other figures of local importance—a slumlord, for instance, who could guarantee access to housing or a municipal corporator who could offer a way of approaching state agencies.

These three legislations introduced three competing registers of tenurial security in the working-class neighbourhoods. The Rent Control Act offered significant rights to tenants, the Slum Areas Act introduced a new form of precarity in urban living and the Urban Land Ceiling Act sharpened the contours of available land. It was against this background that the AMC began acquiring chawls at a very nominal cost across the mill areas for the purposes of slum upgradation. These chawls, thus obtained, were either left unattended, as they largely have been in Gomtipur, or there were attempts to sell them off to residents.[98]

A closer look at the municipal deliberations over the future of Vira Bhagat ki Chaali will allow us to explore the precise ways in which the experience of chawl housing was changing. The chawl had been already acquired by the AMC, when in September 1973 the residents approached the municipal corporation demanding that the existing chawl structures be renovated and individual bathrooms and toilets be added; for these changes, the tenants were willing to agree to an increase in the rent. In response, the commissioner suggested three options—one, a cooperative society be formed by the residents, and the entire row of chawls be sold en masse; two, new quarters be constructed under the state's slum clearance policy, and legal action would be taken against those who did not agree to this plan; and three, the chawl would be partly renovated and partly demolished to make way for new quarters and this new accommodation would be sold to those who could afford it.[99] This points towards a critical change in the experience of housing—through its acquisition of the chawl with the intention of 'slum upgradation', the AMC effectively collapsed the distinctions between slums and chawls. The clear official boundaries between a chawl and a slum were now blurred. With its acquisition as a slum, the chawl's legal status grew increasingly more fragile, for as the earlier illustration indicates, there was a perpetual threat of eviction and displacement. The secure tenancy rights that seem implicit in site upgradation or even in the sale of the dwellings remained ambiguous. Furthermore, the Bombay Rent Control Act, which had so far provided great security to tenants, no longer applied to properties acquired by the government or local authorities.[100] The tensions between forms of legal and informal tenure are, perhaps, best documented by the Slum Networking Project, which, as we discussed in Chapter 4, had allowed for local NGOs to occupy a central mediatory role in urban governance. 'Upgrading' and 'integrating slums into the mainstream of society' and enhanced social status were flagged as objectives and possible outcomes of the project.[101] The contributory structure of project financing, by which the residents provided one-third of the upgradation costs, allowed the inhabitants to enter the scheme as 'partners' rather than as 'beneficiaries'. This sense of ownership and investment, however, had an uneasy relationship with actual legal rights over the land. In a *Times of India* piece on the project, the municipal commissioner was quoted as stating, 'This does not regularise slums ... because we do not give them [the slum dwellers] tenurial rights.'[102] Indeed, the prospects of 'transforming the slum into a colony or society' or, for that matter, the 'increased social status' that the project was expected to engender[103] remained untenable with the mere provision of an 'informal tenure' of ten years. All that 'slum networking' afforded was an assurance that 'those slums and chawls joining the project will not be removed by the AMC for 10 years'.[104] The upward mobility that was offered through the perpetually possible yet ever-postponed promise of secure tenancy rights remained uncertain.

The case of Musa Suleman ki Chaali points to the increasing precarity of chawl residences and also allows us to identify the various intersecting regulatory frames that govern land use and property development in the area. Located behind the vast empty space of Mahendra Silk Mills, popularly called Topi Mills, this chawl looks no different from the hundreds of similar formations dotting Gomtipur. Chawls, reinforced with concrete and plaster, spilled over on to the street. Some with slim verandahs were separated from the narrow pathways with a small iron gate; in others, the door opened onto the streets.

Come evening, the streets of the chawl would be buzzing—older men would sit in companionable silence on the benches installed by the municipal corporation; others would settle cross-legged on the pavement to play never-ending games of *pasha*. This space was clearly gendered. Women did not loiter here—indeed, I can testify that loitering in these areas was a distinctly uncomfortable experience for me—though many women were on the streets, returning from work, carrying shopping, or doing some household work on the threshold of their chawls. Knots of young men gathered around the one pan shop in the chawl, ordering tea from a nearby kitli and buying loose cigarettes and bidis from the stall. On days when there was a cricket match, these local establishments did even more brisk business. On other days, groups assembled to chat and gossip over the sound of the television in this pan stall. The nearby Jhulta Minara, the shaking minarets of Bibiji's Masjid, protected by the Archaeological Survey of India, placed another set of regulations on real estate development in the area. By a notification issued in 1992, construction was prohibited in the 300-metre radius around the *masjid*.[105]

The plot of land popularly known as Musa Suleman ki Chaali, as per the official records, is still registered as agricultural, in the name of the trustee of Vinayakrav Laxmilal Trust and twenty-six others, including one Ghulam Mohammad Musabhai.[106] In 1990, as part of a series on ongoing legal battles, Ghulam Mohammad Musabhai, identified as the owner of Musabhai's chawl behind Topi Mills in Gomtipur, filed a case in the Small Causes Court against his tenant Ujiben Mulabhai. Ujiben was charged with constructing a big room—a permanent structure—without the consent of the owner (which would be grounds for eviction under the Rent Control Act), and being in arrears of the rent of INR 9 since 1 September 1980. Taking recourse to the Rent Control Act, Musabhai appealed to have the tenant evicted. During the proceedings, it was revealed that the chawl had been acquired by the AMC in 1976 and, as such, the provisions of the Rent Control Act no longer applied to this space.[107]

In another related suit, Ghulam Mohammad Musabhai again approached the High Court to reconsider the auction[108] of his chawl by the municipal corporation. He raised issue with both the notice for and the procedure of the auction sale, arguing that the AMC's grounds for appropriating the property for non-payment of taxes was invalid and 'therefore the entire exercise of the auction sale was erroneous'.[109] The petition, however, was denied. This case offers us an illustration of the ways in which the state agencies were entering the mill neighbourhoods. In this case, the rejection of the Rent Control Act actually worked to secure the tenant's rights. But as we see in the following section, the denudation of rent regulations contributed greatly to the remaking of these working-class areas and, as such, presented a rather grim portent of the future of these habitations.

At this moment, then, we can identify two contradictory movements in the mill districts—on the one hand, the attempts towards upward mobility through investments in housing and, on the other, tenurial stability was imperilled by the official marking out of these very areas as slums. The acquisitions of personal property took the form of either individual investments or purchases en masse, when entire lines of chawls were sold together.[110] Accompanying this shift towards property ownership was the proliferation of cooperative housing societies, as upwardly mobile workers moved into residences that were visibly different from the chawls that they had so far lived in. By the early 1980s, the mill areas boasted several established and upcoming residential societies. This shift towards gentrified housing and a visible articulation of upward mobility was occurring at a time when the secure tenancy rights that these areas had enjoyed thus far were being steadily threatened. Established markers of social respectability, such as the ownership of property, gained a new fragility with large parts of these neighbourhoods being officially tagged as slums.

UNSTABLE TENANCY IN THE MILL NEIGHBOURHOODS

From the early 1980s onwards, the textile industry entered a period of crisis from which it would never recover. The mill closures from 1985 onwards resulted in an extensive loss of employment, with nearly 125,000 workers retrenched.[111] The new insecurity introduced by unemployment was further exacerbated by the changes that were taking place in the lived spaces of the city's mill workers. Spatial transformations that were occurring nearly simultaneously marked the city's industrial districts—the closure of textile mills in the city, the extension of the municipal limits to incorporate large tracts of industrial land in the eastern peripheries, the continued appropriation of chawls by the municipal corporation and the intermittent violence in the city which prompted distress sales and property transfers. These moments coincided to make real estate in both the mill districts and the outlying industrial areas not only more profitable but also more precarious.

The mill areas, as we have seen earlier, were witnessing a moment of upward mobility, attendant with changes in ownership as well as in the built form. At the same time, industrial restructuring precipitated multiple forms of insecurities in these neighbourhoods. Compensation for workers was fraught with complications, since the mills declared bankruptcy and the sale of the mill lands were hampered by years of litigation and land disputes. As payments started trickling in, however, the landscape of these neighbourhoods changed dramatically, and one can map the geographies of compensation. The first investment made by the former mill workers was in refurbishing the existing chawls. Workers, who even after fifty years of service had not been able to add a second storey to their chawls, could now afford (although for a brief moment) to invest in renovating their residences.[112] On the foundations of the original low-roofed, white-washed one- or two-roomed structure, two or sometimes three storeys were added. The walls were tiled, cement floors were laid indoors and, most importantly, as a marker of social respectability, an attached toilet and bathroom were added. A new aesthetic was being actively produced in these areas—new furniture was acquired, and shelves were fitted on the walls, which would display the 'good' kitchen articles and decorative items. Over the years, space was made for other markers of social status—a television, often hoisted on a wall, a refrigerator, and studio portraits of the family proudly displayed across the room. This move towards a visible upward mobility in a time of unemployment was even more dramatic than the establishment of the housing cooperative societies a few decades earlier. However, the very act of refurbishment moved these residences into a zone of illegality, since the requisite building permissions had not been acquired from the municipal corporation.

The period from 1985 onwards proved to be significant in even more ways. Coinciding with the closure of the mills, the city experienced prolonged periods of communal violence. The first significant wave of communally motivated transfers of property began at this point, which I discuss in the next chapter. The terrain of these industrial neighbourhoods was indelibly altered with the closure of the mills. The physical structures of the mill buildings were torn down over the next few years, leaving vast empty spaces as reminders. With the mills gone, what would happen to mill neighbourhoods? In other words, how was social space transformed following the changes that accompanied the urban and industrial restructuring of the mid-1980s?

To begin with, there was considerable dispute over the ownership of the lands on which the closed mills stood. These immense tracts of land, in many cases, had been acquired by the mill agents on long-term and even permanent leases. With the closure of the mills, the control of the mill lands was handed over to the official liquidator, as assigned by the Gujarat High Court. The liquidator was tasked with the process of 'winding up', the sale of machinery and auctioning the land. One form of land disputes centred around the 'original landlords' renewing their claims on properties that had been leased out for nearly a century—as did Vishnubhai Fulabhai Desai over the land of Arbuda Mills.[113] The rental rights that the mill companies held were challenged, as in the case of Prasad Mills and Jubilee Mills, on the grounds that as tenants—the mills, their agents or the official liquidator—they had no authority to sell or transfer the lands.[114]

Others involved chawl dwellers asserting their rights over their homes. The disputes surrounding the sale of Vijay Mills powerfully illustrates the tensions at the heart of the process of retrenchment and displacement, allowing us to investigate the multiple dimensions of claim making. It outlines the ambivalence of employment in establishing tenancy rights—documenting the shift from employment relations validating tenancy to the annulment of work relations as central to lawful possession of properties. Vijay Mills closed down in 1988 and was handed over to the official liquidator in 1993.[115] In 2005, the TLA appealed to the High Court seeking an expedient sale of the mill lands and alleging that the official liquidator had allowed an 'encroacher' to take possession of part of the premises. The 'encroacher' was identified in the case documents as M/s Amin Traders owned by one Mr Mansuri. The TLA's case stated Mansuri was neither a tenant of the mill-owned Krishna chawl nor an employee of Vijay Mills, but was 'merely' a contractor for opening empty bobbins. They further argued that he had installed machines, made alterations to the built structures and rented out the premises for marriages and dinner parties. Mansuri responded that he had been in legal possession of the factory and godown for over twenty years, engaged in reeling yarn for Vijay Mills. He had been paying rent since, at least, December 1987 and produced rent receipts from Krishna chawl to verify this. The 'alterations to the construction' that the TLA accused him of were, in fact, the repairs that he had had to undertake after the destruction of his factory and machinery in the violence of 2002. The TLA challenged the veracity of the rent receipts and argued that as a contractor, Mansuri had neither been an employee of the mill nor, as a consequence, a tenant of Krishna chawl. While the court did rule Mansuri to be an unauthorised occupier, it did concede that as a tenant his claims to the property would not cease with the closure of the mill.[116]

Mansuri's claims treaded the ambivalent territory between rights related to employment and the rights stemming from tenancy. In many cases previously, such as in the Gujarat Housing Board quarters, these two forms of rights coincided, with tenancy being linked explicitly to employment. At this point, however, we see a bifurcation of this braided claim, as rightful possession seemed to be increasingly dependent on the tenants *not* having been mill workers.

Another case around the same Krishna chawl echoes this shift, as possession was sought to be confirmed on the basis of independent tenancy and not as former employees. Instead, there was a clear renunciation of claims emerging from employment, as tenants of Krishna chawl explicitly affirmed their status as *tenants* and not as *employees*. In 2008, other residents of Krishna chawl, which is located on the mill premises and was built by the mill company in the late 1930s, appealed to the court seeking protection against eviction notices served to them by the official liquidator the previous year. The residents petitioned claiming that they had never been employees of Vijay Mills, but were instead independent tenants and were therefore protected by the Rent Control Act. They contended that their claims on the chawl were not invalidated, since 'by virtue of the order of liquidation, the relationship between the landlord and the tenant does not come to an end and the applicants continue to be lawful *tenants* of the Mills company in liquidation' (emphasis mine).[117]

The counsel for the office of the liquidator argued, on the other hand, that the chawl was, in fact, constructed for the workers of the mill and the present tenants were either former mill workers or their legal heirs or had derived their titles from them.[118] As such, their claims on this property were curtailed as soon as the mill went into liquidation, since the employer–employee relationship between the residents and Vijay Mills had come to an end.

Following previous court judgments, the Gujarat High Court ruled that the mere possession of rent receipts, tax bills and electricity bills were not sufficient to establish lawful tenancy. In the absence of a valid rental contract, the relationship between the landlord and the tenant continued to be an unsound one, no matter how historically established the possession or occupation of the rental property may be. The rent receipt, which lay at the heart of the operations of rental security, was supplanted by other evidentiary documents. Despite the evidence of possession of the chawls for the last several decades, the court instructed the liquidator to use all means necessary, including coercive police action, should the tenants not leave peacefully.[119] The Rent Control Act, which had so far given the chawls a far greater tenurial security, was now invoked to do precisely the opposite—through section 13 (1)f of the Act which allowed for evictions if the tenancy was based on employment.[120]

These court judgments should have eased the sale of this 27,129 square metre plot of land as all 'impediments' to this sale had been removed. Instead, the Vijay Mills land auction was caught in another imbroglio. This final legal dispute over the future of Vijay Mills opened up broader questions of social rights and workers' compensation. The land was set to be auctioned and advertisements had been placed in the local newspapers when, in 2011, the state of Gujarat appealed to the High Court declaring the auction to be invalid, as the state had already acquired possession of this land under the Urban Land Ceiling Act.[121] News reports stated that this land, thus acquired, was to be allotted to the municipal corporation for the construction of social housing.[122] Though this was challenged by the TLA, the mill lands were never sold and now house a part of the Sabarmati riverfront relocation housing. Layers of property claims and counter claims were inscribed upon this space. Tenancy rights that were ruptured in the process of deindustrialisation were sought to be restored through an abrogation of the residents' connection to the textile mills. The mill workers and their historic claims on chawl lands disappeared in this framing of property relations, leaving only the figure of the tenant as a salient category with which to negotiate this new precarity.

The TLA continued to play an intermediary role, though their involvement in securing compensation has been routinely accused of corruption. The union positioned itself as a mediator, even against the wishes of the former mill workers. In 2004, the TLA petitioned the High Court to take possession of about seventy-two chawls attached to the Amruta Mills Ltd. and to initiate the process of selling them to the present residents.[123] A host of applications were filed countering the TLA's plea—collectively, by the Amruta Mills Tenement Occupier Association, as well as individually—arguing that the union was neither authorised nor competent to approach the court. The Amruta Mills compound in Saraspur, which is a vast expanse of about 138,000 square metres, is now used as a tethering spot for horses, a storage area for construction material, *shamianas* and tents, sorting ground for rubbish, rented out for functions, and so on. On one part of this land were seventy-two chawls that were owned by the Amruta Mills Company. 'The moot question' that the court posed again centred on the employment history of the tenants.[124] The court ruled the tenancy to be unlawful, contending that the occupation of the chawls had been effected through an employer–employee relationship, thus negating the applicants' claim of a tenant–landlord relationship. Tenurial rights were thus enfeebled as the conditions for lawful tenancy were dramatically reconfigured with the mill closures. That there were disputes over property titles was hardly a new development.[125] Across South Asian cities, informality is often embedded in property regimes of the urban poor.[126] From slums, to chawls, to other impermanent or semi-permanent residential structures are suffused with what Appadurai terms 'spectrality', a terrain of fantasy and speculation, overcrowding and improvisation.[127] What was significant for Ahmedabad in this period was, however, the un-making of earlier historic claims and the emergence of new forms of establishing ownership.

In some situations, former mill workers have been able to organise and initiate collective struggles for their homes. Pickers ni Chaali in Saraspur is a case in point. The chawl named after the occupation of most of the residents—production of pickers, a component of the textile loom—was built by the Ahmedabad Fine Spinning and Weaving Company. This work, involving leather, was done mostly by Dalit workers. Himmatbhai, a Congress Party worker and self-identified leader of the residents of Pickers ni Chaali, provided a brief history of the settlement:

Nobody else would work with leather, upper castes wouldn't do this work. They said we will give you a place to settle in permanently, whether the factory is still running or not.... The pickers' workshop shut down because fibre and plastic replaced the leather and leather pickers weren't in demand any more. The factory closed down, but where should the people go? The rent was paid, but nobody would come to collect it.[128]

The key problematic defining residence in this case, as well as the earlier ones that we have examined, is centred around whether claims on the property derived from an employment relationship or one of tenancy. Here too we see that there was considerable overlap of these two forms of claims. However, it was made clear (in the retelling at least, which, in part, signifies the importance of the relationship) that the relationship established between the landlord and the chawl residents was one of tenancy and one that was explicitly *not* dependent on employment.

In 2008, Kishansingh Tomar, a Congress politician and former member of the municipal corporation, came to the chawl claiming that he had bought the land and attempted to evict the residents. He had acquired the closed leather factory and the land attached to it, which included about 350 chawls.[129] He allegedly 'passed derogatory remarks on [the] victims' social status' and 'threatened to burn [our] houses if we don't vacate in a given period of time'.[130] The residents, despite having paid municipal dues and property taxes for the last several decades, were now threatened with eviction. Himmatbhai relied on his superior 'knowledge' from years of political work.[131]

> We pelted him with stones and he ran.... He is a very big man, I go to his house now, drink water there.... But I taught him a lesson.... I lodged the Atrocities Act against him, but then got him out too.... He won't do this again.... It even came out in the papers that he evicted 10 chawls without ever going to prison, but was jailed despite being unable to clear this chawl.[132]

Here, we have a case when residents have been able to wrest control of their homes, not so much by staking a tenurial claim, but by collectively mobilising, drawing on the resources of local leadership while simultaneously citing legal provisions. Unlike in Bombay, where the question of former mill workers' housing rights and chawl redevelopment emerged as a political issue, mill workers in Ahmedabad have mainly fought tiring long battles in court, without gaining any substantial political visibility.

The cases discussed here represent, in a sense, local and fairly routine struggles over land and property. However, when seen in the context of the broader transformations that were occurring in the mill neighbourhoods, they testify to more pervasive changes. In the last decade, the eastern parts of the city have witnessed some dramatic reorganisation of its built environment. Ahmedabad's remaking was in part propelled by urban development missions as the JNNURM. Alongside an expanded slum rehabilitation policy and regulation of urban employment such as street vending, three projects are crucially responsible for the alteration of the landscape of eastern Ahmedabad—the bus rapid transit system, which circles the entire city and opens up access to the erstwhile mill areas; the Sabarmati Riverfront Development Project, which has made a very dedicated attempt to 'clean up' and 'gentrify' the industrial east; and the ongoing redevelopment of the closed mills, which are changing the character of these areas.[133] The Bus Rapid Transit System (BRTS) corridor is considered to be a 'catalyst' for future development of eastern Ahmedabad, stimulating the rejuvenation of former mill lands and promoting new residential and commercial options for the urban poor along its route.[134] Apart from a few mill properties, which were acquired by state agencies for public housing or industrial development, most became sites of gentrified redevelopment, steadily altering the social textures of these former solidly industrial neighbourhoods. As the mill properties entered the land market in the mid-2000s, tentative investments were launched. The image of eastern Ahmedabad as an 'unsafe' and 'unclean' space was vigorously countered, on the one hand, by mega state undertakings such as the Sabarmati Riverfront Development Project and, on the other, through investments by large realty firms. Urban development of this sort has unfolded across India in the recent years and Ghertner, to my mind, points out a critical conceptual slippage in collapsing a vast range of political, economic and regulatory transformations under the rubric of 'gentrification'.[135] While parts of this process as it has occurred in contemporary Ahmedabad have taken the form of 'urban enclosure', by which 'public' lands occupied by the poor are cleared for private development, other dimensions point towards a regime of accumulation by dispossession, underscored to some extent by the logic of gentrification.

The value of mill lands and the ease with which they were disposed of also depended on their location within the area.[136] As Desai convincingly argues in her doctoral dissertation, the politics of 'othering' was certainly influential in determining land prices. Whether a plot was situated in a 'disturbed area' with a history of communal violence or whether it was located at the borders of Hindu and Muslim parts of the neighbourhood mattered. For instance, while the reserve price for Himadri Textile Mills was fixed at INR 140 million,[137] the tenders received quoted only INR 109.5 million. Such low bids were attributed to unattractive locations.[138] In the case of Himadri Textile Mills, however, one can identify a fairly clear trajectory of gentrification. The former textile mill in Saraspur was acquired by Indiabulls Real Estate for the construction of a housing society. The area, otherwise overspread with chawls, is now dominated by concrete towers of Indiabulls Centrum, advertised as an 'urban oasis' with 'an aesthetic blend of lush and luxury'.[139]

Other corporate real estate investments in the industrial east continued, accelerating in the first decade of the twenty-first century. The Safal Group, for instance, has been actively involved in redeveloping mill lands—Jupiter Mills was remade as a business and commercial centre and the Fine Knitting Mill Compound developed as 'designer factory units'.[140] The Arvind Mills group, one of the few surviving mill companies, entered into a partnership with the Safal Group to develop some of their 600-acre holdings in the city. The first project planned by the mill group was a residential and commercial complex on the lands of Rohit Mills.[141] The geographies of urban investment aligned with the broader global shifts, as mill lands were (re)produced as real estate assets.[142] The collapse of the textile industry and the fragmentation of the social, political and legal claims exercised by the mill workers over the land of the industrial east were underscored by a movement from industrial to financial capitalism. This is not to posit an argument for an overarching de-industrialisation of Ahmedabad, but rather to signal the dislocation of industrial production from the inner urban core to its peripheries.

The attempts to remake the industrial east (especially the mill areas) with investments in infrastructure, urban beautification projects, and commercial and affluent housing ventures has resulted in both a shrinking of available land for the urban working poor and an increased tenurial vulnerability. At the same time, urban development policies through slum upgradations and acquisition of mill properties introduced claims which remained in tension with the ways in which space was actually used in these neighbourhoods. Property relations of the working poor are placed within overlapping and, often, contradictory registers of formal and social regulation—that is, the pressures from above in the form of state regulations and legislations and the claims or constraints on space from below, as in the case of the mill lands. In our discussion on the Disturbed Areas Act in the next chapter, we follow the dynamics of property to find a greater interaction and (often cohesion) between the state regulations prohibiting the transfers of property and social forces encouraging or enforcing communal segregation.

NOTES

1 The city's population grew from 116,873 in 1872 to 274,007 in 1921. See Gillion, *Ahmedabad: A Study in Indian Urban History*, 104.

2 Ibid.; Raychaudhuri, 'Colonialism, Indigenous Elites and the Transformation of Cities in the Non-Western World'; *Municipal Taxation and Expenditure for the Bombay Presidency, 1898–99* (Bombay, 1900).

3 Gillion, *Ahmedabad: A Study in Indian Urban History*.

4 Ibid., 120–6.

5 Ibid., 146.

6 Jhabvala, *Closing Doors*, 42.

7 Abigail McGowan, 'Ahmedabad's Home Remedies: Housing in the Re-Making of an Industrial City, 1920–1960', *South Asia: Journal of South Asian Studies* 36, no. 3 (2013): 397–414, 405.

8 Textile Labour Association (TLA), *A Plea for Municipal Housing for the Working Classes in the City of Ahmedabad* (Ahmedabad: Labour Union Press, 1929), 21.

9 McGowan, 'Ahmedabad's Home Remedies', 397–414.

10 Breman, *Making and Unmaking of an Industrial Working Class*, 53.

11 TLA, *A Plea for Municipal Housing for the Working Classes in the City of Ahmedabad*, 3.

12 *AMA Report* 1927–28, 101–02.

13 TLA, *A Plea for Municipal Housing for the Working Classes in the City of Ahmedabad*, 3.

14 *Times of India*, 19 September 1927.

15 TLA, *A Plea for Municipal Housing for the Working Classes in the City of Ahmedabad*, 15.

16 *Report on an Enquiry into Working-Class Family Budgets in Ahmedabad* (Bombay: 1928); TLA, *A Plea for Municipal Housing for the Working Classes in the City of Ahmedabad*, 15; *TLA Annual Report*, 1928.

17 *Report on an Enquiry into Working-Class Family Budgets in Ahmedabad* (1928); *Labour Gazette*, July 1927, 1038.

18 *Report on an Enquiry into Working-Class Family Budgets in Ahmedabad* (1928).

19 *Labour Gazette*, Bombay, January 1927, 339–40.

20 *RCLI* Vol. 1, Part 1, 4.

21 *RCLI* Vol. 1, Part 1, 24; Breman, *The Making and Unmaking of an Industrial Working Class*, 61–62.

22 Interview with Jigneshbhai Waghela, Ahmedabad, 16 November 2011.

23 Arup Kumar Sen, 'Mode of Labour Control in Colonial India', *Economic and Political Weekly* 37, no. 38 (2002): 3956–66.

24 *RCLI* Vol. 1, Part 2, 69–75, 113–116.

25 TLA, *A Plea for Municipal Housing for the Working Classes in the City of Ahmedabad*, 21.

26 *RCLI* Vol. 1, Part 1, 279.

27 *Times of India*, 25 June 1927.

28 *Said Maher Husein v. Haji Alimohamed Jalaludin*, Bombay High Court, 27 November 1933.

29 TLA, *A Plea for Municipal Housing for the Working Classes in the City of Ahmedabad*, 21–32.

30 TLA Note submitted to consulting surveyor general of Bombay in 1937, enclosure 2 in TLA, *A Plea for Municipal Housing for the Working Classes in the City of Ahmedabad*, 3.

31 TLA, *A Plea for Municipal Housing for the Working Classes in the City of Ahmedabad*, 23; see also McGowan, 'Ahmedabad's Home Remedies.'

32 *Times of India*, 24 May 1934.

33 *Times of India*, 15 June 1939. Siddhartha Raychaudhuri argues that some of these interventions in housing were a way of recalibrating workers' neighbourhoods, breaking up older structures of patronage and creating a 'homogenous' working class. This was effected through the spatial strategies of mill owners and the city's elites, primarily through enforced intermixed living in the industrial neighbourhoods. While the AMA's involvement in housing did undoubtedly transform living arrangements in the mill areas, the evidence presented in this book suggests that caste, religion and regional identity continued to be significant in organising housing in the 1930s and 1940s. Please see Raychaudhuri, 'Colonialism, Indigenous Elites and the Transformation of Cities in the Non-Western World', 718.

34 *Times of India*, 13 June 1935.

35 McGowan, 'Ahmedabad's Home Remedies'; Mehta and Mehta, 'Metropolitan Housing Markets'; *Times of India*, 13 June 1935; *Report of the Rent Enquiry Committee*, Vol. 3, Part 4 (Bombay: 1938), 25–30.

36 S. K. Pathan, V. K. Shukla, R. G. Patel, B. R. Patel and K. S. Mehta, 'Urban Land Use Mapping: A Case Study of Ahmedabad City and Its Environs', *Journal of the Indian Society of Remote Sensing* 19, no. 2 (1991): 95–112, 104. The AMA pushed for the inclusion of the eastern suburbs to decrease the 'double taxation'—on raw material entering the city and on the finished product passing through municipal limits to the railway station—that they otherwise had to bear. *Times of India*, 30 August 1932.

37 *Report on an Enquiry into Working-Class Family Budgets in Ahmedabad* (Bombay: 1937), 42.

38 *Times of India*, 19 May 1934. See also McGowan, 'Ahmedabad's Home Remedies'.

39 *TLA Annual Report*, 1949–50.

40 'Six Decades of the TLA: 1917–1977', 42, available at http://www.indialabourarchives.org.

41 *TLA Annual Report*, 1949–50.

42 Ravi Ahuja, 'A Beveridge Plan for India? Social Insurance and the Making of the "Formal Sector"', *International Review of Social History* 64, no. 2 (2019): 207–48.

43 *Times of India*, 15 August 1948.

44 *Times of India*, 1 November 1948.

45 *Times of India*, 2 October 1946. This was in contrast to the spatial form of the Bombay mill chawls, which were, by and large, multi-storeyed buildings with shared facilities. For a detailed account of workers' housing in Bombay, please see Neera Adarkar, ed., *The Chawls of Mumbai: Galleries of Life* (Delhi: ImprintOne, 2011).

46 Desai, *Directory of Ahmedbad Mill Industry 1929 to 1933*, 12; *Majoor Sandesh*, 14 February 1951.

47 TLA note submitted to consulting surveyor general of Bombay, enclosure 2 in TLA, *A Plea for Municipal Housing for the Working Classes in the City of Ahmedabad*.

48 *TLA Annual Report*, 1953, 34.

49 Radha Kumar, 'Family and Factory: Women in the Bombay Cotton Textile Industry, 1919–1939', *Indian Economic and Social History Review* 20, no. 1 (1983): 81–96.

50 Jhabvala, *Closing Doors*; *Majoor Sandesh*, 2 February 1924.

51 Jhabvala, *Closing Doors*, 47.

52 *Majoor Sandesh*, 2 February 1924.

53 Ibid.

54 *Report on an Enquiry into Working-Class Family Budgets in Ahmedabad* (1928); *Report on an Enquiry into Working-Class Family Budgets in Ahmedabad* (1938), 11.

55 Jhabvala, *Closing Doors*, 45–55.

56 Ibid., 27.

57 Ibid., 48.

58 *RCLI* Vol. 1, Part 1, 279.

59 TLA, *Five Decades at a Glance: A Brief Review of the Activities of the Association from 1971 to 1967* (Ahmedabad: TLA, 1971), 25.

60 *TLA Annual Report*, 1950, 47–48.

61 *TLA Annual Report*, 1953, 4.

62 *TLA Annual Report*, 1950, 47–48.

63 Ibid., 46.

64 *Majoor Sandesh*, 6 January 1951.

65 AITUC, *Index Fraud in Ahmedabad: AITUC's Note sent to the Experts Committee on Ahmedabad Index* (New Delhi: AITUC, 1964), 12.

66 *TLA Annual Report*, 1949, 66–67.

67 *Labour Gazette*, Bombay, March 1937, 532; for a similar dynamic in Delhi, please see Anish Vanaik, *Possessing the City: Property and Politics in Delhi, 1911–1947* (Oxford: Oxford University Press, 2019).

68 Referred to select issues of *Majoor Sandesh*, 1951–69.

69 See *Majoor Sandesh*, 31 March 1951; *Majoor Sandesh*, 9 May 1951.

70 *Majoor Sandesh*, 7 March 1951.

71 Bobbio, 'Collective Violence, Urban Change and Social Exclusion', 164.

72 *Majoor Sandesh*, 2 June 1951.

73 Bobbio, 'Collective Violence, Urban Change and Social Exclusion', 159.

74 *Times of India*, 14 March 1914.

75 *Times of India*, 1 September 1933.

76 Douglas E. Haynes and Nikhil Rao, 'Beyond the Colonial City: Re-Evaluating the Urban History of India, Ca. 1920–1970', *South Asia: Journal of South Asian Studies* 36, no. 3 (2013): 317–35.

77 Select resolutions of the Estate Department, AMC. Interview with Amrutbhai Solanki, estate officer, AMC, Ahmedabad, 8 January 2012.

78 *Times of India*, 21 September 1949.

79 *Times of India*, 25 December 1954 and 27 December 1953; AMC resolutions: no. 1083 dated 22 July 1952, no. 892 dated 13 October 1953, no. 1326 dated 19 January 1954, no. 853 dated 26 August 1954; *Majoor Sandesh*, 2 June 1951.

80 See, for instance, Town Planning Scheme 9, Rajpur Hirpur, AMC, 1959.

81 *Majoor Sandesh*, 28 March 1951.

82 *Majoor Sandesh*, 9 July 1958.

83 *O.L. of Aryodaya Spinning and Weaving Mills v. Charansingh Dhupsingh*, Gujarat High Court, 16 April 2004.

84 Bimal Hasmukh Patel, 'The Space of Property Capital, Property Development and Architecture in Ahmedabad' (Berkeley: University of California, 1995), 90; *Chandulal Vadilal v. Government of Bombay*, Bombay High Court, 5 August 1942.

85 Mahesh P. Bhatt and V. K. Chavda, *The Anatomy of Urban Poverty: A Study of Slums in Ahmedabad City* (Ahmedabad: Gujarat University, 1979), 20. Bhatt and Chavda suggest the term 'chawl slum' to capture the similarities between the two forms. Studies reported that there was a variation in the income and occupational profiles of the residents of these two forms of housing.

86 AMC, 'A Report on the Census of Slums', 3.

87 Pandya, 'Land Markets in Ahmedabad Metropolitan Region'.

88 One study records that the majority of the chawl dwellers paid between INR 5 and INR 9, while another reports that most households spent between INR 10 and INR 15 on rents. Exact figures for every year are difficult to arrive at, but one can safely approximate that rents were uniformly low in the mill areas. See Bhatt and Chavda, *The Anatomy of Urban Poverty*; Pramod Verma, *Profile of Labour* (Ahmedabad: Academic Book Centre, 1981).

89 *TLA Annual Report*, 1961–62, 20; *TLA Annual Report*, 1962–63, 24.

90 *TLA Annual Report*, 1964, 22.

91 Bombay Rents, Hotel and Lodging House Control (Gujarat Extension and Amendment) Act, 1963, 266.

92 *TLA Annual Report*, 1963–64, 28.

93 'AMC Revised Development Plan 1975–1985', 13.

94 Shani, *Communalism, Caste and Hindu Nationalism*, 123.

95 Ibid., 122–23; *Times of India*, 16 April 1970.

96 Slum Areas Act, 1973, 135.

97 *Times of India*, 23 December 1975.

98 AMC resolution no. 2012, dated 26 December 1973.

99 AMC correspondence. Reference No. RNTS 253 dated 17 December 1973. This proposal does not seem to have been approved since a later resolution from 1996 again mentions that Vira Bhagat ni Chaali would be protected from eviction for the next ten years. This was an experience with many chawls acquired by the AMC for their slum upgradation project.

100 The Bombay Rents, Hotel and Lodging House Rates Control Act, 1947 (henceforth Rent Control Act), 2528.

101 World Bank. *The Slum Networking Project in Ahmedabad: Partnering for Change, Water and Sanitation Program* (Washington D.C.: World Bank, 2007), 2; *Parivartan and Its Impact: A Partnership Programme of Infrastructure Development in Slums of Ahmedabad City* (SEWA Academy, 2002), 35ff., available at https://www.mahilahousingtrust.org/wp-content/uploads/Parivartan-Impact-Study_Final.pdf, accessed 26 June 2021.

102 *Times of India*, Ahmedabad edition, 8 March 1997.

103 'The Parivartan Slum Upgradation Programme', Gujarat Mahila Housing SEWA Trust, available at http://www.habitat.org/lc/housing_finance/pdf/Ms.Bijal_Brahmbhatt_Housing_Finance_D4.pdf, accessed on 13 November 2015.

104 *Times of India*, Ahmedabad edition, 8 March 1997.

105 Gujarat Government Notification no. F8/2/90 dated 17 June 1992.

106 Form 7/12, accessed 6 April 2013.

107 *Ghulam Mohammad Musabhai v. Ujiben Mulabhai*, Gujarat High Court, 2011.

108 These auctions implied that the AMC could take over these lands at a cost as nominal as INR 1 (interview with Amrutbhai Solanki, AMC, Estate Department, Ahmedabad, 8 January 2012).

109 *Ghulam Mohammad Musabhai v. Chaturbhai Dalabhai heirs and L/R of Moghiben Dalabhai*, Gujarat High Court, 22 February 2011.

110 This proposed practice of selling entire lines of chawls together has continued since. This was particularly visible during property transfers after episodes of communal violence, as more and more residences changed hands.

111 Breman, *The Making and Unmaking of an Industrial Working Class*, 255.

112 Interviews with Jigneshbhai Waghela, 2011–12.

113 For instance, when Arbuda Mills went into liquidation in 1995, Vishnubhai Fulabhai Desai approached the Gujarat High Court to reclaim what he reported were his ancestral lands. He contended that in 1929, when the property was handed over on a permanent lease to Arbuda Mills, it was declared that the company would be a 'tenant' and Desai and his predecessor-in-title were the 'landlords' of the property. Invoking the Bombay Rent Control Act, Desai argued that as tenants, the mills and the official liquidator had 'no authority to transfer, sell, or otherwise dispose of the lands in question'. The TLA was also party to this suit; as the sole representative union, the union had retained its authority to mediate in all legal matters involving the city's mill workers. The court dismissed the appeal, stating that 'the applicants are at most entitled to receive their rent as per the provisions contained in the Lease Deed'. *Desai Vishnubhai Fulabhai v. O.L. of Arbuda Mills*, Gujarat High Court, 9 May 2005, 3.

114 *Jabal C. Lashkari v. Official Liquidator of Prasad Mills*, Supreme Court of India, 29 March 2016; *Anilkumar Vaikuthlal Patel v. Official Liquidator of Ahmedabad Jubilee Mills*, Gujarat High Court, 26 March 2020.

115 Liquidation list, Ahmedabad, available at www.companyliquidator.gov.in.

116 *TLA v. O.L. Vijay Mills*, Gujarat High Court, 22 February 2005.

117 *Rameshbhai Tank and ors v. O.L. of Vijay Mills Ltd*, Gujarat High Court, 13 August 2008, 3.

118 Ibid., 6

119 Ibid.

120 Rent Control Act 1947.

121 *State of Gujarat v. O.L. Vijay Mills*, Gujarat High Court, 28 November 2011.

122 *DNA India*, 24 April 2010.

123 *Textile Labour Association v. O.L. of Amruta Mills*, Gujarat High Court, 30 September 2004, 1.

124 *TLA v. O.L. of Amruta Mills Ltd.*, Gujarat High Court, 30 September 2004, 3.

125 See, for instance, *Smt. Chandrakanta v. Vadilal Bapalal Modi*, Gujarat High Court, 30 March 1989, wherein claims of ownership were articulated through tenancy and rental payments.

126 A rich body of literature has documented and analysed the structures of informality in the production of urban poor settlements. A small selection includes: Ananya Roy, 'Why India Cannot Plan Its Cities: Informality, Insurgence and the Idiom of Urbanization', *Planning Theory* 8, no. 1 (2009): 76–87; D. Asher Ghertner, *Rule by Aesthetics: World-Class City Making in Delhi* (New York: Oxford University Press, 2015); Lisa Björkman, 'Becoming a Slum: From Municipal Colony to Illegal Settlement in Liberalization-Era Mumbai', *International Journal of Urban and Regional Research* 38, no. 1 (2014): 36–59.

127 Arjun Appadurai, 'Spectral Housing and Urban Cleansing: Notes on Millennial Mumbai', *Public Culture* 12, no. 3 (2000): 627–51.

128 Interview with Himmatbhai, Gomtipur, 6 December 2011.

129 *Times of India*, Ahmedabad edition, 14 March 2008.

130 Complainant Laxmi Makwana, quoted in *Times of India*, Ahmedabad edition, 14 March 2008.

131 Here, I use the term 'knowledge' as it was told to me—implying greater awareness and the wherewithal to negotiate with state agencies.

132 *Times of India*, Ahmedabad edition, 28 March 2008. While the news report did mention that Tomar was charged with the Atrocities Act, it did not mention his role in clearing ten other chawls.

133 While in Ahmedabad, this process of land redevelopment has been markedly slower than it was in Bombay, the pace has quickened considerably in the last decade. For detailed accounts of the tensions surrounding mill lands in Bombay, see Darryl D'monte, *Ripping the Fabric: The Decline of Mumbai and Its Mills* (New Delhi: Oxford University Press, 2002); Darryl D'monte, *Mills for Sale: The Way Ahead* (Mumbai: Marg Publications, 2006). AMC, *City Development Plan Ahmedabad 2006–2012: Jawaharlal Nehru National Urban Renewal Mission* (Ahmedabad: Ahmedabad

Municipal Corporation, Ahmedabad Urban Development Authority and CEPT University, 2006), 136.

134 'Leveraging Urbanisation in South Asia: Managing Spatial Transformation', World Bank, 2015, 122. 'BRTS India Experience', available at https://www.trafficinfratech.com/brts-india-experience/2/, accessed on 15 June 2020.

135 D. Asher Ghertner, 'India's Urban Revolution: Geographies of Displacement Beyond Gentrification', *Environment and Planning A* 46, no. 7 (2014): 1554–71.

136 Desai, 'The Globalising City in the Time of Hindutva', 300ff.

137 Ministry of Textiles, *Annual Report 2009–10*.

138 *BusinessLine*, 7 August 2007.

139 See http://realestate.indiabulls.com/centrumahmedabad/overview.php, accessed in July 2015.

140 Safal Promotional Brochure. See also *DNA India*, 14 April 2012.

141 *Times of India*, 1 May 2012.

142 For an interesting comparison of strategies of urban transformation, see Maria Kaika and Luca Ruggiero, 'Land Financialization as a "Lived" Process: The Transformation of Milan's Bicocca by Pirelli', *European Urban and Regional Studies* 23, no. 1 (2016): 3–22.

6

VIOLENCE, LAW AND 'GHETTOISATION'

In October 2012, Ahmedabad hosted India's first-ever 'Muslim' property show. It was a three-day affair showcasing properties in 'Muslim' areas of the city, such as Juhapura, Sarkhej and Vatva. The organiser of this exhibition, Ali Hussein of Ummat, a web portal for Muslim businesses in the city, understands this development as a way of tapping into a potential 'buyer group': 'There was already a mature need for this. Time, even more than me, has contributed to the success of this show.'¹ What exactly has the role of time been in creating this demand for 'Muslim' properties? What are the historical processes that have led to the production of two distinct and separate property markets in the city?

From the histories of chawl housing explored in the previous chapter, we now turn to questions of segregation and ghettoisation, which have critically shaped the dynamics of housing and property in Ahmedabad. A particular focus is placed on the enactment and implementation of the Prohibition of Transfer of Immovable Properties in Disturbed Areas Act of 1986, which, I contend, contributed heavily to the production of communalised spaces in the city. The juridical roots of present-day segregation of Ahmedabad could be traced back to the riots of 1985–86 and the legal strategies that were designed to contain it. What began as caste riots over the issue of reservations soon morphed into communal violence, rapidly gathering momentum in the working-class neighbourhoods of eastern Ahmedabad. This episode of violence (and those that followed) was marked by not just a loss of life and property, but also a reordering of social space, as neighbourhoods became increasingly communally homogenous. This demographic change was fuelled by rampant distress sales, which reached such alarming proportions during the riots of 1985–86 that the Gujarat government placed restrictions on property transfers in notified 'disturbed areas'. Contrary to its professed intentions, this piece of government legislation eventually formed the basis for the communalisation of the city's real estate and became the legal instrument through which ghettoisation was normalised.

Even during casual conversations in Ahmedabad, while taking an autorickshaw, for instance, or discussing where to eat, the notions of 'Hindu' and 'Muslim' areas surface regularly. The very categories of 'Hindu' and 'Muslim' (identities and space), as Desai and Shani argue, are increasingly fixed, naturalised and posed in antagonism to each other.[2] The Sabarmati River cements this dichotomy, with the western areas seen as Hindu and the eastern banks seen as Muslim. These local imaginaries of the city, the binaries of the 'Hindu' and 'Muslim' spaces, Fachandi suggests, articulate a desired outcome rather than an empirical reality.[3] For the demarcation of space is seldom so absolute; Hindus and Muslims live on both banks of the river and cohabitation is visible in some parts of the city. Yet these indexes of marking space are not merely symbolic but rather are produced through a complex of ideological, material and representational factors. This dichotomy is soldered through a legal and bureaucratic apparatus that has progressively limited the possibilities of inter-communal living. Specifically, property relations emerge as a key dimension and vector of social exclusion. Through this focus on property relations, this chapter aims to excavate the ways in which space is deployed as a political instrument.

Segregated living has historically been a part of Ahmedabad's landscape; the earlier architectural form of the pol is a case in point, as Raheel Dhattiwala suggests, which did not necessarily emerge from communal violence.[4] These densely packed residential arrangements in the walled city, while territorially contiguous and close, were often gated and spatially discrete. The beginnings of communally driven displacement in Ahmedabad can at least be traced to the violence of 1969. Formerly mixed areas, like the mill neighbourhood of Amraiwadi, turned predominantly Hindu. Reconstruction of riot-affected homes lagged in these areas—landlords were reluctant to repair damaged constructions as residents sought out other, safer areas to resettle in. The rehabilitation huts that were built by the government were gradually occupied by Hindus.[5] One of the resettlement sites allotted by the AMC was adjacent to the Gujarat Housing Board quarters in Bapunagar, in what grew to become the Indira Garibnagar slum. It was in Indira Garibnagar that one of the worst excesses of the violence of 1985—a day that the report of the Dave Commission described as 'free for all'—took place.[6]

On 22 April 1985, simultaneous to the attacks on newspaper offices,[7] communal violence gathered momentum in the industrial areas. According to the evidence presented to the inquiry commission, there were not only very obvious lapses in policing, but also direct police collusion in rioting. The sectarian violence, which was alleged to be supported by the mutinying police force, almost exclusively targeted working-class Muslims.[8] This episode foregrounds the tensions over urban land and highlights how communal violence and accompanying ruptures of property relations altered spatial demographics. The second part of the chapter focuses on one of the key state responses to incidents such as these—the enactment of the Prohibition of Transfer of Immovable Properties in Disturbed Areas Act of 1986. It draws out the ways in which the implementation, circumvention and expansion of this law reconfigured property regimes and shaped the urban property market. The two parts of the chapter, in a sense, represent two 'points' in the longer history of urban transformation, particularly with reference to communalisation and urban segregation. Or, in other words, the first section discusses one significant manifestation of sectarian tensions while the second traces the subterranean processes of legitimising and normalising spatial communalisation.

THE BAPUNAGAR RIOT AND TENSIONS OVER URBAN LAND

The violence of 1985 can be seen as a prolonged period of simmering caste conflict, punctuated regularly by communal violence. The unrest began in February 1985 against increased reservations and continued for seven months. Ornit Shani makes a convincing case for seeing multiple local conflicts and smaller riots within this long period of violence.[9] Drawing on the evidence presented to the Dave Commission, we can broadly outline five phases of communal unrest—(a) around 18 March, when communal rioting broke out in the walled city; (b) mid-April, when violence began in the walled city, escalated with the killing of a police officer in Khadia and spread towards the mill areas; (c) a few days later with the attacks in the mill locality of Bapunagar; (d) early May, when again rioting erupted over the murder of a police officer in the walled city and following the earlier spatial trajectory; and (e) again in June over the celebrations of religious festivals.[10]

A close reading of the extensively detailed list of incidents of unrest (both communal and anti-reservationist) included in the Dave Commission report indicates certain key aspects of the geography of conflict. Spearheaded primarily by upper-caste students' and parents' organisations—All Gujarat Educational Reform Action Committee (AGERAC), the umbrella anti-reservation group, Akhil Gujarat Navrachna Samiti and the Gujarat Vali Mahamandal (parents' association)—the initial phase of the anti-reservation agitation remained confined mainly to the more affluent, western parts of the city and the violence itself, limited to attacks on government property.[11] Thereafter, it moved to the walled city, particularly to the pols of Khadia. It was only after the first communal riots on 18 March that large anti-reservation protests took place in the mill areas of Gomtipur, Saraspur, Bapunagar and Amraiwadi, among others. There is evidence at this point of the involvement of anti-reservationists in the communal rioting.[12] Throughout this period, the caste agitation was spread out across the city—western neighbourhoods such as Navrangpura, inner-city localities such as Khadia and Kalupur, and some mill neighbourhoods were key sites. The communal unrest, on the other hand, barely ever moved to the western banks of the Sabarmati, barring a few stray incidents. The walled city was one locus of religious strife, while the most damaging episodes of violence occurred in the mill districts. Furthermore, a rather clear spatial dynamic emerges with respect to the movement of the communal conflict. Originating in the walled city, the rioting would then advance towards the mill areas, where it would often escalate.

A closer look at these 'smaller riots' within this period of violence can highlight the interplay between various levels of social and spatial practice of this period. By the 1970s, new circuits of political mediation had emerged. In part, it was connected to the TLA's declining influence, brought on by its political isolation and the crisis of the textile industry. The forms of political mediation that emerged during this period, then, did not necessarily replace but rather were often interlaced with the existing networks of local power and patronage. It was not, however, a mere perpetuation of older forms of mediation—the direction of these newer networks, their structural dynamics, their terms of engagement with the apparatus of the state and formal politics were oriented by the transformations in the city's political economy. The significance of criminality and corruption in the modes of mediation was reinforced in this changed social terrain of a rapidly swelling city and the expanding interstitial spaces and economies that emerged. There remained a tension between the way city space was being planned and governed (which allowed for acquisition, eviction and demolition) and spatial practice (in terms of the ways in which space was used and perceived). It was this very tension that, in turn, allowed for the emergence of a range of figures who had the capacities and clout to negotiate the problems of urban living. Broadly, we can contend that the fundamental shift in political practice and social space in the workers' neighbourhoods was one of increasing informality—an unmooring of mediatory practices from formal structures. By the mid-1980s, workers' livelihoods were threatened by the closure of the mills, while nearly simultaneously their claims on their homes were increasingly imperilled. How can we, then, place this narrative of marginalisation and precarious security against what occurred on 22 April 1985?

The riot itself unfolded at the intersection of various social, political and economic tensions—the material anxieties (in terms of livelihoods and residence) of the large numbers of textile workers, electoral calculations by various political groups, and intensive mobilisation by the Hindu Right (a process that can be traced back to the violence of 1969, and which had gathered momentum through the riots of 1973 and the Nav Nirman agitation). The BJP at this point was engaged in a careful balancing act between the upper and the lower castes and was actively engaged in re-working rather than restoring the Hindu caste order. To some degree, this had been achieved in Ahmedabad through a deep engagement with the social life of the industrial east, partly through the building of patronage networks, and partly through a process of social and ritual inclusion.

Between 21 and 23 April, parts of Bapunagar, located in the heart of the industrial belt, were attacked by armed upper-caste mobs. Indira Garibnagar slum, along with the neighbouring Gujarat Housing Board quarters (in particular, Blocks 16 and 12) were the primary sites of violence. Behind these were the apartment blocks from where many of the initial attacks were launched. These were a series of well-orchestrated, planned incursions directed at the workers' residences that were located between two sets of apartments buildings.[13] The majority of those killed, injured and displaced were Muslims.

According to the testimonies to the Dave Commission, the first violent mobilisations began in the afternoon of the 21st, when a large group of Hindus gathered outside Block 16, shouting slogans.[14] The aggression intensified and concerted assaults were launched in the evening of the following day.[15] Lasting until the early hours of the 23rd, the violence permanently altered the landscape of the area.[16] The attacks came from two directions—an armed crowd flanked by police jeeps that moved through the locality burning homes and businesses, and stone pelting from the nearby middle-class housing society. As the commission reported in its conclusions, this technique of violence was not unique to this particular case but had developed as a template that was deployed across the state. With active police involvement in nearly all incidents, the commission noted: 'There is strong evidence to suggest that Bungalow-walas and Housing Society walas did not like the Jhopadpattis in their neighbourhood and took advantage of this opportunity to burn them so that the poor Harijans and low caste people may be unsettled and settled down elsewhere.'[17]

This dynamic of settling and unsettling—through violence, demographic engineering and urban and industrial planning—was made swiftly and sharply visible in Bapunagar. With the collapse of the textile industry, investments as well as large numbers of former mill workers had shifted to the diamond polishing units.[18] Bapunagar, in particular, had witnessed, through the early 1980s, a phenomenal growth in the diamond polishing industries, which were largely controlled by the Patidar caste group. The Patidars, who had consolidated their position of economic dominance through the cooperative movement in rural Gujarat, were increasingly moving into private enterprise through the 1980s. This trajectory of Patidar economic influence coincided with their political isolation. With their historically dominant position within the Gujarat Congress slipping with the formation of the KHAM alliance, Patels were steadily moving towards alternative political options—from Chimanbhai Patel's Janata Dal to the BJP.[19] In Bapunagar, Patels established workshops and small factories alongside cooperative housing societies. They had interests in the local land market and, according to contemporary reportage, were involved in the rioting of April 1985.[20]

Land, by all accounts, had become increasingly profitable in eastern Ahmedabad. In this part of Bapunagar, a local akhada was alleged to have designs on the slums of Indira Garibnagar.[21] Wider networks of complicity were identified by Engineer, calling attention to the links between powerful local slumlords and political functionaries. The shadowy ties maintained between state agencies, politicians and local strongmen condensed at this point and became visible in the public performance of violence. Reports of this episode suggest active collusion between senior Congress Party members, municipal corporators, 'professional strike breakers' and slumlords in systematically clearing the predominantly Muslim slums of Indira Garibnagar.[22]

The significance of land in orienting the direction of violence has been highlighted in other accounts of the unrest of 1985. The Lok Adhikar Sangh fact-finding report suggests that as the rioting became progressively more widespread, landlords strategically deployed violence to evict settlers.[23] The *Times of India* reported in the aftermath of the violence:

> In mixed localities in Ahmedabad, the dominant group tries to damage the private properties of the rival community to grab land at throwaway prices. In the suburbs of Bapunagar and Saraspur, slumlords had let loose a reign of terror on one community to take possession of land and houses. And these slumlords were actively supported by the police in their dubious designs.[24]

Such an explanation for communal violence—which locates economic competition, more generally, and land grabbing, more specifically, as the prime triggers—is not peculiar to Ahmedabad and has been made for other Indian contexts.[25] However, it would be specious to suggest that these were purely economic motivations disconnected from the political field. The violence in Bapunagar cannot wholly be attributed to the avarice of particular businessmen or to 'vested' interests from outside or to a congealed body of 'anti-socials'. Rather, these actors were local and deeply embedded in the structures of neighbourhood politics. It was precisely because of their place in the city's political economy that the violence took this particular form.

The slumlord, in particular, could be seen in this case as performing a paradoxical role—involved in both settling and un-settling urban land. These two processes may appear opposed to each other, but a closer look can help place them within the web of local power relationships. These figures, as we have seen, had accumulated considerable political authority through mediating security of housing—ration cards and other documentary proof of tenancy were issued as a way of incorporating slum dwellers into electoral structures. Acquisition of official papers, then, became a way of staking a claim on the land, and riots, a way of severing those claims. In Bapunagar, in particular, many of the slums were located illegally on municipal land and were, thus, placed at the intersection of various competing interests.

Yagnik points to other dimensions of the relationship between the grey economy of land and violence, telegraphing the broader changes that were taking place in the city's economy: that is, politically connected slumlords were seeking to free land from Muslim and Dalit occupation for other investments.[26] This was the moment when the textile industry was disintegrating, and smaller, informal workshops and factories were proliferating. The communal violence, in this perspective, could have been used to rupture claims on land, either to make it available for more lucrative investments (for factories and workshops, or different kinds of residential settlements) or to re-order the social composition of such settlements. To suggest that this episode of violence was deeply tied to control over land is not to denude the violence of its ideological underpinnings; rather, it is to stress that property relations emerged as a key site of politics. The Bapunagar riot and the others that followed through the mid-1980s and 1990s altered the social geography of the city. The way social space was seen, property relations spoken of and property rights circulated was communalised, unwritten simultaneously with social, affective and legal markers of community identity.

More than 5,000 people from Bapunagar lost their homes over those two days and sought refuge in the Aman Chowk camp, the largest state-run relief camp in the city. In the testimonies to Dave Commission, it was recorded that the camp remained unattended by the state agencies for two days, while immediate aid was provided by Muslim organisations, and the Aman Chowk relief camp was seen as being established and supported exclusively by them.[27] Following this, Bapunagar was 'partitioned', with 'Hindu' and 'Muslim' parts divided by a border. Mixed neighbourhoods such as Morarji Chowk and Indira Garibnagar were transformed into uniformly Muslim and Hindu spaces.[28] This segregation of social space and the accompanying splintering of property ties were carried out primarily through distress selling.[29]

LAW AND THE REMAKING OF AHMEDABAD

Distress sales became a matter of such pressing concern during this period that the Gujarat government placed restrictions on property transfers in notified 'disturbed areas'. The Gujarat Prohibition of Transfer of Immovable Property and Protection of Tenants from Eviction from Premises in Disturbed Areas Act (the Disturbed Areas Act or 'Ashant Dhaara' as it is commonly known) was intended as a *temporary* measure to prevent ghettoisation after periods of communal violence. Evidence presented to the Dave Commission mentioned tensions over land and property as one of the key reasons for the continuing conflict. The testimony of Keshav Govindnarain Prabhu, a representative of the Nagrik Sangthan,[30] was recorded by the commission as follows:

The witness quoted one important ground for continuation of communal troubles and that is that of the purchase of properties of Hindus in Muslim majority areas. When one Muslim would like to buy the property, he hires gundas to create trouble in addition to nuisance. He quoted the example of Lalbawna Timba where Harijans were evicted. He discussed this with the Chief Minister, Shri Madhavsingh Solanki and he accepted this and immediately brought the legislation the 'Gujarat Prohibition of Transfer of Immovable Property and Protection of Tenants from Eviction from Premises in Disturbed Areas Act'.[31]

This extract relies on and reinforces a dominant prejudice of the mid-1980s and one that continues to resonate in present-day Ahmedabad—that Muslims, with close ties to the underworld, were driving Hindus out of their homes. This highly exaggerated paranoia formed part of the moral justification for the city's segregated spaces. News reports from the mid-1980s as well as scholarly work on the city indicate that scores of families moved en masse to what were perceived as 'safer' areas—essentially, those in which they would not be the minority.[32] Immediately following the violence of 1985–86, commentaries on the city's future imagined a grim fate. Beirut was invoked as the divided city par excellence and seen as the destiny towards which Ahmedabad was hurtling. News reports from the period alluded to a 'Beirut mentality',[33] as did accounts from violence-affected areas, arguing that this 'exodus' was a 'dangerous trend' and 'soon Ahmedabad will be divided like Beirut'.[34] The Nagrik Sangathan representative further deposed to the Dave Commission, stating:

If we continue to encounter this way of living that is allowing people to evict by coercion, force or illegal force, a day will come as is witnessed by him in the last 50 years, Gheekanta Road may be set in as the Green Line, as in Beirut between Christians and Muslims in 2000 AD, meaning thereby all people living eastern to Gheekanta will be Muslims and beyond that Hindus. Similarly, by 2025 AD, Sabarmati River may be the Green Line.[35]

While many accounts of this process suggest that the traffic of populations and the transfer of properties occurred both ways, it is undeniable that the city's Muslims (and the Muslim working classes, in particular) have been steadily dispossessed. The riots of 1969 initiated the first waves of forced displacement, the violence of 1985 further reinforced the patterns of spatial segregation, and the episodes of unrest through the 1990s and the pogrom of 2002 cemented the production of communally homogenous social space.

Tahirbhai's life story suggests a similar movement. A weaver at Nutan Mills, he and his family left their Gujarat Housing Board quarters in Bapunagar after the riots of 1969 to settle in a chawl in Rakhiyal, from which he moved to a chawl in Gomtipur in 1986. In 2003, he moved to a Muslim-majority area, Shamser Bagh, in Gomtipur. His trajectory is a disturbingly familiar one for many working-class Muslims in Ahmedabad—written into their lives, in the second half of the twentieth century and early twenty-first century, was constant and, often, forced movement. The threat of violence as well as the regular imposition of curfews during the mid-1980s motivated workers to shift to 'safer' areas.[36] Such restrictions on mobility and the threat of violence is what prompted former mill worker Rameshbhai Christian to decide to shift in the early 1990s from Shakra Ghanchi's chawl in Gomtipur to a poorly serviced neighbourhood attached to the Catholic Church in Vatva.

Property transfers, especially during moments of violence, were not only one-sided. However, the readjustment of Ahmedabad's population following every episode of violence was tacitly shored up by the practices and policies of urban planning and governance—especially with regard to the distribution of civic services and amenities, and the impetus towards the formation of specific housing arrangements such as cooperative housing societies—which reproduced and fortified community divisions.[37] Muslims facing systemic discrimination were often unable to find housing outside of those areas designated as 'Muslim', producing urban enclaves (or rather, ghettoes) of Muslim concentration that cut across class hierarchies. 'Red-lining' of the city's Muslim areas has resulted in an economic ghettoisation that accompanies the physical separation of communities.[38]

The implication that properties were transferred under the threat of violence was widely discussed and debated. Accounts from legislators, such as those presented during every successive appeal for amendments to the Disturbed Areas Act, framed the question of distress sales in terms of the anxiety and insecurity felt by those in the minority in 'mixed areas'.[39] The acknowledgement of the violence of 1985 as a critical moment in the formalisation of urban segregation is tempered with the suggestion that these property transactions were more or less symmetrical—that is, that the pressures on Hindus and Muslims to relocate were of equal intensity. Other sources suggest that the threats on mixed neighbourhoods were manifold. On the one hand, it came from the dominant community in these areas—in most cases, the majority Hindu community. The intimidation unfolded as the *India Today* reported: 'Even after the riots had died down, local toughs went around threatening the minority in their areas and scaring them into moving to other areas.[40] On the other hand, police persecution and harassment from state forces prompted some of the movement within the walled city—from predominantly Hindu neighbourhoods to Muslim-majority areas such as Jamalpur, Shahpur, and so on—and towards safer localities outside such as Sarkhej.[41]

The ordinance regulating the transfer of properties was issued in March 1985. Its intention presumably was to ensure that properties between communities were transferred without coercion and at a fair price. The larger objective of this legislation was to prevent ghettoisation in the city. Not only did the law fail in this, but it appears, instead, to have facilitated precisely that which it was framed to prevent. In effect, this law ensured that property in the city is signified through communal markers and that communalisation of real estate is given legitimacy. The colloquial understanding of the law, which in itself is revealing of the way the city is imagined, conceives of it as a measure restricting transfers of property between Hindus and Muslims. The use of this law, which consistently frames real estate through the lens of community, has reshaped the contours of housing not just across Ahmedabad but certainly more sharply in the working-class areas. The already limited space available for workers is then parcelled and circumscribed through religious markers.

The eastern part of the city had historically more heterogeneous neighbourhoods, mainly due to the practices of recruitment and settlement among mill workers. Occupation and recruitment in the textile mills were predominantly ordered along caste and community lines, and migration operated through regional networks. This constellation of caste, community and regional ties and similar dietary habits of Dalits and Muslims (the two groups that dominated mill work in Ahmedabad) resulted in somewhat mixed settlements, where one would find clusters of caste groups as well as migrants of one particular region living together.

The memory of the mixed neighbourhood and the narrative (and occasionally, a lament) of its loss dominate discussions of housing and its transformation in the present-day mill neighbourhoods. This is not to imply that the period before the mid-1980s was one of happy harmony—nostalgic narratives that suggest an easy cohabitation are also complicated by stories of segregation within the mills. Scholarly accounts of life in the mills illustrate the ways in which recruitment and employment along caste and religious lines produced a stratified workforce.[42] The TLA launched efforts to eliminate segregation within the mill; however, the very structure of the union, in a sense, bolstered caste and community distinctions within the workplace.

Caste-based segregation, then, appears to have been a part of factory life—for instance, reports published in the *Majoor Sandesh* in the early 1950s document the existence of separate water tanks and canteens for different castes.[43] However, rules for maintaining caste purity did not seem to have operated as rigidly when it came to habitation in the mill neighbourhoods.

Several kinds of accounts suggest that mixed working-class neighbourhoods are not fabricated out of a nostalgia for a lost past. It is the evidence of segregation that points most convincingly to the historic presence of the mixed neighbourhood. It is important to mention at this point that while the transformation of mixed neighbourhoods since the mid-1980s was mentioned to me several times during my fieldwork, the more specific transactions of actual property transfers were rather difficult to pin down. The narrative remained constant, however. In Hindu-majority mill areas, it was maintained that it was Dalits (the dominant caste group in these localities) who have had to leave, while the account is reversed in the Muslim-majority areas. Conversations often signalled that large intra-community property transfers had taken place in Gomtipur. Jeevanbhai marked out several chawls around the Gomtipur post office *chowk* as formerly belonging to Muslims. Khaddawli chawl, where Jigneshbhai Vaghela was born and still lives, had an almost equal distribution of Muslim and Dalit households when he was growing up. With the 'partition of chawls', as Jigneshbhai put it, it had in 2012 only a few Muslim families remaining. Amrita Shah writes of Abu Kasai ni Chaali in Gomtipur as a previously communally mixed space which has become markedly Hindu in the last few decades.[44]

The absence of details regarding the actual transfers and the mystery shrouding them in these designated disturbed areas is also revealing. At one point, I probed the question of property transfers in Gomtipur perhaps a little too forcefully. I was bluntly rebuffed and told that this line of questioning would invariably lead to trouble, when I tried to wrangle over specific details. Many of my interlocutors were reluctant to offer concrete evidence, concerned that they would be seen by other residents as trying to intervene in and foment disturbance in the delicate neighbourhood 'harmony'. These silences do not deny the transfers but, instead, perhaps point to their local significance.

However, we can trace through a comparison of municipal tax records that possession of these properties has certainly traded hands. Municipal property tax records show ownership in the name of members of a certain community, while current occupiers seem to belong to another. Admittedly, records of this kind point more to the complicated terrain of property rather than clarifying the genealogy of ownership or occupancy. While the legal title of the property may still rest with the original landowner, actual occupation and possession may have changed hands several times over, through the provision of 'power of attorney'.[45] Both of these read together can testify to a creeping segregation that has occurred more insidiously in the mill neighbourhoods and with greater visibility in the rest of the city.

The transfer of properties and the relocation of residents occurred between streets and chawl lines in the same neighbourhood.[46] The displacement of Muslim workers is, to some extent, contained within the mill districts, the sites of possible resettlement gradually expanding to include newer 'Muslim' areas such as Vatva and Juhapura. Contemporary Gomtipur, for instance, may give the impression of a 'mixed neighbourhood'. Zooming in, we can identify the pockets of communal homogeneity within these areas, the shifting borders that are signalled by temples and shrines and, sometimes, just a signboard, a gate or a flag, local idiom classifying areas as 'Hindu' or 'Muslim' (or increasingly, as India or Pakistan). Beginning in the mid-1980s and escalating through the 1990s, entire tracts of chawls in Gomtipur have shifted between communities. An already preferred mode of property transactions in the mill districts, the practice of transferring rows of chawls en masse, acquired a sinister charge as previously heterogeneous living spaces were whittled into religiously uniform ones. These transformations were not restricted to Gomtipur but instead resonated across the mill districts of the city.

Nearly all of eastern Ahmedabad, including the mill areas and the walled city, was notified as disturbed areas in the initial ordinance of 1985. News reports from the mid-1980s suggest that since the official numbers of property transfers were not alarming, the ordinance was not implemented very forcefully. Official statistics placed the number of transfers at 18, though unofficial sources indicated that not only had there been conceivably more than 1,000 such transactions, but also that 'the possibility of clandestine transfers could not be ruled out'.[47] By the end of 1986, the *India Today*'s estimates of property transfers were even larger: 'Already, some 2000 families have migrated from the walled city and are now buying or renting accommodation in the suburbs. Hindus and Muslims are steadily moving into areas where their respective communities are in a majority.[48]

Unlike in other areas of the country, such as the northeastern states, where similar legislations are enforced by the Home Department, in Ahmedabad the Disturbed Areas Act is administered by the Revenue Department. In the foreward to the *Collectors' Manual* published in 2007–08, Revenue Minister Anandiben Patel wrote:

> The Revenue Department is related to human beings from his birth to death. Whether he is the owner of land or not, each citizen has to come into contact with the Revenue offices for a major or minor work. Thus, the Revenue Department is the only Department, which has wide contacts with the common mass at large.[49]

This portrayal suggests that the department was involved in rather prosaic, quotidian affairs and the implementation of this 'extraordinary' legislation sat somewhat uneasily with the everyday transactions that the department was otherwise occupied with. First issued as a *temporary* measure to deal with an intensifying communal situation, it was ratified as a law in 1986. Not only has this otherwise provisional ordinance been made the rule, its spatial scope has been progressively expanded over the years, bringing large parts of the industrial east into its purview. It was seen, at one level, as a necessary impediment to further episodes of communal violence.[50] With its continued implementation as part of the Revenue Department's governmental responsibilities, this seemingly 'extraordinary' measure was not only formalised as a routine feature of the urban property market, but has also served to normalise the state of exception that triggered the development of the law.

The Act, which was passed on 26 October 1986, prohibited transfers of all immovable property in disturbed areas and further amended the existing Bombay Rent Control Act of 1947 to protect tenants in such areas from eviction. The original legislation made three critical interventions: One, it retrospectively annulled property transfers carried out between March 1985 (when the ordinance was issued) and October 1986 (when the law was enacted).[51] Two, it declared that no transfers could be made between October 1986 and March 1987 without the prior permission of the collector. For such transfers to be given legal validity, approval was to be sought from the collector's office, which, after an investigation, would declare whether the transfer had been made of the free will of both parties.[52] And three, new directives were added to the Bombay Rent Control Act which placed the responsibility of post-riot rehabilitation and reconstruction on landlords.

Those provisions which had so far entitled landlords to demand a standard rent or allowed eviction for non-payment of rent were suspended for certain periods. After the introduction of the Act by the Madhavsinh Solanki–led Congress government, successive governments have made no attempt to repeal it but have instead expanded its purview. Newer areas were designated as 'disturbed' by the state government, based on the reports of the local police.[53]

Despite the introduction of this Act, transfers had undoubtedly taken place—prompted by a feeling of insecurity and often coupled with coercion. Already by the end of the 1980s, neighbourhoods in the city had become almost entirely homogenous.[54] As this news report from the late 1990s details:

> Respective communities have been silently on the move in Ahmedabad over the past 15 years, turning scores of neighbourhoods with mixed populations into ghettoes of relative safety.[55]

The transformation of erstwhile mixed neighbourhoods, on the whole, has been insidious, stealthy and 'unlawful'. Most property transactions in the disturbed areas do not have the required clearance from the collector's office, nor do they have legal sales deeds. Instead, the transfers are given some amount of documentary proof through the 'power of attorney'. In the assembly debates of 2001, it was suggested that transfers through power of attorney had increased since 1991. Between 1999 and 2001 alone, the number of such transactions was placed at 15,000.[56]

This increase in 'informal' property transfers could be perhaps partly understood as a response to the tighter regulations that accompanied every successive amendment to the Act. In the debates of 1991, the revenue minister of the time, Dalsukhbhai Godani of the Janata Dal, proposed an extension of the law, suggesting that greater powers be given to the collector—every transfer of property would have to be approved of and the value of the property decided by the collector.[57] This proposition was seconded by Ashok Bhatt, the BJP stalwart from Khadia constituency in the walled city. In his argument, he hinted that members of the land mafia would enter neighbourhoods and capture a few properties first. After engineering violence and consequently depressing property values, they would take control of the real estate market of the area—such as in Hindu areas like Tokar Shah's pol, where property prices allegedly dropped from INR 300,000 to INR 30,000. Bhatt advocated for the tightening of the power-of-attorney privilege through which, he claimed, a majority of transfers in the Gujarat Housing Board quarters in Bapunagar were taking place.

The objection to the amendment came from Manubhai Parmar, a Congress leader from Gomtipur and, if we recall, Jeevanbhai's 'patron'. He claimed intimate knowledge of the situation on the ground, living as he did in a 'disturbed area'. Arguing against investing greater powers to the office of the collector, he suggested that placing restrictions on the transfer of properties could potentially endanger and dispossess citizens. If an application for a transfer was denied by the collector, for instance, the resident would have no choice but to leave the chawl to seek shelter in a slum on the banks of the Sabarmati—highlighting the downward mobility that such a move would entail. These assembly debates suggest that the intention of the lawmakers was not so much to prevent ghettoisation but to either protect areas from 'infiltration' or to enable people to move away from mixed areas. In the amended legislation of 1991, the legal connotations of a 'disturbed area' were expanded. The legal definition changed from areas that experienced riots or mob violence between 18 March 1985 and 29 October 1986 to those which were affected by violence for a 'substantial period'. What constituted a 'substantial period' was left open to interpretation by the state government.[58]

Nowhere in the Act is it mentioned that property is not to be transferred between members of different communities. It states instead that all transactions in designated disturbed areas would require the approval of the collector. However, in popular perception (and often in practice), this law has been designed solely to restrict transfers between Hindus and Muslims. The colloquial understanding of the law was revealed as Bashir Sayyid, a lower-middle-class advocate from Vatva, explained the workings of this legislation.

Hindu properties in 'Muslim' areas can't be acquired by Muslims, and Muslim properties in 'Hindu' areas cannot be acquired by Hindus. For this, one has to take the permission of the Collector, take permissions from the Government. It is only after it is approved by the Government, that the property documents are released. First, one has to go to the Collector.... It is all up to the Collector.... Transactions between Muslims, in the same 'disturbed area' are easily sanctioned.

For inter-community transfers, permissions are not so easy to come by. Even if permissions are granted, it is after a lengthy inquiry process. First, there is a police inquiry, then the talati.... If their report is positive, then they give it [the permission].... Transfers happen, though. They happen even in Vatva. For any property transaction, there has to be some kind of documentary proof ... so, a power of attorney is prepared.... There are some kinds of rights on the land ... but these are rights of possession, not of ownership.

If someone were having biryani, their hunger would be satisfied by it ... but if they didn't get biryani, they would have to manage with plain rotis. Similarly, people need homes.... If one can't acquire them legally, they have to do it illegally.[59]

This exchange reveals three key aspects of this law: One, it sharply outlines the popular conception of the Disturbed Areas' Act, a view that has been echoed wherever I have broached this subject—that this law is meant to prevent inter-community transfers. Two, it details the process by which permissions are granted, while throughout underscoring the difficulties of inter-community transfers. Third, the ease with which he suggests the power-of-attorney route, for all manner of difficult transactions, is indicative of the prevalence of this mechanism in areas such as Vatva. As in Vatva, the instrument of the power of attorney is the primary means through which property rights circulate in most localities of the industrial east. Sales deeds, clearances and registrations do not usually form part of the local mechanisms of property transactions. The increasing curbs on this mode of transfers, thus, strikes at the heart of the workings of the local property market.

The legal battle between SNA Infraprojects and the government sub-registrar (Revenue Department) can be used to illustrate not only how the geography of the city is being shaped but also of how the colloquial understanding of the Disturbed Areas Act structures the practice of the law. SNA Infraprojects, headed by a Muslim builder, purchased twenty-nine flats from Hindu owners in Paldi with the intention of converting them into an apartment complex. Permission to register the sale was denied by the sub-registrar on the grounds that the flats were located in a 'disturbed area'. In the meantime, a residents' welfare society also filed a petition opposing the sale, joining the Revenue Department in the suit. The opposition to the sale was framed specifically around the transfer of properties between communities. 'Any transgression by a single Muslim family or individual,' the application of the residents' group stated, 'then ... all will be forced to leave.... [We] are also equally interested to see that the law in force is obeyed and according to the notification, no transfers take place from Hindu people to a Muslim owner.'[60] One of the key issues debated in court was that of the precise contours of what was designated as 'disturbed'. For Mevawala flats, the discussions revolved around whether the building was located within the 'entire area of Kochrab village upto Tagore Hall'—an area that had been notified as 'disturbed'. Revenue, town planning and police maps were respectively marshalled as evidence by both parties. Land records and maps prepared by the local police station, presented by the collector's office, showed that the building did fall under the disturbed area notified in the Act; the town planning maps produced by the counsel for SNA infraprojects, instead, established that Mevawala flats was nowhere near Kochrab village.[61] The revenue authorities, the High Court observed, 'ought to have clarified details of the area', that the authorities 'were not so much clear about the disturbed area', that the demarcations of the area were vague and that more precise maps be prepared so that the 'entire public' may be informed of what exactly lies in a disturbed area.[62] The incongruity of the various maps prepared by different wings of the state testifies to the fuzziness and ambiguity of the implementation of the legislation. The impression that the Act was intended to 'protect' areas was reinforced in another more recent case in 2018, when the collector's office withdrew previously granted permissions for a property transaction in Paldi, Ahmedabad, following protests over the fact that Hindu owners were selling to Muslim buyers.[63]

The discussions between the four key sets of actors—the buyers and sellers, the officials of the state government, the residents' association and the judiciary—revolved centrally around the question of location and the inter-community dynamics of property transfers. The bureaucratic exercise of inquiring, verifying and granting permissions was equally shaped by considerations of community. As the long legal battles over Mevawala Flats revealed, nearby buildings had been transferred between Hindus, without requiring the permission of the collector.[64] Transactions involving Muslims, contemporary news reports suggest, could face considerable delays in getting clearances—first from the local police station, and then from the sub-registrar's office.[65] In case there was any doubt over the intent behind the way the law was enforced, the chief minister of Gujarat recently clarified: 'We have set this rule in place to tell them (Muslims) that they must buy property in their own areas.'[66] In effect, then, the practice of the law corresponds to the popular perception that it is intended to prevent transfers between Hindus and Muslims.[67]

The communalisation of the real estate market is not restricted to Ahmedabad alone, but is also visible elsewhere in Gujarat. A case in point is an incident in Bhavnagar in 2014, when the local VHP unit forced Aliasgar Zaveri to sell his newly purchased house in a predominantly Hindu locality. After facing threats and harassment for over a year, Zaveri transferred the property to a Hindu business concern. The president of the VHP's Bhavnagar unit was quoted in the Hindu as stating: 'A Muslim had purchased the house, but a compromise was brokered and the property was sold to a Hindu three months ago. The VHP has been working for the implementation of the Disturbed Areas Act in Bhavnagar [which prevents inter-community transfers of immovable property] for the last 12 years.'[68] The operation of the Act in Ahmedabad, in a sense, provides a blueprint for the regulation of the property market in other cities of Gujarat.

In 2001, an attempt was made to repeal the law (which was rejected) on the grounds that Ahmedabad had been peaceful for the last ten years and there was no real need to extend the limits of the law. At the same time, it was argued that while the legislation restricted the sale of property, it had not been able to thwart actual transfers. As a result, much of the property transactions in eastern Ahmedabad were done through benaami means and without paying the required stamp duty. The opposition to this proposed repeal was, however, greater. Without this law in place, it was suggested, people from other communities could enter neighbourhoods and coerce residents into selling the property at lower prices.[69] It was proposed that the instruments of property transactions be made even tighter. Gordhanbhai Zadafia, a BJP MLA from the labour district of Rakhiyal, alluded to the power-of-attorney privilege, inferring that this loophole could still be used to acquire property. He instead requested the assembly to introduce measures that would annul power-of-attorney transactions.[70] Since much of the property transfers had already taken place and segregation cemented, this law could be then enforced to prevent the entry of the minority community into a majority-dominated area. The extension of the law—both in terms of its powers as well as its limits—suggests that law itself was used more for the consolidation of homogenous neighbourhoods than for the prevention of distress sales.

In every successive amendment, greater powers were granted. In November 2009, the power-of-attorney provision was annulled, while making the transfer of property in disturbed areas without prior approval a cognisable offence. Collectors were now empowered to hold inquiries into cases of property transfer of their own accord as well as to seize or restrain the transfer of any property, should they feel that it is in violation of the Act.[71] In April 2013, more areas (especially those affected in the riots of 2002, such as Gulberg Society, Naroda Patiya and Vatva) were added. In a recent development, the legislation was amended on 8 July 2019 to extend the powers of the collector to check 'improper clustering' and 'polarisation' in the designated disturbed areas.[72] The penalty for the violation of the legislation was increased from six months to six years of imprisonment, while restrictions were placed on property transfers within a 500-metre radius around the disturbed areas. Above this, the new amendment proposes to appoint a Special Investigation Team comprising the collector, municipal commissioner and police commissioner to evaluate the demographical equilibrium of communities in 'disturbed areas'.[73] The mechanisms of notifying disturbed areas and enforcing the regulation that I have mentioned here are also likely to change. These new amendments are telling, having become significantly more stringent as it were after neighbourhoods have already been made communally homogenous. At present, this list includes over 750 areas, a massive increase from the 167 designated in 1986.[74]

The latest list includes large parts of Vatva, which has emerged as a visibly Muslim space over the last few decades. Through the implementation of this law, which has progressively imposed stricter regulations, 'formal' property transactions (those with registered deeds, leases, and so on) in areas like Vatva would be policed even more rigorously. Neighbourhood borders would be sharply delineated, as the clearly stated intention of the law according to the joint commissioner of police is 'to avoid any situation that can create tension among communities'.[75] In effect, this translates into a reluctance to concede to inter-community transfers in all 'disturbed areas'. The informality that was built into property relations in large parts of industrial Ahmedabad was born of the state's design of strategically notifying 'disturbed areas', pushing increasing numbers of Muslim working poor into property regimes that were unstable and often illegal.

The closure of the textile mills, evictions from mill chawls and urban renewal projects such as the Sabarmati Riverfront Development Project testify to a process by which workers' claims on urban space are being steadily undermined. Other scholarship has demonstrated how the Sabarmati Riverfront Development Project has bludgeoned through the affected slum residents' rights to life, shelter and livelihood.[76] The project which was intended as a self-financing undertaking has instead relied on other state programmes for the urban poor (such as the BSUP housing under the JNNURM) to provide resettlement and rehabilitation. It can be argued, however, that the shrinking spaces of housing in the city centre were accompanied by new areas being opened for low-income housing. Vatva, in particular, has the highest concentration of proposed EWS (economically weaker section) housing. Some of this is counted in the resettlement blocks built for those displaced by the Sabarmati Riverfront Development Project. Others include plots of land reserved through town planning for EWS housing, as I discuss in the following chapter. Notwithstanding these provisions, the land demarcated for EWS housing remains underutilised by the government.[77] Despite the allotment of resettlement land and proposed housing for the economically weak in the city's peripheries, the mill closures, chawl evictions, and so on, have contributed to a broader weakening of workers' claims on urban space. I see this at occurring at two levels: One, with these processes (of factory closures and new investments in eastern Ahmedabad), land in the urban core is increasingly limited for the city's working classes. And two, the judicial interventions around the issues of displacement and resettlement, as Desai has argued, have allowed the state authorities to implement urban renewal projects without attending to the rights of the working poor.[78] When read against this backdrop, the Disturbed Areas Act adds further layers of vulnerability for the urban working populations. The legal category of the 'disturbed area' emerged as a central concern not only for administration and policing, but also for ordering the contours of the urban property market. The enactment and the implementation of the legislation were profoundly tied to dynamic social and spatial relations. The entanglement of legal regimes with the social regulation of urban space was signalled by the ways in which the Disturbed Areas Act splices into dominant views of social and spatial order, both following and reinforcing them. The actual workings of the Disturbed Areas Act—as a tool to solidify spatial zones along communal lines—were closely tied to the rhetoric of 'land jihad', which emerged as a potent election issue for the BJP in 2017.[79] The political geography of the city thus both shaped and was, in turn, produced by this law. The property market of contemporary Ahmedabad, then split along community lines, provided a fertile basis for communal segregation and ghetto-like enclosure.

NOTES

1 NDTV news report, 12 November 2012, available at http://www.youtube. com/watch?v=PI_EczCwEIw, accessed on 22 January 2020.

2 Renu Desai, 'Producing and Contesting the "Communalized City": Hindutva Politics and Urban Space in Ahmedabad', in *The Fundamentalist City? Religiosity and the Remaking of Urban Space*, ed. N. AlSayyad and M. Massoumi (Abingdon, Oxon and New York: Routledge, 2010); Shani, *Communalism, Caste and Hindu Nationalism.*

3 Ghassem-Fachandi, *Pogrom in Gujarat*, 217ff.

4 Dhattiwala, *Keeping the Peace*, 75.

5 *Times of India*, 7 March 1971.

6 *The Report of the Commission of Inquiry into the incidents of violence and disturbances which took place at various places in the State of Gujarat since February 1985 to 18th July 1985* by Justice V. S. Dave (Ahmedabad: Government of Gujarat, 1990) (henceforth referred to as the Dave Commission).

7 In particular, the 'police revolt' targeted the offices of the *Gujarat Samachar*, which had been especially critical of the police brutalities.

8 The police, it was suggested, were leading gangs of 'Hindu goondas', as the unrest spread towards the mill areas. See *Illustrated Weekly of India*, 12 May 1985; *India Today*, 15 May 1985. See also Dave Commission Vol. 1, 251.

9 Shani, *Communalism, Caste and Hindu Nationalism.*

10 Dave Commission Vol. 1, 53.

11 Shani, *Communalism, Caste and Hindu Nationalism.*

12 Ibid., 82.

13 *Illustrated Weekly of India*, 12 May 1985.

14 Dave Commission Vol. 1, 251–55.

15 *Illustrated Weekly of India*, 12 May 1985.

16 Shani, *Communalism, Caste and Hindu Nationalism.*

17 Dave Commission Vol. 2, 10.

18 *Times of India*, 8 June 1989.

19 Harish Damodaran, *India's New Capitalists: Caste, Business, and Industry in a Modern Nation* (Ranikhet: Permanent Black, 2008).

20 Engineer, 'Communal Fire Engulfs Ahmedabad Once Again', 1116–20; Shani, *Communalism, Caste and Hindu Nationalism.*

21 Shani, *Communalism, Caste and Hindu Nationalism*, 126.

22 Protected by Congress MLAs and other senior party members, Ramlal Pehalwan, a slumlord and an active participant in the 1969 riots, and Rajendra Anchal, took part in the Bapunagar carnage. Congress municipal corporators were alleged to have declared that as Hindus, it was their duty to protect the interests of other Hindus. A certain Ramlal had also been named as an attacker by Hasinabibi in her testimony to the Dave Commission (Vol. 1, 254). Engineer, 'Communal Fire Engulfs Ahmedabad Once Again', 1116–20. Other accounts suggest that 'strike breakers' were involved in fomenting the 22 April episode of violence in Bapunagar. The reference to 'strike breakers' could have also been a possible allusion to TLA leaders. Given that the union (as we have seen in Chapter 2) had been involved in thwarting strikes organised by the Left parties, we could perhaps speculate that this hints at the participation of union members in this episode of communal rioting. Nimesh Sheth, Neerav Patel and Roopa Mehta, 'Ahmedabad Riots', *Economic and Political Weekly* 20, no. 24 (1985): 1022.

23 Patel, 'Debacle of Populist Politics', 681–82.

24 *Times of India*, 20 July 1985.

25 For instance, Brass points out that the tensions over land is often offered as a common explanation for communal riots. See Brass, *The Production of Hindu–Muslim Violence in Contemporary India*, 202–16.

26 *Illustrated Weekly of India*, 30 June 1985.

27 Dave Commission Vol. 1, 258.

28 Shani, *Communalism, Caste and Hindu Nationalism*, 127.

29 Lokhande, *Communal Violence, Forced Migration and the State*; Desai, 'Producing and Contesting the "Communalized City".'

30 Nagrik Sangthan was a citizens' organisation established by a group of social activists in the aftermath of the April violence. The group remained ineffective in condemning either caste or communal violence. They, however, continued to play a role in the negotiations between the government and the anti-reservationists (*Times of India*, 21 November 1985). The TLA appeared to have made negligible efforts at any form of peacekeeping. Apart from their own publications, there was no mention of any role that they may have played in diffusing tensions or providing assistance in the working-class areas.

31 Dave Commission Vol. 1, 57.

32 *India Today*, 30 November 1986.

33 *Times of India*, 9 February 1987.

34 *India Today*, 15 March 1986.

35 Dave Commission Vol. 1, 56–57.

36 Interview with Rameshbhai Christian, Ahmedabad, 3 December 2012.

37 Arvind Rajagopal, 'Special Political Zone: Urban Planning, Spatial Segregation and the Infrastructure of Violence in Ahmedabad 1', *South Asian History and Culture* 1, no. 4 (2010): 529–56.

38 Ibid. Red lining refers to the practice of marking out a territory as a bad investment prospect for banks and other financial institutions on the basis of its ethnic make-up.

39 Vidhan Sabha debates, 14 February 1991 and 23 August 2001 (all Vidhan Sabha debates have been translated from the Gujarati original by Siddhi Shah).

40 *India Today*, 15 March 1986.

41 Ibid.

42 Breman, *The Making and Unmaking of an Industrial Working Class*; Patel, *The Making of Industrial Relations*; Salim Lakha, *Capitalism and Class in Colonial India: The Case of Ahmedabad* (Bangalore: Sterling Publishers, 1988).

43 *Majoor Sandesh*, 17 May 1950; *Majoor Sandesh*, 17 January 1951.

44 Amrita Shah, *Ahmedabad: A City in the World* (New Delhi: Bloomsbury, 2015), 113–16.

45 Informal estimates suggest that nearly 60 per cent of property transfers in Ahmedabad happen through the POA route. Interview with Bashir Sayyid, advocate, Vatva, 16 February 2013. For a sample of property tax information, please see Appendix.

46 Dhattiwala, *Keeping the Peace*.

47 *India Today*, 15 March 1986.

48 *India Today*, 30 November 1986.

49 'Collector's Manual', Revenue Department, Government of Gujarat, 2007–08, 1.

50 Vidhan Sabha debates, 23 August 2001, statement by Ashok Bhatt, BJP MLA from Khadia.

51 *Gujarat Samachar*, 22 February 1987.

52 The Gujarat Prohibition of Transfer of Immovable Properties and Provision for Protection of Tenants from Eviction in Disturbed Areas Act, 1986 (henceforth referred to as the Disturbed Areas Act).

53 *Indian Express*, 24 August 2013.

54 Nandy et al., *Creating a Nationality*.

55 *Times of India*, 6 April 1999.

56 Vidhan Sabha debates, 23 August 2001.

57 Vidhan Sabha debates, 14 February 1991.

58 Disturbed Areas Act 1986 and 1991.

59 Interview with Bashir Sayyid, advocate, Ahmedabad, 16 February 2013.

60 *SNA Infraprojects v. Sub Registrar*, Gujarat High Court, 13 May 2011, 4.

61 *SNA Infraprojects v. Sub Registrar*, Gujarat High Court, 13 May 2011.

62 *State of Gujarat v. Nareshbhai Parmar*, Gujarat High Court, 13 February 2012; *State of Gujarat v. Nareshbhai Parmar and Others*, Gujarat High Court, 20 April 2012.

63 *Times of India*, 4 September 2019.

64 *SNA Infraprojects v. Sub Registrar*, Gujarat High Court, 13 May 2011.

65 *The Caravan*, 21 August 2019.

66 *Economic Times*, 27 July 2019.

67 *SNA Infraprojects v. Sub Registrar*, Gujarat High Court, 13 May 2011.

68 *The Hindu*, 22 April 2014 and 8 April 2015.

69 Vidhan Sabha debates, 23 August 2001.

70 Ibid.

71 *Desh Gujarat*, 15 May 2010; *Frontline* 29, no. 3 (11–24 February 2012), available at https://frontline.thehindu.com/cover-story/article30164344.ece, accessed 28 June 2021.

72 *Indian Express*, 10 July 2019.

73 Ibid.

74 *Gujarat Samachar*, 22 February 1987.

75 *Ahmedabad Mirror*, 29 January 2014.

76 Desai, 'Municipal Politics, Court Sympathy and Housing Rights.'

77 Rutul Joshi and Prashant Sanga, 'Land Reservations for the Urban Poor: The Case of Town Planning Schemes in Ahmedabad', Centre for Urban Equity, CEPT University, Ahmedabad, 2009.

78 Desai, 'Municipal Politics, Court Sympathy and Housing Rights.'

79 *Live Mint*, 13 July 2018.

7

SECURITY AND TENANCY AT
THE MARGINS OF THE CITY

The strategic implementation and expansion of the Disturbed Areas Act initiated a bifurcation of the urban property market and a process by which city dwellers could be corralled into communally homogenous enclaves. The legislation as a mechanism for crystallising spatial segregation moved in tandem with widening social distance in Ahmedabad. Affective dimensions of social life and emotional practices facilitated (and even justified) segregation. The idiom of disgust, for instance, as Ghassem-Fachandi has argued, was employed rather effectively not only to other the Muslim, but also to legitimise violence.[1] We are then confronted with a historical moment at which it is virtually impossible for Muslim citizens to acquire property or secure a home outside of the so-called Muslim areas. For the Muslim working poor, access to housing was especially difficult—as property relations ruptured in their older areas of residence (predominantly in the walled city and the erstwhile mill districts) during every successive episode of violence, it grew increasingly arduous to rebuild their lives and homes in their former neighbourhoods.[2] For some it was the memory of the loss they experienced in these areas, for others it was the hostility of their former neighbours and for yet others it was the sheer impossibility of finding new homes in the already congested 'safe' areas in the inner city.[3] The only alternative left, both in terms of security as well as access, was to move to areas that had significant Muslim populations, and it was in these areas that property relations were tentatively forged anew.

Vatva's location at the intersection of the working-class city and the segregated city offers a particularly productive lens with which to approach the forms and patterns of spatial and social exclusion. The forms of proscribed living that are pervasive in the area, however, are continually shifting and historically contingent. This chapter pixelates the landscape of Vatva to trace property and housing dynamics in a situation of segregation and to consider how formal and informal pressures align to make the 'ghetto' an unstable socio-spatial form in Ahmedabad.

THE 'GHETTO' IN AHMEDABAD

The study of the ghetto as a space of segregation has long been a subject of academic inquiry.[4] As an urban formation, the beginnings of the ghetto can be traced to medieval Europe, when Jewish populations were confined to designated zones, and their movements policed.[5] In writing on Muslim localities in Delhi, Jamil foregrounds the dehumanising connotations of the term 'ghetto' and its potential to normalise segregation as an aspect of urban life.[6] In popular usage, one can identify a certain looseness with which this term is applied. Wacquant places a similar charge on conceptualisations of the term, arguing that it is a 'wooly and shifting notion' that has been denuded of analytical charge.[7] The easy application of this category to all manner of urban residential arrangements, he argues, obfuscates the historic relationships of power that contribute to its making. Thus, Wacquant calls for a reformulation of the concept, arguing instead that the spatial form of the ghetto is 'a Janus faced institution of ethnic closure and control'.[8] Its production is then based on a dialectic of both 'external hostility' and 'internal affinity'. It is simultaneously an instrument of confinement and control and a 'protective and integrative device'. This theorisation, while acknowledging the asymmetry of power relations that contribute to its making, also sees the ghetto 'as a cultural combustion engine that melts divisions among the confined population and fuels its collective pride even as it entrenches the stigma that hovers over it'.[9] This taken uncritically would pose a problem, for it may imply a uniformly uncomplicated space of goodwill and community support. In Vatva, for instance, various forms of social distinctions are played out in quotidian life, and while there is an identification of the area as a Muslim space (which is both enforced from outside as well as reaffirmed within the area), this identity is also fractured and fragmented at various levels. Wacquant's understanding of the ghetto does, indeed, offer us a useful framework with which to approach an area like Vatva. While such areas do indicate enforced segregation, a social identity that is marked as 'Muslim', and (gradually in Vatva) class differentiation, there are other dimensions to this sequestering that we should explore.

Most central here is the juridical weight behind the process of segregation. Not only is the separation of communities in Ahmedabad engendered by social and economic practices, but it is also supported by the application of the Disturbed Areas Act. In Hirsch's classic study of the black ghetto in Chicago, we witness the formidable power of the state and local political bodies in producing and reproducing spaces of racial enclosure and containment.[10] The harnessing of legal and municipal power to make bounded territories of racial (or ethnic or communal) homogeneity is, perhaps, most usefully portrayed through the term 'urban apartheid'. Abu-Lughod makes compelling use of the category to understand social spaces of colonial Morocco. Arguing that the South African situation of racial segregation by law was but an 'extreme version of more general colonial policies', she demonstrated how urban planning and local administrative policies were 'effective substitutes'.[11] Or to draw from Wacquant's writing on the United States at the end of the twentieth century, 'domestic Bantustans', which were not autonomous socio-spatial units governed by their internal logics of evolution and change, but were discursively and empirically produced by new 'political articulations of racial cleavage, class inequality and urban space'.[12] In contemporary Gujarat, similarly, we find a constellation of legal, administrative and social practices that serve to constrict the housing market for Muslims. However, the ghetto as a spatial formation implies a sense of spatial fixity. As we shall see, in the case of Ahmedabad, the spatial congregation of Muslims in certain areas was a process that had unfolded over about three decades. The spatial permanence that was ascribed to these areas, however, was precarious and subject to various threats.

To begin our discussion on ghettoisation, let us turn briefly to Juhapura—Ahmedabad's most prominent 'Muslim' space, with the dubious distinction of being the largest Muslim ghetto in India. Located in the southwestern periphery of the city, the settlement was initially built to accommodate slum dwellers from the banks of the Sabarmati, who had been affected by the heavy floods of 1973. Sankalit Nagar, the first resettlement housing initiative in the area was jointly undertaken by Ahmedabad Study Action Group, a local NGO, the civic bodies and housing finance agencies.[13] The area's early residential arrangements were communally mixed. At this point, Juhapura was not yet considered part of the city and, for much of its residents, disconnected from their worksites. Soon after the construction and allocation of homes in Sankalit Nagar, a large majority of residents sold or rented their residences informally and returned to the inner city. By the 1980s, Muslims formed the dominant religious group in the area, and in the episodes of violence that followed, Juhapura expanded to house those displaced from the core of the city. Gradually, with greater investments in real estate in the area, enclaves of affluence were built. Juhapura then represented, as one news report called it, a 'dystopian sprawl', where luxurious gated living coexisted with slums.[14] As Jaffrelot argues, social space in Juhapura is differentiated on the basis of class; it is marked by civic neglect and remains insulated from the rest of the city. In mainstream representations, the area is routinely branded as 'mini Pakistan', stigmatised as a space of dirt and, more recently, as a breeding ground for terrorism.[15]

In recent scholarship, Charlotte Thomas has creatively applied Wacquant's conceptualisation of the ghetto to the socio-spatial formations of Ahmedabad. Juhapura's transformation into a 'ghetto' occurred after the carnage of 2002, precisely because of the in-migration of a large number of affluent Muslims.[16] Having expanded with a much more variegated class profile than Vatva, residents of Juhapura turned 'inwards', developed modalities of 'self-help' and established 'quasi-state' institutions.[17] Education and business appear as crucial ways of both integrating with a majoritarian society and as defence against majoritarian violence.[18]

In tracing the histories of settlement in the area, Jassani identifies a spatial trajectory of migrant Muslim workers from the mill neighbourhoods to Juhapura and a connected spread of ideas of religious reform.[19] Islamic organisations in Juhapura, as in Vatva, had supported the bulk of reconstruction and rehabilitation of riot-affected Muslims after 2002. Relief work extended to the domain of providing services, organising education and propagating reformist ideologies.

Similar to what Thomas has argued for the case of Juhapura, much of Vatva lives under the structures of daily domination and is affected by 'an ethnicisation of citizenship', by which effective citizenship is differentiated by religion.[20] The strategies of daily domination also appear in the absence of public infrastructure and civic amenities. Spatial expansion of Juhapura, she demonstrates, is restricted by the built forms on all four flanks, some having been built after 2002. Much of this resonates strongly with the social conditions in Vatva. Further drawing from Wacquant, we could also argue that both Juhapura and Vatva are engendered by a 'communal segmentation of the housing market'.[21] Vatva, however, lacks the class differentiation and the near-total communal homogeneity of Juhapura. Residential patterns in Vatva, since the 1990s, have tended to crystallise around lines of class and

religion and the area has remained one of the 'poorest Muslim' localities of
Ahmedabad.[22] While it is the story of Vatva that we follow in this book,
Juhapura and Vatva represent two interconnected but distinct socio-spatial
configurations.

SETTLING VATVA

By the late 1960s, Ahmedabad expanded further southeast, towards the
large industrial development estates that had been planned outside the
city limits. These three estates—Vatva, Odhav and Naroda—which were
to be later incorporated into the municipal boundaries, grew as hubs of
small- and medium-scale enterprises. Perhaps a description of Vatva would
be useful to map out the crucial signposts of the area. Present-day Vatva,
which spans nearly 33 square kilometres, stretches from the edges of the
GIDC estate to the Delhi–Bombay highway running through Ahmedabad.
When one enters Vatva from the city, the first encounter with the area is
through the bridge running over the Kharicut canal, a stream of frothing
effluents from the chemical industries in the area. The main road leading
up to Bibi Talab, a pond ringed with *jhuggi*s, is lined with shops. It is along
this road that one finds the more affluent and historically more established
housing societies, such as Silicon City and Jehangir Nagar Society, as well
as the largest high school in the area. The Bibi Talab crossroads provides
an axis of sorts in understanding the geography of Vatva. Following the
road from the city, we move towards Vatva village, which at present is
largely Hindu dominated. The village and the smaller settlements along the
way, such as Maliwada and Saiyyadwada, are the oldest settlements in the
area. Taking a left from the char rasta would lead us to the GIDC and
the Sabarmati relocation flats. Large factory compounds, closed since the
late 1990s, punctuated by barren stretches of land, flank this road. Further
ahead, just before reaching the industrial estate, is the massive relocation
colony built to house those displaced from the Sabarmati riverfront. A little
beyond the main road, adjacent to the older settlements in the area, are the
localities that are the most vulnerable in Vatva—Jain Ashram, Navapura
and Darbar Nagar. Vulnerability in Vatva, especially after the violence of
2002, is usually judged on the basis of how open the borders of particular
settlements are and how easily they can be breached. On taking the right
from the Bibi Talab char rasta, we reach the most densely populated areas

of the neighbourhood, and the ones that have seen the most substantial growth in the last decade. These areas—Chistiya Park, Al Mustafa and Noor Nagar—with mostly informal *jhuggi jhopdi* settlements are mostly populated by migrant labour from Bihar, Uttar Pradesh and Rajasthan (Figure 7.1).

By 1965, Vatva had been designated an industrial area and production was already being nudged towards the outskirts of Ahmedabad—a plan which was intended to ameliorate congestion and industrial pollution in the city.[23] The establishment of the GIDC estate in 1968 and the communal riots of 1969 spurred the initial growth of Vatva. The riots of 1969 forced inner-city Muslims to relocate to outlying areas, of which Vatva was one. Land prices were lower in these suburban areas, and the neighbourhood, thus, appeared more attractive.[24] Post-riot resettlement colonies were established in Vatva, with Tamizben Koreishi, a Congress municipal corporator and honorary secretary of a Muslim women's organisation, building 100 tenements for riot victims.[25] Another speculative theory that surfaced during discussions of the area's growth centred around a rumour that was circulating in the early 1960s. Gandhinagar's selection as the site for the new capital of Gujarat was in jeopardy following the discovery of oil fields in the area.[26] As talks began anew for relocating the capital, there emerged a possibility that the new site may be located towards the southern edges of the city, in which case Vatva would fall en route and land in the area would be in high demand. While the rumour cannot be substantiated with the limited documentary evidence available, it could have very well accounted for some of the early investments in real estate in Vatva.[27]

Through the 1970s and 1980s, industries in Vatva proliferated—the GIDC estate housed small- and medium-scale chemical, plastics and engineering units, while the parts around Jain Ashram had larger factories, such as Ambica Tubes, SLM and Saurashtra Paints—many of which were environmentally polluting.[28] With the involvement of the municipal corporation from 1987 onwards, the civic administration of the area shifted from the Vatva gram panchayat to the AMC. Through this shift, we already encounter the first step towards urbanisation of former agricultural lands. Not only was land use changing from agricultural to industrial or residential use, but farming itself was no longer viable by the early 1990s. The polluting effluents from the industrial units flowed the canals, seeped into the groundwater and turned these fertile lands into arid stretches.[29] Residents like Gulab Khan and his brother had given up farming by the

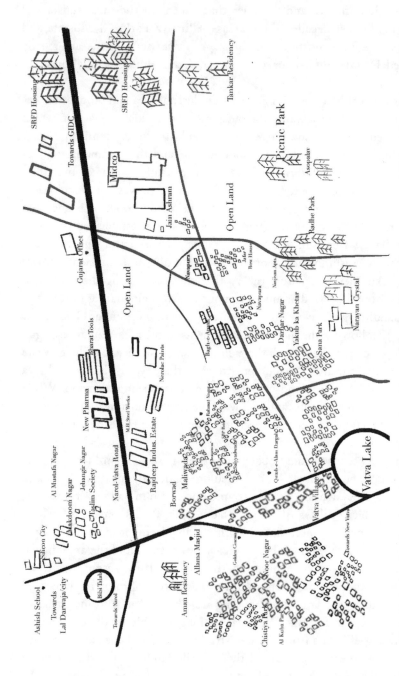

Figure 7.1 Map showing the major landmarks and architectural forms of the south-western parts of Vatva that is discussed in this chapter

Source: Author.

1970s and joined scores of migrant workers in seeking employment in the nearby factories.

Development of real estate in Vatva during this period was nearly all unplanned and unauthorised. Reconstructing the history of habitat in Vatva through oral narratives, it would appear that in the 1950s and 1960s, most of Vatva's population was clustered around the village, and a few scattered settlements were spreading out from the village towards the railway tracks. These densely populated clusters—Maliwada, Borwad, Jain Ashram (named after the adjacent Jain temple)—flow from around the village and the Qutub-e-Alam dargah towards the GIDC estate. These earliest settlements retain visible traces of previous housing structures—kutcha walls, uncemented floors, older toilet and bathroom arrangements.

One of the oldest residents of Jain Ashram, popularly known as Bade Khan Chacha, was born in the same house where he lives now. This house, like many others in the area, is a squat, tin-roofed structure with plastered walls. The entrance overlooks dry, dusty open patches, where goats wander. The small courtyard adjacent has a chulha in the corner, again an anomaly in most urban households. This area, given its shared 'borders' with the adjacent Hindu middle-class residences and the open tracts of 'no-man's land' in between, is considered one of the most insecure in Vatva. Security in Vatva is thus framed along two intersecting lines—that of life and property and that of tenure. Security of life is seen as being somewhat ensured by a certain homogeneity of the population and by location away from the 'borders'. These 'borders' presented a conundrum. On the one hand, these were the zones from which an attack could be launched and, hence, the most vulnerable of all. On the other hand, they also offered the possibility of escape during a situation of violence. Likewise, tenurial security has grown as a significant concern in the last decade or so, since the implementation of the new town plan for the area in the early 2000s. This anxiety is buttressed by real material structures of dispossession, as the municipal corporation has been consistently targeting haphazard constructions in the area. The twin forms of precarity converge to make life and living in Vatva ever more insecure.

When Khan was born in 1936, there were perhaps, as he recollected, five families in the Jain Ashram area, and all of them, his relatives. Unlike many of the other residents who moved from agricultural work to factory work in the industries set up in Vatva, Khan looked cityside for employment. He worked as a peon in the AMC from 1961 until his retirement in 1997.

Around the time that Khan joined the AMC, Seth Harivallabhdas, the owner of the Ambica group, began his tenure as the city's mayor. After having established textile mills in parts of eastern Ahmedabad, the company was in the processes of acquiring land in Vatva for Ambica Tubes, a plant manufacturing steel tubes. Bade Khan's relationship with the mayor was a complicated one. On the one hand, the stratified world of the AMC placed Bade Khan and Harivallabhdas at two ends of the hierarchical spectrum. On the other, Bade Khan was a crucial resource in the company's land acquisition in Vatva. Not only was his family one of the area's oldest residents, but he was also allegedly one of the original owners of the land on which Ambica Tubes stands. To avoid giving out any information, or possibly from being coerced into selling the land, he would religiously avoid the mayor. Eventually, he claims, the land was obtained—some of it bought but mostly acquired through state intervention—and Ambica Tubes, along with SLM Maneklal, became the first industrial units to be established in Vatva.[30]

Bade Khan recollects how his daily cycle journey to the AMC office in the city centre changed when the first paved road was built in 1970, connecting Bibi Talab to the GIDC. Munira Bukhari, another old resident of the area, remembers traffic lights sprouting on the same road in the early 1980s, a development which considerably lengthened her commute to her workplace in western Ahmedabad. The year 1970 or, for that matter, the early 1980s might very well be a misremembrance, but it nevertheless points to the gradual transformation of the area from an agricultural hinterland to being subsumed by the inexorable expansion of the city. Educational facilities were meagre, with only two schools in the area—the AMC-run Gujarati medium one, and another, which was managed privately by the Seva Kutir Samiti.[31] Oral narratives suggest that Vatva was dominated at this point by a few communities—the Saiyyads, Bharwads (a Hindu pastoral caste), Vaghris, Dalits, Patels and Thakors. These caste groups had segregated living arrangements, with each locality being the domain of a particular caste. Running through this narrative of segregation is also a parallel narrative of harmony. While these neighbourhoods were not 'mixed' like they are now (in terms of caste and regional affiliations, since they continue to be deeply segregated according to religion), there was plenty of social interaction despite the restrictions on commensality.[32]

The most enduring memory of Vatva is that of a 'jungle'. This image was presented to me in every inquiry I made about the history of the area's settlements. Among others, one account evoked memories of wading through fields of knee-high grass; another remembered having to shut the windows of the bus to keep out the overgrown vegetation that spilled over onto the narrow streets.[33] These remembrances were then often juxtaposed with the present-day appearance of the area. This sense of shock and disbelief at the remarkable speed at which Vatva has grown is not completely unwarranted given that in only twenty-five years the area has moved from a solidly agrarian zone to being saturated with real estate development options.

BUILDING VATVA: THE MAKING OF SMALL-TIME PROPERTY 'MAGNATES'

While the late 1980s destabilised the landscape of the mill areas and prompted investigations into the legality of workers' housing, erratic growth was taking place further south, in Vatva. The riots of 1991–92 sent another influx of displaced Muslims towards Vatva. This period witnessed the rise of slumlords of a particular variety—what I call the small-time property 'magnate'. These are people, predominantly men, who have managed to establish themselves as major landlords, despite often not having any legal titles to the land. Their realm of influence usually did not extend beyond the boundaries of the neighbourhood, but within this bounded territory, they exercised no small measure of control. They became the dispensers of housing, arbiters of local disputes, negotiators with the municipal corporation, and so on. The career of Suraj Singh Rathore from Vatva demonstrates how these 'magnates' come to be made.

Popularly known as Darbar Chacha (after his caste name), Suraj Singh Rathore moved to Vatva from the walled city after the riots of 1969. He found employment in the A-1 washing company in Vatva village. The company owners, Saiyyads by caste, allowed him to live on their land in Borwad (named after the Bohra Muslims who were some of the early settlers of this locality). Alongside his work at the laundry, he also managed the owner's agricultural land, which was located in what is now known as Darbar Nagar, at present a cobbled space of informal housing with both *pucca* and kutcha houses. In Darbar Chacha's retelling, around the mid-1970s, the Saiyyad owners sold this agricultural land to Hindu Bania businessmen. It was planned that a housing society by the name of Mahavir Nagar Co-operative Housing Society was to be built on this plot, and until such time, Darbar Chacha was employed as the watchman.[34] He remained the watchman until the city witnessed severe riots in 1992, following the demolition of the Babri Masjid in Ayodhya. Then, his role in the real estate market of Vatva changed significantly. He divided the area into plots and sold each one for INR 3,000. He dates the growth of Vatva as a settlement to 6 December 1992, the day the Babri Masjid was demolished. The growth of the area and, more precisely, its transformation from a 'jungle' to a residential locality then is crucially tied to violence that the city has experienced.[35] At this moment, Darbar Chacha, who had clearly amassed some amount of clout in the area, shifted from being a watchman to a proprietor. Mahavir Nagar Co-operative Housing Society was never built, and Darbar Nagar now is an established residential area for working-class Muslims. By publicly declining to sell his land to builders who have repeatedly approached him with plans of constructing low-income residential complexes in Darbar Nagar, he has positioned himself as a patron and defender of his 'tenants'.[36]

The official records, on the other hand, tell another story. The revenue records show that the plot of land that is popularly known as Darbar Nagar is owned by Mahavir Nagar Co-operative Housing Society Limited.[37] The municipal tax records, on the other hand, present Singh as the owner, while the address of the plot is marked as Mahavir Nagar, Darbar Garh (roughly translated as Darbar Fort).[38] Ownership in revenue records or in municipal records does not, however, translate to a legal title on the land. The mutations of land titles are to be registered in the sub-registrar's office; however, these records are maintained only if the sale deed has been registered and if the sale itself has been conducted through legal means. For large parts of working-class Ahmedabad, the legal titles to these lands are difficult to trace. However, revenue and municipal records provide evidence of possession, if not of ownership, and the basis for staking a legal claim on the land, as a consequence, becomes stronger in theory. Other localities in Vatva, such as Jafar Row House and Yakub ka Khetar, have similar trajectories of development. Jafar Row House, one of the 'border' areas of Vatva, was developed by one Jafarbhai, after whom the colony was named. Now a warren of narrow, unpaved and potholed streets, the area is cramped with one- or two-room dwellings. These residences, which were sold in the early 1990s, were certainly not registered and the transfers of property were effected by granting power of attorney affixed on stamp papers.[39] The municipal tax information in 2014 continued to reflect the ownership of one Ghulam Jafar Ghulam Rasool, with the current residents registered as occupiers.[40] This parcel of land, which has neither any of the required clearances for urban development nor secure tenancy, is made doubly insecure by its very location at the edges of 'Muslim' Vatva.

TOWN PLANNING IN VATVA

In contemporary Vatva, security of housing remains one of the most crucial concerns for residents. The violence of 2002 not only ravaged large parts of the neighbourhood, but also left deep spatial traces. The desirability of housing was now judged on the basis of its distance from the 'border areas'. Coupled with this apprehension, most residents of Vatva also have to cope with the perils of spatial restructuring borne out of state interventions. The memory and the threat of communal violence looms over the neighbourhood, while the possibility of displacement through strategies of urban planning is an evermore compelling worry. Retrospective planning measures—that is, town plans that were drafted after the area's growth—reframed land use patterns in Vatva, introducing a persistent threat of eviction and relocation. These two parallel threats coincide to orient the real estate market in very particular ways—areas which are farthest from the border and those which have all the necessary government clearances are the most valued.

The town planning processes in Vatva were initiated with the first consultations with landowners in 1990.[41] At the moment, Vatva has ten town planning schemes, of which nine were sanctioned between 2005 and 2006.[42] With the introduction of the town plans and the subsequent zoning, land was legally primed for urban development. The newer parts of Vatva, such as Chistiya Park, Al Mustafa, Sajid Row House and Noor Nagar, had grown phenomenally after the violence of 2002, when working-class Muslim families relocated in large numbers. Given that local estimates suggest that settlements have since doubled at the very least, it would appear that a significant proportion of construction had already taken place by the time the town plans were sanctioned.

Two regulatory regimes—that of planning and revenue administration—govern land management in Gujarat. For most urban uses, land must be converted from agricultural to non-agricultural and, therefore, this permission is critical for the legal status of the land. The very inclusion of certain areas into the town planning schemes indicates that this land is slated for 'urban development'. By definition, then, this land is now urban and not agricultural. However, each plot of agricultural land must be converted to non-agricultural (NA) status for any development to commence. The process of acquiring an NA certificate is lengthy, daunting and expensive, and requires no less than fourteen no-objection certificates (NOCs) from various government agencies. As a result, this required conversion is ignored and all subsequent construction on the land is placed in a zone of illegality.[43] The town plans imagined space in Vatva in terms of neatly ordered configurations, eclipsing the architectural and social arrangements that had already emerged. The way space is perceived and used remains in tension with how it is conceived in the maps and plans. The mapping exercises isolated and parcelled space as schemas of land use and techniques of zoning overlaid dynamic and embodied spatial practices. Tensions similarly appeared at the crevices of overlapping and, often, competing forms of spatial representations—in sales agreements, ownership documents and tax records.[44] The plans imputed a stable spatial configuration that ignored or deliberately elided actually existing spatial relations to promote a specific form of urban transformation. Implementing these plans then would also necessarily involve a somewhat violent spatial restructuring, as existing built forms would be demolished to make way for the planned spaces envisioned.

The incursions from the state came thick and steady—soon after the town plans were sanctioned, the AMC launched slum clearance drives. Negotiations and resistance, at one level, were effected through civil society organisations and locally influential figures.[45] The relief afforded through such efforts was partial and temporary, producing a fluctuating dynamic of precarity and stability. The civic body escalated their demolition drives through 2011 and 2012, readying the land for state and big investments.[46] Unauthorised constructions were sought to be systematically cleared off reserved land and for carving out and expanding roads and pathways.[47]

While a dense web of permissions and sanctions regulate property ownership, other more oblique ways were often deployed alongside, as a way of securing tenancy. Key to this was regularised access to civic amenities, which emerged as a site for both staking and undermining tenurial claims. Regular water and electricity connections are greatly valued and evidence of bill payments is carefully preserved as they are often assumed to be ways of demonstrating and reinforcing tenure. A PIL filed in 1999 against unauthorised construction in Vatva further elucidates the point. The petition alleged that a group of builders had illegally constructed 2,000 one-room and kitchen dwellings on private agricultural land.[48] Foregrounding the pressures upon the limited civic and public amenities available in the area, the suit aimed to reveal the degrees of informality that lay in the realm of property transactions in Vatva. Evidence presented to the court established competing and conflicting narratives of ownership.[49] Construction had then proceeded without securing the necessary clearances of either a sale deed or land conversion or the requisite building permissions. One set of arguments from the respondents highlighted the tensile spatial relationships between Vatva and older sites of working-class residences. The builders claimed that the dwellings were intended, in part, to accommodate those displaced from Chandtoda Kabrastan in Gomtipur.[50] The petitioner suggested instead that these residences were designated for and sold to 'weaker sections of [the] Society', which, in turn, was said to strengthen the claim for the regularisation of such illegal constructions.[51] Firmly drawing together questions of ownership, building permits as well as civic amenities in deciding the legality of constructions, the court tightened the relationship between the various regimes of land and property regulations. This convergence of the otherwise diffuse mechanisms of land control and service provisions further corroded the precarious security enjoyed by the residents. On the grounds that the constructions had been carried out without permissions, the court ordered the AMC and the Ahmedabad Electricity Company to discontinue all essential services provided.

Another crucial issue that emerges in this case relates to the practices of informality and the networks of mediation that support it. Closely connected to the tactics of political mediation discussed in the earlier parts of the book, collusions between 'builders, head-strong persons' and municipal officials were suggested as a mode of actualising property development. The municipal officers were alleged to have 'joined hands' with the builders, remained 'actively silent' and permitted the constructions to continue unchallenged. Shored up by contacts within the state machinery, these property dynamics appear as a set of interlinkages between state-led processes of planning and urban governance and the informal workings of the urban property market. Undergirding the social relationships that enabled (or impeded) housing initiatives in Vatva, however, lay the material threat of dispossession. Without the necessary paperwork, these residences remain in a state of perpetual insecurity. Thus, some of the key markers of coveted real estate in the area revolve around whether the land is NA and whether it has clearance from the city authorities (the much-valued NOC). The modalities of urban transformation introduced by the Town Plans furthered exacerbated this precarity. Consider the town planning map presented in Figure 7.2.

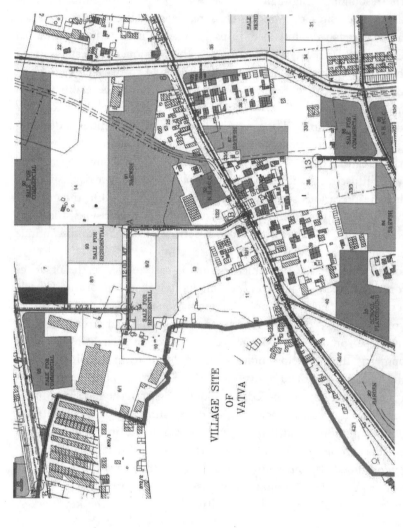

Figure 7.2 Town Planning Scheme No. 86, showing the areas of Jain Ashram, Darbar Nagar, Navapura and Jafar Row House

Source: AMC.

Colour coded to indicate planned land use—pink for community centres or schools, pale yellow for residential, blue for industrial and commercial, ochre for planned housing for economically weaker sections—the draft plans also included sketched blocks to show existing structures on the ground. These orderly representations hardly corresponded to the settlements in Vatva, as I observed during my fieldwork over 2011–13. Industrial spaces of factories and workshops that pepper this locality find no acknowledgement in the plans. Neither do the pathways that are in use. As the plans moved from the drafts to the sanctioned, their modalities of representing space shifted, flattening and erasing pre-existing spatial forms. The imprinting of new land use categories obliterates the complex and enmeshed ways in which the land is actually used and the socio-spatial relations that are tied to this use. The slippage between official representations of space and everyday spatial dynamics points to forms of informality that are inherent in the planning and regulation of urban space. This informality takes on a different political valence when it is produced and operationalised at the intersection of class and religion.

Reading the official map against the built environment of the area shows the dense tangle of socio-spatial relations that the town plan disrupts. Two large parcels of land (plots 91 and 92 in the draft map) which are reserved as housing for the poor and as a 'neighbourhood and community centre' respectively, are represented as two coloured swathes, devoid of any other particularities. By local accounts, parts of these plots were developed in the aftermath of the 2002 violence. Named Bagh-e-Aman, these row houses were built as resettlement facilities for families affected by violence. Around the initial constructions, newer settlements sprouted in plot no.92 and were named Bagh-e-Aman 2. By December 2012, demolitions had begun in Bagh-e-Aman 2, on the grounds of the built structures being unauthorised. During this period, official notices were also issued to residents of adjacent Navapura and Jain Ashram that part of their homes would be razed to extend the road to the planned 18-metre width, setting in motion appeals to the municipal authorities and the intensified involvement of figures such as Suraj Singh Rathore.

Even in this sliver of land, we find not only competing registers of property claims, but also visible tensions between spatial planning and spatial practice, which limit and informalise the expansion of housing. The processes of retrospective planning and the mechanisms by which land use is retroactively transformed further destabilises property relations in the area, circumscribing the possibilities of housing for the Muslim working classes. Parts of the neighbourhood, such as Sana Park (plot 83), developed by builders from Bapunagar in the early 2010s or Navapura (plot 87), expanded by local 'property magnates' in the mid-1990s, both crowded settlements of one or two roomed tenements, are re-categorised as land for schools, playgrounds and housing for the urban poor.

Underlying the tensions that surround retrospective planning in Vatva is another vein of property regulation—the Disturbed Areas Act. The designation of large parts of the locality as 'disturbed'—significant parts of Vatva village and Maliwada—annuls and undermines the power of attorney as a legal instrument of property transactions. The classification of these 'disturbed' areas is themselves imprecise and fuzzy. Suggested by the local police station in Vatva, it includes broad swathes: like the 'area surrounding Golden cinema, Vatva' or Vatva Masjid (which is nomenclature that is confusing for most residents, given that there is no 'Vatva Masjid' per se).[52] The fuzziness of these classifications and the vague territorial demarcations keep these sites and property structures in a perpetual state of ambiguity.

SPATIAL FIXITY/MOBILITY

Vatva as a 'Muslim' area was produced both through a strategic deployment of the Disturbed Areas Act and the severe violence that engendered it. A 'Muslim' property market was *formalised* and *systematised* in Ahmedabad, by which I mean that there was social and legal marking out of the spaces and kinds of properties that Muslims had access to. Within the 'Muslim' property market, we can trace the presence of informal housing arrangements (in the form of slum housing, shanties and tenements which operate without clearances from the regulatory bodies) and formal ones (which arguably are fewer in Vatva and fulfil the necessary government regulations).

Having been signalled out as such, Vatva grew as a site for informal housing for the Muslim working poor and was subsequently promoted by real estate developers as part of the city's formal 'Muslim' property market. The later trajectory of property development is accompanied by an emphasis on authorised and regularised constructions and formal property relations. This remains at odds with the other significant trend in Vatva's real estate market—that is, the informality and ambiguity that marks property transactions in large parts of the area.

The early settlement of Vatva was directed and managed by figures such as Darbar Chacha or Jafarbhai, whereas the recent impetus has come from the more established players in the city's real estate sector. While a distinction between the small-time property 'magnate' and the corporate real estate sector is useful in delineating the types of constructions, the processes of acquisition of residences and security of tenancy, it would be misleading to neatly map planned development from corporate real estate firms with formal property relations, and those from smaller, local-scale players with informal arrangements. Dynamics of informality, illegality and ambiguity surface routinely in both forms of property development in the area.[53] Nevertheless, we witness at this point a curdling of Vatva's real estate landscape, as newer spatial configurations of investments, clearances and tenurial entitlements are separated, to an extent, from the tangled, messy relationships of property and tenancy that otherwise dominate. Operating on a much larger scale and usually with a greater degree of clearances from the state authorities, these constructions, or rather, Vatva's 'formal' real estate sector, is geared towards generating 'Muslim' middle-class housing, while simultaneously being readied as a new site for low-income housing.

That 'Muslims only' property fairs are being organised in the city indicates the ways in which ghettoisation has become profitable. The two property fairs organised by Ali Hussein in 2012 and 2013 showcased homes ranging from INR 1 million to INR 10 million and attracted more than 40,000 potential buyers.[54] The lucrative potential of this emerging market is drawn out by builder Ashvin Patel's statements in the *Indian Express*: 'There is never a recession in the housing market in Muslim areas. There are very few Muslim areas in the city. With choices so limited, the prices of houses rise 10–15 per cent faster than those in Hindu areas.'[55] As an investment opportunity, this has called for new partnerships being forged between Hindu and Muslim builders—as Raheel Dhattiwala reported on the property show held in October 2012: 'For the first time, Gujarati (mostly) Patel builders teamed up with Gujarati Muslims builders to create upscale residential and commercial complexes exclusively for Muslims—of course, within existing Muslim ghettoes and enclaves.'[56] This kind of development is an established trend in Juhapura, in particular. Vatva is an emerging site for formal 'Muslim' housing, with the Narol–Vatva road as a new hub for middle-class Muslim housing, transforming pockets of Vatva into 'hi-fi societies'.[57]

Alongside the investments in 'Muslim' middle-class housing, the introduction of the Town Plans animated a surge of investments in 'formal' or planned low-income housing. This was accompanied, to some extent, by infrastructure constructions—including the laying and widening of inner roads, another facet of retrospective planning, leading to tensions and negotiations between residents and the urban authorities. Recent AMC data on road works also shows a heavy focus on the southern peripheries of the city—including Vatva, Lambha, Ramol and Hathijan. Congruent with accounts from corporate real estate developers, this is perhaps indicative of property development moving further into the urban peripheries—towards areas like Narol and Lambha, and the 'new Vatva' area, extending from Vatva village towards the Ring Road. The Development Plan of 2021 has earmarked zones around the outer Ring Road for affordable housing, which is also beginning to transform the landscape of eastern Ahmedabad. New public housing schemes (such as the Pradhan Mantri Awas Yojana), which privilege private sector participation, are slated for these affordable housing zones, extending the attempts to develop Vatva and beyond as sites of formally demarcated low-income housing.

Private sector investments in organised low-cost housing dovetailed into the broader agenda of the slum-free city that was gaining momentum across the country.[58] Incentivised by the state government, these experiments in housing were often grounded upon the dismantling of existing informal housing arrangements. Developers of low-income housing in Vatva made public commitments to the eradication of slum settlements, offering high-rise affordable housing in its stead.[59] Local accounts, on the other hand, imply that these property developers applied quite a literal interpretation of slum eradication; rumours were afloat that the construction of low-cost housing in Vatva had been stalled because the real estate firms were waiting for the adjacent Navapura and Jafar Row House slums to be cleared first.[60]

Atmiya Developers, one of the prominent investors in low-cost housing in the area, acquired land for their flagship project, Navjivan, in 2007, soon after the town plans were drafted. Located behind Jafar Row House and Darbar Nagar, this set of 423 units is targeted at those earning INR 20,000 and below, and is intended for a 'mixed' occupancy.[61] Accounts from Jafar Row House and Darbar Nagar, however, suggest that these new residences are almost uniformly Hindu. The architectural form and the demographic composition of the Navjivan flats added to the anxieties circulating about the 'border'. For many of the residents of Jafar Row House, Darbar Nagar, Navapura and Jain Ashram—the eastern edge of the predominantly Muslim parts of the area—experienced attacks from the adjacent high-rise, uniformly Hindu housing societies during the violence of 2002. With the establishment of Navjivan, and others like it, the border had inched closer, signalling the limits of 'Muslim' Vatva. The spatial fixing through the imposition of the Disturbed Areas Act and the creation of the 'Muslim' property market is then periodically threatened and eroded through state practices of planning and the forms of property development that followed. While it has become clear that communally unmarked access to housing is almost impossible in the city, Muslim settlements were not necessarily territorially permanent. They could be forcefully displaced, and their 'borders' breached and dislocated.

The demographic uniformity of the anticipated clientele of Navjivan flats was perhaps foreshadowed in the publicity material that the company released (Figure 7.3). For instance, none of the significant Islamic architectural monuments find any mention on the map. Nor do any other markers of 'Muslim' Vatva. All the signposts and landmarks on the promotional brochure are drawn either from the few visibly Hindu establishments or the seemingly neutral ones—Jain Ashram, Radhe Park Society, Midco Industries, and so on.[62]

In the discussion here, we have focused on certain aspects of Vatva's marginalisation. I have written about the neighbourhood as a 'ghetto', living under various intersecting regimes of insecurity. No doubt Vatva was gradually carved out as a 'Muslim' space and experienced immense anxiety over issues of physical security and marginalisation in terms of civic engagement and electoral activity. However, to overstate the isolation of Vatva from the wider social world of Ahmedabad city or to overemphasise the spatial fixity of the area would be problematic. To understand Vatva as a 'city within a city' or a 'separate city', as some commentators have argued,[63] runs the risk of ascribing a complete separateness to the space, of seeing the residents as leading lives that were somehow 'different' from the rest of the city, of viewing these social worlds as sealed, impermeable entities. While it is a powerful polemical comment (and one that needs to be made) which highlights violence, discrimination and segregation in the city and the related social experiences that it produces, it may obscure the social, political and economic ties—contested, conflicting and, at points, fraying—that Vatva maintains with the rest of the city.

Therefore, it is important to address some of the various points of contact that are maintained with the city at present. Kinship and marriage networks, work arrangements, entertainment and bureaucratic engagements, among others, produced possibilities of interaction with the wider social world. That said, it is also important to note that these interactions seem to appear within regulated circuits of engagement. Take, for instance, marital ties. In Vatva,

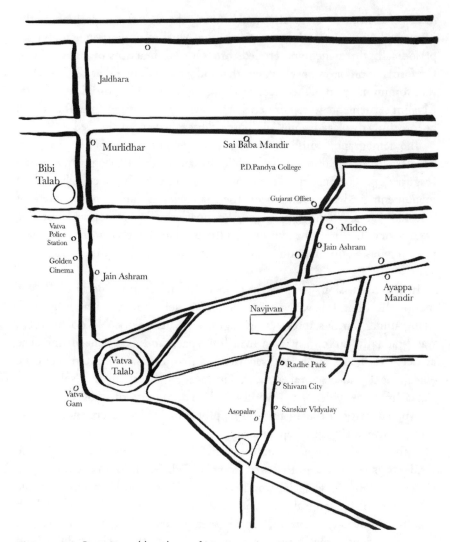

Figure 7.3 Promotional brochure of Navjivan Apartments

Source: Reproduced from the original by author.

these are brokered with the help of matchmakers and inquisitive and involved relatives. For a socially acceptable union, the marital agreement would take place within the same caste group, preferably within the Ahmedabad metropolitan region, for convenience.[64] With the city's Muslims concentrated in certain pockets, the options of spatial mobility through marriage are also rather restricted. The movements implicit in marriage (especially for women in patrilocal living arrangements) and the broader social relationships forged are then ordered through the networks of caste and religion, at one level, and through the geographical distribution of Muslims, at another.

To take another example—of the sorts of jobs that take people outside of Vatva. Autorickshaw driving, a remarkably mobile occupation, is an increasingly popular option. Owning one's auto seems to be a significant aspiration in many working-class families in the area. For most auto drivers, the vehicle is taken on rent for a period of time and is used as shuttle transport between designated points. Shuttle autorickshaws, overstuffed with passengers, leave from the Bibi Talab crossroads to go to three or four destinations—towards Lal Darwaja in the walled city, to the GIDC railway crossing and up to the Narol highway. The legal restrictions on the plying of shuttle autos are circumvented through a well-ordered system of bribery and subterfuge. The codes of the system are familiar to both parties— every month, a new sticker appears on the windshields of the shuttle auto to indicate that the hafta has been paid to the local police. The practices of bribery and corruption as an informal mechanism of regulation aside, the destinations of these shuttle autos are also telling, for all of them are to Muslim-majority areas. For those driving private autorickshaws (as opposed to the semi-public shuttles), considerable reluctance is displayed when engaged for a trip to the western parts of the city. Part of this objection stems from economic considerations, as there is a more than reasonable chance that they might not get a passenger back to Vatva. Drawing upon the material discussed previously, we could also argue that the various struggles waged for access to social welfare and better public amenities, for regularisation of housing and stricter controls over the chemical industries reflect a deep, though undeniably mediated engagement with the state. Therefore, rather than seeing the area through a lens of isolation and containment, it might be more fruitful to consider that the traffic between Vatva and the city—in a literal and social sense—then, seems to occur within regulated circuits.

Vatva's growth as a site of resettlement and recent designation as a 'disturbed area' suggests a process of forced mobility (through displacement) and a subsequent spatial fixity. This fixity, upon closer examination, is revealed to be rather precarious. To put it differently, 'ghettoes' had certainly been created through growing social distance between communities, through communal violence and through legal measures—that is, historical conditions and processes ensured that communities clustered together. However, whether the 'ghetto' itself could be spatially and permanently pinned down is debatable in this context. Partly, this divergence between fixity and mobility is revealed in the dynamic and shifting classifications of the designated 'disturbed areas', which present a historically fluctuating axis within which community clusters could move. Partly, it is revealed in the techniques of urban planning and consequent spatial precarity of settlements such as Vatva. The tensions between spatial fixity (as produced by the implementation of the Disturbed Areas Act) and spatial precariousness (as produced by retrospective urban planning) are manifested in the consistent threats upon the security of these settlements. While areas are marked out for Muslim habitation in the city, a precarious and potentially shifting spatial fix is produced, rather than an absolute one.

The displacement of vulnerable populations through communal violence ensured that people had to find housing in 'safe' areas, of which Vatva was one. The very act of resettling, however, added to the insecurity rather than diminishing it. The progressive undermining of legal instruments of property transfers, through the expansion of the Disturbed Areas Act, has made property transactions 'informal' and illegal. The employment of urban planning measures retrospectively has made the material structures of housing ever more precarious. Far from the enduring, self-reproducing image of the ghetto, Vatva is shaped equally by the designs of the state, institutional logics and politics of exclusion. Segregation in Vatva converged primarily along community and class lines, resembling, to a degree, Wacquant's 'hyperghetto'. Working lives in Vatva are, thus, framed by consistent insecurities of work, residence and even life, presenting us with a spatial configuration of various forms of informality and precarity.

NOTES

1 Ghassem-Fachandi, 'Ahimsa, Identification and Sacrifice in the Gujarat Pogrom', 155–75.

2 Rubina Jasani's research on post-2002 reconstruction also documents the processes by which large numbers of poor Muslims were displaced from the inner city to peripheral areas such as Juhapura. See Jasani, 'Violence, Reconstruction and Islamic Reform', 431–56. On the other hand, Dhattiwala points another crucial dimension of post-conflict living, where many residents in mixed localities of Ahmedabad do not have the (mainly

economic) choice of relocating to 'safe neighbourhoods'. Thus, the current heterogenous neighbourhoods of the city do not indicate a voluntary decision of residents to remain. Dhattiwala, *Keeping the Peace.*

3 Interviews, Vatva.

4 A rich body of scholarly literature, especially from the United States, exists on this subject. In the classic study by Louis Wirth, ghettoes are understood as being produced by almost natural processes, and seen as nearly indistinguishable from ethnic enclaves of largely immigrant populations. In studies produced in the wake of the Civil Rights movement, the naturalising analyses of the Chicago School were countered and complicated. Kenneth Clarke, for instance, writing in 1965, powerfully brought back the question of race into studies of urban geography. The ghetto was then seen as being produced through unequal relationships of power, inscribed in space. The industrial restructuring of the 1970s and 1980s exacerbated the conditions of poverty and 'social dislocation' in black ghettoes. The analysis of such neighbourhoods, by the 1980s, was located ever more sharply at the intersection of race and urban deprivation. With the notion of the 'urban underclass' gaining greater currency, racial segregation was gradually displaced as the key lens through which to approach the ghetto. There was then a blurring of the analytical categories of the urban slum and the ghetto. See William Julius Wilson, ed., *The Ghetto Underclass: Social Science Perspectives* (London: Sage Publications, 1993); Loïc Wacquant, 'Ghetto', in *International Encyclopedia of the Social &Behavioral Sciences*, ed. N. J. Smelster and P. B. Balter (London: Pergamon Press, 2004).

5 Louis Wirth, *The Ghetto* (Chicago: University of Chicago Press, 1956).

6 Ghazala Jamil, *Accumulation by Segregation: Muslim Localities in Delhi* (New Delhi: Oxford University Press, 2017), 34–35.

7 Wacquant, 'Ghetto?', 155–64.

8 In Wacquant's studies of urban marginality, he further sharpens his analysis of the ghetto, drawing a distinction between the American black ghetto and other enclosures of the urban disposed across the world. The predominance of certain ethnic groups in the Parisian banlieues, for instance, is 'accentuated, but not primarily driven, by ethnic discrimination in housing'. See Loïc Wacquant, *Urban Outcasts: A Comparative Sociology of Advanced Marginality* (Cambridge; Malden: Polity, 2010), 192.

9 Loïc Wacquant, 'A Janus-Faced Institution of Ethnoracial Closure: A Sociological Specification of the Ghetto', in *The Ghetto: Contemporary Global*

Issues and Controversies, ed. Ray Hutchison and Bruce Haynes (Boulder: Westview, 2011).

10 Arnold R. Hirsch, *Making the Second Ghetto: Race and Housing in Chicago 1940–1960* (Chicago; London: University of Chicago Press, 1998).

11 Janet L. Abu-Lughod, *Rabat: Urban Apartheid in Morocco* (Princeton, NJ: Princeton University Press, 2014), xvii.

12 Wacquant, *Urban Outcasts*, 47.

13 Jaffrelot and Thomas, 'Facing Ghettoisation in the "Riot City".'

14 Soutik Biswas, 'Why Segregated Housing Is Thriving in India', BBC News, 10 December 2014, available at https://www.bbc.com/news/world-asia-india-30204806, accessed on 5 August 2020.

15 See, for instance, *The Wire*, 13 December 2017 and 17 September 2018; *Sabrang*, 25 November 2017.

16 Charlotte Thomas, 'Being Muslim in Narendra Modi's India Ghetto Life: Between Domination and Resistance', Noria Research, May 2015, available at https://www.noria-research.com/being-muslim-in-narendra-modis-india-ghetto-life-between-domination-and-resistance/, accessed on 17 August 2020.

17 Christophe Jaffrelot and Sharik Laliwala in *The Wire*, 12 September 2018.

18 Thomas, 'Being Muslim in Narendra Modi's India Ghetto Life: Between Domination and Resistance'.

19 Jasani, 'Violence, Reconstruction and Islamic Reform.'

20 Thomas, 'Being Muslim in Narendra Modi's India Ghetto Life, Between Domination and Resistance' .

21 Loïc Wacquant, 'French Working-Class Banlieues and Black American Ghetto: From Conflation to Comparison', *Qui Parle* 16, no. 2 (2007): 5–38, 25.

22 Renu Desai, Darshini Mahadevia, Shachi Sanghvi, Suchita Vyas, Rafi Malek and Mohammad Sharif Malek, 'Bombay Hotel: Urban Planning, Governance and Everyday Conflict and Violence in a Muslim Locality on the Peripheries of Ahmedabad', Working Paper 31, Centre for Urban Equity, CEPT University, Ahmedabad, 2016.

23 *Times of India*, 8 October 1965.

24 Interview with Munira Bukhari, Ahmedabad, 10 December 2012.

25 *Times of India*, 16 April 1970.

26 *Times of India*, 9 August 1960, 10 August 1960 and 13 August 1960.

27 Interviews with Suraj Singh Rathore and Munira Bukhari.

28 *Times of India*, 27 July 1973 and 3 October 1975.

29 *Times of India*, 1 May 1990.

30 *Times of India*, 8 December 1961, 16 December 1963, 13 March 1964 and 17 October 1964.

31 Kutir Vidyalaya was established in the late 1950s.

32 Interview with Munira Bukhari, Ahmedabad, 10 December 2012; Swara Bhaskar's evocative article on Vatva also highlights this invocation of a golden age, arguing that this 'remembered utopia was both agrarian and pre-industrial'. *Himal South Asian*, March 2005.

33 Interviews, Vatva.

34 Interview with Suraj Singh Rathore, Anand, 20 December 2011.

35 Amrita Shah's recent book has an almost tender account of Bombay Hotel, a predominantly Muslim area located between Vatva and the National Highway. She outlines a similar process in the settling of the area: 'This swathe of land, off the Narol Road, was parceled out among a host of small-time, would-be developers. Through the fraught nineties a steady trickle of Muslims arrived from the city. Some even bought a plot as an investment. Bit by bit, the jungle was cut down.' See Shah, *Ahmedabad: A City in the World*, 174–95.

36 Private builders, in particular, have made offers of constructing high-rise tenements on the Darbar Nagar land.

37 Form 7/12 from the sub-registrar's office.

38 See Table A.1 in Appendix.

39 Interviews with Shehnazben, Amnaben and Mumtazben, 2011–12.

40 See Table A.2 in Appendix.

41 The AMC is very proud of its 'participatory' process of urban planning. However, conversations with landowners in the area suggest that the process of consultations with the AMC was far less detailed than is indicated on paper. Darbar Chacha insists that the discussion meetings with the AMC for the adjustment and reservation of plots began only after 2002, as does Bade Khan, who suggests that the town planning scheme discussions were initiated a few years ago, only after he demanded it.

42 AMC and AUDA TPS status, 30 January 2010. See also https://ahmedabadcity.gov.in/portal/jsp/Static_pages/pi_cplanning.jsp, accessed on 3 July 2021.

43 Shirley Ballaney, 'The Town Planning Mechanism in Gujarat, India', World Bank Institute, 2008. For instance, most of the construction work and acquisitions of property that I observed during my research between 2010 and 2013 were conducted without these regulatory clearances. These

ranged from building without permissions, 'buying' homes through power of attorney, and modifying and expanding the built structure.

44 As Vanaik has argued in the case of colonial Delhi, the state's attempts at creating deep connections between various representations of space had limited success. Anish Vanaik, 'Representing Commodified Space: Maps, Leases, Auctions and "Narrations" of Property in Delhi, C. 1900– 47', *Historical Research* 88, no. 240 (2015): 314–32.

45 For instance, the civic body's eviction attempts in 2009 were periodically stalled through court appeals initiated by Jan Sangharsh Manch. See *Indian Express*, 22 June 2009.

46 *Times of India*, 23 February 2012.

47 In August 2011, the AMC razed about 107 illegal row houses in the area. These unauthorised constructions of one-bedroom dwellings had been built partly on land reserved for a public garden and partly on encroached private land. *Times of India*, 30 August 2011.

48 It is, of course, entirely possible that the petitioner, Muhammad Yunus Khan Pathan—described as an ordinary resident of Vatva—was acting more out of a personal interest in the land, rather than out of a sense of civic duty. Nevertheless, it points towards local tensions, whether over civic resources or over the control of land. *Mohammed Yunus Khan Pathan v. AMC, Municipal Commissioner*, Gujarat High Court, 10 May 2000.

49 It was reported that the private agricultural lands had been sold in 1998 to five buyers, including one Sharifkhan Nawabkhan Pathan of Shah Alam Roza. The land records produced in court, however, revealed that the sale had actually not been effected and, therefore, the property did not belong to the group of builders who had commenced construction on the land. Pathan, one of the builders named in the court documents, is one of the partners of Nawab Builders, which operated out of the Shah Alam area. In 1988, he was detained under the Anti-Social Activities Act on charges of being a 'dangerous person'. One of his nephews is the current municipal corporator of the Dani Limda ward. After the carnage of 2002, Nawab Builders were actively involved in resettling riot-affected persons in Vatva. See, for instance, *Times of India*, 8 January 2015; *Mehboobkhan Nawabkhan Pathan v. Police Commissioner, Ahmedabad*, 25 July 1989; and *Mohammed Yunus Khan Pathan v. AMC, Municipal Commissioner*, Gujarat High Court, 10 May 2000.

50 From another property dispute, we can glean that out of the several hundred Muslims squatting on graveyard land in the erstwhile mill district of Gomtipur, about eighty-five families were resettled in Vatva through the

Ahmedabad Sunni Waqf Trust. *Ghulam Mohammad Abdulmajed Ansari v. State of Gujarat*, Gujarat High Court, 18 July 2000.

51 *Mohammed Yunus Khan Pathan v. AMC, Municipal Commissioner*, Gujarat High Court, 10 May 2000, 2.

52 'List of Disturbed Areas of Ahmedabad (City and Rural)', available at http://www.gicl.in/disturbed_area.html, accessed on 3 July 2021.

53 The case of NA constructions is illustrative. The firm was a sponsor at the Vibrant Gujarat Summit in 2013, well regarded as a key player in Ahmedabad's real estate market, having initiated several low-income housing projects across the city. One of these was located in Vatva, adjacent to Jafar Row House and Navapura. By 2015, the developers were charged with fraud. See *Times of India*, Ahmedabad edition, 5 May 2015.

54 Biswas, 'Why Segregated Housing Is Thriving in India'; *Indian Express*, 27 October 2012.

55 Ashvin Patel quoted in 'A House for Mehboob Desai', *Financial Times*, 28 October 2012.

56 *Hindustan Times*, 25 October 2012.

57 This is a fairly new trend. Until 2013, Aman Residency, which was under construction at the corner of Bibi Talab, was one of the few middle-class housing societies.

58 'Ahmedabad: More but Different Government for Slum Free and Livable Cities', World Bank Policy Research Working Paper 6267, World Bank Group, Washington, D.C., 2012.

59 *DNA India*, 24 February 2013.

60 Interview with Foliage Constructions, Ahmedabad, 17 January 2012; interviews, Vatva, 2012.

61 Interview with Foliage Constructions, Ahmedabad, 17 January 2012.

62 This strategy is visible in promotional material produced by other real estate firms in the area. The advertisements for Umang constructions, another low-income housing complex, similarly stripped Vatva of all Muslim spatial markers.

63 Mahadevia, 'A City with Many Borders', 315–40. See also Jaffrelot and Thomas, 'Facing Ghettoisation in the "Riot City"', 43–80; Bobbio, *Urbanisation, Citizenship and Conflict in India*, 132.

64 Interviews, 2011–12.

CONCLUSION

Asiyaben and her husband, Karimbhai, live in Jain Ashram, Vatva, in a two-roomed dwelling painted blue. Asiyaben's family was one of the area's 'original' residents and was said to have owned a large parcel of land, including where the Jain temple and the Sabarmati relocation flats now stand. Karimbhai used to work in the Vatva industrial estate and now drives an autorickshaw; Asiyaben takes in subcontracted sewing work. Their home is decorated in a fashion fairly typical in Vatva—a crockery stand mounted on the wall, displaying the gleaming steel utensils and studio portraits of the family. The greatest attention was devoted to their youngest daughter, Nasreen, whose growth over the years had been lovingly documented, photographed with her parents, her four brothers and a large array of stuffed animals. Nasreen is adopted, and how she became a part of Asiyaben's family is something of a local legend. She was found in 2004, abandoned on the banks of the Sabarmati, still bloody from the birth, wrapped in nothing but a plastic bag with the name 'Nidhi Hospital, Satellite'. The date is important—it was two years after the Godhra *kand*, as Asiyaben stressed. While narrating this story to me, Karimbhai mentioned several times that he was quite certain that Nasreen had been born to a rich Hindu family. He gleaned this from the address of the hospital where she is assumed to be born. For there are no Muslims in Satellite—a neighbourhood in western Ahmedabad. The way Karimbhai and Asiyaben perceive the city sets up certain binaries—between Hindus and Muslims, the rich and the poor, the eastern and western banks of the Sabarmati. The congruence of these categories, as this book has shown, is complicated by many other coordinates—of class, employment and histories of residence. Yet the binary framing of identity remains a potent one in the ways in which urban life is experienced and articulated.

One's place in the city, as the above anecdote shows, is historically contingent. This book has explored how workers' claims on the city were forged and transformed over the course of the twentieth and early twenty-first centuries. This is an attempt to demonstrate the centrality of the city's working classes in Ahmedabad's political and spatial history. By focusing on the neighbourhood, I have aimed to connect a range of everyday processes and activities to wider shifts in the city's political and economic history. The close attention to the dynamics of neighbourhood life has allowed me to trace the shifting interactions of spatial practice and politics across nearly a century of the city's history. At one level, this work has empirically delineated how local politics and property relations play out in Ahmedabad's labour spaces. This has not just been an exercise in zooming in, of magnifying the micro, but rather, I hope, an exercise in connecting local matters—of sewage and sanitation, property ownership and distress selling, dadagiri and social work—with the administrative and discursive regimes of the state. The issues that I have discussed in this book can be seen along three interconnected themes.

MEDIATION

The actors of mediation appear in this book as representatives of local political textures, operating at the porous threshold between formal control and informal authority. The focus on mediation draws together a range of everyday concerns of the urban working classes—from the world of union politics and access to land and housing, to supply of civic amenities, networks of electoral participation and negotiating moments of violence—while being attentive to the temporality and the spatiality of social practice. In a crucial way, this relates to the presence or absence of state institutions and functionaries in workers' neighbourhoods, by way of municipal governance, electoral representation, service provision and urban planning. At the risk of belabouring the point, I would like to emphasise that my understanding of the different configurations of political mediation discussed in Part I is not based on a model of linear transition. The three chapters introduce these mediatory forms at the particular historical conjunctures at which they are rendered most visible; however, one form of mediation did not naturally flow into another. Instead, there were also considerable overlaps between them; they often coexisted and conflicted. Mediation was as central to the associational form of the TLA as it is in negotiating life in Vatva. This book has demonstrated that the practices of political mediation linked different scales of social, political and state authority, thereby producing historically contingent, spatially located circuits of power. The practices of political mediation and the figure of the intermediary, thus, present an unstable and shifting interface between the formal and informal registers of local authority.

Accounts of the carnage of 2002 suggest that India's 'mediated state' structure offered the possibilities of organising the violence.[1] Much of this book historicises the field of forces that facilitated riot production. In his study of eastern Ahmedabad, Berenschot identifies the existence of 'institutionalised riot systems', which were equipped with a range of figures performing specialised functions—riot organisers, provocateurs, fire tenders, riot specialists, and so on.[2] These networks were not necessarily forged with the intention of organising violence, but were instead predicated on the more everyday practices of mediating state agencies. The practices and politics of mediation that Berenschot has elaborated on for contemporary Ahmedabad are elongated here to provide an account of how the figure of the pratinidhi or the dada or the social worker and the networks which they were part of were historically produced, transformed and reproduced. An understanding of the forms of mediation (and the figure of the intermediary) is key to understanding the geographies of urban transformation and social experience.

INFORMALITY

I suggest that to understand the histories of urban working-class neighbourhoods, it is essential that we trace the processes of informalisation that have occurred. An overarching argument of this book suggests that this was not restricted to the realm of industrial production and labour relations, but impacted the economy at large as well as the structure of politics. The chapters have followed, on the one hand, the ways in which the figure of the intermediary, while continuing to play a crucial role in local politics, was gradually unmoored from more formal political and electoral structures and, on the other, detailed the shrinking of formal, legal rights of the urban working classes over their living spaces.

The process by which the city's working poor are dispossessed and their claims on urban land and housing denuded follows what David Harvey has elsewhere termed 'accumulation by dispossession'.[3] The industrial neighbourhoods of Ahmedabad, as we have seen, were shaped by a complex interaction between legal regimes, planning mechanisms, social conflict and employment relations. In the mill districts, we find a steady erosion of legal rights of residence. The brief moment of tenurial security afforded by the Rent Control Act was gradually dismantled from the 1970s onwards. Through property transfers that took place via legally dubious means, changing urban policy and new land and property regulations, social and legal connotations of housing in the mill areas were being remade and new forms of residential precarity introduced. For instance, with the imposition of the Urban Land Ceiling Act, access to land for the city's working poor grew more contentious or, for that matter, the Slum Clearance Act or the Disturbed Areas Act, which governed property relations with greater rigour. After the collapse of the textile industry, the chawls that stood on mill lands were caught in litigation and long battles over ownership. There emerged a new ambivalence of employment relations in securing tenurial rights; evidence of mill employment was no longer adequate to establish a claim on chawl property. Rather, it was the reverse, as lawful claims were made on the basis of a denial of any connection to mill employment, rather than on proof of its confirmation.

The role of the state in these transformations of urban property is revealed, at one level, through its direct interventions in acquiring mill chawls or in the sale of closed mills, making this land available to private capital for commercial or industrial use. More so than large-scale land grabs, the state's role in this process of accumulation has been through its legislative and bureaucratic apparatus. Thus, one vector of spatial dispossession has been through the techniques of urban planning and legal regimes governing land use. The other was the exacerbation of communal conflict and the state-led measures designed to curb it. The two dovetailed to produce a stratified and a segregated city.

EXCLUSION

The institutionalisation of exclusion, as Mahadevia points out, was significant in allowing a communal ideology to flourish.[4] Apart from the dynamics of exclusion implicit in modes of urban governance in contemporary Ahmedabad, one of the key ways in which this book has addressed this question is with regard to the deep segregation of social space. The legal and material bases of urban segregation, I suggest, were tied, to a great degree, to the application of the Disturbed Areas Act. The intention of this legislation was ostensibly to *prevent* ghettoisation, by regulating distress sales of property. Three repercussions can be identified. First, the tightening of regulations *after* most areas have already been reordered along community lines suggests that certain legal limits are placed on inter-communal living. We have enough evidence to show that spatial segregation along Hindu and Muslim lines has occurred and has become deeply entrenched since the 1990s. The early years of the legislation's implementation were marked by administrative indifference and the initially *temporary* ordinance was progressively expanded and normalised, leading to an urban property market that is split along communal lines. Second, with the processes of acquiring clearances of inter-community transfers, undeniably labourious, 'formal', registered property transactions with all official clearances, in present-day Ahmedabad, can possibly only be concluded within communally uniform areas. And third, for ongoing property transfers in 'mixed' areas, the only recourse was often 'informal', legally suspect transactions. This, to my mind, is valid for the entire city. For the working-class districts, the implications of this Act may be even more pernicious. With the legal instrument of the power of attorney, arguably the most common mode of property transactions in the workers' districts, progressively curtailed through this legislation, the extension of the Act further pushes these properties into a zone of illegality.

Therefore, the implementation, consistent circumvention and periodic expansion of the legislation, instead, ascribed religious markers to real estate, and facilitated the production of two separate communally inscribed property markets. The material dispossession that occurred during the violence of 2002 further reinforced, on the one hand, the distinctions in the city's real estate market and, on the other, the significance of intermediary figures in acquiring 'safe' housing. The Act, which was intended to provide security of tenancy in situations of violence, paradoxically exacerbated the insecurity. Unable to prevent distress sales, the legislation produced a property market (especially for the city's Muslims) that was largely informal and precarious.

These forms of social exclusion were invariably shored up the state machinery, in acceding or denying permissions for transfers, in its tacit approval of social segregation and in its often biased application of the Disturbed Areas Act. Accumulation through dispossession, in this case, was grounded in a communal logic through the rupturing of heterogeneous spatial arrangements and the subsequent spatial enclosure and the progressive weakening of property rights of the Muslim working poor. The dynamics of social and spatial exclusion, while unfolding gradually over decades, have nevertheless been systematic and consistent enough to produce clearly demarcated 'Muslim' spaces in the city. In the mill areas, this segregation of social space was more subtle, as large pockets of the neighbourhood were marked as either Hindu or Muslim, while spatial divisions in the rest of the city were even more stark.

The initial impetus of property development in areas marked out as 'Muslim', such as Vatva—the provision and mediation of housing, negotiations with state agencies—was managed by slumlords or the small-time property 'magnates'. Retrospective planning, regulatory frameworks of building and construction permits, and new formal real estate investments introduced new dimensions of possible dispossession. While it is beyond the scope of this book to go into great detail over this, it is worth mentioning that the Sabarmati riverfront development relocation flats in Vatva have also introduced new quotidian tensions in the area, in terms of both their (mixed) communal composition and conflicts over resources. The provision of civic amenities in the flats has emerged as a flashpoint for tensions between residents, local service providers and the municipal corporation, while there is increasing anxiety over growing crime in the area. Furthermore, according to local accounts in 2012, the resettlements and informal transfers have been such that the predominantly Muslim blocks are the farthest from the 'Muslim' parts of Vatva, such as Jain Ashram. There was tension, in particular, around attempts to conduct Friday prayers in an open ground around the resettlement flats. Opposed by the Hindu residents, many would then have to walk a considerable distance, crossing Hindu-majority blocks, to the mosque in Vatva. The threat of a rather violent spatial re-structuring (and possible dislocation) lurks upon these neighbourhoods, while borders and frontiers undulate, thereby complicating the notion that a ghetto is necessarily permanently rooted in one particular location. Therefore, the Muslim residents of Vatva appear to be precariously fixed to their spatial location—their mobility greatly limited (unless it occurs within the clearly demarcated circuits of the city's 'Muslim' areas) and their spatial fixity jeopardised by the planning and regulatory processes, allowing us to perhaps advance a conceptualisation of a 'mobile ghetto'.

In focusing on the more intimate histories of the working-class neighbourhoods, this book has no doubt overlooked other important aspects of city politics, urban transformation and social change. These include, among others, state- or national-level political tactics, operational minutiae of political parties and questions of middle-class participation in social and political movements. I have, furthermore, not addressed the transformation of the western parts of the city—the more elite, affluent spaces where, too, the interaction between Hindutva politics and processes of globalisation are sharply visible.

The main intention of this book is to offer a historical account of mediation, informalisation and exclusion in Ahmedabad's labour spaces. The unavoidably linear process of writing has meant a separation of the entangled processes of political and spatial practice into two distinct segments of the book. The differential registers and rhythms of political participation, which draw from both historic engagement with formal political structures and their current position within Ahmedabad's political landscape, were connected to the hierarchised production of social space that has contributed to and is, in turn, shaped by social marginalisation and material dispossession. Politics, property and precarity emerge, in the end, as the matrix for this troubled history of Ahmedabad.

NOTES

1 Berenschot, 'Riot Politics: Communal Violence and State-Society Mediation in Gujarat, India.'
2 Ibid., 236ff.
3 David Harvey, *The New Imperialism* (Oxford: Oxford University Press, 2003).
4 Mahadevia, 'Communal Space over Life Space', 4858.

APPENDIX

Table A.1 Sample of property tax information for Darbar Nagar

Address	Owner	Occupier
Mahavir Society, Darbargarh, Near Jafar Row House, Vatva	Surajsing Udesing	Mumtazbibi
		Asma Ahmadbhai
		Mohammed Sabir Abdulrahim
		Zakirbhai Huseinbhai
		Muhamad Zakirkhan Chauhan
		Idris Nasirbhai
		Nahibbibi Anvarkhan
		Seemaben Udesing Rathod
		Aslambhai Pirbax
		Islambhai Malek
		Salman Ansari
		Rasulahmed Mukhtyarahmed
		Aamirkhan Pathan
		Omarhussein Ahmadkhan

Source: Table complied by author from AMC, available at www.egovamc.com, accessed on August 2020.

Note: All names have been anonymised.

Table A.2 Sample of property tax information for Jafar Row House

Address	Owner	Occupier
JAFAR RAW HOUSE NR JAIN ASHRAM VTAVA AHD [*sic*]	Mohammad Jafar Shaikh	Afjalbhai Shaikh
		Hasinaben Aamirkhan Pathan
		Sabeena Ansari
		Nasreenben Ghanchi
		Saimaben Desai
		Rahul Mohamad Sheikh
		Rohansingsing Bablusing Sisodiya
		Zainabben Tamboli
		Danish Shaikh
		Fatima Azamkhan
		Saiyeeda Begum
		Sajjad Khan
		Ikrambhai Khudabux
		Hamidbhai Rathod
		Muneerbhai Ahmad Khan
		Yasmin Begum
		Yusuf Khan
		Rihan Khan

Source: Table complied by author from AMC, available at www.egovamc.com, accessed on August 2020.

Note: All names have been anonymised.

GLOSSARY

adda	a gathering spot for conversation; alternatively used to imply a drinking den
akhada	gymnasium
bandh	general strike
benaami	property held or transactions concluded in the name of another person
bidi	leaf rolled cigarettes
char rasta	crossroads
charpai	cot
chowk	junction
chulha	open fire wood stove
daku	bandit
goonda	a violent, aggressive person; goon; hoodlum
hafta	a regular payment of bribes
hukkah	water pipe for smoking tobacco
jhuggi-jhopdi	shanties, semi-permanent housing
kand	incident
kund	a tanning pit
kutcha	makeshift; impermanent
mukadam	foreman, recruiter of labour
nagarseth	the position of the leading businessman of the city

pan shops	small stalls or shops selling betel leaves, areca nuts and cigarettes, among other things
panchayat	elective village council
prakhand	a division of a party
pucca	permanent dwellings
rathyatra	Hindu ceremonial chariot processions; also used for political mobilisations and demonstrations
saraf	banking and financing families and communities
*shakha*s	branches
swadeshi	related to one's own country; political movement or commitment to boycott foreign goods and consume domestic products
taluka	administrative sub-division of a district
yatra	pilgimage

BIBLIOGRAPHY

REPORTS

Ahmedabad Municipal Corporation. *A Report on the Census of Slums in Ahmedabad.* Ahmedabad: Ahmedabad Municipal Corporation, 1976.
———. *AMC Revised Development Plan 1975–1985.* Ahmedabad: Ahmedabad Municipal Corporation, 1975.
———. *Statistical Outline of Ahmedabad City.* Ahmedabad: Ahmedabad Municipal Corporation, 2003–06.
Ahmedabad Municipal Corporation and Ahmedabad Urban Development Authority with technical assistance from the Centre for Environmental Planning and Technology (CEPT). *Ahmedabad City Development Plan 2006–2012.* Ahmedabad, 2006.
Bhattacharjea, Ajit. *Report on Ahmedabad.* Ahmedabad: Sampradayikta Virodhi Committee, 1969.
Concerned Citizens' Tribunal. *Crime Against Humanity: An Inquiry into the Carnage in Gujarat.* Vols 1, II and III. Bombay, 2002. Available at http://www.sabrang.com/tribunal/index.html, accessed 13 May 2020.
Dave, Justice V. S. *Report of the Commission of Inquiry: Into the Incidents of Violence and Disturbances Which Took Place in Various Places in the State of Gujarat since February, 1985 to 18th July, 1985.* Vols I, II and III. Ahmedabad: Government of India, 1990.
Election Commission of India. *Statistical Report on General Elections to the Legislative Assembly of Gujarat, 1975–1998.* New Delhi: Election Commission of India. Available at https://eci.gov.in/statistical-report/statistical-reports/, accessed May 2019–June 2020.
Government of Gujarat. *Collectors Manual, Revenue Department.* Government of Gujarat, 2007–08.

Government of India. *Annual Report of the Ministry of Textiles, 2009–10*. Available at http://texmin.nic.in/sites/default/files/ar_09_10_english.pdf, accessed 15 July 2021.

Human Rights Watch. *Politics by Other Means: Attacks against Christians in India*. Available at https://www.hrw.org/legacy/reports/1999/indiachr/christians804.htm#P393_83982, accessed 20 October 2015.

Indulal Yagnik Papers relating to Ahmedabad Police Firing Inquiry Commission, 1958. Nehru Memorial Museum and Library.

Islami Relief Committee, Gujarat. *Islami Relief Committee Report upto 2004*. Ahmedabad: Islami Relief Committee, Gujarat, 2004.

Miyabhai, N. M.. *Report of the Commission of Inquiry into the Prohibition Policy in Gujarat*. Ahmedabad: Government of Gujarat, 1983.

———. *Report of the Laththa Commission of Inquiry*. Ahmedabad: Government of Gujarat, 1978.

Labour Office. *Report on an Enquiry into Working-class Family Budgets in Ahmedabad*. Bombay: Government Central Press, 1928.

Labour Office. *Report on an Enquiry into Working-class Family Budgets in Ahmedabad*. Bombay: Government Central Press, 1938.

Labour Bureau, Government of India. *Report on Family Living Survey Among Industrial Workers in Ahmedabad 1958–59*. Nasik: Government of India Press, 1965.

Papers relating to Ahmedabad Police Firing Inquiry Commission, 1958. Nehru Memorial Museum and Library.

Reddy, Pingle Jaganmohan, N. K. Vakil and Akbar S. Sarela. *Report: Inquiry into the Communal Disturbances at Ahmedabad and Other Places in Gujarat on and after 18th September 1969*. Gandhinagara: Gujarat Government Press, 1971.

Report of the Laththa (Hooch) Commission of Inquiry. Ahmedabad: 2008.

Report of the Rent Enquiry Committee, Vols I, II and III. Bombay: Government Central Press, 1939.

Sampradayikta Virodhi Committee. *Ahmedabad Riots: X-Rayed*. Ahmedabad: Sampradayikta Virodhi Committee, 1970.

Sedgwick, L. J. *Census of India*, Vol. IX, Part I: *Cities of the Bombay Presidency*. Poona: Superintendent, Government Printing, 1922.

Textile Labour Association. *A Plea for Municipal Housing for the Working Classes in the City of Ahmedabad*. Ahmedabad: Textile Labour Association, 1929.

———. *Annual Reports of the Textile Labour Association*. Ahmedabad: Textile Labour Association, select issues.

Whitley, J. H. *Report of the Royal Commission on Labour*, Vol. I, Part 1. London: H. M. Stationery Office, 1931.

NEWSPAPERS AND MAGAZINES

DNA: Daily News and Analysis
Gujarat Samachar
Hindu, The
Hindustan Times
Illustrated Weekly of India
India Today
Indian Express
Outlook
Majoor Sandesh
Times of India

COURT PROCEEDINGS

Abdul Latif Abdul Wahab Sheikh v. B.K. Jha and Others. Gujarat High Court. 9 February 1987.

Abdul Razak Abdul Wahab Sheikh v. S.N. Sinha, Commissioner of Police. Gujarat High Court. 3 March 1989.

Anilkumar Vaikuthlal Patel v. Official Liquidator of Ahmedabad Jubilee Mills. Gujarat High Court. 26 March 2020.

Ayub alias Pappukhan Nawab Khan Pathan v. S.N. Sinha and Another. Gujarat High Court. 7 August 1990.

Desai Vishnubhai Fulabhai v. O.L. of Arbuda Mills. Gujarat High Court. 9 May 2005.

Ghulam Mohammad Abdulmajed Ansari v. State of Gujarat. Gujarat High Court. 18 July 2000.

Ghulam Mohammad Musabhai v. Chaturbhai Dalabhai heirs and L/R of Moghiben Dalabhai. Gujarat High Court. 22 February 2011.

Ghulam Mohammad Musabhai v. Ujiben Mulabhai. Gujarat High Court. 4 July 2011.

Harji Hira Rabari v. E. N. Renison, Dy. Comm of Police. Gujarat High Court. 25 April 1968.

Jabal C. Lashkari v. Official Liquidator of Prasad Mills. Supreme Court of India. 29 March 2016.

Mehboobkhan Nawabkhan Pathan v. Police Commissioner, Ahmedabad. Gujarat High Court. 25 July 1989.

Mohammed Yunus Khan Pathan v. AMC, Municipal Commissioner. Gujarat High Court. 10 May 2000.

O.L. of Aryodaya Spg. and Weaving Mills Co. Ltd. v. Charansingh Dhupsingh. Gujarat High Court. 16 April 2004.

Pravinbhai Jashbhai Patel v. The state of Gujarat. Gujarat High Court. 5 August 1995.

Rajubhai Kumavati Marwadi v. Sabarmati River Front Development Corporation Limitation. Gujarat Hight Court. 13 June 2012.

Rameshbhai Tank and Others v. OL of Vijay Mills Ltd. Gujarat High Court. 18 March 2008.

Said Maher Husein v. Haji Alimohamed Jalaludin. Bombay High Court. 27 November 1933.

Smt. Chandrakanta v. Vadilal Bapalal Modi. Gujarat High Court. 30 March 1989.

SNA Infraprojects v. Sub Registrar. Gujarat High Court. 13 May 2011.

State of Gujarat v. Nareshbhai Parmar. Gujarat High Court. 13 February 2012.

State of Gujarat v. Nareshbhai Parmar and Others. Gujarat High Court. 20 April 2012.

State of Gujarat v. O.L. Vijay Mill. Gujarat Hight Court. 28 November 2011.

Textile Labour Association v. O.L. of Amruta Mills. Gujarat High Court. 30 September 2004.

Textile Labour Association v. O.L. Vijay Mills. Gujarat High Court. 22 February 2005.

UNPUBLISHED THESES

Berenschot, Ward. 'Riot Politics: Communal Violence and State–Society Mediation in Gujarat, India'. PhD thesis, University of Amsterdam, 2006.

Bobbio, Tommaso. 'Collective Violence, Urban Change and Social Exclusion: Ahmedabad 1930–2000'. PhD thesis, University of London, 2010.

Desai, Renu. 'The Globalising City in the Time of Hindutva: The Politics of Urban Development and Citizenship in Ahmedabad'. PhD thesis, University of Berkley, 2008.

Kansara, Bharti P. 'Business, Labour and Opposition Movements in the Politics of Ahmedabad City, 1960–72'. PhD thesis, SOAS, University of London, 1975.

Masihi, Edwin. 'Trade Union Leadership in Textile Industry of Ahmedabad'. PhD thesis, Gujarat University, 1976.

Parikh, Manju. 'Labor–Capital Relations in the Indian Textile Industry: A Comparative Study of Ahmedabad and Coimbatore'. PhD thesis, University of Chicago, Department of Political Science, 1988.

Patel, Bimal Hasmukh. 'The Space of Property Capital, Property Development and Architecture in Ahmedabad'. PhD thesis, University of California, Berkeley, 1995.

BOOKS AND ARTICLES

Abu-Lughod, Janet L. *Rabat: Urban Apartheid in Morocco*. Princeton: Princeton University Press, 2014.

Adarkar, Neera, ed. *The Chawls of Mumbai: Galleries of Life*: Delhi: ImprintOne, 2011.

Ahuja, Ravi. 'A Beveridge Plan for India? Social Insurance and the Making of the "Formal Sector"'. *International Review of Social History* 64, no. 2 (2019): 207–48.

———. 'A Freedom Still Enmeshed in Servitude: The Unruly "Lascars" of *SS City of Manila* or, a Micro-History of the "Free Labour Problem"'. In *Working Lives and Worker Militancy: The Politics of Labour in Colonial India*, edited by Ravi Ahuja, 97–133. New Delhi: Tulika Books, 2013.

———. 'Mobility and Containment: The Voyages of South Asian Seamen, C. 1900–1960'. *International Review of Social History* 51 (2006): 111–41.

———. *Pathways of Empire: Circulation, Public Works, and Social Space in Colonial Orissa (C. 1780–1914)*. Hyderabad: Orient Longman, 2009.

Alter, Joseph S. *The Wrestler's Body: Identity and Ideology in North India*. Berkeley: University of California Press, 1992.

Appadurai, Arjun. 'Spectral Housing and Urban Cleansing: Notes on Millennial Mumbai'. *Public Culture* 12, no. 3 (2000): 627–51.

Ballaney, Shirley. 'The Town Planning Mechanism in Gujarat, India'. Washington, D.C.: World Bank Institute, 2008.

Barua, Rukmini. 'The Textile Labour Association and Dadagiri: Power and Politics in the Working-Class Neighborhoods of Ahmedabad'. *International Labor and Working Class History* 87 (Spring 2015): 63–91.

Basu, Amrita. 'The Long March from Ayodhya: Democracy and Violence in India'. In *Pluralism and Democracy in India: Debating the Hindu Right*, edited by Wendy Doniger and Martha C. Nussbaum, 153–173. Oxford: Oxford University Press, 2015.

Baviskar, Amita. 'Between Violence and Desire: Space, Power, and Identity in the Making of Metropolitan Delhi'. *International Social Science Journal* 55, no. 175 (2003): 89–98.

———. *In the Belly of the River: Tribal Conflicts over Development in the Narmada Valley*. Delhi: Oxford University Press, 1999.

Baviskar, Amita, and Nandini Sundar. 'Democracy Versus Economic Transformation?' *Economic and Political Weekly* 43, no. 46 (2008): 87–89.

Berenschot, Ward. 'On the Usefulness of Goondas in Indian Politics: "Moneypower" and "Musclepower" in a Gujarati Locality'. *South Asia: Journal of South Asian Studies* 34, no. 2 (2011): 255–75.

———. *Riot Politics: Hindu–Muslim Violence and the Indian State*. Delhi: Rupa Publications, 2013.

———. 'The Spatial Distribution of Riots: Patronage and the Instigation of Communal Violence in Gujarat, India'. *World Development* 39, no. 2 (2011): 221–30.

Bhan, Gautam. 'This Is No Longer the City I Once Knew'. Evictions, the Urban Poor and the Right to the City in Millennial Delhi'. *Environment and Urbanization* 21, no. 1 (2009): 127–42.

Bhargava, G. S. 'Mobilizing Women for Change: Case Study of Sanjaynagar, Ahmedabad'. Working Paper 7, Centre for Urban Equity, CEPT University, Ahmedabad, 2010.

———. 'Structure of a Riot'. *Seminar* 125 (1970): 18–20.

Bhatt, Mahesh P., and V. K. Chavda. *The Anatomy of Urban Poverty: A Study of Slums in Ahmedabad City*. Ahmedabad: Gujarat University, 1979.

Bhattacharya, Debraj. 'Kolkata "Underworld" in the Early 20th Century'. *Economic and Political Weekly* 39, no. 38 (2004): 4276–82.

Björkman, Lisa. 'Becoming a Slum: From Municipal Colony to Illegal Settlement in Liberalization-Era Mumbai'. *International Journal of Urban and Regional Research* 38, no. 1 (2014): 36–59.

Bobbio, Tommaso. *Urbanisation, Citizenship and Conflict in India: Ahmedabad 1900–2000*. London and New York: Routledge, 2015.

Brass, Paul R. *The Production of Hindu–Muslim Violence in Contemporary India*. Seattle and London: University of Washington Press, 2003.

Breman, Jan. 'Anti-Muslim Pogrom in Surat'. *Economic and Political Weekly* 28, no. 16 (1993): 737–41.

———. 'Communal Upheaval as Resurgence of Social Darwinism'. *Economic and Political Weekly* 37, no. 16 (2002): 1485–88.

———. *The Labouring Poor: Patterns of Exploitation, Subordination, and Exclusion*. New Delhi: Oxford University Press, 2003.

———. *The Making and Unmaking of an Industrial Working Class: Sliding Down the Labour Hierarchy in Ahmedabad, India*. New Delhi: Oxford University Press, 2003.

———. 'The Study of Industrial Labour in Post-Colonial India—the Formal Sector: An Introductory Review'. *Contributions to Indian Sociology* 33, nos 1–2 (1999): 1–41.

———. 'The Study of Industrial Labour in Post-Colonial India—the Informal Sector: A Concluding Review'. *Contributions to Indian Sociology* 33, nos 1–2 (1999): 407–31.

Breman, Jan, and Parthiv Shah. *Working in the Mill No More*. New Delhi: Oxford University Press, 2004.

Brenner, Neil. 'The Limits to Scale? Methodological Reflections on Scalar Structuration'. *Progress in Human Geography* 25, no. 4 (2001): 591–614.

———. 'The Urban Question: Reflections on Henri Lefebvre, Urban Theory and the Politics of Scale'. *International Journal of Urban and Regional Research* 24, no. 2 (2000): 361–78.

Burman, B. K. Roy. 'Social Profile'. *Seminar* 125 (1970): 33–38.

Caru, Vanessa. 'The Making of a Working-Class Area, the Worli Bdd Chawls (1920–40)'. In *The Chawls of Mumbai: Galleries of Life*, edited by Neera Adarkar, 26–36. Delhi: ImprintOne, 2011.

Chakrabarty, Dipesh. *Rethinking Working-Class History: Bengal, 1890–1940*. Princeton: Princeton University Press, 1989.

Chandavarkar, Rajnarayan. 'The Decline and Fall of the Jobber System in the Bombay Cotton Textile Industry, 1870–1955'. *Modern Asian Studies* 42, no. 1 (2008): 117–210.

———. 'From Neighbourhood to Nation: The Rise and Fall of the Left in Bombay's Girangaon in the Twentieth Century'. In *History, Culture and the Indian City*, edited by Rajnarayan Chandavarkar, 121–90. Cambridge and New York: Cambridge University Press, 2009.

———. *Imperial Power and Popular Politics: Class, Resistance and the State in India, 1850–1950*. Cambridge: Cambridge University Press, 1998.

———. *The Origins of Industrial Capitalism in India: Business Strategies and the Working Classes in Bombay, 1900–1940*. Cambridge: Cambridge University Press, 1994.

———. 'The Perils of Proximity: Rivalries and Conflicts in the Making of a Neighbourhood in Bombay City in the Twentieth Century'. *Modern Asian Studies* 52, no. 2 (2018): 351–93.

———. 'Workers' Politics and the Mill Districts in Bombay between the Wars'. *Modern Asian Studies* 15, no. 3 (1981): 603–47.

Chandhoke, Neera. 'Civil Society'. *Development in Practice* 17, nos 4–5 (2007): 607–14.

———. 'Civil Society in Conflict Cities: The Case of Ahmedabad'. Crisis States Working Paper, LSE 64 (2009), 2009.

Chatterjee, Partha. 'Beyond the Nation? Or Within?' *Social Text* 56 (Autumn 1998): 57–69.

———. 'Democracy and Economic Transformation in India'. *Economic and Political Weekly* 46, no. 16 (2008): 5362.

———. *The Politics of the Governed: Reflections on Popular Politics in Most of the World*. New York: Columbia University Press, 2004.

Chauhan, Uttara, and Niraj Lal. 'Public–Private Partnerships for Urban Poor in Ahmedabad: A Slum Project'. *Economic and Political Weekly* 34, nos 10–11 (1999): 636–42.

Cox, Kevin R. 'Representation and Power in the Politics of Scale'. *Political Geography* 17, no. 1 (1998): 41–44.

———. 'Spaces of Dependence, Spaces of Engagement and the Politics of Scale, Or: Looking for Local Politics'. *Political Geography* 17, no. 1 (1998): 1–23.

Damodaran, Harish. *India's New Capitalists: Caste, Business, and Industry in a Modern Nation*. Ranikhet: Permanent Black, 2008.

D'Monte, Darryl. 'Ahmedabad's Alienated Textile Workers'. *India International Centre Quarterly* 29, no. 2 (2002): 129–40.

———. *Mills for Sale: The Way Ahead*. Mumbai: Marg Publications, 2006.

———. *Ripping the Fabric: The Decline of Mumbai and Its Mills*. New Delhi: Oxford University Press, 2002.

Das, Suranjan. 'The "Goondas": Towards a Reconstruction of the Calcutta Underworld through Police Records'. *Economic and Political Weekly* 29, no. 44 (1994): 2877–83.

De Neve, Geert. *The Everyday Politics of Labour: Working Lives in India's Informal Economy*. New Delhi: Social Science Press, 2005.

Desai, Kiran, and Ghanshyam Shah. *Gujarat: When Patels Resist the Kshatriyas*. New Delhi: Routledge, 2009.

Desai, Natvarlal Nandlal. *Directory of Ahmedabad Mill Industry, 1929 to 1933*. Ahmedabad: Commercial News, 1935.

Desai, Renu. 'Municipal Politics, Court Sympathy and Housing Rights: A Post-Mortem of Displacement and Resettlement under the Sabarmati Riverfront Project, Ahmedabad'. Working Paper 24, Centre for Urban Equity, CEPT University, Ahmedabad, May 2014.

———. 'Producing and Contesting the "Communalized City": Hindutva Politics and Urban Space in Ahmedabad'. In *The Fundamentalist City?*

Religiosity and the Remaking of Urban Space, edited by N. AlSayyad and M. Massoumi, 99–124. Abingdon, Oxon and New York: Routledge, 2010.

Desai, Renu, Darshini Mahadevia, Shachi Sanghvi, Suchita Vyas, Rafi Malek and Mohammad Sharif Malek. 'Bombay Hotel: Urban Planning, Governance and Everyday Conflict and Violence in a Muslim Locality on the Peripheries of Ahmedabad'. Working Paper 31, Centre for Urban Equity, CEPT University, Ahmedabad, 2016.

Dhattiwala, Raheel. 'Cooperation and Protection in a Peaceful Neighbourhood'. Paper presented at conference on Re-visiting the Working-Class Neighbourhood in South Asia, University of Göttingen, Göttingen, 11–12 July 2014.

———. 'The Ecology of Ethnic Violence: Attacks on Muslims of Ahmedabad in 2002'. *Qualitative Sociology* 39, no. 1 (2015): 1–25.

———. *Keeping the Peace: Spatial Differences in Hindu–Muslim Violence in Gujarat in 2002*. New Delhi: Cambridge University Press, 2019.

———. The Puzzle of the BJP's Muslim Supporters in Gujarat'. The Hindu Centre for Politics and Public Policy, Policy Report 5 (2014).

Doshi, Harish. 'Industrialization and Neighbourhood Communities in a Western Indian City—Challenge and Response'. *Sociological Bulletin* 17, no. 1 (1968): 19–34.

———. 'Traditional Neighbourhood in Modern'. In *A Reader in Urban Sociology*, edited by M. S. A. Rao, C. Bhat and L. N. Kadekar, 179–208. New Delhi: Orient Longman, 1991.

Dupont, Véronique. 'Slum Demolitions in Delhi since the 1990s: An Appraisal'. *Economic and Political Weekly* 43, no. 28 (2008): 79–87.

Economic and Political Weekly. 'Gujarat-Communal Divide'. *Economic and Political Weekly* 22, no. 8 (1987).

Engineer, Asghar Ali. 'Communal Fire Engulfs Ahmedabad Once Again'. *Economic and Political Weekly* 20, no. 27 (1985): 1116–20.

———. 'Communal Riots in Ahmedabad'. *Economic and Political Weekly* 27, nos 31–32 (1992): 1641–43.

———. 'Communal Violence and Police Terror'. *Economic and Political Weekly* 21, no. 9 (1986): 382–83.

———. 'Gujarat Burns Again'. *Economic and Political Weekly* 21, no. 31 (1986): 1343–46.

———. *The Gujarat Carnage*. New Delhi: Orient Blackswan, 2003.

———. 'Gujarat Riots in the Light of the History of Communal Violence'. *Economic and Political Weekly* 37, no. 50 (2002): 5047–54.

Erdman, Howard L. *The Swatantra Party and Indian Conservatism*. New York: Cambridge University Press, 1967.

Fischer-Tiné, Harald, and Jana Tschurenev, eds. *A History of Alcohol and Drugs in Modern South Asia: Intoxicating Affairs*. London: Routledge, 2014.

Franco, Fernando, Jyotsna Macwan and Suguna Ramanathan. *Journeys to Freedom: Dalit Narratives*. Mumbai: Popular Prakashan, 2004.

Gellner, Ernest. 'Civil Society in Historical Context'. *International Social Science Journal* 43, no. 3 (1991): 495–510.

Ghassem-Fachandi, Parvis. 'Ahimsa, Identification and Sacrifice in the Gujarat Pogrom'. *Social Anthropology* 18, no. 2 (2010): 155–75.

———. *Pogrom in Gujarat: Hindu Nationalism and Anti-Muslim Violence in India*. Princeton and Oxford: Princeton University Press, 2012.

Ghertner, D. Asher. 'Analysis of New Legal Discourse Behind Delhi's Slum Demolitions'. *Economic and Political Weekly* 43, no. 20 (2008): 57–66.

———. 'India's Urban Revolution: Geographies of Displacement Beyond Gentrification'. *Environment and Planning A* 46, no. 7 (2014): 1554–71.

———. *Rule by Aesthetics: World-Class City Making in Delhi*. New York: Oxford University Press, 2015.

Gillion, Kenneth L. *Ahmedabad: A Study in Indian Urban History*. Berkeley and Los Angeles: University of California Press, 1968.

Goel, Shiv Kumar. *Gandhian Perspective on Industrial Relations: A Study of Textile Labour Association, Ahmedabad, 1918–48*. Delhi: Shipra Publications, 2002.

Gooptu, Nandini. *The Politics of the Urban Poor in Early Twentieth-Century India*. Cambridge: Cambridge University Press, 2001.

Gudavarthy, Ajay. *Re-Framing Democracy and Agency in India: Interrogating Political Society*. London: Anthem Press, 2012.

Gupta, Akhil. 'Blurred Boundaries: The Discourse of Corruption, the Culture of Politics, and the Imagined State'. *American Ethnologist* 22, no. 2 (1995): 375–402.

Gupta, Dipankar. *Justice before Reconciliation: Negotiating a 'New Normal' in Post-Riot Mumbai and Ahmedabad*. Abingdon and New Delhi: Routledge, 2013.

Hansen, Thomas Blom. 'Recuperating Masculinity: Hindu Nationalism, Violence and the Exorcism of the Muslim "Other"'. *Critique of Anthropology* 16, no. 2 (1996): 137–72.

———. *Violence in Urban India: Identity Politics, 'Mumbai', and the Postcolonial City*. Delhi: Permanent Black, 2005.

———. *Wages of Violence: Naming and Identity in Postcolonial Bombay*. Princeton: Princeton University Press, 2001.

Hansen, Thomas Blom, and Oskar Verkaaik. 'Introduction—Urban Charisma: On Everyday Mythologies in the City'. *Critique of Anthropology* 29, no. 1 (2009): 5–26.

Harriss, John. 'Antinomies of Empowerment: Observations on Civil Society, Politics and Urban Governance in India'. *Economic and Political Weekly* 42, no. 26 (2007): 2716–24.

Harvey, David. *The New Imperialism*. Oxford: Oxford University Press, 2003.

Haynes, Douglas E., and Nikhil Rao. 'Beyond the Colonial City: Re-Evaluating the Urban History of India, ca. 1920–1970'. *South Asia: Journal of South Asian Studies* 36, no. 3 (2013): 317–35.

Heitmeyer, Carolyn, and Edward Simpson. 'The Culture of Prohibition in Gujarat, India'. In *A History of Drugs and Alcohol in Modern South Asia: Intoxicating Affairs*, edited by Jana Tschurenev and Harald Fischer-Tiné, 203–17. London: Routledge, 2014.

Heuzé-Brigant, Gérard. 'Populism and the Workers Movement: Shiv Sena and Labor in Mumbai'. *South Asia: Journal of South Asian Studies* 22, no. 2 (1999): 119–48.

Hirsch, Arnold R. *Making the Second Ghetto: Race and Housing in Chicago 1940–1960*. Chicago and London: University of Chicago Press, 1998.

Holmström, Mark. *South Indian Factory Workers: Their Life and Their World*. Vol. 20. Cambridge: Cambridge University Press, 1976.

Howell, Jude, and Uma Kambhampati. 'Liberalization and Labour: The Fate of Retrenched Workers in the Cotton Textile Industry in India'. *Oxford Development Studies* 27, no. 1 (1999): 109–27.

Human Rights Watch. *India: Compounding Injustice: The Government's Failure to Redress Massacres in Gujarat*. Human Rights Watch (HRW), 2003. Available at https://www.hrw.org/reports/2003/india0703/, accessed 13 July 2021.

Jaffrelot, Christophe. 'Gujarat: The Meaning of Modi's Victory'. *Economic and Political Weekly* 43, no. 15 (2008): 12–17.

———. 'The Hindu Nationalist Reinterpretation of Pilgrimage in India: The Limits of Yatra Politics'. *Nations and Nationalism* 15, no. 1 (2009): 1–19.

———. *Religion, Caste, and Politics in India*. Delhi: Primus Books, 2011.

Jaffrelot, Christophe, and Charlotte Thomas. 'Facing Ghettoisation in the "Riot City": Old Ahmedabad and Juhapura between Victimisation and Self-Help'. In *Muslims in Indian Cities: Trajectories of Marginalisation*, edited by Laurent Gayer and Christophe Jaffrelot, 43–79. London: Hurst and Co., 2012.

Jamil, Ghazala. *Accumulation by Segregation: Muslim Localities in Delhi*. New Delhi: Oxford University Press, 2017.

Jani, Manishi. *The Textile Workers: Jobless and Miserable*. Ahmedabad: SETU, 1984.

Janmohamed, Zahir. 'Muslim Education in Ahmedabad in the Aftermath of the 2002 Gujarat Riots'. *Studies in Ethnicity and Nationalism* 13, no. 3 (2013): 466–76.

Jasani, Rubina. 'A Potted History of Neighbours and Neighbourliness in Ahmedabad'. In *The Idea of Gujarat: History, Ethnography and Text*, edited by Edward Simpson and Aparna Kapadia, 153–67. Hyderabad: Orient Blackswan, 2010.

———. 'Violence, Reconstruction and Islamic Reform: Stories from the Muslim "Ghetto"'. *Modern Asian Studies* 42, nos 2–3 (2008): 431–56.

Jaswal, Parmjit S. 'India: Judicial Review'. In *Preventive Detention and Security Law: A Commparative Survey*, edited by Andrew Harding and John Hatchard, 71–104. Dordrecht: Martinus Nijhoff Publishers, 1993.

Jhabvala, Renana. *Closing Doors: A Study on the Decline of Women Workers in the Textile Mills of Ahmedabad*. Ahmedabad: SETU, 1985.

———. 'From the Mill to the Streets: A Study of Retrenchment of Women from Ahmedabad Textile Mills'. *Manushi*, no. 26 (1985).

Jones, Dawn E., and Rodney W. Jones. 'Urban Upheaval in India: The 1974 Nav Nirman Riots in Gujarat'. *Asian Survey* 16, no. 11 (1976): 1012–33.

Jones, Katherine T. 'Scale as Epistemology'. *Political Geography* 17, no. 1 (1998): 25–28.

Joshi, Chitra. 'Histories of Indian Labour: Predicaments and Possibilities'. *History Compass* 6, no. 2 (2008): 439–54.

———. *Lost Worlds: Indian Labour and Its Forgotten Histories*. Delhi: Permanent Black, 2003.

———. 'On "De-Industrialization" and the Crisis of Male Identities'. *International Review of Social History* 47, no. S10 (2002): 159–75.

Joshi, Rajendra, Pooja Shah, Keren Nazareth and Darshini Mahadevia. 'From Basic Service Delivery to Policy Advocacy: Community Mobilisation in Pravinnagar-Guptanagar, Ahmedabad'. Working Paper 6, Centre for Urban Equity, CEPT University, Ahmedabad, 2010.

Kaika, Maria, and Luca Ruggiero. 'Land Financialization as a "Lived" Process: The Transformation of Milan's Bicocca by Pirelli'. *European Urban and Regional Studies* 23, no. 1 (2016): 3–22.

Kalhan, Promilla. *Gulzarilal Nanda: A Life in the Service of the People*. New Delhi: Allied Publishers, 1997.

Kamath, M. V., and V. B. Kher. *The Story of Militant but Non-Violent Trade Unionism: A Biographical and Historical Study*. Ahmedabad: Navajivan Mudranalaya, 1993.

Kannappan, Subbiah. 'The Gandhian Model of Unionism in a Developing Economy: The TLA in India'. *Industrial and Labor Relations Review* 16, no. 1 (1962): 86–110.

Karnik, Vasant Bhagwant. *Indian Trade Unions: A Survey.* Bombay: Popular Prakashan, 1966.

Khare, Harish. 'Social Tensions in Ahmedabad'. Paper presented at the Ahmedabad 2001–Imperatives Now Towards a New Metropolitan Management Strategy, 1988.

Kidambi, Prashant. *The Making of an Indian Metropolis: Colonial Governance and Public Culture in Bombay, 1890–1920.* Aldershot: Ashgate Publishing Ltd., 2007.

Kohli, Atul. *Democracy and Discontent: India's Growing Crisis of Governability.* Cambridge: Cambridge University Press, 1990.

Kothari, Rajni, and Rushikesh Maru. 'Caste and Secularism in India: Case Study of a Caste Federation'. *Journal of Asian Studies* 25, no. 1 (1965): 33–50.

Kumar, Radha. 'Family and Factory: Women in the Bombay Cotton Textile Industry, 1919–1939'. *Indian Economic and Social History Review* 20, no. 1 (1983): 81–96.

Kumar, Ravindra. *Life and Work of Sardar Vallabhbhai Patel.* New Delhi: Atlantic Publishers & Distributors, 1991.

Lakha, Salim. *Capitalism and Class in Colonial India: The Case of Ahmedabad.* Bangalore: Sterling Publishers, 1988.

——. 'Character of Wage Labour in Early Industrial Ahmedabad'. *Journal of Contemporary Asia* 15, no. 4 (1985): 421–41.

Lefebvre, Henri. 'Reflections on the Politics of Space'. In *State, Space, World: Selected Essays,* 167–84. Minneapolis: University of Minnesota Press, 2009.

——. *Rhythmanalysis: Space, Time and Everyday Life.* London: Continuum, 2004.

——. 'Space: Social Product and Use Value'. In *State, Space, World: Selected Essays,* 185–95. Minneapolis: University of Minnesota Press, 2009.

Lokhande, Sanjeevini Badigar. *Communal Violence, Forced Migration and the State: Gujarat since 2002.* New Delhi: Cambridge University Press, 2015.

Mahadevia, Darshini. 'A City with Many Borders: Beyond Ghettoisation in Ahmedabad'. In *Indian Cities in Transition,* edited by Annapura Shaw, 315–40. Hyderabad: Orient Longman, 2007.

——. 'Communal Space over Life Space: Saga of Increasing Vulnerability in Ahmedabad'. *Economic and Political Weekly* 37, no. 48 (2002): 4850–58.

——. 'Unsmart Outcomes of the Smart City Initiatives: Displacement and Peripheralisation in Indian Cities'. In *The New Companion to Urban Design,* edited by Tridib Banerjee and Anastasia Loukaitou-Sideris, 310–24. London: Routledge, 2019.

——. 'Urban Land Market and Access of the Poor'. In *India: Urban Poverty Report 2009,* edited by Ministry of Housing and Urban Poverty Alleviation, 199–221. Delhi: Oxford University Press, 2009.

Mahadevia, Darshini, Bijal Bhatt and Neha Bhatia. 'Resident Welfare Associations in BSUP Sites of Ahmedabad: Experiences of Mahila Housing SEWA Trust (MHT)'. Working Paper 25, Centre for Urban Equity, CEPT University, Ahmedabad, September 2014.

Mahadevia, Darshini, Neha Bhatia and Bijal Bhatt. 'Decentralized Governance or Passing the Buck: The Case of Resident Welfare Associations at Resettlement Sites, Ahmedabad, India'. *Environment and Urbanization* 28, no. 1 (2015): 294–307.

Mahadevia, Darshini, Renu Desai, Shachi Sanghvi and Suchita Vyas. 'Vatwa Resettlements Sites: Basic Services and Amenities; Deprivations and Infrastructural Conflicts'. Ahmedabad policy brief 2, Centre for Urban Equity, CEPT University, Ahmedabad, 2015.

———. 'Vatwa Resettlements Sites: Thefts, Robberies and Burglaries'. Ahmedabad policy brief 3, Centre for Urban Equity, CEPT University, Ahmedabad, 2016.

Mahadevia, Darshini, Renu Desai, Shachi Sanghvi, Suchita Vyas and Vaishali Parmar. 'Vatwa Resettlements Sites: Constrained Mobility and Stressed Livelihoods'. Ahmedabad policy brief 1, Centre for Urban Equity, CEPT University, Ahmedabad, 2015.

Marston, Sallie A. 'The Social Construction of Scale'. *Progress in Human Geography* 24, no. 2 (2000): 219–42.

Marston, Sallie A, and Neil Smith. 'States, Scales and Households: Limits to Scale Thinking? A Response to Brenner'. *Progress in Human Geography* 25, no. 4 (2001): 615–19.

Massey, Doreen. 'Politics and Space/Time'. *New Left Review* 1, no. 196 (November–December 1992): 65–84.

Mazumdar, Ranjani. *Bombay Cinema: Archive of the City*. Minneapolis: University of Minnesota Press, 2007.

McFarlane, Colin. 'The Entrepreneurial Slum: Civil Society, Mobility and the Co-Production of Urban Development'. *Urban Studies* 49, no. 13 (2012): 2795–816.

McGowan, Abigail. 'Ahmedabad's Home Remedies: Housing in the Re-Making of an Industrial City, 1920–1960'. *South Asia: Journal of South Asian Studies* 36, no. 3 (2013): 397–414.

Mehta, Dinesh and Meera Mehta. 'Housing in Ahmedabad Metropolitan Area by 2001 AD: Certain Policy Imperitives'. Paper presented at Seminar on Ahmedabad 2001—Imperatives Now Towards a New Metropolitan Management Strategy, Ahmedabad, 1–3 December, Times Research Foundation, 1988.

————. 'Metropolitan Housing Markets: A Case Study of Ahmedabad'. *Economic and Political Weekly* 22, no. 40 (1987): 1701–09.

Mehta, Makrand. *The Ahmedabad Cotton Textile Industry: Genesis and Growth*. Ahmedabad: New Order Book Co., 1982.

Menon, Meena and Neera Adarkar. *One Hundred Years One Hundred Voices: The Millworkers of Girangaon: An Oral History*. Kolkata: Seagull Books Pvt Ltd, 2004.

Michelutti, Lucia. 'Wrestling with (Body) Politics: Understanding "Goonda" Political Styles in North India'. In *Power and Influence in India: Bosses, Lords and Captains*, edited by Pamela Price and Arild Engelsen Ruud, 44–69. New Delhi: Routledge, 2010.

Mookherjee, Surya. 'Unions in Industries in Downturn: A Study of Cotton Textile in Gujarat and Role of TLA'. *Indian Journal of Industrial Relations* 40, no. 2 (2004): 213–41.

Nandi, Sugata. 'Constructing the Criminal: Politics of Social Imaginary of the "Goonda"'. *Social Scientist* 38, nos 3–4 (2010): 37–54.

————. 'Respectable Anxiety, Plebeian Criminality: Politics of the Goondas Act (1923) of Colonial Calcutta'. *Crime, Histoire et Sociétés/Crime, History and Societies* 20, no. 2 (2016): 77–99.

Nandy, Ashis, Shikha Trivedy, Shail Mayaram and Achyut Yagnik. *Creating a Nationality: The Ramjanmabhumi Movement and Fear of the Self*. New Delhi: Oxford University Press, 1998.

National Labour Organisation. 'Powerloom Factories and Workers Therein'. National Labour Organisation, Ahmedabad, 1986.

Oommen, T. K. *Reconciliation in Post-Godhra Gujarat: The Role of Civil Society*. New Delhi: Pearson Education India, 2008.

Pai, Sudha. 'Transformation of the Indian Party System: The 1996 Lok Sabha Elections'. *Asian Survey* 36, no. 12 (1996): 1170–83.

Pandya, D. G. 'Land Markets in Ahmedabad Metropolitan Region: The Demand, Supply and Pricing Scenario, 2001 AD'. Paper presented at Seminar on Ahmedabad 2001—Imperatives Now Towards a New Metropolitan Management Strategy, Ahmedabad, 1–3 December, Times Research Foundation, 1988.

Parry, Jonathan P. '"The Crisis of Corruption" and "the Idea of India"'. In *Morals of Legitimacy: Between Agency and System*, edited by Italo Pardo, 27–56. New York: Berghann Books, 2000.

————. 'Nehru's Dream and the Village "Waiting Room": Long-Distance Labour Migrants to a Central Indian Steel Town'. *Contributions to Indian Sociology* 37, nos 1–2 (2003): 217–49.

Patel, B. B. 'Workers of Closed Textile Mills'. New Delhi: Oxford/IBH Publishing, 1988.

Patel, Sujata. *City Conflicts and Communal Politics: Ahmedabad 1985–86*. Delhi: Oxford University Press, 2006.

———. 'Class Conflict and Workers' Movement in Ahmedabad Textile Industry, 1918–23'. *Economic and Political Weekly* 19, nos 20–21 (1984): 853–64.

———. 'Collapse of Government'. *Economic and Political Weekly* 20, no. 17 (1985): 749–50.

———. 'Contract Labour in Ahmedabad Textile Industry'. *Economic and Political Weekly* 21, no. 41 (1986): 1813–20.

———. 'Debacle of Populist Politics'. *Economic and Political Weekly* 20, no. 16 (1985): 681–82.

———. *The Making of Industrial Relations: The Ahmedabad Textile Industry, 1918–1939*. Delhi: Oxford University Press, 1987.

———. 'Nationalisation, TLA and Textile Workers'. *Economic and Political Weekly* 20, no. 49 (1985): 2154–55.

Pathan, S. K., V. K. Shukla, R. G. Patel, B. R. Patel and K. S. Mehta. 'Urban Land Use Mapping: A Case Study of Ahmedabad City and Its Environs'. *Journal of the Indian Society of Remote Sensing* 19, no. 2 (1991): 95–112.

R.S.S. Resolves 1950–2007: Resolutions Passed by A.B.P.S and A.B.K.M. Of R.S.S. From 1950 to 2007. New Delhi: Suchi Prakashan, 2007.

Rajagopal, Arvind. 'Special Political Zone: Urban Planning, Spatial Segregation and the Infrastructure of Violence in Ahmedabad 1'. *South Asian History and Culture* 1, no. 4 (2010): 529–56.

Raychaudhuri, Siddhartha. 'Colonialism, Indigenous Elites and the Transformation of Cities in the Non-Western World: Ahmedabad (Western India), 1890–1947'. *Modern Asian Studies* 35, no. 3 (2001): 677–726.

Roy, Ananya. 'Why India Cannot Plan Its Cities: Informality, Insurgence and the Idiom of Urbanization'. *Planning Theory* 8, no. 1 (2009): 76–87.

Roy, Tirthankar. 'Sardars, Jobbers, Kanganies: The Labour Contractor and Indian Economic History'. *Modern Asian Studies* 42, no. 5 (2008): 971–98.

RoyChowdhury, Supriya. 'Industrial Restructuring, Unions and the State: Textile Mill Workers in Ahmedabad'. *Economic and Political Weekly* 31, no. 8 (1996): L7–L13.

Ruparelia, Sanjay. 'India's New Rights Agenda: Genesis, Promises, Risks'. *Pacific Affairs* 86, no. 3 (2013): 569–90.

Sanchez, Andrew. 'Capitalism, Violence and the State: Crime, Corruption and Entrepreneurship in an Indian Company Town'. *Journal of Legal Anthropology* 2, no. 1 (2010): 165–88.

————. 'India: The Next Superpower? Corruption in India'. *IDEAS Reports: Special Reports*, edited by Nicholas Kitchen. LSE IDEAS. SR010 (2012), 50–53.

Sanghavi, Nagindas. 'From Navnirman to the Anti-Mandal Riots: The Political Trajectory of Gujarat (1974–1985)'. *South Asian History and Culture* 1, no. 4 (2010): 480–93.

Sarkar, Sumit. 'The Return of Labour to South-Asian History'. *Historical Materialism* 12, no. 3 (2004): 285–313.

Sarkar, Tanika. 'Semiotics of Terror: Muslim Children and Women in Hindu Rashtra'. *Economic and Political Weekly* 37, no. 28 (2002): 2872–76.

Sassen, Saskia. *The Mobility of Labor and Capital: A Study in International Investment and Labor Flow.* Cambridge: Cambridge University Press, 1990.

Sen, Arup Kumar. 'The Gandhian Experiment in Ahmedabad: Towards a Gramscian Reading'. *Economic and Political Weekly* 27, no. 37 (1992): 1987–89.

————. 'Mode of Labour Control in Colonial India'. *Economic and Political Weekly* 37, no. 38 (2002): 3956–66.

Sen, Samita. 'Commercial Recruiting and Informal Intermediation: Debate over the Sardari System in Assam Tea Plantations, 1860–1900'. *Modern Asian Studies* 44, no. 1 (2010): 3–28.

————. *Women and Labour in Late Colonial India: The Bengal Jute Industry.* Cambridge: Cambridge University Press, 1999.

Shah, Amrita. *Ahmedabad: A City in the World.* New Delhi: Bloomsbury, 2015.

Shah, Ghanshyam. 'The 1969 Communal Riots in Ahmedabad: A Case Study'. In *Communal Riots in Post-Independence India*, edited by Asghar Ali Engineer, 175–208. Hyderabad: Sangam Books, 1991.

————. 'Anatomy of Urban Riots: Ahmedabad 1973'. *Economic and Political Weekly* 9, nos 6–7–8 (1974): 233–40.

————. 'BJP's Rise to Power'. *Economic and Political Weekly* 31, nos 2–3 (1996): 165–70.

————. 'Communal Riots in Gujarat: Report of a Preliminary Investigation'. *Economic and Political Weekly* 5, nos 3–4–5 (1970): 187–200.

————. 'Polarised Communities'. *Seminar* 470 (1998): 30–35.

————. *Protest Movements in Two Indian States: A Study of the Gujarat and Bihar Movements.* Delhi: Ajanta Publications, 1977.

————. 'Tenth Lok Sabha Elections: BJP's Victory in Gujarat'. *Economic and Political Weekly* 26, no. 51 (1991): 2921–24.

Shaheed, Zafar. *The Labour Movement in Pakistan: Organization and Leadership in Karachi in the 1970s.* New Delhi: Oxford University Press, 2007.

Shani, Ornit. 'Bootlegging, Politics and Corruption: State Violence and the Routine Practices of Public Power in Gujarat (1985–2002)'. *South Asian History and Culture* 1, no. 4 (2010): 494–508.

———. *Communalism, Caste and Hindu Nationalism: The Violence in Gujarat.* Cambridge: Cambridge University Press, 2007.

———. 'The Rise of Hindu Nationalism in India: The Case Study of Ahmedabad in the 1980s'. *Modern Asian Studies* 39, no. 4 (2005): 861–96.

Sharma, Sita Ram. *Municipal Administration and Education.* Vol. 2. New Delhi: Mittal Publications, 1994.

Sheth, Nimesh, Neerav Patel and Roopa Mehta. 'Ahmedabad Riots'. *Economic and Political Weekly* 20, no. 24 (1985): 1022–22.

Singha, Radhika. 'Punished by Surveillance: Policing "Dangerousness" in Colonial India, 1872–1918'. *Modern Asian Studies* 49, no. 2 (2015): 241–69.

Spodek, Howard. *Ahmedabad: Shock City of Twentieth-Century India.* Bloomington and Indianapolis: Indiana University Press, 2011.

———. 'Crises and Response: Ahmedabad 2000'. *Economic and Political Weekly* 36, no. 19 (2001): 1627–38.

———. 'From Gandhi to Modi: Ahmedabad, 1915–2007'. In *The Idea of Gujarat. History, Ethnography and Text*, edited by Edward Simpson and Aparna Kapadia, 136–52. New Delhi: Orient Blackswan Private Limited, 2010.

———. 'From Gandhi to Violence: Ahmedabad's 1985 Riots in Historical Perspective'. *Modern Asian Studies* 23, no. 4 (1989): 765–95.

———. 'In the Hindutva Laboratory: Pogroms and Politics in Gujarat, 2002'. *Modern Asian Studies* 44, no. 2 (2010): 349–99.

———. 'The Manchesterisation of Ahmedabad'. *Economic Weekly* 17, no. 13 (1965): 483–90.

———. 'The Self-Employed Women's Association (Sewa) in India: Feminist, Gandhian Power in Development'. *Economic Development and Cultural Change* 43, no. 1 (1994): 193–202.

Srinivas, Lakshmi. 'Land and Politics in India: Working of Urban Land Ceiling Act, 1976'. *Economic and Political Weekly* 26, no. 43 (1991): 2482–84.

Sud, Nikita. 'Secularism and the Gujarat State: 1960–2005'. *Modern Asian Studies* 42, no. 6 (2008): 1251–81.

Tarlo, Emma. *Unsettling Memories: Narratives of India's Emergency.* Delhi: Permanent Black, 2003.

Tripathi, Dwijendra. *Slum Networking in Ahmedabad: The Sanjay Nagar Pilot Project.* University College London (UCL), Development Planning Unit (DPU), 1999.

Valiani, Arafaat. *Militant Publics in India: Physical Culture and Violence in the Making of a Modern Polity*. Basingtoke and New York: Palgrave Macmillan, 2011.

Vanaik, Anish. 'Representing Commodified Space: Maps, Leases, Auctions and 'Narrations' of Property in Delhi, C. 1900–47'. *Historical Research* 88, no. 240 (2015): 314–32.

———. *Possessing the City: Property and Politics in Delhi, 1911–1947*. Oxford: Oxford University Press, 2019.

Varadarajan, Siddharth. *Gujarat, the Making of a Tragedy*. New Delhi: Penguin Books, 2002.

Varshney, Ashutosh. 'Civic Life and Ethnic Conflict: Hindus and Muslims in India'. New Haven: Yale University Press, 2002.

———. 'Ethnic Conflict and Civil Society: India and Beyond'. *World Politics* 53, no. 3 (2001): 362–98.

Vasavada, Shyam Prasad. *Majoor Charwal*. Ahmedabad: Textile Labour Association, 1968.

Verma, Pramod. *Profile of Labour*. Ahmedabad: Academic Book Centre, 1981.

Wadhva, Kiran. *Role of Private Sector in Urban Housing: Case Study of Ahmedabad*. Vol. 2. New Delhi: Human Settlement Management Institute (HUDCO), 1989.

Wacquant, Loïc. 'A Janus-Faced Institution of Ethnoracial Closure: A Sociological Specification of the Ghetto'. In *The Ghetto: Contemporary Global Issues and Controversies*, edited by Ray Hutchinson and Bruce Haynes, 1–31. Boulder: Westview, 2011.

———. 'Ghetto'. In *International Encyclopedia of the Social and Behavioral Sciences*, edited by N. J. Smelster and P. B. Balter. London: Pergamon Press, 2004.

———. *Urban Outcasts: A Comparative Sociology of Advanced Marginality*. Cambridge and Malden: Polity, 2008.

———. 'French Working-Class Banlieues and Black American Ghetto: From Conflation to Comparison'. *Qui Parle* 16, no. 2 (2007): 5–38.

Watt, Carey Anthony. *Serving the Nation: Cultures of Service, Association, and Citizenship*. New York: Oxford University Press, 2005.

Wilson, William Julius, ed. *The Ghetto Underclass: Social Science Perspectives*. London: Sage Publications, 1993.

Wirth, Louis. *The Ghetto*. Chicago: University of Chicago Press, 1956.

Wood, John R. 'Extra-Parliamentary Opposition in India: An Analysis of Populist Agitations in Gujarat and Bihar'. *Pacific Affairs* 48, no. 3 (1975): 313–34.

Yagnik, Achyut. 'Paradoxes of Populism'. *Economic and Political Weekly* 18, no. 35 (1983): 1505–07.

———. 'Spectre of Caste War'. *Economic and Political Weekly* 16, no. 13 (1981): 553–55.

Yagnik, Achyut, and Suchitra Sheth. *Ahmedabad: From Royal City to Megacity.* New Delhi: Penguin, 2011.

Yagnik, Indulal. *The Autobiography of Indulal Yagnik.* Translated by Devavrat N. Pathak, Howard Spodek and John R. Wood. Vol. 3. New Delhi: Manohar Publishers & Distributors, 2011.

Yang, Anand A. 'A Conversation of Rumors: The Language of Popular "Mentalitès" in Late Nineteenth-Century Colonial India'. *Journal of Social History* 20, no. 3 (1987): 485–505.

Zaidi, S. Hussain. *Dongri to Dubai: Six Decades of Mumbai Mafia.* New Delhi: Roli Books, 2012.

INDEX

Adani, Ratubhai, 41
Advani, L. K., 48, 118
Ahmad, Nur, 85
Ahmedabad
  British influence over, 32
  conceptualisation as 'shock city', 13
  Congress Party's dominance in, 37
  differentiation of workers, 15
  fable about, 1
  hegemonic domination, 13
  historiography of, 12–18
  incidence of communal violence, 16–18
  labour-capital relations, 14
  mapping practices in, 10
  morphology, 3
  municipal limits, 7–8
  notions of 'Hindu' and 'Muslim' areas,
    214, 225, 228–229, 238
  population of, 3
  property transfers, legislation, 220–233
  proportion of textile workers in, 4
  textile mill industry, 3–4
  worker neighbourhoods, 6
Ahmedabad Millowners Association
  (AMA), 5, 13, 33, 44–45, 52n11, 72
Ahmedabad Municipal Commission, 32
Ahmedabad Municipal Corporation
  (AMC), 37, 49–50, 59n92, 63, 107, 112,
  253–254
  community development, 137
  constitution of, 52n6
  cooperative housing scheme, 182
  demolition of unauthorised
    constructions, 250, 264n47
  elections, 50–51
  grounds for appropriating property, 195
  'participatory' process of urban
    planning, 263n41
  policy on rehabilitation and
    resettlement, 176n5
  slum networking project, 136
Ahmedabad Parivartan (Slum
  Networking Project), 137
Akhil Bharatiya Vidyarthi Parishad
  (ABVP), 58n81
Akhil Gujarat Navrachna Samiti, 216
Ala, Chhagan, 100
alcohol/hooch poisoning, 98, 101,
  103, 124n1. *See also* bootlegging/
  bootlegger
  hooch deaths, 98–101
alcohol/hooch prohibition, 85, 97, 99, 101
Ali, Manjur, 121
All Gujarat Educational Reform Action
  Committee (AGERAC), 216
Aman Chowk camp, 220
Aman Chowk relief camp, 220
Ambica group, 246
Ameen Society, 63
Amraiwadi, 6, 63, 83, 214, 216

Amruta Mills Tenement Occupier
    Association, 200
Anti-Goondas Act, 96, 113–115, 129n90.
    See also Prevention of Anti-Social
    Activities Act (PASA)
    Calcutta Goondas Act of 1923, 113
anti-reservation agitation, 44, 46
anti-social elements/goondas, 18, 58n81,
    69n11, 70, 77, 79, 82, 86, 96–98, 101,
    103, 105, 113–114, 116, 120, 132n133,
    134, 163
Arvind Mills, 136
Asarwa, 44, 76, 168n54

B. J. Medical College, 44
Babri Masjid demolition, 48–49, 248
badli, 15
Banias, 42
Banker, Shankarlal, 4, 24n12, 32, 73
Bapunagar, 6, 222, 228, 254
    riot, 215–220, 235n22
    workers' housing and slums, 136, 192,
        214
Barot, Navinchandra, 105
Barot, Sameer, 158
Basic Services for the Urban Poor
    (BSUP), 173–174, 176n5, 233
Basu, Amrita, 161
Bauddha Sampradaya, 46
Bavchas, 5
Berenschot, 18
Berenschot, Ward, 68n10
Bhagat, Kacharabhai, 31, 33
Bharatiya Janata Party (BJP), 17, 43, 45–46,
    116, 147, 217, 227, 233
    anti-reservation protests, 46, 58n81
    'Ashok-Harin' era, 119
    campaign rhetoric, 51
    electoral campaigns, 122
    electoral success, 47–48, 51, 117
    hard-line Hindu image, 48
    Hindutva ideology, 48, 50

internal conflicts within, 49
Muslim supporters, 61n130
polarised local politics, 116–123
politics of 'inclusion', 45–48
socio-political activities, 118
violence against minorities, 50–51
Bharatiya Kranti Dal (BKD), 57n69
Bhartiya Dalit Vargha Sangh, 46
Bhatt, Ashok, 45, 57n61, 117, 120, 122, 227
Bhoot, Manga, 100
Bibi Talab, 141, 242, 246, 259, 265n57
Bollywood films, 71
Bombay Improvement Trust, 89n16
Bombay Industrial Disputes Act, 1938, 73
Bombay Industrial Relations Act, 1946,
    28n61, 38
Bombay Presidency, 24n23
Bombay Rent Control Act of 1947, 186,
    190, 193, 195, 199, 226, 269
Bombay textile industry, 12
bootlegging/bootlegger, 40, 67, 79, 82, 87,
    97–105, 107, 114–116, 120–121, 129n86,
    134, 157–159, 162
Brahmins, 42
Breman, Jan, 14–16, 74
Bus Rapid Transit System (BRTS), 202

caste
    based occupational groupings, 5
    BJP's politics of 'inclusion', 45–48
    political significance of, 42–45
caste violence, 44, 46–47
    anti-Christian attacks, 50
Chandavarkar, 67
Chatterjee, Partha, 21, 135, 138, 161–162
Chaudhary, Amarsinh, 45, 103, 114–115
Chavda, Harisinh, 101
Chawl owners, 110
chawls, 187, 190–191, 193
    distinctions between slums and,
        188–193
    ownership of, 191

private, 181
rights over, 198–199
transfer of, 191–192
chawl slum, 208n85
chemical industry, 6
Chhagan Ala, 100
Chhotalal, Ranchhodlal, 32
Chimanbhai, Chinubhai, 52n11, 53n28
Chiranjeevi Yojana scheme, 149–150
Chowdhury, Supriya Roy, 25n24
Citizens for Justice and Peace, 151
civil society, 134–138, 159–163, 170n91
    forms of engagement, 152–159
    relationship between Hindu Right and,
        161
    resettlement and rehabilitation efforts
        in, 150–152, 174–175
    theorisation of, 161–162
    vs political society, 162–163
communal harmony, 65
communalisation of city space, 176
communalism, 1, 17
communal polarisation, 19
communal violence, 6, 16–18, 45, 49–51,
        96–97, 103, 121–122, 146, 197, 214–215
    of 1969, 39
    Bapunagar riot, 215–220
    Gujarat pogrom, 2002, 49–51, 60n105,
        146
    pogroms, 2
    rioting, 12, 103
    riots of 1969, 16, 39, 41, 83, 120,
        160–161, 170n90, 214, 217, 221–222,
        243, 247
Communist Party of India (Marxist), 41
Congress (O), 39, 104
Congress Party, 31–35, 40, 52n1, 55n42,
        64, 87, 121, 123, 153, 155, 157, 178
    alliances with caste and communities,
        42–46
    relationship with Kshatriya Sabha,
        42–43

social work and, 157–158
    split, 1969, 39, 105
Congress Party and
    Textile Labour Association (TLA)
        and, 31–37, 39, 87
Congress (R), 41
Congress Socialists, 72, 89n11
contract workers, 15, 154

dadagiri, 82, 98, 106–107, 150
    making of dada, 82–88
Dalits, 45–47, 102, 117
Darji, Jinabhai, 41
Dave Commission, 215–217, 220–221
Delhi Agreement of 1935, 72
Desai, Khandubhai, 34, 77, 188
Desai, Laxman, 45, 117, 120
Desai, Renu, 17
Desai, Thakorbhai, 56n59
detention laws, 113–115, 129n90
Development Plan of 2021, 256
Dhattiwala, Raheel, 18, 69n10
Dheds, 5
diamond polishing, 6, 218
Disturbed Areas Act of 1986, 22, 111–112,
        129n89, 204, 220, 222, 229, 231, 233,
        269–270
doffers' union, 38, 54n30

Ekta Nagar, 151–152
Emergency period, 1975, 42
Engineer, 17
Environment and Planning Collaborative
        (EPC), 173
ethno-religious mobilisation, 48–51

floods of 1927, 179
footloose labour, 15
formal sector work, 14–15

Gandhi, Indira, 39, 41, 105, 192
Gandhi, Mahatma, 4, 13–14, 31

Gandhi, Rajiv, 130n112
Gandhian ideology of labour relations, 4,
    12–14, 76–79, 99, 134
Gandhinagar, 5, 243
gentrification, 203
ghetto, 239–242
ghettoisation, 18, 22, 176, 213–214, 220,
    222–223, 228, 240, 255, 270
Ghia, Kantilal, 105
Godani, Dalsukhbhai, 227
Gomtipur, 6, 8, 19–21, 64, 82–83, 86–87,
    107, 112, 117–119, 144, 153–154, 163,
    188–189
Gujarat Industrial Development
    Corporation (GIDC), 6, 138, 143, 145,
    166n29, 174, 242–243, 245–246, 259
Gujarat pogrom, 2002. *See under*
    communal violence
Gujarat Pradesh Congress Committee
    (GPCC), 106
Gujarat Slum Areas Act in 1973, 192
Gujarat State Textile Corporation
    (GSTC), 25n24
Gujarat Vali Mahamandal (parents'
    association), 216

Hansen, Thomas Blom, 103
Harivallabhdas, Jaykrishna, 52, 52n11, 246
Harji Rabari, 98–100
harmony, 66
Hindu–Muslim conflict, 16, 18. *See also*
    communal violence
Hindu nationalism, 17, 31
Hindu right-wing politics, 48–51
Hindutva, 2, 13, 16–17, 20, 48–51, 118–119,
    123, 135, 159, 272
hooch poisoning case of 1977, 100
housing arrangements and property
    claims, 173
    in industrial areas, 185–186
    low-cost housing, 256
    property ownership, 196–198

relationship between employment and
    residence, 183
tensions around tenancy and rents,
    186–187
housing cooperative societies, 182, 197
Hussein, Ali, 213, 255

Ibrahim, Dawood, 122
India Development and Relief Fund, 50
Indian National Trade Union Congress
    (INTUC), 39, 104
Indira Garibnagar slum, 214, 217–218, 220
industrial neighbourhoods, 12
industrial restructuring, 1, 13–15, 160,
    196–197, 261n4
industrial transformations, 1
informalisation, 268–269
informal sector work, 6, 14–15, 25n25
institutionalised riot systems, 29n70
investments, 6
Islami Relief Committee (IRC), 150–151

Jadeja, Pradeepsinh, 147
Jadeja, Santokben, 124n5
Jaiswal, Dhirajlal, 129n86
Jallianwala Bagh incident, 32
Janata Dal, 48
Janata Morcha, 43
Janata Parishad, 55n42
Janata Party, 43, 101, 118
Janata Samiti, 55n36
Jan Sangh, 41–42
Jan Vikas, 151
Jayprakash Narayan's movement, 42
jobber system, 74–75, 90n26
Joshi, Chitra, 84
Jwaharlal Nehru National Urban
    Renewal Mission (JNNURM),
    173, 202, 233

Kamdar Sangram Samiti, 38, 81
KHAM coalition, 43–44, 218

Khan, Shahrukh, 115
Khare, Harish, 104
Kisan Mazdoor Lok Parishad (KMLP),
    43, 56n59, 57n61
Kolis, 5, 42
Koreishi, Tamizben, 243
Kshatriya identity, 42
Kshatriya Sabha, 42

labour retrenchment, 104, 184, 198
Lakha, Salim, 12
Lala Dana, 75
Lalbhai, Kasturbhai, 32, 52n11
land
    agricultural, 111
    ownership patterns and tenurial
        relationships on private lands, 109
    redistribution policies, 110
    tenancy, 22, 77, 111, 176, 186–187, 191, 194,
        196, 198–201, 211n125, 219, 249–250,
        255, 270
    urban, 45, 109–111, 165n23, 166n25, 173,
        193, 215, 219, 268
    vacant land, appropriation of, 65, 109,
        187
land grab scandals, 103
Latif, Abdul, 45, 47, 103, 116–117, 120–122,
    132n141
latta mahajans, 73, 76, 187
Lattha Commission report, 98
Lefebvre, Henri, 11
liberalisation policies of 1991, 6
liquor prohibition, 99
Lok Adhikar Sangh, 218
Lok Dal, 43
Lok Sabha elections of 1991, 49
Lokswaraj Manch, 48

Maha Gujarat Janata Parishad (MGJP),
    36–37, 54n28, 81
Maha Gujarat movement, 1956, 35–41
mahajans, 4

Mahavir Nagar Co-operative Housing
    Society, 247–248
Majoor Mahajan Sangh, 4. See also Textile
    Labour Association (TLA)
Majoor Sandesh, 75, 110, 185, 224
Mandal agitation, 48
Mandal Commission, 60n101
Marathas, 5
masculinity, 85
mediation, 267–268
Mehta, Chablidas, 101
Mehta, Dinkar, 38
Mevawala flats, 230
migration and migrant labour, 60n105,
    139, 223, 225, 241
mill closures, 117
Mill Kamdar Union (or Lal Vavta), 38, 72,
    89n11
mill neighbourhoods, 12, 70
    dada culture of, 82–88
    overcrowding of workers' settlements,
        183–184
    property arrangements, 5
    tenancy in, 196–204
    tenements in, 5
    workers' accommodation and social
        welfare in, 179–185
Miyan, Nur, 107
Modi, Narendra, 47, 49, 51, 65, 119, 123, 147
Mookherjee, Surya, 29n62
morality, 155
Muslim League, 34
Muslim political leadership, 123
Muslim properties, 213

nagarseth, 32
Nagrik Paksh (Citizens Party), 53n28
Nagrik Samiti, 41
Nagrik Sangthan, 220, 235n30
Nanda, Gulzarilal, 33–34, 53n13, 76–77
Narmada Valley Project, 56n54
Naroda, 5, 109, 139, 150–151, 232, 242

Nath, Manek, 1
National Labour Party (NLP), 39
National Security Act of 1980, 114
National Textile Corporation (NTC),
    25n24
Nav Nirman agitation, 42, 108
Nawab builders, 112
New Cotton Mills Circle, 63
New Textiles Policy, 1985, 25n24
Non-cooperation movement, 32, 113
non-governmental organisations (NGOs),
    134, 136–137, 145, 151, 163
no-objection certificates (NOCs), 249–251

Odhav, 5, 139, 174, 242
Oza, Ghanshyam, 41

Padmashalis, 5
'Paksh' alliance, 43
Pandit Deendayal Upadhyaya Antyodaya
    Slum Networking Project, 136
Parmar, Girishbhai, 106
Parmar, Jeevanbhai, 64–67, 82–83, 105,
    107, 153
    associates, 85–86
    career as a dada-turned-politician,
        83–86
Parmar, Karsandas, 38, 54n30
Parmar, Manubhai, 105–106, 154, 228
Parmar, Sailesh, 106, 153
Parmar, Sanjaybhai, 81
Patel, Atul, 147–149
Patel, Babubhai, 48
Patel, Bimal, 173
Patel, Chimanbhai, 41–42, 48, 56n54, 96,
    103, 122, 218
Patel, Himmatsinh, 50
Patel, Keshubhai, 48–49, 123
Patel, Popatlal, 114–116, 130n110
Patel, Sejalben, 147
Patel, Sujata, 13–14
Patel, Vallabhbhai, 31–33, 114–115, 178

Patel leadership in Gujarat, 48
Patels, 5, 44, 46
Pathak, Harin, 45, 57n61, 116, 118–120, 122
Patidars, 5, 42–44, 218
polarised local politics, 116–123
political leadership, 123, 124n4
political mediation, 163
political society, 162–163
pol panchs, 134
Praja Socialist Party, 55n36
pratinidhis, 79–82, 84–87, 89n7, 103–108,
    110
Prevention of Anti-Social Activities Act
    (PASA), 113–116. See also Anti-
    Goondas Act
Prevention of Terrorist Activities Act, 116
Prohibition of Transfer of Immovable
    Properties in Disturbed Areas Act of
    1986, 129n89, 213, 215, 220
property ownership, 22, 140, 196, 250, 267
    disputes, 197–198
    employment relations and tenancy
        rights, 198–199
property rights, 111, 151, 271
property transfers, 22, 129n89, 149, 196,
    210n110, 213, 220–233, 236n45, 260,
    269–270
public housing, 183
public–private partnership model, 135–138,
    149

Quit India movement, 34
Qutub-e-Alam, 6

Rabari, Harji, 98–100
    externment orders against, 99
Rajkot, 49, 114, 116, 130n110–111
Rajubhai v. Sabarmati Riverfront
    Development Corporation Ltd., 175
Rakhiyal, 105, 222, 231
Ram Shila Pujan, 48, 118
Rana, Mahendrasinh, 45

Ranchhodlal, Chhotalal, 32
Rashtriya Swayamsevak Sangh (RSS), 18,
    46–47
Rathore, Suraj Singh, 247–248
rent control, 183, 186, 190–191, 193–195, 199,
    210n113, 226, 269
Bombay Rent Control Act of 1947, 186,
    190, 193, 195, 199, 226, 269
resettlement and rehabilitation, 150–152,
    165n18
rights of workers, 4, 13, 82, 233
    housing rights, 196–204
rights to resettlement, 174
riots networks, 171n105
Rowlatt Acts, 32
Royal Commission on Labour, 74

SAATH, 136
Sabarmati Nagrik Adhikar Manch,
    173–174
Sabarmati Riverfront Development
    Corporation Limited (SRFDCL),
    173
Sabarmati Riverfront Development
    Project, 173, 203, 232–233, 271
Salt March, 32
Sangh Parivar, 45–46, 48, 50, 159
    social work and, 158–159
Sangram Samiti, 55n41, 81–82
Sangram Samiti agitation, 39
Sanjay Nagar, 136
Sanjay Nagar project, 137
Sankalit Nagar, 240
Sarabhai, Ambalal, 32, 52n11
Sarabhai, Anasuyaben, 4, 23n11
sarafs, 32
Saraspur, 76, 111, 121, 154, 200–201, 203,
    216, 219
sectarian violence, 10
segregated living, 214
Self Employed Women's Association
    (SEWA), 64, 68n5, 134

seva, 76, 134, 163
Sewa Bharati, 50
Shah, Amit, 147
Shah, Sultan Ahmad, 1, 3
SHARDA (Strategic Help Alliance for
    Relief to Distressed Areas), 136
shared urban experience, 9
Sheikh, Imdad, 63–66
Sikh Sampradaya, 46
Singh, Ajay, 82–83, 105
Singh, Lohre, 83
Singh, Megh, 128n84
Slum Areas Act of 1973, 108, 193
Slum Clearance Act, 269
Slum Clearance Board, 112
slumlord, 109, 111, 149, 219
    as intermediaries in securing housing
        and official documentation, 111
Slum Networking Project, 194
slums, 109–110, 188, 190
    clearance, 188, 192–193
    definition, 108, 190
    distinctions between chawls and,
        188–193
    upgradation, 193
SNA Infraprojects, 229–230
social exclusion, 17–18, 214, 269–272
social metric, 11
social space, 10–11
social workers, 18, 21, 37, 78, 87, 135,
    142–143
    political ambitions of, 152–159
social work (samajik kaam), 102, 112,
    134–135, 143–144
    in Vatva, 143–150
Solanki, Madhavsinh, 42–46, 103, 110,
    227
    KHAM strategy, 43–44
    reservations for postgraduate medical
        students, 44
spaces of dependence, 10
spaces of engagement, 10

Spodek, Howard, 13, 97
Swadeshi Mills, 81
Swadeshi movement, 32, 52n9
Swatantra Party, 43

tenancy rights, 21–22, 188, 190, 193–204, 269
textile industry, 1–2
  decline of, 6
  recruitment in, 74
  women's participation, 6
Textile Labour Association (TLA), 4–5, 13–15, 21–22, 28n62, 50, 70–71, 86–87, 100, 154, 162, 184, 198, 200
  Central Executive Committee, 73–74
  channels of patronage, 103–108
  civic and political activities, 71, 77, 96–98
  Congress Party and, 31–37, 39, 87
  contractors and, 80–81
  control over workforce and local politics, 81
  distinction between model worker anti-social element, 79–80
  influence of housing and urban service provision, 108–112
  institutional apparatus, 72–76
  involvement in rent issues, 186–187
  latta khatta, 76
  loss of political power, 40
  membership, 93n73
  neighbourhood-level associations, 73
  *pratinidhi*s, 79–82, 84–87, 89n7, 103–108, 110
  primary objectives, 72
  righteous struggle, 14–15, 86
  worker representation, 35
Thackeray, Bal, 123
Tomar, Kishansinh, 111
Town Wall Committee, 32
trade unionism, 12

Umeed, 145–147, 149
Ummat, 213
United Nations Development Programme (UNDP), 137
Urban Land Ceiling and Regulation Act (ULCRA), 109–110, 193, 200, 269
urban working classes, 2

Vaghela, Jigneshbhai, 112, 224
Vaghela, Jitu, 66, 88, 159
Vaghela, Shankarsinh, 49
Vaghris, 5
Valiani, 18
Valliulah, Rauf, 122
Vankar Co-operative Housing Society, 182
Vankars, 5
Vasavada, S. P., 35, 39, 184
Vasavada, S. R., 39
Vatva, 6, 8, 12, 19–21, 135, 138–150, 228, 232, 238
  civil society organisations in, 144–145, 150–152
  employment options available in, 174
  as industrial area and production, 243
  investments in real estate in, 243–245
  legislative assembly constituency, 147–148
  micro-credit and savings group in, 145–147
  Muslim parts of, 147, 149, 175, 254–255, 257, 263n35, 271
  political patronage for working-class Muslims in, 149
  population clusters, 245
  post-riot resettlement colonies, 243
  present times, 242–254
  relationship between social worker and politicians, 148–150
  resettlement and rehabilitation efforts in, 150–152

security in, 245

segregated living arrangements, 246

self-help groups, 145

small-time property 'magnates' of, 247–249

social work in, 144–150

spatial fixity/mobility, 254–260

town planning in, 249–254

violence in, 166n29

vulnerability in, 242

violence against Muslims, 51

Vira Bhagat ni Chaali, 193, 209n99

Vishva Hindu Parishad (VHP), 46–47, 231

Vivekananda Mills, 174

Wacquant, Loïc, 239–241, 260, 261n8

weavers, 5, 72, 89n9

women workers, 25n26, 89n7, 154, 184

working-class housing, 2, 176, 180, 182–184, 202

working-class neighbourhood, 8–12, 66–68, 206n33

'making' and 'unmaking' of industrial working class, 16

micro-level politics of, 66

notion of scale, 9–11

political arrangement in, 33–34

rural ties and primordial connections, 9

socio-spatial relations within, 10–11

workers' participation in local governance, 33–34

working-class neighbourhoods, 193

Yagnik, Indulal, 37–38, 44, 54n31, 81, 103, 219